RICHARD DANBURY read philosophy at Cambridge University and trained as a barrister before practising criminal law. In a bid for freedom in 1998 he escaped to South America to reinvent himself as a travel writer, spending six months on the continent researching the first edition of this book. He first visited South America in 1992 and has also hiked in North America, Asia, Africa and Europe.

Married to Trailblazer author, Melissa Graham, with whom he wrote *The Rough Guide to Chile*, he now lives in London and works for the BBC.

ALEXANDER STEWART researched and updated this edition of *The Inca Trail*. Born in England, he left for Kenya aged only three months and spent the next 15 years shuttling between Africa, Australia and Europe. The wanderlust instilled during his formative years has never left him and he has now visited more than 30 countries in six continents. He has followed Peruvian spirits over high Andean passes, seen the sunrise from the roof of Africa, been airlifted from the Alps and fallen through the floor of a Vietnamese hostel. He's been spat at by llamas, assaulted by orang-utans but, undeterred, he continues to explore, producing articles and photographs for various magazines and newspapers.

Alexander is currently based in London where he is Senior Buyer at Stanfords, the renowned map and travel bookshop. He is also the author of Trailblazer's *New Zealand – The Great Walks* and is currently updating *The Rough Guide to Chile*.

The Inca Trail, Cusco & Machu Picchu
First edition 1999; this third edition 2005, reprinted with amendments Aug 2006

Publisher
Trailblazer Publications
The Old Manse, Tower Rd, Hindhead, Surrey, GU26 6SU, UK
Fax (+44) 01428-607571, info@trailblazer-guides.com
www.trailblazer-guides.com

British Library Cataloguing in Publication Data
A catalogue record for this book is available from the British Library

ISBN 978-1-873756-86-7

Editor: Harry Adès
Series editor: Patricia Major
Layout: Anna Jacomb-Hood
Proof-reading: Anna Jacomb-Hood and Patricia Major
Cartography: Jane Thomas (trail maps) and Nick Hill (town plans and colour maps)
Index: Jane Thomas

Warning: mountain walking can be dangerous
Please read the notes on when to go (pp19-20) and on mountain safety (pp34-6 and
pp174-180). Every effort has been made by the authors and publisher to ensure that
the information contained herein is as accurate and up to date as possible. However,
they are unable to accept responsibility for any inconvenience, loss or injury sustained
by anyone as a result of the advice and information given in this guide.

Printed on chlorine-free paper by
D2Print (☎ +65-6295 5598)

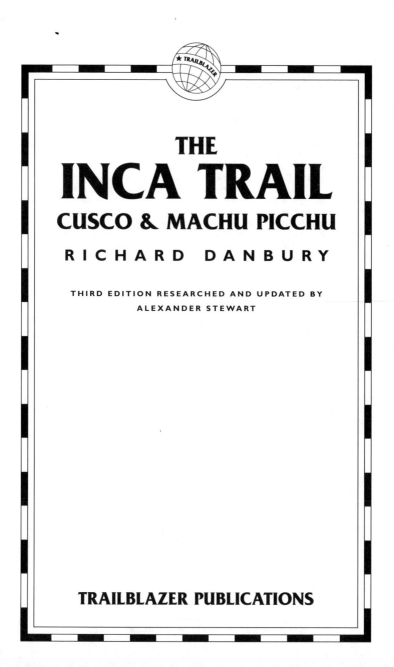

THE
INCA TRAIL
CUSCO & MACHU PICCHU

RICHARD DANBURY

THIRD EDITION RESEARCHED AND UPDATED BY
ALEXANDER STEWART

TRAILBLAZER PUBLICATIONS

Richard Danbury dedicates this book to the memory of his parents

Acknowledgements

From Richard At the risk of sounding like an Oscar winner, there are many people, both in the UK and in Peru, to whom I owe thanks. For providing help and information in London: Giovanna Salini at the Peruvian Embassy, the DTI and FCO, and Marcia Walker at the Peru Support Group. In Peru I must thank the INC, the SAE and Infotur. The staff at Humanities 1 in the British Library provided great help with general research, and in more specific fields Samya Beidas Emanuel gave a hand with economics, and doctors Chris Danbury and Gus Gazzard helped with medical stuff. I was also lucky enough that another type of doctor, Dr Ann Kendall, found time to help with information about the Cusichaca. Thanks to Richard Derham for checking the maps and not getting lost, and to his sister Katie. For this third edition, enormous thanks again to everyone at Trailblazer and, in addition, thanks to Alexander Stewart for researching and updating the text.

And to Melissa: 'Se van tiñendo con tu amor mis palabras. Todo lo ocupas tú, todo lo ocupas.'

From Alexander Thanks go to all those who willingly gave of their time to answer my questions and keep me abreast of developments regarding elements of the book. In particular, thanks to all those at the INC and SAE who proved to be invaluable sources of information. Also thanks to Pia Portillo, and Julio Vidallon at PromPeru. Special thanks to Mike Weston for his time and boundless enthusiasm and to Timoteo Auccapuma for his efforts on my behalf. Others meriting a special mention include Bianny Mendoza, Karla Fernández, Jesús Cardenas, Julio César Camacho, Leo Cusi and Juan Carlos Carlotta.

At home, a big thank you to Bryn Thomas and to Richard Danbury for the opportunity to take on this project and for the support of all those at Trailblazer involved in its production: Harry Adès for scrupulous editing, Anna Jacomb-Hood for layout and Jane Thomas and Nick Hill for working on the maps. Finally, huge, heartfelt thanks to Dad for volunteering to trek to Machu Picchu with me, to Mum for generously letting him go and special thanks as ever to Katie for her support and encouragement, and for ensuring that coming home is still the best bit of every journey.

A request

The author and publisher have tried to ensure that this guide is as accurate and up to date as possible. Nevertheless things change. If you notice any changes or omissions that should be included in the next edition of this book, please write to Richard Danbury at Trailblazer (address on p2) or email him at richard.danbury@trailblazer-guides.com. A free copy of the next edition will be sent to persons making a significant contribution.

Updated information will shortly be available on the Internet at
www.trailblazer-guides.com

Front cover: Machu Picchu (photo © Richard Danbury)

CONTENTS

GOLD BREASTPLATE FROM CUSCO

INTRODUCTION

Declared both a natural and a cultural World Heritage Site by UNESCO, the **Machu Picchu Historical Sanctuary** is truly a rare and wonderful place. Where else in the world can you walk for days through cloud forests and over razor-sharp passes, in country that's been inhabited for thousands of years by civilizations only discovered by Europeans less than five hundred years ago? Where else could you have such a breathtaking goal to your trek: the magical, lost city of Machu Picchu which rises from a high spur of mountain, like a stage set in a green amphitheatre of forest-clad hills?

THE INCA HERITAGE

For thousands of years the people of South America developed separately from the rest of the world. Their culture culminated in the Incas, a people whose empire was centred on Peru and which stretched further than that of the Romans, yet who governed without having discovered iron, the wheel or writing. Like the Romans, the Incas left behind them monumental stone constructions, built for the most part without mortar yet strong enough to withstand centuries of earthquakes that have toppled more modern edifices. Also like the Romans, they left behind them one of the most extensive road networks in the ancient world, for the most part paved and drained, which linked every part of their realm.

Many of these roads have been rediscovered and some of them have been cleared. The **Inca Trail** is one such road, part of a network that once penetrated the thick rainforest which grows either side of the river Urubamba. Walkers who follow it today pass over high-altitude wind-blown grassland and down to steamy encroaching jungle. At the end of the road is **Machu Picchu**. On these grasslands and in this jungle is an abundance of plant, bird and animal life, and beside this ancient Inca road are recently rediscovered castles and remote fieldstone inns.

The Incas also left their capital, **Cusco**, which for the most part has been spared the complete destruction suffered by Mexico, capital of that other great ancient American people, the Aztecs. It's still possible to wander along Cusco's Inca alleyways which run between walls of perfectly hewn stone and visit the remains of the magnificent Sun Temple, once the religious heart of an empire. And the 'new' buildings such as the Cathedral and the Compañía, built in the 16th century by the Spanish colonizers, are beautiful in their own right.

VISITING CUSCO AND MACHU PICCHU

In the days of the Incas, Machu Picchu was a long hard walk from Cusco. *Chasquis*, Inca messengers, ran the roads of the Inca Trail and herders drove llama trains laden with maize and potatoes over the high passes. Today Machu Picchu is only four hours from Cusco by train, along a railway that's been pushed through the jungle along the banks of the Urubamba river.

However, you can still walk. The high tableland around Cusco leads down to the fringes of the Amazon rainforest, and the area is criss-crossed with roads and tracks, ancient and modern, passing through unrivalled natural and ancient beauty. As you walk you'll pass dazzling high glaciers and remote corries, along trails lined with original Inca canals and dotted with remote unvisited ruins where countless orchids grow in the clear Andean air.

ABOUT THIS BOOK

The book is designed to take you from your armchair to these cities of the Incas, Cusco and Machu Picchu, and to guide you along the Incas' trails, stretches of some of the best hiking in the world. The book includes information on getting to Peru, a guide to Peru's capital Lima, background material on modern Peru; there's a chapter devoted to the Incas and their predecessors, and chapters on Cusco and Machu Picchu. Detailed trekking maps are included, as are site plans and descriptions of what's known about the abandoned ruins you'll pass on your way.

For this edition the trekking section of this book has been expanded to include full details of two new treks: the Santa Teresa trek, which avoids the regulations and bureaucracy associated with the Inca Trail but which arrives at Machu Picchu all the same, after a glorious hike through diverse landscapes; and the splendid trek to the Inca ruins at Choquequirao, a remote site that resembles Machu Picchu, perched on a ridge above the sheer Apurímac valley. Also covered is the wonderful walk to the last refuge of the Incas at Vilcabamba, the ruins of which now lie abandoned and overgrown in a heavily forested valley. The hike traverses some stunning scenery, from lofty mountain passes, via pampa, puna, pasture, dwarf forest and cloud forest to thick lowland rainforest, the 'eyebrows of the jungle', that smothers and engulfs the lost, ancient stones of Vilcabamba.

RESPONSIBLE TRAVEL

Sadly, as with many tourist sites, the paradox of tourism means that the trails, ruins and cities of the Sanctuary are at risk, threatened by their own beauty. It's this beauty that draws the tourists who bring much needed money but at certain times of the year the main trails have become overcrowded and the fragile environment and old ruins damaged by thoughtless visitors who fail to behave with sensitivity. Such damage is not inevitable and this book contains a section suggesting how on your visit you can help preserve this beautiful environment.

Peru is full of wonders. Its beauty is breathtaking, and its culture fascinating. If you are sensitive to the place, it can have a greater impact on you than you have on it. So, in the words of Rudyard Kipling:

> 'Something hidden. Go and Find it. Go and look behind the Ranges
> Something lost behind the Ranges. Lost and waiting for you. Go!'

(From *The Explorer,* which inspired the man who rediscovered Machu Picchu, Hiram Bingham).

PART 1: PLANNING YOUR TRIP

With a tour group or your own guide?

So you've decided to take one of the greatest walks on the planet. The first question to ask yourself always used to be, 'Am I going to do this with a tour or on my own?' Sadly, independent trekking in the Machu Picchu Historical Sanctuary isn't an option any more as in 2001 the Peruvian government brought in new rules about who can walk the trail and how they can do it. Briefly, you can now walk the trail only with a tour company or in the company of a guide.

I said 'sadly', but some of the changes are for the best. In the past there were too many people walking the trail, causing too much damage, litter and erosion, and the regulations will help stop that. This doesn't mean the end of the road for the independent trekker, as you can still walk to Machu Picchu via the Santa Teresa trek (see p25) or to Vilcabamba (see p25) and Choquequirao (see p26) on your own – just not any of the Inca Trails.

Prices have gone up because of the changes, but the good news is that for an organized trek it's still pretty good value. Walking the classic Inca Trail now costs from US$270 to US$350 (£145-190) for the four-day trip which works out to be about US$67-87/£35-47 a day. These are the lowest prices but there are also discounts for students.

When and where to book

Nowadays, the first thing you need to think about is making a booking as soon as possible. The days of turning up in Cusco on spec and joining a tour that's just about to leave are all but over. With the Inca Trail regulations (for more details see box p182), only about 180 tourists are allowed to begin the route each day, and they must have permits to do so, booked and paid up in advance. Competition for permits is fierce and at the busiest time of year (July and August), you might have to book more than three months in advance to get one. The upshot is that you should be looking to make a reservation as soon as you're sure of a date for your trek – the permits are inflexible and cannot be changed later on.

For most, therefore, it'll be easiest to make a booking from home over the internet or by phone. Since only licensed Peruvian agencies are entitled to book permits, you'll be cutting out a middle-man and probably a fat commission if you deal with one of these directly. There are other advantages too: you'll be in contact from the outset with the people leading your trek and your money will go straight into the local economy, rather than into Western pockets. For a list of operators in Cusco, see box pp140-1; most have their own websites and online booking facilities. Alternatively, there are also lots of tour companies outside Peru who'll be happy to make arrangements for you, at a price – see pp12-16.

PLANNING YOUR TRIP

If you're unlucky with your booking and you don't manage to secure a permit, there are plenty of other wonderful treks on offer that aren't subject to the regulations, including the Santa Teresa trek (see p25) which also leads to Machu Picchu, the Vilcabamba trail (see p25) and the Choquequirao trek (see p26), all covered in detail in this book.

Group or private tours

When you make your booking, you'll need to decide whether you want to be on a 'group-service' or a 'private-service' trek. Most people plump for the standard group trek, which involves joining a group of up to 16 people. This is a cheap (typically US$270-350) and sociable way of doing the trek, but the downside is that the groups can sometimes feel a bit large and the mix of abilities may mean you have to walk at a slower pace than you enjoy. It's usually a great way to make new friends, but there's always a chance that you're thrown together with people you'd rather not be spending your holiday with.

This won't happen on a private trek, which is arranged just for you and your chosen companions. If there's a small number of you, it's going to be expensive. Two people on a private trek would expect to pay around US$650 each, while four people might pay around US$450 per person. For larger groups the differences aren't so great: parties of six to nine will cost around US$350 per head, ten to twelve about US$325, and thirteen to sixteen (the maximum) US$300. You'll probably be treated to better service and added comforts for the extra outlay than group trekkers will receive. A private trek is also the surest guarantee of getting a place because the tour agency is able to reserve permits as soon as you book because the numbers are fixed (agencies have to book permits for the entire group in one go). With group-service tours, agencies tend to wait as long as possible to build up numbers before bagging the permits; very occasionally they wait too long and miss the boat – there are no permits left and your trek gets cancelled.

Just the ruins

You can, if you don't want to do the walk, just visit the ruins. Most of the companies mentioned below do straightforward tours to Machu Picchu, and you need never see a pair of hiking boots and a rucksack.

It's as easy to get to the ruins by public transport as it is to get to the trailheads. A passenger train runs regularly between Cusco and the valley floor below Machu Picchu (see p293). From the valley floor there's a bus up to the ruins.

TOUR OPERATORS AND TREKKING AGENCIES

Agencies in Cusco usually charge about US$270-350/£145-190 for the standard four-day trek to Machu Picchu, although there are some cheaper options – see box pp140-1 for more information. Alternatively, travel companies at home can sort everything out for you; prices are in the region of US$2160-4320/£1500-3000 and tours range from two to three weeks. The Peruvian consulate in your home country (see p299) can supply you with the names and telephone numbers of other operators.

Agencies in the UK and Ireland

● **Amazonas Explorer** (☎ 01437-891743, 🖳 www.amazonas-explorer.com) is based in Peru (see p306). Offers the Inca Trail and the Choquequirao trek through their agents in the UK, USA and Switzerland.

● **Andes** (☎ 01556-503929, 🖳 www.andes.org.uk), 37a St Andrew's St, Castle Douglas, Dumfries & Galloway, Kirkendbrightshire, DG7 1EN. Tailor-made treks and climbs.

● **Andean Trails** (☎/🖹 0131-467 7086, 🖳 www.andeantrails.co.uk), The Clockhouse, Bonnington Mill Business Centre, 72 Newhaven Rd, Edinburgh EH6 5QG. Organize treks for small groups and also offer tailor-made itineraries.

● **Audley Travel** (☎ 01869-276210, 🖳 www.audleytravel.com), 6 Willows Gate, Stratton Audley, Oxon OX27 9AU, offers tailor-made tours.

● **Charity Challenge** (☎ 020-8557 0000, 🖳 www.charitychallenge.com), 7th Floor, Northway House, 1379 High Rd, London, N20 9LP. Offer charity treks on the Inca Trail.

● **Classic Journeys** (☎ 01773-873497, 🖳 www.classicjourneys.co.uk), 33 High St, Tibshelf, Alfreton, Derbyshire, DE55 5NX. The Classic Inca trek and others.

● **Condor Journeys and Adventures** (☎ 01700-841318, 🖳 www.condorjour neys-adventures.com), 2 Ferry Bank, Colintraive, Argyll, PA22 3AR. Offer a variety of Inca Trail treks.

● **Discover Adventure** (☎ 01722-718444, 🖳 www.discoveradventure.com), Throope Down House, Blandford Rd, Coombe Bissett, Salisbury, SP5 4LN. Organize ordinary treks as well as treks for charity.

● **Exodus** (☎ 0870-240 5550/020-8675 5550, 🖳 www.exodus.co.uk), Grange Mills, 9 Weir Rd, London SW12 0NE. A well-established, long-running company.

● **Explore Worldwide** (☎ 0870-333 4001/01252-760000, 🖳 www.explore.co .uk), 1 Frederick St, Aldershot, Hants GU11 1LQ. This is a large company doing the Classic Inca trek and the Choquequirao route amongst others.

● **Footprint Adventures** (☎ 01522-804929, 🖳 www.footprint-adventures.co .uk), 5 Malham Drive, Lincoln, LN6 0XD, run a number of treks in the region.

● **Great Walks of the World** (☎ 01935-810820, 🖳 www.greatwalks.net), Salcombe House, Long St, Sherborne, Dorset DT9 3BU, do the Classic Inca trek, the Mollepata trek and the Vilcabamba trail.

● **Guerba Expeditions** (☎ 0845-130 1770, 01373-826611, 🖳 www .guerba.com), Wessex House, 40 Station Rd, Westbury, Wiltshire BA13 3JN.

● **HF Holidays** (☎ 020-8905 9556, 🖳 www.hfholidays.co.uk), Imperial House, The Hyde, Edgware Rd, London NW9 5AL, offer a number of treks.

● **High Places** (☎ 0114-275 7500, 🖳 www.highplaces.co.uk), Globe Centre, Penistone Rd, Sheffield S6 3AE, operate two trips including the Inca Trail.

● **The Imaginative Traveller** (☎ 0800-316 2717, 🖳 www.imaginativetrav eller.com), 1 Betts Ave, Martlesham Heath, Suffolk, IP5 3RB. Agents for Tucan (see p14), a major operator in the area.

● **Journey Latin America** (☎ 020-8747 8315, 🖳 www.journeylatinamerica .co.uk), 12-13 Heathfield Terrace, Chiswick, London W4 4JE. Also in **Manchester**: 12 St Ann's Square, 2nd Floor, Manchester, M2 7HW (☎ 0161-

832 1441, ▤ 0161-832 1551). One of the market leaders for tours to South America, with two Inca Trail trips a month between March and December.

● **KE Adventure Travel** (☎ 017687-73966, ▢ www.keadventure.com), 32 Lake Rd, Keswick, Cumbria, CA12 5DQ. Another big operator with branches in North America.

● **Last Frontiers** (☎ 01296-653000, ▢ www.lastfrontiers.com), Fleet Marston Farm, Aylesbury, Bucks HP18 0QT.

● **Maxwells Travel** (☎ 01-677 9479, ▤ 01-679 3948, ▢ maxwelltravel@eir com.net), D'Olier Chambers, 1 Hawkins St, Dublin 2, is an agent for Explore but also tailor-make trips to the region.

● **Naturetrek** (☎ 01962-733051, ▢ www.naturetrek.co.uk), Cheriton Mill, Cheriton, Alresford, Hants SO24 ONG, offer a Macaws and Machu Picchu trek.

● **Peregrine Adventures** (☎ 01635-872300, ▢ www.peregrineadventures .co.uk), First Floor, 8 Clerewater Place Lower Way, Thatcham, Berkshire RG19 3RF, an Australian company offering a variety of trips to the area.

● **Pura Aventura** (☎ 0845-225 5058, 01273-676712, ▢ www.pura-aventura.com), 18 Bond St, Brighton, BN1 1RD.

● **Ramblers Holidays** (☎ 01707-331133, ▢ www.ramblersholidays.co.uk), Box 43, Welwyn Garden, Herts AL8 6PQ, has a Six Faces of Peru trip which includes the Inca Trail.

● **Red Spokes** (☎ 020-7502 7252, ▢ www.redspokes.co.uk), 29 Northfield Rd, London, N16 5RL. Organize cycling trips in Peru as well as the Inca Trail trek.

● **South American Experience** (☎ 020-7976 5511, ▢ www.southamerican experience.co.uk), 47 Causton St, Pimlico, London SW1P 4AT. Mainly does flights (see p18) but also arranges tailor-made tours.

● **Spirit of Adventure** (☎ 01822-880277, ▢ www.spirit-of-adventure.com), Powder Mills, Princetown, Yelverton, Devon PL20 6SP. The Inca Trail with white-water rafting, mountain-biking or other activities.

● **Tucan Travel** (☎ 01473-667337, ▢ www.tucantravel.com), 19 Gloster Rd, Martlesham Heath, Suffolk IP5 3RB, is one of the largest operators in the area.

● **Walks Worldwide** (☎ 01524-242000, ▢ www.walksworldwide.com), 12 The Square, Ingleton, Carnforth, LA6 3EG, have a 14-day trip including the Inca Trail.

● **White Peak Expeditions** (☎ 01279-654401, ▢ www.whitepeakexpedi tions.co.uk), Hockerill AEC, Dunmow Rd, Bishops Stortford, CM23 5HX, offer the Inca Trail plus the Choquequirao trek and/or mountain biking.

● **World Expeditions** (☎ 0800-074 4135, 020-8870 2600, ▢ www.worldexpe ditions.co.uk), 3 Northfields Prospect, Putney Bridge Rd, London SW18 1PE. See also p16.

Agencies in Continental Europe

● **Austria** El Mundo Reiseburo (☎ 0316-810698, ▢ www.elmundo.at), Schmiedgasse 16, A-8010 Graz.

● **Belgium** Allibert Voyages (see France opposite); **Joker** (☎ 02-426 4030, ▢ www.joker.be), Verdilaan 23/25, 1083 Brussels-Ganshoren; **Divantoura** (☎ 09-223 0069, ▢ www.divantoura.be), Bagattenstraat 176, B-9000, Gent; also St

Jacobsmarkt 5, 2000 Antwerpen (☎ 03-233 1916). Agents for Explore Worldwide, see p13.

● **Denmark** **Inter-Travel** (☎ 33-150077, 🖳 www.inter-travel.dk), Frederiksholms Kanal 2, DK-1220 Kobenhavn K. Agents for Explore Worldwide, see p13.

● **France** **Allibert Voyages** (☎ 08.25.09.01.90, 🖳 www.allibert-voyages.com) has branches in Chamonix, Chapareillan, Paris, Toulouse and Brussels; **Club Aventure** (☎ 08.26.88.20.80, ☎ www.clubaventure.fr), 18 rue Séguier 75006 Paris; also at Le Néréis, Ave André Roussin, Saumaty-Séon, 13016 Marseille; **Tamera** (☎ 04.78.37.88.88, ☎ www.tamera .fr), 26 rue du Boeuf, 69005 Lyon.

● **Germany** **Reise Theke** (☎ 351-471 6222, 🖳 info@reisetheke.de), Mensa Reichenstrasse 1, Dresden 1069; **Explorer Fernreisen** (☎ 0211-99 49 02, 🖳 www.explorer-fernreisen.com), Huttenstrasse 17, 40215 Dusseldorf.

● **Netherlands** **Trotamundos** (☎ 043-350 0308, 🖳 www.trotamundos.nl), Postbus 1695, 6201 BR Maastricht; **Adventure World** (☎ 023-5382 954, 🖳 atc @euronet.nl), Muiderslotweg 112, Haarlem 2026 AS. Agents for Explore Worldwide, see p13.

● **Switzerland** Amazonas Explorer (see p13).

Agencies in the USA
● **Adventure Center** (toll free ☎ 1-800-227-8747, 🖳 www.adventurecenter .com), 1311 63rd St, Suite 200, Emeryville, CA 94608. Agents for Explore Worldwide (see p13).

● **Adventure Travel Network** (☎ 619-544-0800, toll-free ☎ 1-800-467-4595, 🖳 www.atntravel.com), 7 Horton Plaza, San Diego 92101; branches also in San Francisco (☎ 415-247-1800; #143, 595 Market St, CA 94105) and Seattle (☎ 206-322-0396; 715 Broadway Avenue East, WA 98102). Agents for Tucan, one of the largest operators in the area.

● **Holbrook Travel** (☎ 352-377-7111, toll free ☎ 800-541-7111, 🖳 www.hol brooktravel.com), 3540 NW 13th Street, Gainesville, FL 32609-2196. Ruins-only tours, but they do stay in the upmarket Machu Picchu Pueblo Hotel (see p167).

● **Wilderness Travel** (☎ 510-558-2488, toll-free ☎ 1-800-368 2794, 🖳 www .wildernesstravel.com), 1102 9th St, Berkeley, California 94710-1211. A very good company.

● **World Expeditions** (☎/🖳 415-989-2212, toll-free ☎ 1-888-464-TREK, 🖳 www.worldexpeditions.net), 6th Floor, 580 Market St, San Francisco, CA 94104.

Agencies in Canada
● **G.A.P Adventures** (☎ 416-260-0999, toll-free ☎ 1-800-465-5600, 🖳 www .gapadventures.com), 35 Eglinton Avenue, East Toronto, ONT M4P 1M5. This is a very large, well-run organization that offers many tours on the Inca Trail and they also have an office in Cusco.

● **Trek Holidays** (☎ 780-439-9118, toll-free ☎ 1-888-456-3522, 🖳 www .trekholidays.com), 8412-109th St, Edmonton, Alberta T6G 1E2. Agents for Explore Worldwide (see p13) and other companies.

● **Trek Escapes** (☎ 1-866-338-TREK, 🖳 www.trekescapes.com) is a group of companies formed from Westcan Treks, Adventure Center and Fresh Tracks. They have offices in: **Calgary** (☎ 1-800-663-5132, 🖳 calgary@trek escapes.com; 336 14th St NW, Alberta T2N 1Z7); **Vancouver** (☎ 604-734-1066, 🖳 vancouver@trekescapes.com; 1847 West 4th Ave, BC V6J 1M4); **Edmonton** (☎ 1-800-387-3574, ☎ 780-439-0024, 🖳 edmonton@trekescapes .com; 8412 109 St, Alberta T6G 1E2) and **Toronto** (☎ 1-800-267-3347, 🖳 tor onto@trekescapes.com), 223 Carlton St, Ontario, M5A 2L2.

World Expeditions (toll free ☎ 1-800-567 2216, ☎ 613-241-2700, 🖳 www .worldexpeditions.ca, www.expeditionmonde.com) has a branch in Montreal (☎ 514-844-6364, 🖳 info@expeditionmonde.com; 1705 St Denis St, Quebec H2X 3K4) and a sales agent in Toronto (☎ 416-633-5666, 1770 Sheppard Avenue West, Suite 45, ONT M3K 2A3).

Agencies in Peru
See Cusco, box pp140-1.

Agencies in South Africa
● **Shiralee Travel** (☎ 028-313 0526, 🖳 www.harveyworld.co.za), 32 Main Rd, PO Box 1420, Hermanus, 7200. Agents for Explore Worldwide, see p13.

Agencies in Australia
● **Adventure Associates** (☎ 02-9389 7466, 🖳 www.adventureassociates.com), 197 Oxford Mall (PO Box 612), Bondi Junction, Sydney, NSW 2022. Mainly does long tours, but one of their South American options is the Km88 trek.
● **Adventure World** (☎ 02-8913 0755, 🖳 www.adventureworld.com.au), Level 20, 141 Walker St, North Sydney NSW 2060. This company is an agent for Tucan, a large operator in the area.
● **Inca Tours** (☎ 02-4351 2133 or toll-free ☎ 1-800 024 955, www.incatours .net), 3 Margaret St, Wyong NSW 2259.
● **Peregrine Adventures** (☎ 03-9663 8611, 🖳 www.peregrine.net.au), 258 Lonsdale St, Melbourne, Victoria 3000.
● **World Expeditions** (☎ toll-free 1300 720 0000, 🖳 www.worldexpeditions .com.au) has branches in: **Sydney** (☎ 02-8270 8400, 🖳 enquiries@worldexpe ditions.com.au; Level 5, 71 York St, NSW 2000); **Melbourne** (☎ 03-8631 3300, 🖳 travel@worldexpeditions.com.au), 1st Floor, 393 Little Bourke St, Melbourne, Victoria 3000; **Brisbane** (☎ 07-3216 0823, 🖳 adventure@world expeditions.com.au), Shop 2, 36 Agnes St, Fortitude Valley, Queensland 4006; and **Perth** (☎ 08-9485 9899, 🖳 holiday@worldexpeditions.com.au), Level 1, 849 Hay St, Perth, WA 6000.

Agencies in New Zealand
● **Adventure World** (☎ 09-524 5118, 🖳 www.adventureworld.co.nz), 101 Great South Rd, PO Box 74008, Remeura, Auckland.
● **World Expeditions** (☎ 09-368 4161, toll-free ☎ 0800-350354, 🖳 www .worldexpeditions.co.nz), Level 2, 35 High St, Auckland.

PORTERS, ARRIEROS (MULETEERS) AND GUIDES

On most of the walks in this book you'll be going with a tour company and they'll provide guides and porters. The exceptions are the Santa Teresa, Vilcabamba and Choquequirao treks, where you can go it alone and you can organize your own arriero (muleteer) to carry some of your kit and act as your guide.

You can arrange things in Cusco but I prefer finding help in the villages on the trail rather than using a tour agency for a number of reasons: you know you're not exploiting the locals and are paying a fair price for a fair service; also, you're putting your tourist dollars directly into the local economy and not lining the pockets of already flourishing Cusqueños or Limeños. And anyway, it's more personal. For more information on porter welfare see the box on p172.

You can pick up a muleteer and mules in Mollepata (see p218) before embarking on the Salcantay or Santa Teresa treks, Huancacalle (see p244) on your way to Vilcabamba or in Cachora (see p267) at the start of the Choquequirao trek. Remember when negotiating – and most arrieros only speak Spanish and Quechua – that you'll need to discuss where he's going to sleep; if he has to rely on the villagers en route for accommodation then how far you walk per day will largely be dictated by where he will be able to find lodging.

You should also discuss whether you are going to provide food for him, or whether his fee includes an allowance for him to buy his own before departure. Finally, don't forget to factor into his wages a sum for his return journey; he may only be walking with you for four days, but it will probably take another two or three for him to return back home.

The **going rate** (at the time of writing) for a porter or for an arriero is s/20-30 per day, which is about US$6-9/£4-6. A **tip** is expected: 5-10% is customary but porters and arrieros are usually very ill-paid so be generous.

Hiring arrieros

It sounds simple enough, but it took no end of argument and persuasion...to convince these worthy arrieros that they were not going to be everlastingly ruined by this bargain. Hiram Bingham, 1922, *Inca Land*

Some things never change. Even today arrieros drive a hard bargain and will convince you that, however much you pay, you're stealing the bread from their children's mouths. If you're hiring an arriero, don't be surprised if he insists on taking two mules. Since the dawn of time, muleteers all over the world have refused to take only one animal. It's not a rip-off, it's an insurance policy should one of the mules go lame or should you become exhausted and need a ride.

Getting to Peru

BY AIR

The following main airlines fly to Lima: Aeroflot, Aerolíneas Argentinas, Air France, Alitalia, American Airlines, Avianca, Continental, Copa, Delta, Ecuatoriana, Iberia, KLM, Lan Chile, Lan Peru, Lloyd Aéreo Boliviano, Lufthansa, Servivensa and Varig. Many of the tour operators mentioned above (pp12-16) can get you tickets. Note that flights connecting Peru and Chile are now subject to a tax of US$50, payable at the airport.

Airpasses covering Peru are available; as the exact details of the offers change regularly, you should check with your travel agent. At the time of writing, a five-coupon Lan Peru airpass costs US$390/£270, and a two-coupon pass US$173/£120.

For a website guide to flights to/from Lima, visit 🖳 www.traficoperu.com.

From Europe

There are currently no direct flights from London. The main gateway is Madrid but there are also flights from Amsterdam. From all other European cities connections must be made. The main market for discount flights is the UK, and the cheapest cost from £500 in the low season to £650 in the high season. Check for cheap deals at Internet sites such as 🖳 www.opodo.co.uk, 🖳 www.ebookers .com, 🖳 www.expedia.co.uk, or 🖳 www.cheapflights.com.

● **Journey Latin America** See p13. As well as organizing tours this company often has good deals on flights.
● **South American Experience** See p14. A specialist in South America, this company mainly offers flights.
● **STA Travel** (☎ 0870-166 7686, 🖳 www.statravel.co.uk). One of the largest budget-flight companies in the world with branches all over the place.
● **Trailfinders** (🖳 www.trailfinders.com) has branches in London; Birmingham; Cambridge; Manchester; Glasgow; Bristol; Newcastle; Belfast and Dublin.

From the USA and Canada

The main gateways are Miami and New York, though there are also flights from Dallas, Los Angeles and Houston. Expect to pay at least US$1300-1500 from the States and C$1000-1500 from Canada.

● **Air Brokers International** (☎ 1-800-883-3273, 🖳 www.airbrokers.com), 685 Market St, Suite 400, San Francisco, California 94105.
● **STA Travel** (🖳 www.statravel.com) has branches countrywide including: **New York** (☎ 1-212-627-3111) and **Los Angeles** (☎ 1-800-781-4040). Also in **Vancouver** (☎ 1-604-806-4040).
● **Travel CUTS** (☎ 1-866-246-9762, 🖳 www.travelcuts.com), found in all the major Canadian cities as well as in California.

From Australia and New Zealand

There are currently no direct flights to Peru from Australia or New Zealand. From Australia, the cheapest fare is about A$2000. From New Zealand, expect to pay from NZ$2400.

● **Flight Centre** (🖳 www.flightcentre.com.au). Many branches in **Australia**, including Melbourne (☎ 03-9650 2899), 19 Bourke St, Melbourne, and in **New Zealand** (☎ 09-358 4310), 350 Queen St, Auckland.

● **STA Travel** (🖳 www.statravel.com.au), found in most major cities including Melbourne (☎ 03-9639-0599) and Wellington (☎ 04-385-0561).

● **Trailfinders** (🖳 www.trailfinders.com.au). Branches in Brisbane (☎ 07-3229 0887); Sydney (☎ 02-9247 7666); Cairns (☎ 07-4041 1199); Perth (☎ 08-9226 1222), and Melbourne (☎ 03-9600 3022).

OVERLAND

It's very difficult to get to Peru overland from Central America, because of the swampy region in Colombia known as the **Darien Gap.** The Pan-American highway, which links most of the rest of the two continents, stops either side of this fearsome natural obstacle. It's much easier to get to Peru and Cusco overland from neighbouring countries. There are buses from La Paz in **Bolivia** that cross Lake Titicaca on a ferry and reach Cusco via Puno.

From **Brazil**, there's a 10-day ferry ride up the Amazon from Manaus to Peru's Amazonian port of Iquitos, from where you can fly to Cusco. In the past you could also take a boat up the river to Cusco but it's not safe because of bandits.

From **Ecuador** in the north and **Chile** in the south there are major bus routes into Peru along the Pan-American highway.

Budgeting

The price of a **guided tour** on the Inca Trail to Machu Picchu is around US$270 -350/£145-190 for four days, although if you're a student you may be able to get a cheaper package. These tours should include the price of a ticket for the trail (US$25-60: see p182). **Day-to-day costs** will be around US$20-25/£10-15 a day for basic living; on US$40/£25 a day you will have a very comfortable time. To get some perspective on the costs below, a housemaid gets on average US$70 a month, a teacher around US$300 and a doctor about US$1000.

The cheapest **hotels** cost US$3.50/£2.50 per person per night. At the other end of the scale, the most expensive hotels can cost over $300/£155.

In terms of **food**, a local will pay around US$1/£0.50 for a filling lunch and a backpacker will pay about US$4/£3 for a light one in a tourist café. You can easily eat more expensively though not necessarily much better: breakfast at Machu Picchu Sanctuary Lodge costs US$30/£20, and dinner at one of Lima's more flashy restaurants can cost US$60/£40 per person (without wine).

A 24-hour luxury **bus ride** from Lima to Cusco will set you back about US$30/£22, and a **flight** to Cusco will cost up to US$80/£50.

You're inevitably going to be tempted to buy **souvenirs**. The cost of these will depend on how good you are at bargaining and the quality of the thing you're buying: cheap Andean pan-pipes cost about US$2.50/£1.60 but prime quality handwoven textiles can cost hundreds of dollars.

When to go and for how long?

WHEN TO GO

The best time to go is in late April or May. The trekking season is April/May to October. In June/July the trails become very, very busy, and it's sometimes difficult to get on a tour, and if you do it'll be difficult to find a spot to pitch your tent. At other times of the year the trails will be less crowded but be prepared for some serious rain and impassable roads: the Vilcabamba Trail may be so washed out at this time that you probably won't find a guide willing to take you.

Avoid February: the classic Inca Trail **is closed for the duration of February**, although Machu Picchu remains open to visitors as usual. The shorter Km104 trek (see p205) and the Trekkers' Hotel also remain open.

LIMA – CLIMATE CHARTS

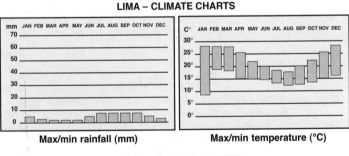

Max/min rainfall (mm)   Max/min temperature (°C)

CUSCO – CLIMATE CHARTS

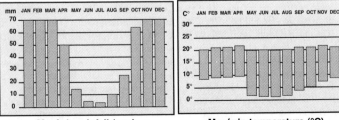

Max/min rainfall (mm)   Max/min temperature (°C)

FOR HOW LONG?

The longest walk in this book takes two weeks and the shortest only two days. The basic Inca Trail from Km88 takes four days – see below for more details.

To work out how long your Peruvian trip's going to be, you should add five days to the length of the trail you're thinking of walking. This allows a day to fly to Cusco from Lima (more if you're travelling overland), a day to fly back, a day just in case there's a problem with the flights, and a couple of days acclimatizing to the altitude in Cusco. If you're not already booked on the classic Inca Trail you should allow up to four weeks to secure a place on the trail because of the regulations (see p182). If you want to tackle one of the other routes allow two to five days to make the necessary arrangements.

Acclimatizing is very important. If you don't spend a little time allowing your body to get used to Cusco's thin air you can expect a thoroughly miserable and exhausting time, and you might also be risking your life. See pp175-7 for more information.

Route options

(**See Route Options map overleaf**). All but five of the trails in this book end up following the ancient Inca road from the village of Huayllabamba to Machu Picchu, the route trekkers call 'The Inca Trail'. In 1911 the Hiram Bingham expedition began to uncover this route and Dr Paul Fejos discovered more of it in 1944. The trails that don't follow this route are the two-day route to Machu Picchu from Km104, the Riverside Trail from Km88 (for both see 'Shorter trails', p204), the Santa Teresa trek (see p226), the Vilcabamba Trail (see p238) and the Choquequirao trek (see p263).

THE CLASSIC INCA TRAIL (3-4 days)   (see pp185-200)

The classic Inca Trail starts at kilometre 88 (Km88) on the railway line that runs from Cusco to the jungle town of Quillabamba – the foot of Machu Picchu mountain is at Km113. The first part of the walk, from Km88 to the village of Huayllabamba, is a relatively gentle stroll taking you through eucalyptus groves and past the extensive ruins of Patallacta. The hike from Huayllabamba is more gruelling but it's a superb walk through varied scenery and vegetation, travelling from barren grassland to encroaching jungle, through stone-hewn tunnels

> ❏ 'OLD MARTIN: *You call them the Andes. Picture a curtain of stone hung by some giant across your path. Mountains set on mountains: cliffs on cliffs. Hands of rock a hundred yards high, with flashing nails where the snow never moved. Scratching the gashed face of the sun'.*
> **Peter Shaffer**, *Royal Hunt of the Sun*
> (Act 1 Scene 7)

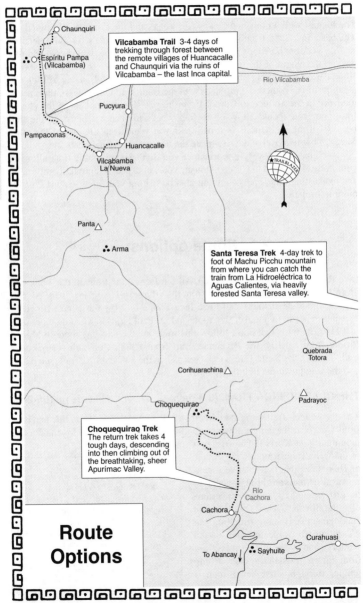

Chaunquiri

Vilcabamba Trail 3-4 days of trekking through forest between the remote villages of Huancacalle and Chaunquiri via the ruins of Vilcabamba – the last Inca capital.

Espíritu Pampa (Vilcabamba)

Rio Vilcabamba

Pucyura

Pampaconas

Huancacalle

Vilcabamba La Nueva

TRAILBLAZER

Panta

Arma

Santa Teresa Trek 4-day trek to foot of Machu Picchu mountain from where you can catch the train from La Hidroeléctrica to Aguas Calientes, via heavily forested Santa Teresa valley.

Quebrada Totora

Corihuarachina

Padrayoc

Choquequirao

Choquequirao Trek The return trek takes 4 tough days, descending into then climbing out of the breathtaking, sheer Apurímac Valley.

Río Cachora

Cachora

Curahuasi

Route Options

To Abancay

Sayhuite

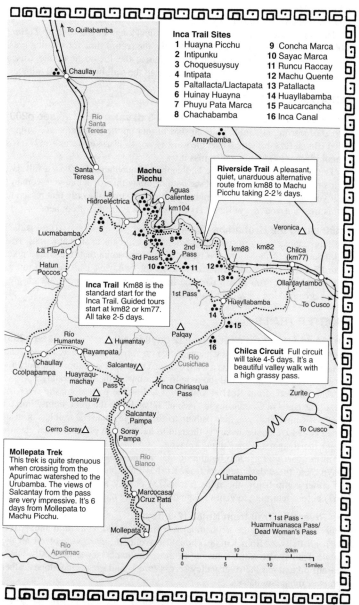

Inca Trail Sites
1 Huayna Picchu
2 Intipunku
3 Choquesuysuy
4 Intipata
5 Paltallacta/Llactapata
6 Huinay Huayna
7 Phuyu Pata Marca
8 Chachabamba
9 Concha Marca
10 Sayac Marca
11 Runcu Raccay
12 Machu Quente
13 Patallacta
14 Huayllabamba
15 Paucarcancha
16 Inca Canal

Riverside Trail A pleasant, quiet, unarduous alternative route from km88 to Machu Picchu taking 2-2½ days.

Inca Trail Km88 is the standard start for the Inca Trail. Guided tours start at km82 or km77. All take 2-5 days.

Chilca Circuit Full circuit will take 4-5 days. It's a beautiful valley walk with a high grassy pass.

Mollepata Trek
This trek is quite strenuous when crossing from the Apurímac watershed to the Urubamba. The views of Salcantay from the pass are very impressive. It's 6 days from Mollepata to Machu Picchu.

* 1st Pass - Huarmihuanasca Pass/Dead Woman's Pass

and over 4200m/13,750ft-high passes. At the end of your journey lies the legendary Machu Picchu, Lost City of the Incas.

The walk's tough: it's only 43km (26½ miles) long but you walk up 2150m/7000ft and down 2100m/6880ft. Incidentally, the record time for running (yes, running) the trail is held by Edgar Rodríguez, the President of the Cusco Athletic League, who is said to have completed the trail in 3 hours 50 minutes.

VARIATIONS ON THE CLASSIC TRAIL

Chilca (Km77) along the Urubamba (4-5 days)   (see p200)
Instead of starting at Km88, you can start further up the Urubamba at a village called Chilca (at kilometre 77 on the railway, so it's also known as Km77). It's a small place – blink and you'll miss it.

The hike from here along the Urubamba to Huayllabamba takes a full day, but it's not really worth it – you'll see nothing along this route that you wouldn't see if you started at Km82. Although it's a pleasant stroll, the only real reason to do this trek is if you've got time to burn, or if your tour starts from here.

Km82 along the Urubamba (3½-4½ days)   (see p202)
The compromise between starting at Km88 and Chilca is to start at Km82. This walk takes you further along the banks of the Urubamba than the Km88 hike, rewarding you with wonderful views down the valley; it isn't so wearing as starting at Chilca. You'll also pass the Inca hill fort, Inca Raccay, which provides a breathtaking view over Patallacta.

SHORTER TRAILS

Km104 and the Purification Trail (2 days in all)   (see p205)
The path from the Inca site of Chachabamba (at Km104) to Huinay Huayna and the last part of the Inca Trail is a short exposed walk across an open hillside, not worth doing if you can afford the time to walk one of the other routes.

Alternatively, from Km104 you could follow the path along the river for 3km to the ruins of Choquesuysuy (see p207) and take the three-hour climb up the 'Purification Trail', an Inca path up to Huinay Huayna. The trail has been so named because Choquesuysuy is thought to have been a place of ritual cleansing for those approaching Huinay Huayna.

In the past you used to be able to stay at the Trekkers' Hostel at Huinay Huayna, but these days trekkers from Km104 must push on to Machu Picchu and either camp below the ruins (see p278) or stay at Aguas Calientes (see p167) before returning to visit the site the following day.

The Riverside Trail from Km88 (2-3 days)   (see p237)
Rather than following the Urubamba river from Km104, you could simply follow it all the way from Km88. Though it avoids the passes involved on the Classic Trail it also misses out on all those dramatic views; it's really just a pleasant hike along the river valley across forest- and grass-clad slopes rather than over mountain passes.

CHILCA (KM77) UP THE SILQUE VALLEY (5-7 days)   (see p208)

This is a very beautiful valley walk on which you're unlikely to meet many gringos. The area around here was once the land of the Bethlemites, the wealthiest religious group in the province, and the walk up the verdant Silque valley takes you through their rich and fertile old farmland. There's a 4700m-/15,740ft-high pass to climb, and if you tell people you're walking that way they'll think you're mad – it's much quicker to get to Huayllabamba along the Urubamba.

THE MOLLEPATA TREK (6 or 7 days)   (see p217)

Along with the Vilcabamba Trail (see below), this is the most difficult and most dramatic of the hikes in this book. You start in the village of Mollepata, and walk from the valley of the Apurímac to the valley of the Urubamba, over the shoulder of Mt Salcantay. There's a 4950m-/16,235ft-high pass, and you pass within touching distance of the glacier that gives birth to the river Cusichaca. If you're a glutton for punishment you can start in the desert heat down by the river Apurímac and add another day to this hike.

THE SANTA TERESA TREK (3-4 days)   (see p226)

Closed by giant landslips in 1988, this recently reopened alternative route to Machu Picchu is not subject to the Inca Trail regulations (see p182), and has consequently become popular with those who have fallen foul of the rules. It is also less heavily used than the traditional route.

The trek begins from Mollepata and climbs over a pass (4700m/15,420ft) on the shoulder of Mt Salcantay before descending into the beautiful forested Santa Teresa valley. From here it clambers over a ridge into the Aobamba Valley and then joins the Urubamba valley, finishing at the foot of Machu Picchu mountain. Although there are few Inca ruins along the way, it is a very scenic walk through some of the region's most picturesque landscapes and it does finish at one of the finest archaeological sites in the Americas.

THE VILCABAMBA TRAIL (6-9 days in all; 4 days walking) (see p238)

This trail takes you between the remote villages of Huancacalle and Chaunquiri via the ruins of Espíritu Pampa, believed to have been the site of Vilcabamba, the legendary last capital of the Incas.

This is a much tougher challenge than the classic Inca Trail: there are no designated campsites, the path is often very muddy in places and can be overgrown and the ruins themselves are nowhere near as spectacular as Machu Picchu. It's the trek itself that makes this route really worthwhile, a remote and beautiful hike through many of Peru's vegetation zones. Much of the trek is low-lying: altitudes range from 3800m/12,465ft down to 1000m/3300ft.

While there are only about four days of actual walking involved, you'll need to add on the time it takes to get to and from the trail, plus perhaps a couple of days in Quillabamba or Huancacalle, meaning that the whole expedition could take anything between six and nine days to complete.

THE CHOQUEQUIRAO TREK (4 days)   (see p263)

This trek goes from Cachora to the ruins at Choquequirao, the first major Inca site uncovered outside Cusco, yet one which remains largely unexplored. Having reached the ruins at the end of the second day, you then retrace your steps and walk out along the same trail.

The trek is physically quite demanding as it involves a steep descent of 1500m/4920ft into the Apurímac valley to cross the river, followed by an 1800m/5900ft haul up the other side. It's hot and dry, and there are few water sources along the route. However, the vertiginous Apurímac valley is spectacular and the ruins themselves, perched on a magnificent ridge like Machu Picchu, are fascinating.

COMBINING OR ALTERING ROUTES

There's scope for linking together many of these routes, or doing different bits of them, or doing them in a different order. See the map on pp22-3. There are also many other hikes you could take in these hills and many other places to explore. However, you should bear in mind that the park authorities don't allow you to start at Machu Picchu and walk in the direction of Huayllabamba.

Two obvious alternative hikes are a **Chilca circuit**, and a hike from **Mollepata to Machu Picchu via Chilca** (see p236).

What to take

The golden rule is to travel light. If you're in doubt, leave it out and take more money with you. The more that's in your bag, the more weight you'll have to carry and the more you'll curse yourself. Wherever you go in Peru, don't wear military clothes or carry military-style equipment as people might mistake you for a soldier or a terrorist. For hiking it's still a good idea to travel light but if you want to be fully equipped you're going to have to carry much more. What follows is a list of what you'll need for safe and comfortable hiking.

BOOTS

Good boots, well broken in, are essential. Don't skimp on them – the more you pay, the better quality you'll get. There are two main types: **Fabric boots** are generally lined with Gore-Tex (if they're not, don't look at them) and are waterproof and immediately comfortable. They're not as tough as leather boots and don't last as long. **Leather boots** are tough and last ages, but to keep them water-resistant you have to keep rubbing in dubbin or some other waterproofing agent. **Plastic boots** for mountaineers are not necessary or suitable for the hikes in this book.

CLOTHES

Back in 1922, to avoid frostbite, Bingham had to order each man in his party to put on four pairs of thick woollen socks and three pairs of longjohns. Modern fabrics, however, are light and keep you warm and dry without being too bulky.

Most hikers wear several layers of clothing, rather than just a thick jumper or an enormous jacket. The advantage of doing this is that you can peel off layers as you walk and still keep comfortable, or you can combine the layers to prepare yourself for all kinds of weather from damp heat to dry cold.

● **Jacket** If you can afford it, buy a waterproof jacket made from Gore-Tex, a material that is breathable (ie it lets your sweat out) and highly waterproof. It's effective but not quite the all-purpose fabric the advertisements would have you believe. There are other similar fabrics on the market that are similar, such as Sympatex, but I don't find them quite as good.

● **Down jacket/fleece top** Under your waterproof you should wear a warmth layer. Some people wear fleeces (tightly woven nylon) because they're light and warm, but I find them bulky. The alternative is a down (feather-stuffed) jacket, very light, very warm, very compact but also very expensive and completely useless should it get wet.

● **Jersey** Some people take a woollen jumper, although there are some good micro-fleeces around which are warm, lightweight and quick drying.

● **Shirts** Light shirts with long sleeves and collars are best; synthetic ones dry faster than cotton, but I prefer the latter. Many people take T-shirts and end up with burnt necks in the fierce sun. Two or three shirts should be enough.

● **Trousers/pants and skirts** Poly-cotton travellers' clothing of the sort sold by Rohan is good since it dries quickly but it's expensive. Don't take jeans. They absorb water and sweat like a sponge, and take ages to dry. They're heavy and bulky and for the same weight you can pack both a pair of warm and a pair of light trousers. Women should not wear shorts or short skirts.

 The bare necessities?
From here to the top, we were to carry only such things as were absolutely necessary. They included the Mummery tent with pegs and poles, the mountain-mercurial barometer, the two Watkins aneriods, the hypsometer, a pair of Zeiss glasses, two 3A Kodaks, six films, a sling psychrometer, a prismatic compass and clinometer, a Stanley pocket level, an eighty-foot red-strand mountain rope, three ice axes, a seven-foot flagpole, and American flag and a Yale flag. In order to avoid disaster in case of storm, we also carried four of Silver's self-heating cans of Irish Stew and mock-turtle soup, a cake of chocolate, and eight hard-tack, besides raisins and cubes of sugar in our pockets.
Hiram Bingham, 1922, *Inca Land*

● **Inner layer/underwear** The important thing about a skin layer is that it draws sweat away from your body and dries quickly. Cotton isn't very good: T-shirts get sopping wet and then cling to you, and the moment you stop walking you freeze. I recommend thermal underwear – silk thermals are warmest but the most expensive. For normal underwear, three changes of whatever you usually wear is fine.

● **Socks** Three pairs of thick socks is enough.

● **Hat** A sun hat with a wide brim is important protection against the heat during the day. A woolly hat (the locally knitted hat is known as a *chullo*) is essential at altitude and on cold evenings.

● **Gloves or mittens** Cheap woollen gloves are available in the tourist shops in Cusco and are essential.

● **Swimsuit** Useful when you're washing in the open or for visiting the hot springs in Aguas Calientes.

EQUIPMENT

Backpack
This is another thing you shouldn't skimp on. You'll be wearing it for days on end so make sure it fits your back well, is tough and has the right capacity for you.

There are two types of rucksack, **internal frame** (the bag incorporates a rigid back-piece) and **external frame** (with the bag hung from a frame). You hardly ever see external-frame rucksacks in Europe anymore, but they're still common in the US. Leading makes are Karrimor, Berghaus and Lowe.

It's vital to line your backpack with at least one strong plastic bag to keep everything dry, and a good idea to pack everything inside it in plastic bags, too.

Sleeping bag and mat
Down **sleeping bags** are lighter and pack up tighter than foam-filled ones but they're more expensive and difficult to dry if they get wet. You'll need at least a three-season bag, possibly a four-season if you feel the cold. Some people bring a **sleeping bag liner**, made from a folded sheet sewn up on two sides. This can be easily washed so helps keep the sleeping bag clean; it also makes it warmer.

Sleeping-mats do two things: obviously they cushion you, but more importantly they insulate you from the chilly ground. A **foam sleeping-mat** is OK, but the self-inflating air-mats made by **Therm-a-rest** are much more comfortable. They do tend to puncture, however, so take a repair kit, too. You can hire mats and bags in Cusco.

Tent
Don't bother with anything but a free-standing tent – the ones with metal poles that you can pitch anywhere. These are so much better than the old A-frame tents which are a waste of money these days. Make sure you buy one that packs up tightly and is light, and don't forget to seal the seams before your first night out in the rain.

Tents are expensive, and if you're not planning many other trekking holidays it's not really worth buying one. You can hire them in Cusco and agencies are obliged to provide them for their groups.

Stoves, pans and crockery

Although **butane gas stoves** like the camping-gaz ones that run on the little blue cylinders don't normally work at altitude, you can buy cylinders for them containing a butane-propane mix which is completely satisfactory. They sell these cylinders in Cusco. Unless they're able to run on a wide range of fuels, **liquid fuel stoves** are next to useless in Peru, because the proprietary fuel on which they run is unobtainable and they get clogged up on Peru's filthy petrol. If you bring a liquid fuel stove it must be able to run on as many fuels as possible, and be easy to clean.

Bring a couple of **aluminium pans** that can be stored nestling inside each other. Some people don't bother with plates, as you can eat out of the pans. Do bring **cups** and **cutlery**, and a wire scrubber for cleaning off your burnt-on porridge. You can hire or buy these things in Cusco.

General equipment

Other essential items include **matches** and a couple of **lighters**, **sunglasses** (mountain or skiing sunglasses are good because they enclose your eyes and reduce glare), a **torch** (a head torch is recommended because it leaves your hands free), **spare batteries** (easy to forget, impossible to do without), a **whistle** (to summon help), a **small sewing kit**, **plastic bags**, a **penknife** (with scissors and a tin opener), **water bottles** (carry two litres capacity per person; the Platypus system, a pouch connected to a tube from which you can drink as you walk along, is popular with trekkers everywhere and recommended because it encourages you to drink more), **water purifying tablets** (chlorine doesn't kill all the bugs, iodine's much better – see p179) a **sun hat**, **toothpaste**, **toothbrush**, **loo paper**, **sanitary towels** (for what they're designed for, and to deal with any serious bleeding injury), **sun block**, **lip balm**, **soap** and a **medical kit** (see p31). All toiletries are readily available in Cusco.

If you're planning to walk the Mollepata trek or from Chilca up the Silque valley, or the Vilcabamba trail a **compass** is essential.

Useful items include **spare bootlaces**, **spare buckles** for your rucksack, **candles** (for when your spare batteries run out), **string** (for a clothes line), **compact binoculars**, **paper and pen** (many hikers bring a **diary**), **insect repellent** (particularly if you're heading to Vilcabamba or to Choquequirao), a **small trowel** for burying your turds, and a small, thin **towel**. You could bring **biodegradeable washing liquid** although you can clean just about anything from your pans with a wire scouring pad. Some people find a **collapsible plastic bucket** useful for washing thereby not polluting the water source.

Some people like taking a walking stick or ski pole, useful for stiff descents, but sticks used on the Inca Trail from Huayllabamba to Machu Picchu must have rubber bungs fitted over the metal tips to prevent damage to the path.

You don't need mountaineering equipment (ice-axes, ropes, crampons) on these treks.

Cameras and photography

Some people don't carry cameras, feeling that carrying a camera turns them from a participant into a mere observer, but whenever I've left my camera at home I've regretted it. A slim **compact camera** will be fine for snapshots, but if you're more ambitious you should take an **SLR** with a polarizing filter and a wide-angle lens. It'd be good to take a portrait lens too but you shouldn't weigh yourself down too much. If you take a **digital camera** or any camera with rechargeable batteries you'll need to take spares as there's nowhere to recharge batteries on the trails.

As for **film**, because the light's so strong you needn't bother with anything faster than 200ASA unless you're travelling in the wet season. Although it's best to bring all the film you need from home, you can buy print and slide film in Cusco and Lima although you can't be sure that it hasn't been left lying around in the sun (which degrades the chemicals in the film). When flying never put film in baggage that goes in the hold as this may be X-rayed (or even lost). Remove film from your hand luggage before it is X-rayed. The official may simply point to a label on the machine that says 'Film Safe' but you should not believe this and request a hand search.

Because of the strong light, the best time to take photos is in the early morning or late afternoon. If you want to take someone's picture always ask them first. Like you they value their privacy (see p173).

If you're buying videos in Peru note that the system used is NTSC not PAL. This is used in the USA and is not compatible with the UK's system.

FOOD

Bring some dehydrated or vacuum-packed trekkers' food from home and use it as emergency rations or a treat, but don't load yourself up as you'll be able to buy all the main food you need in Cusco. When you're off up the mountains, take food that doesn't weigh much but which provides large amounts of carbohydrate, sugary food and little treats to raise your spirits. Examples of good food to take, all of which you can buy out there are dehydrated potato, polenta, *quinoa* (an Andean grain), porridge, milk powder, dried noodles and packet soup. Also take some dried fruit and nuts, chocolate, boiled sweets, sugar, stock cubes, salt, pepper (keep them in used film canisters), dried sausage or tinned meat. Ground cinnamon and cloves go well in the porridge. All of this is light and nutritious. It helps greatly if you divide the food into a separate plastic bag for each day, and then you won't have to empty your whole rucksack looking for the last packet of soup.

MEDICAL KIT

Mine contains: assorted **plasters**, different sizes of **sterile gauze**, a **triangular bandage**, a **crêpe bandage**, **elastic knee supports** (essential, particularly if you've had knee problems in the past as the steep descents place enormous strain on knees), some **moleskin** or **compeed** (for blisters), **antiseptic** cream and wipes, **antihistamine cream** and **antihistamine tablets**, **ibuprofen**, soluble **aspirin** tablets (for sore throats), a **spare lighter**, **spare needle and thread**. You might also want to take **acetozelomide** (Diamox) for altitude sickness (see p175) and for diarrhoea **loperamide** (Imodium) and **re-hydrating powders**.

Some people carry a course of antibiotics which they get from their doctor at home. Note that overuse of antibiotics can create super bugs that are resistant to treatment so you should use them only if it's really necessary. If you take prescription medicine at home make sure to bring sufficient stock with you as it may not be so easy to come by in Peru.

MAPS

The IGN (Instituto Geográfico Nacional) in Lima sell good maps of the region, which you can also buy from the South American Explorers' Club (see p118). The maps you want, which are on a scale of 1:100,000, are: 2444 (27-r) and 2344 (27-q), while for Vilcabamba you'll also need the north-western corner of map 2344 (27-q), as well as 2244 (27-p) and 2245 (26-p) and for the Choquequirao trek you'll need maps 2343 (28-q) and 2344 (27-q). Watch out for old editions of 27-q since the bottom of the map is incomplete and does not include Mollepata, the starting point for both the Mollepata and Santa Teresa treks; it is on the new edition of this map.

Should you be contemplating the link-up trek from Cachora to Machu Picchu you'll need maps 2343 (28-q) and 2344 (27-q). To get from Cachora to Espíritu Pampa use 2343 (28-q), 2344 (27-q), 2244 (27-p) and 2245 (26-p). There's also a 1:200,000 map of the region to the north of Cusco that's of no use for hiking because the scale's too great and it's inaccurate. However, it does give a general overview of the region.

These maps are now available at some specialized map shops outside Peru. Stanfords has them and takes mail orders on its website (🖳 www.stanfords .co.uk, 12-14 Long Acre, London WC2).

RECOMMENDED READING

Guidebooks

My favourite guidebook is *The Rough Guide to Peru* but *Peru Handbook* (Footprint) and Lonely Planet's *Peru* are both excellent. Hilary Bradt's *Backpacking and Trekking in Peru and Bolivia* (Bradt Travel Guides in the UK, Globe Pequot Press in USA) is the classic guide to trekking in these two countries. Charles Brod's *Apus & Incas* (Inca Expeditions, 1989) is a very good guide to hiking in the area around Cusco but difficult to obtain. There's also Peter Frost's *Exploring Cusco*. The only widely available phrase book in Quechua is published by Lonely Planet.

General books on Peru

The Peru Reader (Duke University Press 1995), edited by Orin Starn and others, is an interesting introduction to all of Peru, past and present. For analyses of modern Peru, read *Fujimori's Peru* edited by John Crabtree and Jim Thomas

(Institute of Latin American Studies 1998), and *Shining Path,* Simon Strong (HarperCollins 1992). *A Fish in the Water* by Mario Vargas Llosa (English translation Faber & Faber 1994) is a description of his 1990 election campaign.

The Incas and their ancestors

Richard Burger's lavishly illustrated *Chavín and the Origins of Andean Civilisation* (Thames and Hudson 1992) is the seminal book on how it all started. *The Incas and their Ancestors* by Michael Moseley (Thames and Hudson 1992) is a good survey of where it went from there.

In the 19th century, Prescott and Markham wrote famous histories of the Incas but the best book on the subject is John Hemming's *The Conquest of the Incas,* (Penguin 1983, Papermac 1993). This book is excellent reading and a thorough piece of scholarship. *The Incas* by Terence D'Altroy, Blackwell 2002, is a recent survey of Incan culture.

There are hundreds of other books on the Incas, ranging from children's pop-up books to academic tomes. The best place to start looking for a reading list is in the bibliography of Rebecca Stone-Miller's art history book *Art in the Andes,* (Thames and Hudson 1993). *The Cities of the Ancient Andes* by Adriana von Hagen and Craig Thomas (Thames and Hudson 1998) also has a good reading list.

Machu Picchu

Machupicchu, Devenir Histórico y Cultural, Efrain Chevarria Huarcaya, (UNSAAC 1992) is a guide to Machu Picchu and its position in Peru's history and culture (available only in Spanish). *Machu Picchu* by John Hemming (Readers' Digest *Wonders of Man Series*) 1981) is the best book in English on the subject. *The Machu Picchu Guidebook*, Ruth Wright and Alfredo Zegarra, Johnson Books, 2004, is a good modern guide to the site.

Worth a read are *The Sacred Centre,* Johan Reinhard (Nuevas Imágenes 1991), which gives an alternative view of what Machu Picchu's about, and Jim Bartle's and Peter Frost's attractive coffee-table book, *The Machu Picchu Historical Sanctuary* (Nuevas Imágenes 1995). An even more delightful coffee-table book is *Realm of the Incas* (Idlewild 2003) by Max Milligan, former owner of the Cross Keys pub in Cusco. The photos are simply gorgeous.

Lost City of the Incas, Hiram Bingham, (Weidenfeld & Nicholson, 2002), is a reprint of Bingham's classic account of the discovery of Machu Picchu including his original photographs and some beautiful modern ones.

Vilcabamba

A copy of Vincent R Lee's *Forgotten Vilcabamba – Final Stronghold of the Incas* is by far the best and most comprehensive on the subject. If you're planning on walking the Vilcabamba trail, it will enhance the pleasure of your walk tenfold; Benjamin Cobos at the Sixpac Manco Hostal in Huancacalle has a copy that he sometimes lends out. Lee's first book, the much shorter *Sixpac Manco – Travels among the Incas*, is also a good read and covers a lot of the same information. Both of these books contain detailed diagrams of the ruins. Gene Savoy, the man who finally established the location of the ancient capital of the rebel

Incas (see p105) wrote up his explorations in *Antisuyu* (Simon and Schuster 1970). The last few chapters of John Hemming's classic *Conquest of the Incas* are also very relevant to this trail. Hugh Thomson's *The White Rock* has good historical detail and provides more recent descriptions of the ruins.

Travelogues and expedition reports

Early descriptions of Peru include *Peregrinations of a Pariah* by Flora Tristan and the beautifully illustrated 1877 book *Peru. Travel and Exploration in the Land of the Incas* by E George Squier (Macmillan). Hiram Bingham's most accessible account of his travels is *Inca Land* (Constable & Co, 1922) and of the discovery of Machu Picchu is *The Lost City of the Incas* (Duell, Sloan and Pearce 1948). This last book is available in a reprint all over Cusco, and there's also a larger format edition (see books on Machu Picchu, opposite). Dr Paul Fejos explored what's now called the Inca Trail and published the results in *Publications in Anthropology #3: Archaeological Explorations in the Cordillera Vilcabamba* (The Werner Gren Foundation, The Viking Fund 1944).

Cut Stones and Crossroads (Penguin 1984) is a good modern travelogue by Ronald Wright (sadly now out of print); and Matthew Parris's *Inca Kola* (Weidenfeld & Nicholson, 1990) is characteristically well-written.

Other books

The *Royal Hunt of the Sun*, Peter Shaffer, is a play about the fall of the last Inca Atahualpa (see pp101-2). *The Heights of Machu Picchu,* Pablo Neruda, (Jonathan Cape 1966) is an extended piece inspired by the ruins by the Nobel Prize-winning Chilean poet. Colin Thubron's novel, *To the Last City* (Chatto and Windus, 2002), follows five travellers on the Vilcabamba Trail, brilliantly evoking this challenging hike. *Three Letters From the Andes* by Patrick Leigh Fermor (John Murray, 2005) is an enthralling, lyrical account of the author's trip to Machu Picchu that captures the country's people and magnificent landscape perfectly.

Two good books on keeping yourself healthy are *Bugs, bites and bowels,* Dr Jane Wilson Howarth (Cadogan Books 2002) and *Medical Handbook for Mountaineers,* Peter Steele (Constable 1993).

For more information on the effects of high altitude, there's an accessible guide aimed at non-medics: *Altitude Illness, Prevention & Treatment* by Stephen Bezruchka MD (Cordee 1994).

Field guides

It's difficult to find a good but compact field guide for Peru. For birds there's John Dunning's *South American Birds*, the comprehensive *Birds of the High Andes* (Jon Fjeldsa and Niels Krabbe) or the *Field Guide to the Birds of Peru* by James Clements and Noam Shany (see 🖳 www.ibispub.com). Perhaps most useful, but tricky to come by, is the *Field Guide to the Birds of Machu Picchu* by the expert birder and Cusco resident Barry Walker (to order copies try 🖳 www.hbw.com). For an all-round book that features superb illustrations of more then 500 of Peru's most common insects, amphibians, reptiles, birds and mammals, try *The Travellers' Wildlife Guide to Peru* by David Pearson and Les

❏ **Internet sites**
Peru
For general information try 💻 **www.travel-library.com** (an excellent travel site with listings and links for Peru). Be aware that many sites claiming to be 'official' are nothing of the sort, but just agencies offering tours and trips.

Cusco
💻 **www.cuscoperu.com** is a listings site for Cusco in English, and another good site in Spanish is 💻 **www.cuscoonline.com**. Also worth a browse is 💻 **www.unsaac. edu.pe/cusco/**, run by the local university.
There are a number of good sites on Machu Picchu and the Inca Trail. One, with links all over the web, is 💻 **www.ex.ac.uk/~RDavies/inca**. A personal favourite is the ultra-informative Andean travel web, 💻 **www.andeantravelweb.com.** The site of Gene Savoy, one of the discoverers of Vilcabamba, is at 💻 **www.genesavoy.org/**, and Vincent R Lee, another Vilcabamba traveller, can be found on-line at 💻 **www.bliss-net.com/~sixpacmanco/books.htm**. Also worth a look is 💻 **www.pacaritam bo.com**, an informative (if a little odd) site specializing in ancient South American cultures.

General information
💻 **www.traficoperu.com** (detailed information on as diverse things as flights and restaurants, lodging and car hire), 💻 **www.paginasamarillas.telefonica.com.pe** (Peru's yellow pages online). 💻 **www.saexplorers.org** is the website of the South American Explorers' Club (see p118). A good general Latin-American travel site is 💻 **www.amerispan.com/lata**.

Beletsky. There's a good section on orchids and birds in Peter Frost's and Jim Bartle's *Machu Picchu Historical Sanctuary*, to which Barry Walker has also contributed.

Pre-departure health preparations

FITNESS

Obviously it shouldn't need saying but one of the most important health prepa-rations is to get reasonably fit. You don't have to be a marathon runner, but you'll enjoy yourself much more if you're in good shape.

INOCULATIONS

Before you travel you should make sure that you've been immunized against the following diseases: **tetanus, polio** and **diphtheria, tuberculosis, yellow fever, hepatitis A** and **typhoid.** Check that the shot you had is still effective and that you do not need a booster. There was a serious outbreak of cholera in Peru in

1991 but there's not much point being inoculated against it as the cholera germ has become resistant to the vaccine. If you're going to the jungle (below 2000m) or planning on taking either the Vilcabamba trail or Choquequirao trek you should take a course of anti-**malaria** tablets.

If you're walking the longer trails, consider having a **rabies** inoculation too. It's expensive and you need to leave a month between injections, but as you will be a couple of days' walk from the nearest transport to the nearest hospital and the locals' dogs aren't usually friendly, it's wise to have one. The inoculation won't, however, prevent the disease, it'll only buy you more time to get to hospital.

To check on the latest requirements, look at the **US Center for Disease Control** website (⌨ www.cdc.gov), or ask a doctor. Travel clinics, however, are usually better informed than your local doctor. Up-to-the-minute health information and an on-the-spot vaccination service is available in London at **Nomad Travellers Store & Medical Centre** (☎ 020-8833 4114, STA Travel, 40 Bernard St, WC1N 1LJ). There are also clinics run by **Trailfinders** (see p18) and **British Airways** (☎ 020-7606 2977 to find one near you). Note that while some inoculations are available on the NHS in the UK, you'll have to pay for all inoculations at travel clinics.

HIGH-ALTITUDE TRAVEL

The effects of high altitude

You should be aware of the possible ill effects of high altitude before you go, and people with heart and lung problems or high blood pressure should get advice from their doctor before travelling. Children are more susceptible to altitude sickness than adults, and, if young, may not be able to tell you they're feeling sick, in which case they should not be taken to high altitudes at all. Young adults (in their teens or early twenties) are also more susceptible and extra days should be allowed for acclimatization. Cusco is at 3360m/11,000ft above sea level, and the highest pass described in this book is 5000m/16,400ft.

The altitude can do funny things to you. The first thing you'll notice is that you're always short of breath, but you may also lose your appetite, have difficulty sleeping and sometimes wake up feeling as if you've been slightly smothered. You might also notice your companions' breathing becoming increasingly shallow as they sleep, before an enormous grunting breath reassures you they're still alive. Don't worry, all this is normal. It's caused by your body having to deal with less oxygen at a lower pressure than it's used to at lower elevations. Almost everyone who comes to Cusco notices some of these things, and it's so common that the better restaurants and hotels have oxygen available.

You might notice several other things happening, too, in your first days up there with the gods. Your hands, face and ankles may swell up, and you may fart and burp more than usual. You're most likely to get a headache. Rarely, some people suffer from fainting fits, but these aren't serious on their own.

Having given you all the bad news, I should reassure you that the most obvious effect of altitude you'll notice, once you're acclimatized, is a feeling of clearness and health.

❑ **Dealing with dogs**
It's worth noting that if a dog does run up to you barking you should do as the locals do: pick up a stone and throw it in the dog's direction. If there's no stone nearby simply making as if to pick up a stone will usually scare off the dog.

Acclimatization

Altitude sickness can be fatal but is entirely preventable. The key to avoiding problems is to acclimatize (see p175). The biggest mistake to make is to belt up from Lima (which is at sea level) and then expect your body to do everything that it normally does when you're breathing richer air. Take a couple of days lazing around Cusco while your system catches up with you. After two weeks, you'll hardly notice the altitude.

For more information on health and safety while trekking see p175.

INSURANCE

You should take out travel insurance before you leave or check you're covered by your domestic policies. In the US and Canada, your domestic health insurance, home owners' insurance or rental insurance may cover you on this trip; check with your insurer.

Many travel insurance policies will cover you for trekking the routes described in this book but some won't. Check the small print before you sign up. For added safety, take out insurance specially tailored for trekkers or mountaineers. The British Mountaineering Council (☎ 0870-0104878, 🗎 0161-445 4500, 🖳 www.thebmc.co.uk), 177-179 Burton Rd, Manchester M20 2BB, does this type of insurance for members.

PART 2: PERU

Facts about the country

Peru is an amazing country. Within its borders there's part of the largest jungle on earth, the planet's driest desert and a large section of the world's second highest mountain range. The seas around Peru are no less impressive – there's a thousand times more food in Peru's coastal waters than in the average ocean. Because it's a land of such extremes, Peru has an immense range of life forms: you can find 20 out of the planet's 34 life zones in Peru, more than any other country in the world.

Peru's attractions are not only geographical: it possesses a rich cultural tradition, both ancient (Peru is the source of the ethereal Andean music) and modern (exemplified by the novelist, Mario Vargas Llosa, and the poet César Vallejo).

But Peru's not just a place of fascinating geography, natural history and cultural interest: it's also a country that's emblematic of modern South America. Struggling to maintain economic stability, Peru is trying to live with the atrocities of a past conflict while struggling to entrench democracy.

GEOGRAPHICAL BACKGROUND

Peru covers 1,280,000 square kilometres and is divided into three basic zones: *costa* (coast), *sierra* (highlands) and *selva* (jungle).

Geographical regions

The Pacific Ocean is circled with a 'ring of fire' of soaring mountains and active volcanoes that are created when the massive plates forming the skin on the earth's core of molten rock ram into each other. These plates can rise into the air and form mountains or can sink deep into the planet's crust and melt. When this melted rock rises to the surface again it causes volcanoes to form. This is how the Andes, the mountain range that separates Peru's Amazon rainforest from the Pacific coast, were formed and this is the cause of Peru's frequent earthquakes.

Costa   The geography of Peru's coast is dominated by the **Humboldt (or Peru) current**. This is a cold stream of water, so cold that it creates above itself a wide mass of chill coastal air. This air forms a barrier that the warm moist winds of the Pacific can't penetrate, so scarcely any rain falls on the coast. Because the coast's so parched, the **Atacama desert** has formed – a long thin strip of scorched land that extends far down into Chile. The Humboldt current is also rich in nutrients and supports a vast amount of sea life.

Sierra There are two branches of the Andes in Peru, the *Cordillera Blanca* (White Range) fronting the Amazon and the *Cordillera Negra* (Black Range) which parallels the coast. Between the two ranges is the *altiplano* (high plateau), an enclosed plain 800km long, which is characterized by high grasslands called *puna* whose fertile topsoil has been scraped off by glaciers. It's too cold up here for this soil to be replaced naturally, so it's pretty barren land.

Selva The eastern slopes of the Andes are covered by the edge of the Amazonian rainforest, which the locals call the *cejas de la selva* or 'eyebrows of the jungle'. The selva itself is largely unexplored.

Climate

Peru carries the curse of El Niño. Usually the country's climate is predictable; it's always dry on the coast and there's regular rainfall in the mountains but a couple of times in a decade El Niño hits.

El Niño is a change in the weather brought on by a change in the currents of the Pacific Ocean. What happens is that the coast becomes bathed in warmer waters that have made their way across the Pacific. The Humboldt current disappears, and the fish that bless Peru's coast swim south to colder waters. Damp winds roll from the sea over the desert, causing heavy rains that drench the land and cause serious flooding. Many people die or are made homeless. The effects aren't limited to South America. On the other side of the world, El Niño inverts usual weather patterns and causes devastation. Whilst the mechanics of this scourge are understood, the cause isn't. It seems to come in seven-year cycles but until we know why El Niño happens, there's no way of predicting exactly when it will come back.

The phenomenon was first noticed to occur around Christmas, and so called *El Niño* (the boy) after Jesus. El Niño has an opposite called *La Niña* (the girl), when the seas are unusually cold. El Niño shows that Peru's climate isn't static, but there's more to it than just these short-term disturbances. About 12,000 years ago most of Peru was covered by massive ice sheets, and even within the past 4000 years there have been cycles of heating and cooling; just 300 years ago

---

El Niño and the fall of the Moche and Tiahuanaco
The periodic climatic upheaval of El Niño causes great damage. The last major one, in 1998, killed at least 900 people, destroyed hundreds of thousands of domestic animals and caused an estimated US$90 billion worth of damage across the world. In the past, however, El Niño's done worse. It's probable that it finished off two ancient Peruvian civilizations and prompted the expansion of a third.

Samples of ice taken from a Peruvian glacier suggest that there was an El Niño about the time of the decline of the Moche civilization (see p80), which supports theories that the Moche were wiped out by massive climatic change. It's also likely that the same phenomenon caused the fall of the greatest of pre-Inca civilizations, the Tiahuanaco, and a similar environmental catastrophe destroyed the fertile lands of the Chimú and spurred them on to conquer their neighbours (see p84).

Peruvians were growing plants at 4200m that you can only grow today at 3700m. The one thing that's static about Peru's climate is the fact that it changes.

● **Costa** Summer is from December to April. The temperature ranges from 25°C to 35°C, and rainfall is extremely rare. Winter comes from May to November, when the temperature drops by about 10°C and there's lots of fog and cloud and a little rain too.

● **Sierra** There isn't really a summer and winter in the sierra, more like a rainy and a dry season. April/May to October is the dry season, when temperatures range from 25°C by day to -20°C by night. November to March is the wet season; the temperature's pretty much the same by day, but it's much warmer at night.

● **Selva** The wet and dry seasons are the same as the Sierra, but it's hot just about all the time.

HISTORICAL OUTLINE

For Peru before the Spanish see Part 3, pp74-107.

Peru under the Spanish

In 1542, after the Spanish authorities consolidated their power by mopping up a brief revolt by some rebellious *conquistadors* (the name given to the Spanish conquerors of the Americas), they created the Viceroyalty of Peru. It was a massive, immensely rich place, governing all of South America except Venezuela and Brazil. Peru was the jewel in the crown of Spanish South America, the centre of law, administration and commerce for a whole continent. Lima became one of the most important cities in the hemisphere; the highest court in the continent was in Lima, and if you were a trader anywhere between Quito and Chile your goods could only leave the continent through Lima's port, Callao. This happy state of affairs for the Spanish Peruvians was made even happier with the discovery in 1545 of a mountain of silver called Potosí, in what's now Bolivia.

Spanish rule in theory

The Spanish Crown tried to rule humanely, protecting the Indians from the excesses of the settlers. The principles of rule were fiercely Roman Catholic and profoundly nationalistic, not surprising considering that Spain had just emerged from under the heel of the Moors. The theory was that the Crown was supreme, and no government should be left to the locals, be they conquistadors or *cabildos* (town councils). Everything was owned by the Crown and was supposed to revert to the Crown. Spaniards were permitted to hold *encomiendas* (land, and

❑ Bishop la Casa, a contemporary supporter of the Indians, wrote: '...long before they [the Indians] had heard the word Spaniard they had properly organized states, wisely ordered by excellent laws, religion and custom... [they were ruled by] laws that at very many points surpass ours, and could have won the admiration of the sages of Athens... Now what belief will be placed in the Spaniards – greedy, violent, and cruel men who put unarmed and harmless Indians to the sword and rob them with extraordinary avarice?'

with it the benefit of the labour of any Indians who lived on it) only if they spread Christianity, and they were not permitted to live on their property, nor could they leave it to their children. Indians were not slaves; they were equals who simply hadn't learnt of the Gospels, and they should be treated as such. Crown agents, called *corregidors*, were appointed as supervisors.

Spanish rule in practice It didn't, of course, work like that on the ground. Spain was making too much money really to want to emancipate the Indians, and even if Spanish intentions had not been compromised by greed, it was too far away to supervise the implementation of the laws. In any case, the *encomenderos* (owners of encomiendas) were out for all they could get, wouldn't have obeyed laws that deprived them of their labour force. Consequently many Indians were worked to the bone (the silver mines at Potosí – see boxed text below – were particularly horrific places), and much of the glory of Imperial Spain was built from the sweat and blood of the children of the Incas.

However, it wasn't simply a case of the European power raping Peru and Peruvians (though there's no doubt they did both), and from Don Cristóbal Paullu Inca onwards some Indians did very well out of the conquest.

La Leyenda Negra

The stories of the great atrocities inflicted by the Spanish on the Incas are called by some La Leyenda Negra (The Black Legend). Anglo-Saxons, looking south with envious eyes, have always been prepared to believe the worst about the Spanish Empire, and stories of great evils perpetrated on the noble Peruvians have been frequently told by historians such as Markham and Prescott, who described the treatment of Atahualpa as one of the darkest chapters in Spanish Colonial History. In the 19th century, the Inca civilization became for many in the Romantic movement a golden age of harmony, violated by the conquistadors.

Spaniards maltreating Incas
FELIPE HUAMÁN POMA DE AYALA

The truth is more complicated, of course. The Incas didn't run a perfect society: they were ferocious and merciless in war, and Atahualpa (see p101) admitted that if he'd captured the Spaniards he would have enslaved them and had them castrated. But the bottom line has to take account of the horrors of Spanish rule, especially the horrors associated with the silver mines of Potosí, Bolivia. It was there that hundreds of thousands of Indians met their deaths, suffocated in the depths of the mountain or maddened by the chemicals used to extract the silver itself. Convoys of pressed labour made their way here from all over the old Inca Empire, men separated from their families, and tied together by the neck. If these poor sufferers were too weary to continue, or if they fell, the Spaniards didn't waste time loosening their bonds, they simply cut their bodies from the yoke with swords. These were days of great suffering.

The empire in decline The flower of Peru's and Lima's glory held the seeds of the decline of the Viceroyalty, and Peru's pre-eminence was one of the causes of the decline of the Spanish Empire. For example, it was incredibly inefficient to have the continent's only port in Callao; this caused smuggling to become commonplace and Spain's laws to be flouted. Disregard for the mother country extended further: the colonists did not like the benevolent attitude of the Crown to Indians or the fact that locally born Spaniards (Creoles) were denied any power – such positions were reserved for newcomers from Spain. It didn't help matters that less money was coming in from mining and that pirates were scourging the coast.

The empire rallies and Peru declines A historian has described the 18th century, when the Bourbons replaced the Hapsburgs on the Spanish throne, as a second conquest. The colonies were once again ruled with vigour, and South America was transformed. Power was consolidated by the tightening of the regulations prohibiting Creoles from holding public office, and the Jesuits were expelled. Peru ceased to be the only Viceroyalty in the continent, and became just one of many: the Viceroy of new Granada deprived Peru of its northern territory in 1718, the Viceroyalty of Río de la Plata (Argentina, Paraguay and Uruguay) cut off its eastern provinces in 1776 and Chile became a virtually autonomous captaincy general. The trade system was reformed removing Lima's monopoly as a port, and old taxes were put up and new ones imposed.

Days of rebellion This caused problems. In 1780 a prosperous Indian called José Gabriel Condorcanqui took the name of the last Inca, Tupac Amaru (see p134), and revolted against the authorities. He said – to start with at least – that he was loyal to the Spanish Crown and Church, and was rebelling against increased taxation and oppressive labour. Then his movement began to mean something more: it began to be an attempt to recreate the rule of the Incas. He was captured and executed in 1781 (his execution took seven hours), but his revolt carried on till 1783.

These events were seen amongst Europeans (for example Baron von Humboldt, the German naturalist after whom the sea current was named) as a war waged by the forces of civilization against those of barbarism. It's now seen rather differently as the stalking horse of Peruvian Independence.

Liberation

The turn of the 18th century was a time of revolution in America and France – something that wouldn't have escaped the notice of the Spanish colonies in South America. Then, in 1808, Napoleon invaded Spain who, desperate to resist the French, asked for help from its empire, and the price of Spanish American support was more recognition of the rights of Creoles. And so, partly because of the revolutionary atmosphere of the time, and partly because of the abasement of Spain, Spanish America began to taste independence.

Peru was very loyal to the Crown, because it had done very well out of the empire. It's no surprise then, that it was liberated by outsiders rather than being the seat of sedition. What is surprising is that in the wars of liberation there were more Peruvians in the monarchist army of Spain than in the liberating army of South America.

Peru was freed by the two great South American liberators: **San Martín** and **Simon Bolívar**. Two more different men it's difficult to imagine. San Martín was a refined, cautious, cold Argentinian; Bolívar was a heated, hairy, impulsive Venezuelan but both were equally brilliant generals. San Martín started the ball rolling by kicking the Spanish out of Argentina and Chile, but he needed to secure his victory by denying Spain the wealth of Potosí and access to the port of Callao. In other words, he needed to liberate Peru. He landed in Pisco from Chile in 1818 and fought his way up to Lima, entering the city and declaring Independence in 1820 just as the Viceroy was escaping with the remains of the royalist army.

San Martín travelled north to meet Bolívar, from whom he sought help in defeating the Viceroy. Bolívar refused, wanting all the glory for himself, so San Martín abandoned the country to his northern colleague. Bolívar finished off the royalists at the battles of Junín (6 August 1824) and Ayacucho (9 December 1824).

First steps in independence

Bolívar was made political supreme chief in 1824 but the Peruvians feared absorption into his 'greater Colombia' and abandoned him soon thereafter. Sadly there was a reluctance by civilians to take power because there was no tradition of self-government in the country and so, in a coup that was to mark a pattern in the rest of Peru's history, the *caudillos* (military leaders) seized control. A soldier called **Gamarra** became president, and the die of Peru's history was cast.

In 1835-6, Peru was promptly invaded by the dictator of Bolivia, Santa Cruz, who planned to create a confederation with Bolivia. Chile and Argentina put a stop to these plans at the battle of Yungay in 1839, and recreated Peru's independence. Gamarra became president again, and retaliated by invading Bolivia; his army was defeated and he was killed at Yngavi in 1841.

One revolt later an honest and tolerant man, **Ramón Castilla**, became president. His presidency coincided with the exploitation of *guano* (bird excrement fertilizer) in the Chincha islands and the nitrate of Tarapacá, so he had wealth to play with. He built railways and invested in the education of the Indians, abolished the system of tribute, and emancipated black slaves. Prosperity and stability weren't to last, and the next president, **Balta** (1868-72), encouraged by Castilla's example, spent vast sums on the Andean railways, money the country could ill afford. He hung the albatross of Peru's national debt around its neck.

War with Spain

Then in 1864 came war with Spain, which had never formally let go of the colonies. A Spanish squadron seized the valuable Chincha islands. The Peruvian president, Pezet, would have been happy to pay a ransom to get them back, but he was quickly replaced as leader by a man called Prado who, in alliance with Chile, Ecuador and Bolivia, went to war against the Spanish. The Spanish bombarded Callao and the Chilean port of Valparaíso in 1866, then slunk off home, but it wasn't until 1871 that an armistice was signed. Not till 1879 did Spain finally acknowledge Peruvian independence.

War of the Pacific

Having beaten off the Spanish, Peru didn't have much time to enjoy peace. The price of guano, a main Peruvian export, fell after the invention of chemical fertilizers so Peru's finances got worse. Prado decided to make the sale of nitrates a government monopoly and he arranged compensation for the mine owners; the Chileans who owned the mines didn't think he paid them enough.

Their government was spoiling for a fight anyway, and Prado's action antagonized them. Bolivia and Peru, aware of this, had entered into a half-secret alliance against the Chileans in 1873.

War broke out between Chile and Bolivia in 1879, and surprisingly, when Peru offered to mediate between the two, the Chileans declared war on Peru. To start with, all went well for the Peruvians. They won the battle of Iquique sinking the Chilean ship, the *Independencia*, but then it all went wrong and they lost Arica. By 1881 the Chileans had occupied Lima, and a humiliating peace treaty was signed at Ancón in 1883, which ultimately resulted in Peru losing its southern provinces.

Picking up the pieces

If Peru was in a bad way before the War of the Pacific it was desperate after and by 1890 couldn't pay its foreign debt. The British bondholders who held this debt formed the **Peruvian Corporation**, an organization which undertook to pay it off in return for annual payments, a 66-year lease of the railways and guano concessions. The Peruvians hated this arrangement but despite the humiliation, relative peace followed, and the country was buoyed up by rising copper production. Reforms were introduced such as direct suffrage, public education programmes and municipal elections. One of the main presidents of this time was **Leguía**, who ruled from 1908 to 1912 and then from 1919 to 1930. He began well, but when he was conciliatory to Chilean claims for Peruvian land in the south and Ecuadorian claims in the north he lost the sympathy of his people.

The dance of APRA and the army

The Depression finished off Leguía, and he was ousted in a coup in 1931, but a more interesting fish was being fried far from the centre stage of Peruvian politics. This was the **APRA party** (*Alianza Popular Revolucionaria Americana*) formed by Victor Raul Haya de la Torre. APRA was to dominate Peru right through to the 1980s, either through being in power or being suppressed by the army.

APRA started off Marxist and was bent on integrating the oppressed minorities of Peru, resisting what they called the economic imperialism of the US, and founding a union of Latin American states. Haya de la Torre first stood for president in 1931 and lost. APRA cried foul, and in 1932 staged an **uprising in Trujillo**, during which they killed 50 army hostages. Up to 5000 people were then taken out into the desert by the army and shot. APRA retaliated by assassinating the president in 1933.

Banned by the authorities, APRA continued to operate covertly and endorsed a presidential candidate in the 1936 elections. However, just as their candidate was about to win, Congress annulled the elections and gave General Benavides dictatorial powers. He was followed by Dr Manuel Prado Ugarteche who, except in his relations with Ecuador, was a pan-Americanist: Peru followed the USA and belatedly declared war on Germany and Japan in February 1945.

In 1941 Ecuador and Peru had a **border war** which Peru won, causing Ecuador to cede parts of its southern territory. The war still festers: it last erupted in 1995 but a deal in 1998 seems to have brought the two countries to peace.

In the 1945 election, APRA was legalized and got a majority of the seats in the lower house and half of the seats in the upper house. However, shortly after the election, President Bustamente (elected on an APRA ticket) went independent so APRA staged an uprising in Callao. They were banned again and suppressed so fiercely that Haya de la Torre had to seek sanctuary in the Colombian embassy for the next five years.

Land reform – 1963
In the 1950s, the power of APRA declined. In a bizarre marriage of convenience, they sided with their old enemies, the army, in support of Manuel Prado in the 1956 election. About this time the pressures from landless *campesinos* (peasants) increased, and there was a bloody revolt in the Cusco area led by Hugo Blanco.

After the inconclusive 1962 election, a military junta rather predictably seized power but they permitted another election in 1963 that was won by **Belaúnde Terry**. By this stage everyone was worried by the campesinos' volatility, so agrarian reform was implemented, 500,000 acres of land being distributed. This was an important step, and the campesinos of Peru, who had from time immemorial worked the land for a distant landlord – the Incas, the encomenderos, the hacienda owners – finally worked the land for themselves. Whether you think they have thrived or withered since depends on your politics.

The military take control
The military didn't hold back for long, and in 1968 they forced the resignation of Belaúnde, imprisoned politicians and suspended rights. It was a time of friendship with Soviet Russia and of censorship. Nationalization of industry followed and with the agrarian, mining, and industrial laws the government seized control of Peru's industries. More land was given to the campesinos and in 1973 the government reformed the education system, recognized the equality of women, built rural schools (permitting children to be taught in Quechua and Aymara) and gave autonomy to the University. The national debt grew, increased by the cost of agrarian reform and a decline in the price of fishmeal and copper.

Things fall apart
The army allowed elections again in 1978 and after a new constitution was drafted, Haya de la Torre was finally elected President. He didn't last long, however, beaten in the 1980 elections by Belaúnde Terry who reorganized the economy along free-market lines.

Terrorism in Peru

The two main terrorist groups in Peru are the Communist Party of Peru, (Sendero Luminoso or Partido Comunista de Perú) and the Tupac Amaru Revolutionary Movement (MRTA). The **Sendero Luminoso**, founded in the 1970s by philosophy professor Abimael Guzmán Reynoso (aka 'Comrade' or 'Presidente Gonzalo'), are Maoists intolerant of global capitalism and the Peruvian government. They draw their support from dissatisfied campesinos (of which there are many), particularly those who live in the highlands around Ayacucho.

The Sendero ruthlessly persecute those who don't support their ideology. If you're not with them, you're against them, and any other group is a target: in 1991, for example, they killed four mothers and their children because they were distributing free milk to children. In the 1980s and 1990s members numbered in their thousands; today they're much less active and only number a couple of hundred, but they still occasionally make their presence felt: in March 2002 a car-bomb attributed to them exploded by the American Embassy in Lima killing 10 people, and in July 2003 a patrol of marines was ambushed in Sendero heartlands near Ayacucho and seven people died. The Sendero still garners support abroad from some quarters, and has an old website 🖳 www.blythe.org/peru-pcp, and 🖳 www.csrp.org. Guzmán has been in prison since 1992; Nicholas Shakespeare's novel, *The Dancer Upstairs*, which was subsequently made into a film, is based on his arrest. Following a 2003 ruling that his trial by an anonymous military panel was unconstitutional, Guzmán was retried and convicted. Hundreds of other terrorist-related verdicts delivered by anonymous judges in the 1990s during the presidency of Alberto Fujimori have also been annulled.

The other Peruvian terrorist organization, the **MRTA**, was little-known abroad until they took over the residence of the Japanese ambassador in December 1996, having got in disguised as waiters. More than 450 people were taken hostage including Fujimori's brother, several of Peru's highest-ranking officials and the Japanese ambassador; it was only by chance that Fujimori, himself of Japanese ancestry, wasn't there too. The MRTA are a more moderate left-wing terrorist group, but they've never been as strong as the Sendero. The Japanese ambassador's siege gained them notoriety, and then won Fujimori support when four months later, in April 1998, he sent in the military to resolve the situation. The building was stormed and all but one of the hostages were released unharmed. All the terrorists were killed, as were two soldiers. In 2003 the soldiers who stormed the embassy were tried for executing the terrorists in cold blood. Forensic evidence showed that eight of the rebels had been shot in the back of their necks and a Japanese diplomat said that he'd seen three captured alive. The soldiers were acquitted on the basis that they'd been involved in a military confrontation. Either way, the MRTA remain today a spent force.

It was about now that things started to go seriously wrong. In 1982-3, an El Niño hit the fishing industry, and the terrorist movements **Sendero Luminoso** (The Shining Path) and the **MRTA** (*Movimiento Revolucionario Tupac Amaru,* Tupac Amaru Revolutionary Movement) built up a head of steam. Peru's currency, the sol, collapsed, and inflation ran riot. In 1983 APRA were elected and **President García** tried to remedy the situation by not paying more than 10% of Peru's foreign debt, a move that caused the international banks to refuse to make any further loans to Peru. The situation got steadily worse. García's administration became increasingly characterized by graft and human rights abuses, which peaked when the *Rodrigo Franco Commando* (a right-wing death squad) started fighting the terrorists with extreme violence. The people who suffered were those caught in the middle, the campesinos.

The economy got steadily worse, and in 1987 García moved to nationalize the banks, a move that caused strikes and inflation. The country descended into a spiral of misery.

1990s – Peru under Fujimori

The 1990 election was, therefore, one of the most important for a century. With the economy and society in tatters, the novelist **Mario Vargas Llosa** (see p53) stood for President as a moderate right-wing candidate against APRA. Hardly anyone noticed another contender, a provincial agricultural engineer of Japanese ancestry, called **Alberto Fujimori**. Against the odds, Llosa lost, and Fujimori won.

In 1992 Fujimori shut down the Congress and dismissed the Supreme Court, and in 1993 the constitution of Peru was rewritten. Fujimori then embarked on economic and legal reform which he claimed would enable the country's economy to grow and assist in the crushing of the Sendero Luminoso. It also allowed him to stand for another term in office.

It's been called the **President's coup**, for that's what it was: a bloodless coup d'état. However, it did bear some good fruit when in 1992 Abimael Guzmán, the leader of the Sendero, was arrested by the police and the economy was brought under control. The Peruvian people obviously thought that Fujimori's actions were justified since nearly two out of three of them voted for him in the 1995 elections, when he beat the former head of the United Nations, Javier Pérez de Cuellar. A negotiated peace with Ecuador followed, and Fujimori managed the economy to the satisfaction of the IMF and USA but at considerable cost in terms of human rights.

Then Fujimori tempted fate. He re-wrote the constitution yet again to allow him a further term. His opponent this time was a man called Toledo, a former shoe-shine boy and one time economist with the World Bank. After an election of dubious fairness, Fujimori won. But just as he was settling in to his unprecedented third term in office, the wheel of fortune turned and his past caught up with him. His shadowy right-hand man, Vladimiro Montesinos, who had been his eyes and ears as the head of the state intelligence agency ('Servicio de Inteligencia Nacional', or SIN), fell from grace.

A video tape of Montesinos bribing a member of Congress was leaked to the press. The tape led to the revelation that Montesinos had bribed or threatened most of the Peruvian establishment to garner support for Fujimori; around 2700 so-called '*vladivideos*' have since come to light showing the man engaged in underhand activity. Montesinos fled abroad, and it was only when he'd left that it was discovered he'd salted away some US$48 million in various foreign banks.

Fujimori held onto power for a couple of months, declaring he intended to track Montesinos down. But he left the country on a run-of-the-mill tour, and stopped off in Japan. He's never left. In November 2000, he faxed congress his resignation as president of Peru and much to the irritation of Peruvians, he said that he'd always been a Japanese national. Only a Peruvian national can be president of Peru – this revelation meant that he'd been an illegal president for 10 years.

Toledo in power

Fresh elections were called. Alan García, the man who had caused such economic chaos in the late 1980s, stood against Fujimori's challenger, Alejandro Toledo. The centrist Toledo narrowly won, standing on a manifesto that promised to create a million new jobs while keeping a prudent hold of the country's purse strings. He also vowed to bring Fujimori back to Peru to face charges of corruption, human rights' violations and murder.

Toledo is of Andean Indian ancestry, a fact that he exploited skilfully throughout the campaign, even adopting the nickname 'Pachacutec' after the great Inca emperor. There are those in Peru who believe that it would take a ruler of the Inca Pachacutec's capability to solve the country's many problems; so far the president has not lived up to his namesake. In broad terms, the economy appears to be on the mend, but most Peruvians feel that the benefits have not filtered down to them yet and have accused Toledo of failing to deliver on his election promises. His pledge to create a million jobs remains unfulfilled: unemployment and underemployment continue to be serious problems. Taxes have risen but his commitment to double teachers' pay has not been carried through. For these and other reasons, he has become very unpopular. Crippling strikes and violent street demonstrations during 2003 prompted him to declare a state of emergency but the protests have continued regardless.

Toledo has tried hard to win back support, not least by reducing his salary three times and repeatedly relaunching his administration. It hasn't helped. His approval rating flounders at a meagre 11%, lower even than the disgraced Fujimori (31%), while the popularity of Peru's first woman prime minister,

Clearing up the Fujimori mess

Fujimori now faces an international arrest warrant. Peru formally petitioned Japan for his extradition in July 2003, to face charges of bribery, corruption and being an illegal president. There are also allegations that he made a US$15 million pay-off to Montesinos, Fujimori's Rasputin, when he lost his job; set up a campaign of forced sterilization of campesino women; and was linked to the Grupo Colina death-squad, who were responsible for a number of assassinations and kidnappings in the early 1990s. Japan has no extradition treaty with Peru, however, so it's very unlikely that the former president will be brought to book. On the other hand, Montesinos was tracked down to Venezuela and brought back to Peru, where in 2003 he was convicted of embezzlement (on relatively minor counts) and sentenced to nine years' imprisonment; he has since received a further tariff of five to eight years on additional counts, but this is not the end of it. He's on trial again for his alleged involvement in the death-squad killings as well as running guns to the Colombian rebel group, the FARC, apparently with CIA support. Montesinos denies the charges.

Beatriz Merino, soared to 60%. This might explain why Toledo sacked her, his third prime minister, at the end of 2003, though she was also dogged by allegations of corruption (and lesbianism), which she denied. Meanwhile, evidence of Fujimori's enduring appeal – he even broadcasts an hour-long radio show on Radio Miraflores every Saturday, which he records from his current home in Japan – has spurred him into campaigning for the 2006 presidential election, an election that looks set to be as dramatic as any in Peru's recent past.

THE PEOPLE

Most (70%) of Peru's 27.6 million people live in modern cities, but the society is deeply rooted in its past; about half the population is **Quechua**, the descendants of the Incas. The blood of the Incas was mixed with that of the Spanish from the first days of the conquest, and a third of the people are the products of these unions: **mestizo**; a fifth are **Caucasian**.

The others that make up Peru include the significant minority of **Aymara** around Lake Titicaca, and about 250,000 **indigenous people of the Amazon rainforest**. There's also a small **black** population, based south of Lima, who are the descendants of those unfortunates brought to Peru as slaves (in the first century alone after the conquest as many as 10,000 were brought to Peru).

The Quechua who farm the highlands prefer to be called campesinos (rural labourers) and not *indios* (Indians), which they consider an insult.

Education and literacy

About one in ten adult Peruvians is illiterate. Almost a third of Peru's population is under 14 and education's now free and compulsory up to the age of 16. It's difficult to enforce this in rural areas, but the government estimates that most of Peru's children have primary education, two-thirds of children go to secondary school and a quarter are in tertiary education. The government spends 9.3% of its budget on education, but publicly funded schooling doesn't have a good reputation and those who can afford it send their children to private schools.

Language

(For useful words and phrases see p294). **Spanish** is the main language today, but **Quechua** (or *Runasimi*, 'the people's mouth') is spoken by about 10 million people concentrated around Cusco and southern Peru, two million of whom don't speak anything but Quechua. In the main tourist areas in Lima and Cusco English is understood by some people. Around Lake Titicaca, the ancient language *Aymara* survives; it dates from before the Incas.

Quechua, the language of the Incas, was not written down till the 16th century so there are many different ways of transcribing it. It's difficult to be consistent, as different words have become familiar in different spellings: Inca can be written Inka, Sacsayhuaman as Saq'saywaman, and Cusco as Cuzco or Q'osqo. I've tried to be consistent in my spelling of Quechua words, using Dr Ann Kendall's work as a guide, except where a particular spelling of a word has become so familiar that spelling it another way looks bizarre.

Pilgrimage to Qoyllor Riti
This pilgrimage is a good example of what has been called Pagan Catholicism. Qoyllor Riti is a village in the Nevado (snow-capped peak) Ausangate near Cusco, and once a year in early June many people climb the hills on a pilgrimage there. The Christian basis for the festival is that Christ appeared here to a young shepherd called Marianito in the 18th century but the festival dates back to the days before Christianity arrived in Peru, back to the days when pilgrimages were made to the Apus or spirits of the mountains who needed to be placated with human sacrifice. Some say that to this day there's always a death on the pilgrimage: a baby freezes to death on the glacier, or a campesino falls from a precipice and the Apu is satisfied.

Religion
Ninety-five per cent of the population are **Roman Catholic**, and the Peruvian church is the cradle of 'liberation theology', a socialist interpretation of Christianity. However, in more rural areas the people have been better described by the anthropologist, Robert Randall, as '**Pagan Catholics**' whose Catholicism is mixed with indigenous beliefs, placing a veneer of Christianity on ancient ceremonies and substituting saints for local spirits. Various **Protestant** churches are active in Peru, and they're considered predatory by some Catholics: you'll often see stickers in people's front windows telling Protestant canvassers to go away. Some of these churches are the charmless North American imports that have spread all over the world, but some are indigenous, such as the IEP (Evangelical Church of Peru), which has been in the country for a hundred years.

POLITICS AND ECONOMICS

Politics
The president hires and fires ministers and is elected every five years with the 120 members of congress. The country is divided into 25 departments, governed by prefects who are also appointed by the president. Departments are divided into provinces, which are sub-divided into districts, each governed by a mayor elected every five years.

Current politics
Toledo, leader of the centrist party *Perú Posible*, won just 52% of the final vote in the 2001 elections against García's 48% – one of the narrowest victories ever, and one that ensures that García will continue to have a strong voice in parliament as leader of the opposition party *Alianza Popular Revolucionaria Americana* (APRA), which was originally a revolutionary left-wing party. Even though he lost, the election and his return to the heart of Peruvian politics still represent quite a comeback for García following nine years in exile in Colombia waiting for corruption charges dating back to his tenure as president to expire.

Other political parties are: *Acción Popular* (AP) – centre right; Fujimori's old party, *Cambio 90*, that has all but ceased to exist, although it may still resurface in another form; *Izquierda Unida* (IU) – a left-wing umbrella group, now split by internal division and the *Partido Popular Cristiano* (PPC) – a right-wing, pro-business party centred around Lima. There is widespread disillusionment with traditional political parties in Peru.

Human rights

In the late 1980s and 1990s, there were some very unpleasant things going on in Peru. Both the Shining Path (see p45) and the government were responsible for methodical campaigns of killing, maiming and intimidation which caused immense suffering for the hundreds of thousands caught up in the conflict. After he came to power, Toledo set up a Truth and Reconciliation Commission, which began hearings in April 2002 in an attempt to close the door on the country's horrific past. A spokesman summed up the Commission's task, when he said: 'What is absolute, what is definitive is that people were unjustly killed and human rights were violated. We are not trying to open Pandora's box, we are trying to air things that have been forgotten and stink.'

The Commission's report of August 2003 made grim reading: 69,000 Peruvians died or disappeared during the civil war, making it one of the worst in Latin America's history. The killing was centred around Ayacucho and three-quarters of the victims were campesinos. Both the government and the Sendero Luminoso were responsible. The Sendero killed and tortured to force villagers to support them, the government tortured and killed to force them not to. Toledo has promised to spend US$820 million helping those most affected by the tragedy.

The issue of forced sterilizations on campesino women is now the subject of a Parliamentary Commission. It's estimated that as many as 300,000 sterilizations were carried out between 1995 and 2000.

The economy

Peru is blessed with abundant mineral resources, seas teeming with fish and a wide range of climates that means just about anything can be grown there, but in the past hyperinflation and political instability practically ruined the country. The situation's better now and the economy is thriving, but there are still enormous differences in wealth and opportunity between the richest and poorest Peruvians.

The Fujimori administration privatized large chunks of state-owned industry, reforming the tax system and eliminating many price controls and import tariffs. Toledo, too, is following a pro-market agenda. The economy is now largely free market and, following the reforms, the growth rate for real GDP was as high as 13%; it was a more realistic 7.4% in 1997. However, with the catastrophes of 1998 – El Niño and the Asian economic crisis – this halved. In 2000 the growth rate for real GDP stood at 3.6% and the uncertainty that characterized the end of Fujimori's reign further damaged the outlook. The 2003 estimate for real GDP was 4% and the target for the end of 2005 was 4.5%.

Since 2001 Peru's economy has been one of the fastest growing in Latin America. In 2004 it enjoyed 5% growth, its best performance in seven years, and the forecast continues to be favourable. However, unemployment remains around 9% and foreign investors are concerned that the unpopularity of the Toledo administration threatens the hard-won fiscal stability of the country.

Peru's chief exports are minerals and metals; it's traditionally been a mining economy and mining accounted for 55% of Peru's total exports in 2004, a share of the market which has exposed the economy to global price fluctuations. Peru is also the world's leading fishmeal producer, and agricultural products are important too. The largest proportion of Peru's trade is done with the United States (28%) and the EU (25%), but Japan is heavily involved and China is also growing in importance.

Domestically, manufacturing makes up the biggest individual slice (21%) of GDP, followed by trade and agriculture. Other significant activities are mining and construction. Annual inflation is around 3.7%.

Coca and cocaine

It's been said that coca leaf has as much to do with cocaine as elephants have to do with ivory – it's the raw material from which the refined product comes, nothing more. Coca leaf has been chewed in the Andes for thousands of years, and it's as central to Andean culture as coffee is to the Arabs and tea is to people from the Indian subcontinent. Once, coca leaf was reserved for the Incas themselves, but in the days of the Spanish Empire it was chewed almost incessantly by overworked labourers. It was one of their few reliefs from cold and hardship.

The quid of leaves is chewed with a mixture of lime or quinoa and potash called *llipta*, releasing a natural anaesthetic that relieves hunger, and, in some way that's not understood, relieves the effect of altitude. It also provides the recommended daily dose of iron, calcium, vitamin A and phosphorous so it's hardly surprising that local people still believe that it's a universal panacea. Coca leaf has a long history in Andean culture, and you can see the characteristic quid in the cheeks of some portrait pots from the days of the Nazca (see p81), and implements associated with its use have been found from the Moche culture (see p80).

But the coca leaf is most famous around the world today because of its derivative, cocaine. This alkaloid was first isolated by a scientist called Gaedake in the 19th century, and when it was discovered it seemed an unalloyed benefit to humanity – a pain-relieving drug of great potency. However, over the years its abuse and restriction have created the demon that cocaine is today. In Peru, the main problem centres on the enormous profits that cocaine production can bring, and the growing of coca leaf to produce cocaine is organized by largely Colombian gangs of narco-terrorists, whose anarchic rule subjugates swathes of Peru's remote jungle. Up until 1996 Peru was the world's largest coca-leaf producer, and now it's second only to Colombia.

The USA's Drug Enforcement Agency (DEA) seem set to try to solve the world's cocaine problem by eradicating all coca-leaf growing in the Andes. Sadly, this ignores both the traditional nature of the leaf in Andean society and the poverty that drives campesinos to try to make money from growing it; they can get up to US$6 for a kilo of coca leaf but only a little over a dollar for a kilo of coffee. When the DEA torch remote fields that campesinos have spent months cultivating, they create hatred. The campesinos see cocaine as a problem of the urban West rather than rural Peru, and believe that the US's 'War On Drugs' is cynically fought in the highlands of Peru rather than where it could have more effect – in the USA itself – because there are no votes to lose in Peru.

PERU

De Soto's diagnosis
One of Peru's most eminent economists, Hernando de Soto, has suggested that there is a structural problem at the heart of Peru's (and the rest of the developing world's) economic troubles. In *The Mystery of Capital: Why capitalism triumphs in the West and fails everywhere else* (London, Bantam Press 2000), he suggests that capitalism succeeds in the West because people can liquidate the value of the land they occupy, by mortgages, for example. They can do this because they can prove they own the land. In other countries where it's difficult to prove title to land, the wealth bound up in your property is frozen and inaccessible. He estimates that in the developing world as a whole, US$29,000 billion of wealth is tied up. This figure has come in for criticism as being too high, and the book itself has come in for criticism for not suggesting a practical way of registering land claims.

Continuing economic problems Underemployment is a serious problem in Peru: estimates suggest that a staggering 94% of Peruvians don't have a proper job, and Peru's wealth and income are still highly concentrated in the hands of a few old families, a source of festering discontent. According to the Peru Support Group (a NGO), just under half the population earn less than a dollar a day. More than half the population is under the poverty line, and the richest 10% hold a third of the country's wealth.

On the international side of things, Peru's national debt is still large at five times the annual income from exports – a fifth of all the money Peru makes from its exports is spent on paying the interest on this debt.

The environment

Peru has its share of environmental problems as the country tries to balance the need for economic growth with ecological sensitivity.

The current hot potatoes are proposed oil developments in Peru's wildernesses. In 2003 the Peruvian state granted the international oil industry greater access to indigenous ancestral lands throughout almost all of the Peruvian Andes, while the jungle regions are also under intense pressure. The largest development there is the Camisea Project: in 1998 Shell considered the exploitation of oil reserves in the selva to the north of Quillabamba, and this caused concern amongst environmental NGOs. There's 11 trillion cubic feet of oil and gas under the forest, and exploiting it would create US$500 million to US$1 billion. However, the area is rich in bio-diversity and is populated by indigenous people who have little or no contact with the outside world. Shell, stung by international reaction to their Nigerian activities, abandoned the project but a gas-production consortium have taken it on. The construction of two 800km gas pipes has opened up the forest to settlers and all the associated problems of deforestation, environmental degradation and social pressures, while its extremely steep route has caused massive landslides and soil erosion. It's also feared that the project is jeopardizing the health and safety of Machiguenga indigenous communities living along the Urubamba river.

PERU

Another significant environmental development over the past 30 years has been the shrinking of Peru's glaciers. The country has more tropical glaciers than any other in South America, but in recent years scientists have recorded they have lost a quarter of their area. This is because they are melting in the dry season more quickly than they can be replenished in the wet – probably the result of global warming. In the short term the worry is that the large chunks of glaciers may break off and drop into glacial lakes, causing them to overflow. This happened in Huaraz in 1941 and the resulting flood killed 5000 people. In the longer term, people are concerned about the opposite outcome, desertification. In the dry season, Peru's rivers are fed predominantly by glacier melt-water. If the glaciers continue to shrink, at some point they'll disappear. And with them will go many of Peru's rivers.

CULTURE

Writing

Peru has a vibrant and powerful literary tradition, from the days of the conquest on. Many of the conquistadors left records of their battles, and on the Inca side there's the work of **El Inca Garcilasco de la Vega**, and **Felipe Huamán Poma de Ayala**. Today **Mario Vargas Llosa** is Peru's most famous writer, a man whose books can stand up against the South American Titan, Gabriel García Márquez. Vargas Llosa was born into a middle-class family and is related to an ex-president of Peru. He writes narratives woven with the complexity of Andean fabric: try *Conversación en la Catedral* (Conversation in the Cathedral), or *La casa verde* (The Green House). **César Vallejo** (1892-1938) is one of the Spanish language's greatest modern poets. Vallejo broke linguistic rules to write poetry that appears rough but has magnificent imaginative power.

Visual arts

The most significant form of **painting** to come out of Peru is the **Cusco school**, which flourished in the 17th and 18th centuries. The Cusco school consists of paintings of formal European subjects, such as religious themes, which have been re-interpreted by indigenous artists. There is a lot of decorative flower and bird patterns, and the use of applied gold on the canvas pre-empts Klimt, but the things that most tourists notice are the bizarre details such as angels armed with muskets. These paintings are still made and sold in the San Blas district of Cusco (see p137). Christopher Isherwood came across these pictures and commented in *The Condor and the Cows* (1948): 'In the lounge, there are some beautiful and absurd Colonial religious paintings. My favourite represents an angel, a fairylike little girl with a sword and golden butterfly skirts, who has her foot coquettishly planted on a sprawling demon. The demon, who is old enough to be her father, is obviously loving it. He is leering and caressing her foot with the enthusiasm of a boot-fetishist'.

Peruvian **cinema** has never reached the heights of other Latin American countries such as Mexico or Brazil, but in Cusco in 1955 Manuel Chambi set up a pioneering film club. The name Chambi is also famous in **photography** –

Martín Chambi was a pioneering Cusqueño photographer, who took, in 1920, the first iconic shot of Machu Picchu. The Smithsonian Institution published a collection of his photographs in 1990, entitled *Martín Chambi – Photographs, 1920-1950*. Although difficult to come by in the UK, it is still available in the bookshops in Cusco. Phaidón also published a collection of his photographs in 2002.

Music and dance

Music and dance are a breathing part of everyday campesino culture. The music's going to be familiar to you, either from Andean buskers who play in shopping malls all over the world, or from songs like Simon and Garfunkel's hit *El Condor Pasa*. Many people think that they composed the tune, but it's in fact a traditional Andean melody that was written in the 18th century to mark the execution of the rebel Tupac Amaru II (see p41).

The basic instruments played are the *queña,* a simple flute with a notched end, and the *charango,* a mandolin originally made from the shell of an armadillo. You'll also see panpipes, drums, guitars and – occasionally – harps. Pipes of old didn't have the full scale, so tunes jumped from one player to another, but today they're made with a full complement of notes. The most widely available modern version of traditional Andean music is the Chilean group Inti Illimani.

More traditional musical styles come in different forms, such as the almost waltz-like **huayno** from the highlands with vocals soaring over high-pitched instruments or the more sultry **crillo** from the coast; a song called *La flor de la canela* sung by Chabuca Granda used to be the soul of Lima. Today they play **chicha** in the *pueblos jóvenes* (shanty towns), a music that's a fusion of Colombian dance with Andean music. Also watch out for brass bands pumping out oompa-oompa music at any major festival; it's usually an unforgettable cacophony of a dozen or so different bands blasting away at different tunes in different tempos all at the same time.

Media

The main **newspapers** are *El Commercio* and *La República*, and there are numerous tabloids that decorate their cover pages with bare-bottomed women and fill the insides with gruesome stories of car crashes (with pictures) and horrific murders.

In Lima and Cusco there is a wide range of cable **TV** stations including the predictable CNN and BBC World. There are five domestic TV stations: Televisión Nacional de Perú (Canal 7; the state broadcaster), America TV, Panamericana, Andina TV and Frecuencia Latina (Canal 2). The airwaves are stuffed with Mexican soaps and US movies. The media is now relatively free, though in Fujimori's day the owners of two of Peru's most popular television stations were bribed for favourable coverage, while journalists who were critical of the government were at best harassed, and at worst killed. Seven lost their lives.

The airwaves are packed with **radio** stations, and in the mountains they're the only way people can get the news. In addition to the state-run Radio Nacional, there are three national radio stations, all based in Lima: Radio Programas de Perú, a talk station, Radio Panamericana, a music station; and Radio Americana, a news and music station.

Sport

This is South America, so **football** (soccer) is all that matters. The main teams are Alianza, Universitario, and Sporting Cristal, but in 2004, Cusco giantkillers Cienciano won the Copa de Sud America against Argentinian favourites Boca Juniors, sparking wild celebrations in the city. Don't mention the World Cup: Peru missed out in 1994, 1998 and again in 2002. The 1998 campaign was particularly gutting for Peruvians, as Chile squeezed into the finals ahead of Peru by the smallest of margins and in 2002 they lost out once more to another old enemy, Ecuador. At the time of writing, their chances didn't look too good for qualifying in 2006 either. Learn the names of a couple of Peruvian footballers (their star striker, Claudio Pizarro, plays in Germany, and Nortberto Solano plays for Aston Villa in the UK) and you'll never be at a loss for conversation. If you want more on Peruvian football, visit 🖳 www.FutbolPeruano.com.

Practical information for the visitor

DOCUMENTS AND VISAS

To stay in Peru for up to 90 days no tourist visa is needed by citizens of EU countries, the US, Canada, Australia, and New Zealand. Nevertheless, check with a Peruvian embassy (see p299) that this is still the case.

You should have proof that you've got enough money to finance your stay in Peru and a return ticket to show you're going to leave again, though you're not likely to be asked for these. You'll be given an Embarkation and Disembarkation card (TED) when you arrive, valid for 60 to 90 days. Always keep it, or a copy of it, on you and don't lose it or you'll be fined s/12 (US$3.40/£2.30). You can extend your stay by applying at the Immigration and Naturalization Department (DIGEMIN, see p118 and p145), or by leaving and re-entering the country. They'll give you another 30 or 60 days, and charge US$20.

For those that need a tourist visa, it will cost around US$35 (prices vary according to your nationality), and two passport photos, a return ticket, and 'proof of economic solvency' are required.

MONEY

Currency

The currency is the *nuevo sol*, often just called the sol, whose symbol is **s/**. A nuevo sol is divided into 100 *céntimos* (or cents), and is pretty stable.

Notes in circulation are s/200, s/100, s/50, s/20, s/10. Coins in circulation are s/5, s/2, s/1, s/0.50, s/0.20 and s/0.10.

> ❑ **Airport tax**
> When you leave Peru, you'll have to pay US$28 (about £16). On internal flights (such as Lima–Cusco) there's an airport tax of s/20 (US$6/£4).

PERU

❏ **Rates of exchange**

	Peru Nuevo Sol
Aus$1	s/2.48
Can$1	s/2.67
Euro€1	s/4.02
NZ$1	s/2.25
UK£1	s/5.80
US$1	s/3.25

For up-to-the-minute rates of exchange check the Internet: 💻 www.oanda.com/convert/classic or www.xe.com/ucc

Hoard your s/10 and s/20 notes and avoid any with a value of over s/50 as you'll have difficulty getting change, but don't accept 'no change' as an excuse to rip you off. Don't get landed with damaged notes, as no one else will take them off your hands. You can often use US dollars instead of soles but watch out for forgeries; there are many in circulation.

There was horrendous inflation in the early 1990s (7600% in 1990), and the currency was twice devalued. Be careful that you don't get handed these worthless old notes when you exchange money. They are called *intis* and, rather confusingly, *soles*; there's no need to worry because they look completely different from nuevos soles – and nuevos soles have 'nuevos soles' written on them. All mentions of 'soles' in this book mean nuevos soles.

Other forms of money

There are many **ATM**s (cash machines) in Lima and Cusco where you can get money on your Visa or MasterCard, and many shops where you can use them as **credit cards**. Visa is the more useful. Using your **bank/debit card** through an ATM linked to the Cirrus, Maestro or Plus systems it should be possible to get cash advances direct from your bank account. Check the logos on your card and the logos on the ATM. And to avoid nasty surprises when you return home, it's a good idea to know what handling fee your bank charges on cash withdrawals.

It's much safer to carry **travellers' cheques** than cash but avoid the less well-known brands and take only US dollars – the number of soles you can buy for £1 sterling is sometimes half the amount you can buy for one US dollar because of high commission charged on other foreign currencies. American Express dollar travellers' cheques are by far the most commonly accepted.

Banks and cambios

Exchanging money and travellers' cheques is easy; there are many **banks** (opening times vary, but are generally weekdays 9am-12 noon, 4-6pm) and **cambios.** Take your passport with you when you change money as you will need to prove your identity. There are often *cambistas* (money changers) on street corners, some of them wearing waistcoats that say they're regulated by the municipality. They seldom provide a better rate of exchange than the banks and cambios, and they're more likely to short-change you.

GETTING AROUND

Travelling between cities

The main way of travelling overland is by **bus**, and they're very cheap. Buses range from Chilean-style comfort wagons, the most luxurious road transport

I've ever used, to broken old rattletraps. Always check where the departure terminal is, as it's often in a different place from the ticket office. There are hundreds of bus lines competing with each other, but the main ones are **Cruz del Sur** and **Ormeño**.

Where no buses run you can often **hitch** on a truck, but payment is often expected. It's wiser not to hitch alone.

There are some passenger **trains** still operating, notably the run from Arequipa and Puno to Cusco (called the Southern Railway) and the run from Cusco to Aguas Calientes (below Machu Picchu). But following privatization of the railways in the late 1990s, trains are no longer the cheap option they used to be, particularly as tourists are now forbidden from taking the local trains. There are also remains of a railway from Lima to the highlands (the Central Railway) which wasn't running at the time of writing, though has done so intermittently over the past couple of years. For details of times and prices see p301.

Planes fly regularly between Cusco, Lima and other towns (see p128 and p155), although the domestic industry was in turmoil throughout 2004 and early 2005. The main domestic airline is LanPeru (☎ 213 8200, 🖵 www.lan.com, Av Jose Pardo 513, Miraflores, Lima), which started operations in late 1999. Tans (Av Arequipa 5200, Miraflores, Lima, ☎ 213 6000, 🖵 www.tans.com.pe), also flies to Cusco. AeroCondor (Juan de Arona 781, San Isidro, Lima, ☎ 614 6000, 🖵 www.aerocondor.com.pe) services a small selection of cities including Arequipa, but not Cusco. The **helicopter** that connected Cusco with Machu Picchu has been suspended since 2002 for environmental reasons.

In theory you can cadge a lift with Grupo Ocho – the Air Force – but the schedules aren't reliable and priority is given to locals anyway, so few tourists bother with it.

Local transport

In Peru **taxis** don't use meters and will normally charge what they can get away with, so fix the price before you step into the cab. If you're not sure what the price should be, either ask a passer-by or offer to pay half to three-quarters of the price the *taxista* is asking. Tipping isn't usual or expected.

Buses in cities tend to be beaten-up old crocks, but they're cheap; they charge flat fares. Disorganized though the system may appear, they'll cover just about every part of a city, and travelling by bus is a great way of meeting people, but beware of pickpockets and bag-slashers.

You can also travel by **colectivo** – enormous, chuntering old Dodges or spanking-new Japanese minibuses that speed along set routes filled to the gunwales with paying passengers. They have their routes written on the windscreen.

Hiring a car

Don't drive in Lima unless you've got a strong stomach and a forceful personality, and if you drive outside Lima expect bad roads and aggressive drivers. For car-hire companies and rates, see p115 (Lima) and p139 (Cusco). You need an international driving licence valid for 30 days; you can get one from your country's automobile association.

ACCOMMODATION

Price

The hotels listed in this book are divided into three classes: **budget**, **mid-range** and **expensive**. All prices change, and hotel prices change particularly quickly, so the chances are they'll be higher when you visit than they were when this book was researched. However, you'll still be able to make comparisons between the relative expense of different hotels.

When giving prices in the text, **sgl/dbl/tpl** refers to single, double and triple rooms. The hotel price is always followed by information in brackets: '**att**' means there is an attached bathroom and '**com**' means there is a shared or communal bathroom. If breakfast is included in the cost of the room, that's mentioned too, although in Peru it's normal for breakfast to be extra.

In the **budget** class are hotels that charge up to s/30 for a room. **Mid-range** hotels are those that charge from s/30 (US$8.50) to US$60. The class is wide, so hotels of a similar price are listed together within the class. **Expensive** hotels charge more than US$60, and may add another 10% for service and 18% for tax on top of the price of the room (prices in this book include this extra charge). The rate is usually negotiable; you should get a bargain if the hotel is empty. Try saying '*tiene algo un poco más económico*' (have you got one a little cheaper)?

Standards

A Peruvian hotel can call itself a *residencial*, a *hostal*, a *hotel*, a *pensión* or a *hospedaje*, and by law must display a plaque outside indicating its type – though it makes no difference to the standard of what's on offer. The cheapest hotels offer a plank bed in a dirty room in a dangerous part of town run by a threatening manager, or they may provide a sunny room in an old colonial mansion, so ask to see a room before you part with your money. You won't get plank beds in any hotels listed in this book and expensive hotels will be up to the international standard you'd expect.

Availability

You'll have no problem finding somewhere to stay unless you turn up on a major holiday or festival (see p62), and even then you'll probably find somewhere, it'll just be more expensive.

FOOD

Peruvian food can be excellent. There's a tradition of good eating and drinking that goes back to the days of the Incas. Pedro Pizarro reported that when the Inca Atahualpa ate: 'Ladies brought in his meal and placed it before him on tender thin green rushes. ... They placed before him all his vessels of gold, silver and pottery on these rushes. He pointed to whatever he fancied and it was brought. One of his ladies took it and held it in her hand while he ate.'

Meat

You will get bored with *lomo* (beef loin steak) cooked *cordon bleu* (stuffed with cheese and ham), *milanesa* (beaten into a thin steak, rolled in breadcrumbs and fried), and *a lo pobre* (fried with an egg on top). Chicken is often cooked in these ways too, or just plain roasted. *Parilladas* (a mixed grill and a restaurant that sells grilled meat) are generally very good and filling, if lacking in imagination.

More interesting dishes are *lomo salta-do* (strips of beef cooked in onions, peppers, tomatoes and soy sauce, served with rice), *anticucho* (heart (beef) kebabs), *causa rellena* (a very slightly spiced potato cake mixed with tuna or chicken), *aji de gallina* (shredded chicken stewed in a gently spiced cream sauce) and the artery-hardening *chicharrones* (deep-fried chunks of pork or pork skin).

> ❏ **Pet food**
> In the Cusco area, you'll see *cuy* (guinea pig) on offer – it tastes a bit like duck and has a tough skin. Cuy is laid flat on your plate, as if it had been run over by a bus then peeled off the wheel. They say it's cooked in one piece to prevent someone trying to dish you up cat.

Fish

The coast of Peru has truly excellent fish: *congrio* (a pacific conger eel), *lenguado* (sole), *corvina* (sea bass) and shellfish. Try *jalea* (fried whitebait), *chupe de camarones* (special prawn chowder), and especially the traditional Peruvian dish *ceviche* (raw white fish marinated in lemon and onion and served with two types of maize). Ceviche originated when coastal slaves weren't allowed to cook food on fires and had to prepare their fish in another way – they invented cold cooking with lemon juice.

Other dishes

The potato was first cultivated in Peru as long as 10,000 years ago. Today, scientists have identified more than 4000 potato varieties, many of which are only found in Peru. Not surprisingly Peruvians have come up with many ways of cooking them. Some of the waxy, firm beauties you eat out here will put to shame the humble spuds you get at home. You could also try *chuño*, which is potato that's been freeze-dried. Freeze-drying is a traditional way of preserving potatoes for leaner times by leaving them out in the bitterly cold Andean nights.

Peru is also home to around 35 types of maize, more than anywhere else on earth. Corn has been cultivated in Peru since at least 1200 BC. You can find it on the cob, *choclo* (often served at markets or train stations with a hunk of fresh cheese, *choclo con queso*), boiled, ground, toasted or fermented into *chicha* (see p61). Corn is also used to make cornmash, pastries called *tamales* and *humitas*, which can come in a wide range of colours (green, brown and yellow) and flavours (sweet and savoury).

Peruvians are good at replicating other country's cuisines: pasta is often freshly made and first-class (Cusco is famous for its pizzerias) and Chinese food (*Chifa*) is also good.

Dessert

For dessert, there are *picarones* (light fried doughnuts on a plate of honey) and *mazamorra morada* (a sweet-tasting dish derived from purple maize), which looks like jelly.

DRINK

Non-alcoholic

> **❏ Maté de coca**
> Coca leaf, even in tea bags, is a prohibited drug in most countries, and if you try to take some home you risk jail (in the UK coca leaf is a Class A drug, the importation of which carries a long prison sentence).

Tea is usually served without milk but with sugar and lemon. **Herb teas** are often available. In Cusco you should try *maté de coca*, which is made from coca leaves and said to help alleviate the symptoms of altitude sickness. It's available in most restaurants.

Coffee is usually served as coffee essence that you add to hot water; instant coffee is better. In some places you can now get a cappuccino or espresso. Don't drink **water** from taps or streams without first purifying it (see p179). Alternatively you can buy bottled mineral water. Coke, Pepsi, Fanta and Sprite are widely available. You're going to have to try the ubiquitous home-grown soft drink, **Inca Cola**, at least once – the name's too intriguing to miss. It tastes like bubblegum.

Alcoholic

Avoid Peruvian **wine**, it's not very good, and drink Chilean or Argentinian wine instead. However, the Peruvian spirit **Pisco** (distilled from grapes) is a gift from the gods. Be prepared: it's strong though usually drunk diluted in the refreshing cocktail Pisco Sour. The Chileans claim that they were the ones who invented Pisco, but it's probably Peruvian.

> **❏ Pisco Sour**
> 2 fl oz Pisco
> ¹/₂ lemon (Peruvian lemons are very small so make this ¹/₄ of a normal one)
> 1 egg white (whisked)
> 2 dessertspoons of sugar
> The spirit, egg and lemon juice are shaken together then served over crushed ice with a dash of Angostura bitters.

The **beer** is watery lager and it all seems to taste the same; brands include Cristal, Cusqueña, and Arequipeña.

Chicha (see box opposite) is a **maize wine/beer** that dates back to the time of the Incas – you can identify houses that have chicha for sale because they fly red flags or bin-bags from sticks. The historian Prescott described it as sparkling champagne, but then he'd never tasted it. Another historian, John Hemming, more realistically describes it as murky pale cider.

Health

(Also see pp175) Drink only purified or bottled water and avoid ice in drinks. If you can't peel it, wash it in purified water, cook it or shell it, then don't eat it, otherwise you run the risk of getting diarrhoea. Avoid things like salads, raw vegetables, unpeeled fruit, ice cream, unpasteurized dairy products and anything that's not been freshly cooked. You can make a solution for washing vegetables by putting 12 drops of iodine in a litre of water.

Tax and tipping

Expensive restaurants sometimes add another 10% for service and 18% for tax to the bill. The service element in this should make its way to the waiter, so the-

Chicha

The 'champagne of the Incas' is still widely drunk today. Different areas of Peru make chicha in different ways; the chicha from the Cusco region is made as follows: Maize grains are soaked overnight, and then put in the sun to germinate. When they are part-germinated, they are boiled up, and then strained through a sieve. The liquid produced is called *upi*, and it's put to one side. The maize grains left in the sieve are boiled once more, and then sieved again, which produces a liquid called *seque*. The seque and the upi are then mixed to produce chicha, and the residue is fed to animals. Chicha is often flavoured with cinnamon and cloves, and sweetened with molasses.

oretically there's no need to tip, although the reality is that the money will go straight into the manager's pocket.

ELECTRICITY

220 volts AC, 60 cycles. Expect power cuts and power surges, and don't touch the bare wiring you'll see in your shower!

TIME

Peru is five hours behind GMT (UK winter time).

POST AND TELECOMMUNICATIONS

Telephone and fax

You can make international calls directly from public phones in the street, but you'll need a phonecard to pay, which you can buy from women who hang around phones selling them or in shops that display a sign saying *tarjeta telefónica* (telephone card). There are two sorts: the regular phonecards and the increasingly popular and better-value 147 cards, where you dial 147 and follow the instructions given by the operator. You can also make a call from telephone company offices but this will be more expensive. The number to dial for the operator is 100; for information it's 103 and for the international operator it's 108. However, the cheapest way to dial abroad from Peru is to use a computer and dial through the Internet. Internet cafés in both Cusco and Lima can help you out with this, and the cost should be no more than a couple of soles per hour.

To phone Peru from abroad dial your international access code, then 51. Add 1 for Lima, or 84 for Cusco. To dial home from Peru, first dial the international access code 00, then add your country code (UK 44, USA and Canada 1, Australia 61, New Zealand 64), then your STD and number required.

You can send and receive faxes from hotels and telephone company offices.

Email

Email has replaced other forms of communication for travellers. However, internet cafés spring up like mushrooms and die like mayflies, so check websites such as 🖥 **www.cybercafes.com** for the latest picture. If you don't already

PERU

❑ **Holidays and festivals**

1 January	New Year (all Peru)
6 January	Fiesta de Ollantaytambo (Cusco)
14 January	Feria de Pampamarca (Cusco): a large agricultural fair
April	Maundy Thursday, Good Friday and Easter (all Peru)
1 May	Labour Day (all Peru)
7-9 June	Qoyllur Riti (Cusco): an Apollonian pilgrimage to the glaciers of the high Andes
June	Corpus Christi (all Peru, but especially Cusco): statues of saints are paraded around Cusco's packed streets; it takes place on the Thursday after Trinity Sunday (ninth Thursday after Easter)
24 June	Inti Raymi (Cusco): the old Inca festival of the winter solstice, which was suppressed by the Spanish and recreated in 1944; elsewhere the celebration is called Peasants' Day
29 June	St Peter and St Paul (all Peru)
15-17 July	Fiesta de Paucartambo (Cusco): a Dionysiac festival to honour the Virgin of Carmen of Paucartambo (a village near Cusco) with masked dancers
28/29 July	Independence Day (all Peru)
30 August	Santa Rosa de Lima (all Peru)
7 October	Battle of Angamos (all Peru)
18 October	El Señor de los Milagros (Lima): a day of religious processions
1 November	All Saints' Day: (all Peru): the day when Peruvians remember their dead
8 December	Immaculate Conception (all Peru)
24 December	Santorantikuy (Cusco): originally a market which sold objects for Nativity Scenes, this is now a large market for practically anything; elsewhere, the day is a pre-Christmas holiday
25 December	Christmas (all Peru)

have a free address with one of the companies such as hotmail or yahoo you can easily set up an account at an internet café.

Post

Post is slow but generally reliable, and stamps for a postcard outside the Americas will cost about s/3.80; they're usually available where you purchase your post-cards. Main *correos* (post offices) have **poste restante**, and American Express offices also hold letters addressed to their clients. It helps if the people who are sending you letters underline your surname, and when looking for your letters you should check under *all* the names on the envelope; they're often misfiled.

SHOPPING

Fabrics

Fabrics are profoundly important to Andean peoples, and they always have been. The Inca wore clothes made from the most delicate and beautiful fabrics possible. Pedro Pizarro described Atahualpa's clothes: 'He was ... wearing a

dark brown tunic and cloak. I approached him and
felt the cloak, which was softer than silk. I asked
him "Inca, of what is a robe as soft as this made?"
He explained that it was from the skins of [vampire] bats that fly at night.'

The highest-quality cloth in
Inca times was produced
by the weavers of the
Acclawasi (House of the
Chosen Women)
FELIPE HUAMÁN POMA DE AYALA
(c1590)

You can't get bat skin anymore, but woollens
made from **alpaca** (a relative of the llama, domesticated for its beautiful wool) are widely available.
The quality varies greatly: if you burn a couple of
fibres and it smells of plastic, it's not made from
alpaca but acrylic, and if it stinks when slightly
wet, it's not alpaca, it's **llama**. You might also find
fabrics made from **vicuña** wool, a beautiful, fine
silken fibre that used to be reserved for the Inca
himself. This stuff is incredibly expensive (the
poor beasts are rare and were almost hunted to
extinction), but very beautiful. If you do buy
vicuña make sure it's come from a reputable
source, as the animals are endangered.

Fabrics dyed using traditional techniques tend
to be more expensive and more subtle than those that use modern dyes. You can
pick them up at one of the tourist markets, such as Chinchero (see p162), Pisac
(p160) and Ollantaytambo (p164).

Arts and crafts

You can buy other traditional crafts such as Andean pipes and cheap copies of
Moche erotic pots (see p80). Never be tempted to buy the framed insects and
stuffed animals you'll be offered in Cusco, as the trade in them depletes the
resources of the forest. Many of them are protected species anyway, and either
Peruvian Customs or your own will confiscate them. Any 'Inca' artifacts you're
offered are probably fake, and if they're not it's illegal to try to export them.

Rip offs

Peru is not, as a character said in Peter Shaffer's play *The Royal Hunt of the
Sun*: 'a silent country, frozen in avarice', but if you feel you've been taken for
a ride contact the **Tourist Protection Service**, called **Indecopi** (☎ 0800 4 2579,
and it's a free call, not available from pay phones), at Portal Carrizos 250, Plaza
de Armas in Cusco. This organization is run by the government to deal with
tourists' complaints.

SAFETY

'The Prefect had been very solicitous about our welfare, and, although we
assured him that we preferred to travel without a military escort, he insisted that
a sergeant and at least one soldier should accompany us as long as we were in
his Department.... There was no danger, and highway robbery is unheard of in
Peru.' *The Lost City of the Incas*, by Hiram Bingham, 1948. Whatever it was like

in Bingham's day, Peru now has a crime problem, so you need to be careful. But being careful doesn't mean being paranoid, and most of the guide books to Peru are so liberally spiced with warnings that it seems you're entering a war zone. You're not, and you will have no trouble provided you take sensible precautions:

● **Don't flaunt your valuables** It's wisest not to travel with anything you might be upset to lose. Leave expensive jewellery at home and bring a wrist watch that looks obviously cheap. Leave your passport and wads of money in your hotel safe.

● **Be aware** Don't go to dodgy areas, take care when travelling at night. Be aware of people around you and beware of any who are paying you undue attention. It helps to walk around in groups, at least until you've got your bearings and feel secure. Take taxis when you arrive in a new place.

● **Take precautions** Wear a money belt and carry your money in a couple of different places on your body. Some people stick a US$100 bill under the insole in their shoe for emergencies, or put one in an elastic bandage on their leg. Make sure your luggage is secure – you could put chicken wire inside your bag to prevent slashing razors, or buy a flour sack and sew your rucksack into it to secure easily opened pockets. (Don't use a fishmeal sack for this, as they stink.)

● **Don't fall for tricks** Common scams involve catching your attention and then picking your pocket; someone might spit on you or stick chewing gum on your shirt, or an old lady might collapse under your feet. There'll be an accomplice who's standing behind you, and when you're not on your guard they will whip out your wallet. Also be on your guard against fake policemen; always ask to see an ID. Whilst on the subject of the police, be careful of corrupt policemen as they might try to plant drugs on you, and never get into a police car if you can avoid it, but insist on walking to the police station.

In Cusco they've taken the art of distracting you to the limit. Be on your guard. As in all countries there is the occasional mugging.

● **If the worst happens** Remember, they're probably after your money, so stay calm and hand it over – it's worth much less than your life. If you are unlucky enough to be a victim of crime, go to the **Tourist Police** (see p118 and p144) who speak English and are helpful. Get a police report for insurance.

Having said all that, you should remember that hundreds and thousands of people visit Peru each year without any problems at all. Nothing's likely to happen to you if you take care. As for the risk from **terrorism**, as the SAEC (see p118) say, you're more likely to be run down by Lima's mad traffic than come to grief from the Sendero Luminoso or the MRTA.

DRUGS

For many people, there's nothing that needs to be said about this. But for others, you should know that buying or using drugs can land you in prison for the next 15 years, and the person you're thinking of buying them from may be a police informant. Think long and hard about it – is it really worth the risk?

Sobralia dichotoma
Flor del Paraíso Orchid

Leguminosae
Lupin

Calceolaria engleriana
Ladies' slipper

Epidendrum secundum
Huinay Huayna orchid

Masdevallia veitchiana
Huakanki orchid

Labiateae
Salvia

Datura arborea
Moonflower

Begoniaceae
Begonia

Cantua buxifolia
Kantu

Centre photo © Bryn Thomas. Centre right photo © Henry Stedman
All other photos © Alexander Stewart

Lythraceae cuplea

Lantana

Culcitium

Arum Lily

Puya

Dahlia

Veronica

Commelina

Trimezia

All photos © Henry Stedman

Flora and fauna

'*In the variety of its charm and the power of its spell, I know of no other place in the world which can compare with it. Not only has it great snow peaks looming above the clouds more than two miles overhead, gigantic precipices of many-coloured granite rising sheer for thousands of feet above the foaming, glistening, roaring rapids; it has also, in striking contrast, orchids and tree ferns, the delectable beauty of luxurious vegetation, and the mysterious witchery of the jungle.*' (**Hiram Bingham**, *Lost City of the Incas*)

The Machu Picchu Historical Sanctuary is an area of wilderness banded to the north by the watershed of the Mt Veronica massif, in the east and west by the Cusichaca and Aobamba Valleys, and in the south by the ridgeline of the Salcantay massif. This area, some 325sq km in all, was declared a Protected Natural Area in 1981. Two years later, in 1983, it was pronounced a World Heritage Site by Unesco. Unusually, it is a World Heritage Site for both architecture and wildlife. A tenth of Peru's plant and animal species are represented within the confines of the Sanctuary. This includes around 200 species of orchid, more than 700 kinds of butterfly and almost 400 species of bird, nearly 5% of the world's total.

The reason for this amazing diversity of life is the great variety of ecosystems found inside the Sanctuary. The mouth of the Aobamba river lies at 1725m/5660ft, while 20km away the peak of Mt Salcantay grazes 6271m/20,568ft, and the range of temperatures and microclimates within this 4546m-/14,908ft-altitude span sustains 10 distinct 'life zones', extending from the permanent snows of the high peaks, past two types of high-altitude grassland to seven zones of forest. The best-known and most-recognized habitats are ***puna***, a treeless, mountain grassland environment, and **cloud forest** (which actually encompasses four separate life zones), a beguiling mass of lichen-smothered trees, vines, bromeliads, ferns and dense vegetation speckled with orchids. As you would guess from the name, these forests get most of their moisture from fog and clouds rather than rain. At higher altitudes, you'll see smaller, stumpier ***polylepis*** woodland by slopes, gullies and rocky outcrops; the Inca Trail passes through a *polylepis* forest during the ascent to Dead Woman's Pass.

FLORA

Many of the plants you'll see in the Sanctuary have relatives that are commonly grown in Europe and North America. There are **lupins**, **fuchsias**, **daisies**, **elders**, **buttercups** and **cacti**. **Broom** (*Spartinum junceum*) was introduced from Spain in 1580 and thrives in grasslands up to 3500m/11,480ft. Its bright flowers are used medicinally to treat rheumatism, dropsy, oedema, liver diseases and abscesses, and in parades as confetti. **Begonias** (*Begonia bracteosa*) also flourish within the Sanctuary and the red, white or pink flowers of various species can be seen on numerous dry, sunny, stepped slopes. Around boulders in grassy areas, you might find *Bomarea dulcis*, a type of **lily** which produces between two and five dangling, reddish pink, two-inch flowers resembling tubular bells. The Quechua name for this plant is *milli milli*, meaning 'twins' and describes the two flowers often seen hanging together. The 2m shrub **calceolaria** (ladies slipper) is very common. Its flowers, resembling tiny slippers, give the plant its name in several languages: the Latin *calceolus* means 'slipper'; in Quechua it is *pucllu*, which means 'bag' or 'sack'; and its Spanish nickname is *globito*, meaning 'little bubble', because you can pop them between your fingers. Various species are used by local people in tea as a cure for uterine problems or as a diuretic.

Less familiar, but equally distinctive is *Brachyotum grisebachi*, found on the edges of the cloud forest near to water. This 2.5m shrub produces masses of dangling purple-violet flowers, which are occasionally used by local people as rudimentary earrings. Look out for two striking varieties of **bomarea** too; the showy orange flowers of *Bomarea aurantiaca* and the deep red flowers of *Bomarea coccinea* are particularly visible in the humid cloud forest around Phuyu Pata Marca on the Inca Trail and in the jungle surrounding the Santa Teresa valley. In rocky or wooded areas, you may see the **wild potato** (*Solanaceae sp*), identified by its five-pointed violet flowers with protruding yellow anthers. More unusual are the large trumpet-shaped blooms of the **moon flower**, *Datura arborea*, which is toxic, but has long been used by shamans to induce hallucinations. The flower is either white or orange-red.

Orchids

One of the more exotic plants that you will come across in the Sanctuary is the orchid. Around 200 species thrive here, especially within the moist, humid confines of the cloud forest. There are said to be up to 3000 orchid species just in Peru alone and new species are discovered each year.

The diversity in the Sanctuary alone is boggling: the tallest orchid, *Sobralia dichotoma*, also known as the Flor del Paraíso, can be seen around Machu Picchu, where it grows up to 5m tall and has garish flowers that are 8cm long, while at the other end of the scale the flower of a *Stelis* is barely 2mm wide, one of the world's smallest.

You can spot orchids at any time of year, but most flower during the rainy season from October to March. The most widespread and populous genus is *Epidendrum*, of which there are around 30 species in the Sanctuary. The most common is *Epidendrum secundum*, known locally as **Huinay Huayna**, meaning 'forever young', a reference to the fact that it flowers almost all year-round. This small, starburst of a flower is particularly noticeable around the ruins near the end of the Inca Trail to which it gives its name. Other species include the delicate and fragrant *Epidendrum ciliare*, which grows on trees and rocks at the lower elevations, and *Epidendrum coronatum*, which favours open areas amidst other plants at altitudes between 2800m/9185ft and 3200m/10,495ft. Also commonly seen on the forest border and on open slopes are the distinctively shaped, bright yellow flowers of *Odontoglossum sp*.

One of the most striking orchids is *Masdevallia veitchiana*, known locally as **Huakanki**, which means 'you'll cry'. Its beautiful purple and orange flowers with three delicately pointed petals appear between May and July, and can be spotted at Huinay Huayna and in open sunny areas on moss rugs over rocks. Once prolific, this species has been collected almost to extinction, one of many orchids that are in danger in the Sanctuary from plant hunters and the destruction of their habitat. Intipata on the Inca Trail is a case in point (see box p198).

Trees and shrubs

There are a number of beautiful trees found throughout the cloud forest. Some, such as the 20m **aliso** (*Alnus jorullensis*), which is frequently found on riverbanks between 2500m/8200ft and 3800m/12,465ft, have provided locals with building material for centuries. Both the Incas and the Spanish used its large trunks as beams and lintels in buildings and today, doors, windows and fruit crates are made from its yellow-white wood. The **molle** (*Schinus molle*) is similarly useful and was cultivated by the Incas in the region of Mollepata, giving the town its name. They collected its resin to embalm their mummies, but nowadays its wood is used in carpentry, its ashes for tanning and to make soap, its oil for perfumes and toothpaste, and its small red fruits to flavour honey, vinegar, and other condiments.

You'll probably see **llaulli** (*Barnadesia horrida*), a thorny bush, which locals cultivate as hedgerows and weave it into a lattice on which to lay roof tiles, high up in the ravines adjoining the Urubamba valley. Its pink, daisy-like flowers are used for alleviating respiratory problems and bronchitis. The town of Chilca, also in the Urubamba valley, gets its name from the **chilca** bush (*Bacharis latifolia*), which grows abundantly in the area and can be identified by the generous clusters of white flowers at the end of its branches. The leaves and flowers are used to make a yellow-green dye for wool and its ash is mixed with calcium and made into balls, called *llipta*, which locals chew with coca leaves.

The Cusichaca valley is a good place to spot the thorny **tara** tree (*Caesalpina spinosa*), most easily recognized by its orange-red seedpods which resemble tough-skinned broad beans. The tara is unusual for bearing fruit all year-round; the fruits are used to tan leather and, strangely, to ease throat pain. The smaller **chamana** (*Dodonaea viscosa*) is also found in the Cusichaca valley, and is the perfect plant for binding the soil on the steep mountainsides. The wood burns well even when fresh as it contains a flammable oily sap. As you enter the valley on the early stages of the Inca Trail, you won't miss the abundant pink flowers of the **chacpa** (*Oreocallis grandiflora*), which can grow up to 6m tall. Baskets are made from its small, flexible branches and locals chew the leaves in order to prevent tooth decay. Look out for the attractive **rata rata** (*Abutilon sylvaticum*), found around Huayllabamba and the Cusichaca Valley; it's also planted in city plazas and gardens for its bold displays of conical pink-and-white flowers.

The **unca** (*Myrcanthes oreophyl*), which grows up to 15m tall, is another pretty tree for its large white flowers. The Incas used to make *keros*, ceremonial vases, from its heavy white wood, and people still craft furniture from it. The bright red splashes of colour visible around the towns of Pisac, Calca and Urubamba in the Sacred Valley are likely to be flowering **pisonay** (*Erythrima edulis*), a giant tree native to the high jungle but introduced to much higher elevations by the Incas, who considered it sacred. But the real giant of the forest is the 30m **eucalyptus** (*Eucaliptus globulus*) tree, which is not native to the Andes, but is now used for everything from furniture to railway sleepers. It is farmed not only for the benefit of the construction and mining industries, but by food and drug companies for the menthol in its leaves.

Finally, keep your eyes peeled for the **kantu** (*Cantua buxifolia*), the national flower of Peru. It's a tall shrub with red and yellow flowers which grows above 2300m/7545ft. The Incas dedicated this plant to the sun god and used the pattern of its flower on their pottery, textiles and ceremonial vases.

Other plants

Bromeliads, relatives of the pineapple, can be seen throughout the Sanctuary's cloud forests. In drier mountain areas, you'll see several types of **cacti**; the **agave cactus** (*Agave americana*) is one of the most widespread and the Incas used its fibres to make sandals, ropes and suspension bridges. The **prickly pear** cactus is cultivated as a home for the cochineal, a parasitic insect, which is crushed to obtain the vivid red dye of the same name. The fruits of the cactus are delicious and are sold in many of the towns in the Sacred Valley.

There are two types of common **grasses**. Tussocks of golden or brown *Stipa Ichu* grow all over the puna, and its tough blades are used to thatch roofs, insulate beds and tents, and as animal feed. *Certaderia nitida* stands much taller and looks like a fox tail. A type of succulent grass, *Plantago rigida*, grows in round, rigid cushions, which you'll probably encounter as stepping stones across boggy areas. Its inflexible leaves grow in star shapes in high swampy areas above 4500m/14,760ft and are the favoured foodstuff of alpacas.

FAUNA

Mammals

The star of the Sanctuary, but an animal that you'll be extremely lucky to see, is the **Andean (or Spectacled) bear** (*Tremarctus ornatus*). These large bears pose no threat to trekkers as they are both shy and herbivorous. On the contrary they are the ones threatened by the inroads we make into their habitat. The bear's favourite food is the bromeliad; it will even construct rudimentary platforms to get at these plants. Having feasted and safe in the knowledge it has no natural predator (except man), the bear often just falls asleep.

Don't expect to see any **puma** (*Felis concolor*), the fanged cat of Peru, because they are very, very rare. You're more likely to see the **Colpeo fox**, a bold scavenger that lives in these hills and preys on the ill and the dying, or an Andean **skunk**, a weasel, or if you're lucky a **White-tailed deer**. The Sanctuary also boasts **pudu** (pygmy deer, also known as *sachacabra* in Quechua), timid little nocturnal beasts that are rarely seen during the day.

The Peruvian Paso
Horses were native to South America, but they died out many thousands of years ago. They were re-introduced by the Spanish, who used them to great effect in battles against the natives. Some of the descendants of the mounts of the conquistadors have been developed into a breed of horse called the Peruvian Paso, or Peruvian Stepping Horse. It's famous for its characteristic way of walking, with high-stepping forelegs and powerful hind legs, which makes it comfortable to ride. It has great stamina, being able to maintain a regular speed of about 11mph (18kmph) over rough country.

Keep a look out for mountain **viscachas** – there are hundreds of these rabbit-like rodents living in the Machu Picchu ruins and you'll see their pellet-like droppings everywhere, even if you can't see the viscachas themselves.

The animals you'll see most frequently (apart from horses) are **llamas** and **alpacas**, cousins of the camel that have been domesticated for thousands of years for their meat, wool and ability to carry cargo. Llamas are the most common and strongest, standing 1.9m tall and able to haul up to 60kg. The alpaca, known as *pacocha* in Quechua, has a smaller and more rounded silhouette than a llama. Llamas and alpacas have two wild relatives: **guanacos** (big with a white belly, more common in Chile and Argentina) and **vicuña** (gentle-looking with inquisitive eyes, a furry chest and the finest animal wool in the world), both of which are rarely seen in the Machu Picchu Sanctuary but are more common in the south. Poaching has heavily diminished vicuña numbers and they are now a protected species in Peru.

Birds
The Incas considered birds to be the messengers of the *apus*, the spirits of the *cordillera* (mountain range), and the mighty condor represented the great snow peaks while the lesser birds represented lesser mountains.

Many birds have relatively small altitudinal ranges meaning that each of the Sanctuary's 10 habitats is home to species that are found in no other zone. Up to 400 species are known in the Sanctuary and more than 200 of these can be readily observed along the Inca Trail or on the treks to Vilcabamba and Choquequirao. The *polylepis* woodland contains some of the rarest birds, including tit-spinetails and high-altitude hummingbirds, but the cloud forest is home to the greatest diversity and here you can expect to see tinamous, guans, parakeets, hummingbirds, wrens, jays, swallows, quetzals, woodpeckers, fly-catchers and tanagers.

The best times to spot them are first thing in the morning or at dusk, when they are singing and most active. Binoculars will help no end in picking out birds up in the forest canopy.

For further information on the birds of Peru, consult 🖳 www.inrena.gob.pe, the website of the Instituto de Recursos Naturales (Spanish only).

ANDEAN CONDOR

● **Andean Condor** The Andean Condor (*Vultur gryphus*) is actually an enormous vulture that averages well over a metre from its bill to the tip of its tail and has a 3m/10ft wingspan.

In the air, apart from its sheer size, a condor is easily identifiable by its distinctive wing pattern and characteristic forward-pointing finger-feathers at the end of its wings, its white ruff and bald head. Despite its reputation as a mountain bird it's not common here and is more usually found on the coast where it can find more carrion. It's had a bad press over the years, and stories have been told of its attacking travellers, carrying away goats and killing small children. The great writer and traveller Bruce Chatwin relates in his book, *In Patagonia*, an unlikely story about being harried by a condor and George Squier (*Peru – Travel and Exploration in the Land of the Incas*, 1877) includes

GEORGE SQUIER FENDS OFF A CONDOR

a picture of himself almost being attacked by one of these massive birds, just managing to see it off with a shot from his pistol.

Hiram Bingham recounted in *Lost City of the Incas* that local shepherds had to wage a constant battle with condors that had no difficulty in carrying off a sheep. One glimpse at the feet of a condor (usually only possible when you come across a stuffed one) tells you that this is impossible, as instead of sharp, evil talons, condors have what look like oversized chicken feet. They couldn't grasp anything, let alone carry away a small struggling child or sheep.

● **Birds of prey** The large birds that you'll see are more often than not birds of prey. You're likely to catch a glimpse of an **American Kestrel** (*Falco Sparverius*), an **Aplomado Falcon** (*Falco femoralis*) or a **Mountain Caracara** (*Phalco-boenus megalopterus*). The kestrel is quite a small bird, averaging just under 30cm from beak to tail, with grey wings a grey head, white cheeks and a brownish breast and tail. The falcon is about 10cm longer and has light brown wings and tail and a paler breast. The caracara is larger still, 50cm from beak to tail, and has characteristic black, white and grey wings, a black and white tail and the bare skin of its face is an orangey colour.

MOUNTAIN CARACARA

You might also get to see the **Black-chested Buzzard Eagle** (*Geranoaeus melanoleucus*) and various different types of **hawk**. The buzzard eagle is big, 70cm from beak to tail, and is predominantly a grey colour, with black edges to its wings and a black neck and head. The feathers on the tips of its wings do not spread forward as much as those of the condor.

BLACK-CHESTED
BUZZARD EAGLE

● **Tanagers** Amongst the most common and visible forest birds, tanagers often congregate in small flocks near human habitation to feed in fruit trees. Few other species can match the broad spectrum of colours splashed across their plumage. There are 135 species recorded in Peru, the most common along the Inca Trail are the **Blue-and-yellow Tanager**, the **Blue-grey Tanager**, the **Saffron-crowned Tanager**, the **Fawn-breasted Tanager** and the **Silver-beaked Tanager**.

● **Trogons** Although less well known than other gaudy birds, trogons are often considered to be the most visually impressive.

The largest of the species, the **quetzals**, are the most dazzling. Males are consistently more colourful than the females and have metallic or glittering green, blue or violet heads, backs and chests. Their breasts and undersides are contrasting bright red, yellow or orange. The females usually have darker brown or grey backs and heads, but they share the brightly coloured chests of the males. The long characteristic tail is squared off and stripped black and white on the underside.

Look out for the green-headed **Collared Trogon** (*Trogon collaris*) and the similar **Masked Trogon** (*Trogon personatus*), which can be distinguished by the thicker bars on its tail feathers.

● **Motmots** These beautifully coloured birds are related to kingfishers and live in all types of forest as well as on open areas of grassland. They have long, broad bills that are curved down at the end, but their most distinctive feature is a pair of flamboyant tail feathers which trail far behind them.

The **Highland Motmot** (*Momotus aequatorialis*) grows up to 48cm and has a turquoise-blue forecrown and green underparts. It can be seen all along the Urubamba Valley, often perched on riverside boulders, and around Aguas Calientes. Similar, but slightly smaller and with brown underparts, is the **Blue Crowned Motmot** (*Momotus momata*).

● **Guans** These large pheasant-like birds can be seen or more frequently heard, crashing about in the trees of the humid montane forests. The most common is the **Andean Guan** (*Penelope montagnii*). This turkey-sized bird, with orange-brown plumage and a red wattle, lives in the trees and feeds on fruit, seeds and other vegetable matter, rarely descending to the ground.

● **Waterfowl** In streams, lakes and ponds as well as along the Urubamba river you can find the famous **Torrent Duck** (*Merganetta armata*) of Matthew

Parris's book *Inca Kola*. Male torrent ducks are a stripy black and white with red beaks, and females have reddish-brown chests and grey backs.

Andean Gulls (*Larus serranus*), the only gull to be found in the high Andes, also live along the Urubamba or can be seen on highland lakes. You might also come across **Andean (or Ruddy) Ducks**, red with a spiky black tail, dark head and wide bill; the **Crested Duck**, a sleek grey with a touch of red on the wings; **Andean Geese**, with a rather menacing grey stripe around the eye; and black and white **Giant Coots**.

Elegant **Puna Ibis** (*Plegadis ridgwayi*), which have dark feathers, a white face and a red bill, can often be seen around Cusco and along the first stages of the railway trip to Machu Picchu.

● **Wrens** These are small, brownish birds that tend to skulk in thick undergrowth. The Latin name of the genus, *Troglodytes*, refers to a cave dweller, a reference to the wren's predilection for nesting in holes and crevices. They are very vocal and sing beautifully.

At Machu Picchu you're bound to hear the song of the **Inca Wren** (*Thryothorus eisenmanni*), which is endemic to Peru and whose distinctive spotted breast marks it out from its relatives.

● **Hummingbirds** Of the smaller birds, the ones that cause the most excitement are the various types of hummingbird, which fizz through the air in a streak of iridescent metallic greens, reds, violets and blues. These tiny, nectar-drinking birds rely entirely on their wings for locomotion since their feet and legs are too weak for anything but perching.

The most commonly spotted hummingbird along the Inca Trail or in the gardens of Cusco is the **Sparkling Violetear** (*Colibri coruscans*), a tireless singer with a violet-blue chest and violet ear that extends to its chin. The slightly larger **Green-and-white Hummingbird** (*Leucippus viridicauda*) is regularly recorded around Machu Picchu, where it can be identified by its white chest.

The world's largest hummingbird is the surprisingly dull coloured **Giant Hummingbird** (*Patagonia gigas*), which can reach a massive (for a hummingbird) 24cm from the tip of its bill to the end of its tail.

You might also come across **Sunangels**, **Sapphirewings**, **Coquettes**, **Goldenthroats**, **Sunbeams** and **Coronets**, each of which is as stunning as its beautiful name suggests.

● **Other birds** One of the most famous birds in the Sanctuary – and Peru's national bird – is the **Cock of the Rock** (*Rupicola peruviana*), a **cotinga** which sports a stunning head-dress of red-orange feathers reminiscent of the red fringe that the Inca used to wear as a badge of his rank.

Frequently seen along the railway tracks near Machu Picchu, it is also common in the forests around Espíritu Pampa. Another resplendent, noisy bird is the **parakeet**, which can often be seen and heard around Aguas Calientes or in the forests along the Vilcabamba Trail.

On the ground you can see **partridges**, which at one stage were so common that they gave their name to a town (the name Pisac, a town in the Sacred Valley, means partridge).

In the skies watch out for **swifts** and **swallows** with their distinctive swept-back wings and pointed tails. In woodland look out for **woodpeckers** and in particular the attractive **Andean Flicker** (*Colaptes rupicola*), a largish bird (33cm from beak to tail) with a beige head, grey and dark brown body and a yellow breast that is also fairly common in puna and scrubland.

Reptiles

Few reptiles are known about, as the forest tends to be so dense and inaccessible. Keep a look out for snakes; **coral snakes**, **bushmasters** and the **fer-de-lance** are native to the Sanctuary. They are all poisonous and should not be approached if encountered. Snakes of the *Elapidoe* family and **frogs** of the genus *Atelopus* also live in the forest above 2000m/6560ft.

Insects

Peru is justifiably famous for its **butterflies**. One of every five species of butterfly is found here. Some 1300 species have been recorded in the community of Pakitza, in Manu National Park and over 1200 species have been noted at a community 235km away on the Tambopata river. Incredibly, only 60% of these species overlapped.

Scientists estimate that there must be more than 4000 species in the country, only about 3600 of which have currently been registered. Considering that North America and Europe can barely muster 1120 species between them, this is a truly enormous number.

Most butterflies prefer the warmer tropical forests to the chilly Andean highlands, and on the Vilcabamba Trail you're likely to see a diverse array, occasionally encountering huge clouds of shimmering colour.

Unfortunately, you are also likely to become very well acquainted with the **midges** that can be encountered throughout the Sanctuary.

PART 3: THE INCAS

Pre-Inca civilizations

Peru is a place of great antiquity. The Incas were only the third empire to dominate the Andes. Before they built their roads and terraces, before they counted on their *quipus* (string used for record-keeping – see p91) and before they worshipped the sun, other cultures had flourished in the barren deserts and soaring mountains of this part of South America. The first pan-Andean civilization, the **Chavín**, thrived about 2500 years ago, the second, the **Huari-Tiahuanaco**, about 1000 years ago, and between these times of cultural unity many smaller peoples rose and fell. The glories of the Inca state, the architecture, the textiles, the roads, the agriculture, and the social organization were developed out of the foundations of these more ancient civilizations of Peru.

IN THE BEGINNING

Paleo-Indians, the first settlers of the Americas, walked over the tundra some 20,000 years ago, chasing their migrating food across the land bridge that joined the continents of Asia and North America. This was possible because in those days the world was much colder than it is today, and massive ice sheets froze the oceans into glaciers, making the sea level much lower. The waters have now risen again, and the land bridge is lost beneath the Bering Straits.

Early days in South America

How long it took for humans to work their way down to South America is something about which archaeologists don't agree, but the generally accepted view is that we've been on the continent for between 9000 and 11,000 years. It has been suggested that the first settlers arrived in South America about the same time as they arrived in North America, making a pretty swift migration down the two continents, though this view is disputed.

There's more agreement about what the first people were like: they hunted to survive, eating ancient American horses, which are now extinct, mastodons and the wild relations of the llama. After about 2000 years, differences developed between people on the coast and those living in the highlands.

The highland people

Digging in the floor of a deserted old cave in the Callejón de Huaylas called the Guitarrero Cave; archaeologists have discovered that agriculture began here in the highlands in about 8500BC. By 4000BC animals were being domesticated, and by 3000BC highlanders were planting and eating a wide variety of foods such as maize, gourds, squash, some tubers and grains. As well as telling us about the foundations of agriculture, the Guitarrero Cave has also unveiled what may be the first example of Andean art: a small rock wrapped in textile in about 5500BC. It's from these humble beginnings that the glory of South American cloth arose.

The coastal people

The coastal settlers had the benefit of the lush pastures of the Pacific Ocean (one archaeologist has suggested that as many as 6,500,000 people could have been fed by the anchovy schools swimming in the chill Pacific), so they didn't need to develop agriculture or domesticate animals until much later than the people living in the highlands. At first the coastal dwellers caught their food by angling and scavenging for shellfish but in time they fished with a spear headed by a delicate stone point. This spearhead, which was carved like a slender willow leaf, is called a Paijan point.

Chinchorros   About 5000BC an interesting people, the Chinchorros, lived on the desert coast around Tacna and Arica. They were quite sophisticated, inventing bone fishhooks and living in stable communities. About 7000 years ago, long before the ancient Egyptians, they started to mummify their dead.

❏ **Earliest mummies**
The custom of mummifying the dead to prepare them for the after life goes back at least 7000 years in South America. Bodies were usually placed in a foetal position, seated in a basket and wrapped in many layers of embroidered textiles.

   The mummies have been preserved, partly because they were buried in the dry sands of the Atacama Desert, but partly because of the preservation techniques used by the Chinchorros. The bodies of the dead were wrapped in fabric, bound with reeds and a facemask of clay was placed over their skulls. Some of these mummies, the oldest in the world, are on display in the museum near Arica in northern Chile. The Chinchorros' mummies started a Peruvian tradition, continued by the Incas some 6500 years later.

PRE-CERAMIC PEOPLES (3000 TO 1800BC)

Unlike the rest of the world, civilization evolved in Peru before the invention of pottery. This wasn't realized at first. There are many large temples on the coast in which archaeologists couldn't find any ceramic remains, and these temples were dated by other pottery that was found nearby, pottery that was scattered around by much later inhabitants. Carbon dating, however, such as was performed in 2002 at the site of Caral, shows that the old temple complexes were far more ancient than these ceramics, and the civilizations that built them must have existed without pottery. We now think these are the oldest complex sites in the Americas.

The oldest temples were built about the time of the Old Kingdom of ancient Egypt (about 3000BC), many years before the rise of the other most ancient American civilization, the Olmecs of Mexico. Some of these structures are almost as huge as the Egyptian Pyramids; it's estimated that 2,000,000 workdays were needed to use 100,000 tons of stone in constructing the nine vast complexes at El Paraíso by the river Chancay to the north of Lima.

Kotosh

Most of the decoration of these temples hasn't survived but at one site, Kotosh, by the headwaters of the river Marañón, you can still see the type of thing that adorned these places. Kotosh dates from 2000BC to 1000BC and consists of two mounds, in one of which there's the **Temple of the Crossed Hands**. This is an adobe room with trapezoidal niches, a design that was to become so characteristic of the Incas. Under one of the niches there's a sculpture of a pair of crossed arms.

The decoration has survived because, for a reason that's not understood, at some stage in the past the sculptures were carefully protected with sandbags before the whole complex was buried.

What were these people like?

That these people were traders and travellers is evident from the finding of Ecuadorian shells in a grave at a site called Aspero, between the rivers Chancay and Huarmey. They had reasonably advanced techniques for dealing with their environments: in the highlands a 4000-year-old irrigation canal has been found, and on the coast archaeologists have dug up the remains of fine cotton fishnets and floats made from gourds.

Delicate textiles have been reconstructed from debris found at Huaca Prieta, north of the river Moche, with painstaking work recreating complicated patterns showing birds of prey with snakes on their breasts and crabs that dissolve into smiling snakes.

All this is informative but it's the imposing temples that tell us most about these people. To build the temples, these cultures must have been sophisticated enough to have developed a system of division of labour that provided enough surplus food to supply the workers; but archaeologists disagree as to whether the enormous temples indicate centralized, authoritarian regimes or a loose confederation of peoples performing communal labour. Perhaps there was a mixture of both systems as with the Incas themselves.

THE INITIAL PERIOD (1800BC TO 1000BC)

The years from 1800BC to 1000BC are called the 'Initial Period' because it used to be thought that this was when Peru's cultures started becoming more sophisticated; the rise of sophisticated cultures always being linked with the development of pottery and these were the days in Peru's history when pottery was being invented. The ball of civilization actually started rolling long before but the name has stuck.

The invention of pottery

The coastal people cracked the problem of pottery at a different time from those who lived inland, but both were quite late considering that people had been firing clay dolls for hundreds of years (one was found above the niche of the crossed hands in Kotosh, see p76) and the Ecuadorians had been making pottery for a thousand years or so.

Pottery styles of the coast On the coast the first pots were fired at places like La Florida in Rímac but they're pretty basic as ceramics go, thin-walled and with a mottled finish, their shape based on the gourds that they replaced. In time they became more sophisticated, and the northern Cupisnique culture developed the stirrup-spout pot (two arms leading to a single spout, which prevents the pot making a glugging noise). The Cupisnique are also famous for their hallucinogenic-inspired portrait pots, psychotropic drugs derived from the San Pedro cactus being very important in ancient Peru.

The making of pottery coincided with the development of coastal agriculture, metalwork and smelting (small bits of beaten copper dating from before 1000BC have been found at Mina Perdida, just south of Gargay), and the construction of even larger public buildings than had hitherto been built. The largest such as the La Florida complex would have taken one man about seven million days to build, and the structure at Moxeke is thirty metres high and has a base that covers the same area as three and a half football pitches. There are two basic designs of building – those south of the Chancay River were built with U-shaped courtyards, and north of the river they have sunken circular courtyards. They're all grey-brown mounds now, but originally all these buildings were painted with bright dazzling colours: reds, pinks, yellows, white and greyish-blue, which illuminated the clay sculptures that were moulded onto the walls. These buildings were either tombs of important people, centres of religion, or sites of oracles.

Inland pottery styles Highland pottery was influenced by the styles and techniques of the jungle where the standard was apparently quite advanced; as an early example of ceramics the highland style at Kotosh is relatively sophisticated. Shards of these early pots (indicating a trade connection) have been found in the jungle in a place called the Cave of the Owls, which makes archaeologists suspect that there's a lost jungle civilization from which the highland people learnt the art of pottery. This suspicion is strengthened by the fact that these pots are often decorated with jungle animals like jaguars, spider monkeys and snakes.

The technique of working gold was being discovered inland at the same time as that of making pots. At Waywaka, in the south-central highlands, the body of a man who lived sometime between 1900BC to 1450BC has been found holding in his hands foils of beaten gold. In the same way as the coastal people, the inlanders left significant footprints, both literal (two footprints were carved into a boulder at a place called Pacopama during this period) and metaphorical, such as a 9km-long irrigation canal cut into the bedrock.

The people

These were pretty violent times. In the Río Casma valley, north and east of Huanuco, there's a site called **Cerro Sechín** that consists of over 300 carvings of mauled soldiers: heads lie on the ground, bleeding from their eye-sockets, and severed torsos try to stop their guts from spilling on the ground. In the **Huaca de los Reyes** mound at a place called Caballero Muerto (Dead Horseman) in the lower Moche valley, there are the remains of a two-metre (six-foot) high clay head of a snarling catman.

However, it was not all blood and gore. On the south coast, the **Paracas** left behind some of the most beautiful fabrics ever to be discovered in Peru. These people wrapped their dead in layers of cloth, and the dry sands of the Atacama Desert preserved both the dead and the textile. The fabric is amazing, made from alpaca wool and rich in colour and intricate pattern.

CHAVÍN (1000 TO 200BC)

The Chavín were the first pan-Peruvian civilization, unparalleled in their unification of the multitude of peoples of Peru. They lived in a society that venerated gold, used llamas for cargo carriers, had highly developed textiles and built enormous public buildings in dressed stone. Their influence lasted about 800 years, and it was from this source that the Incas grew.

The cult of Chavín

The Chavín extended their influence over an area twice the size of modern Portugal, but they probably weren't a trading empire or a military power. They were a cult group. Characteristic Chavín iconography, such as the Chavín fanged cat, spread out from the centre of the culture, an oracle called Chavín de Huántar. What sort of cult were they?

Some have suggested they were evangelists and say that the icons of Chavín made their way into many different places in the same way as the cross of Christianity makes its way today into places as different as the Vatican and small altiplano villages in Bolivia. However, Richard Burger (the author of a beautiful book on the Chavín, see p32) thinks that the cult was rather like the

The role of hallucinogenic drugs in Chavín religious life

Hallucinogenic drugs, from the San Pedro cactus or the Vilca seed, have been used in Andean religion since the earliest times. In the capital of the Chavín civilization, there's a fascinating representation of their use. The walls of the sunken courtyard of **Chavín de Huantar** were decorated with carved heads, set deep into stone, resembling gargoyles that are found on European cathedrals. These carvings, fixed onto a wall in tiers, are three dimensional carvings of men and beasts, showing the transformation of a man into a snarling feline.

Some of the carved heads have mucus pouring from the nose, something that happens when hallucinogenic snuff is snorted. This has led Chavín scholar, Richard Burger, to suggest that these heads represent a drug-taking shaman transmuting from man to possessed prophet.

Pachacamac cult in Inca times: it was an organization superior to but also complementary to domestic religions just as the Oracle of Delphi in ancient Greece did not supplant other pagan faiths.

The essence of the Chavín style of carving is found on objects at **Chavín de Huántar** such as the Raimondi Stela, El Lanzón and the Tello Obelisk, all of which can be seen today in museums in Lima (see p112). The Chavín style may be adapted by local cultures, but it's all essentially the same and can be found in various guises on pottery, goldwork and textiles across Peru.

Skilled engineers

The spread of the Chavín influence indicates that trade was becoming more common and people were moving around. Rare Ecuadorian shells are often found in tombs of the Chavín era, as is precious lapis lazuli from the Atacama Desert in Chile. There were other developments too. The construction of the Castillo (castle), the central building at Chavín de Huántar, shows not only that the people of this time could organize labour forces, but also that they had engineers.

The Castillo is a high structure that is honeycombed with watercourses, which would make the whole building resonate and rumble with sound when water flowed in them. Designing a building that could 'speak' like this would have needed well-developed engineering skills.

MASTERCRAFTSMEN (200BC TO AD700)

From about 200BC the time of the Chavín peace was over. A village was built on the site

The **Raimondi Stela** depicts the duality of the Chavín god of agriculture and fertility. Here he stands with his feet firmly placed on the ground. Turn the picture upside down to view the god as a many-faced animal figure descending from heaven to earth.

THE INCAS

of the Castillo at Chavín de Huántar, whose stones were reused as hut walls, fortifications were built where previously none had been needed, and trade diminished. These were days of violence, made manifest in the discovery of headless and armless bodies buried during this period. Chaos reigned.

But these weren't entirely black days. Between 200BC and AD700 some of the most impressive civilizations in Peruvian history thrived, creating some of the country's finest art, hence the name 'Mastercraftsmen period'. In the south, the **Huarpa** built sophisticated clay-lined irrigation canals, metres wide and kilometres long. In the Callejón de Huaylas the Recuay made fine polychrome pots and squat statues, and on the coast the oracle of Pachacamac was founded by people of the Rímac River. However, the high-water marks of this period were left by two of the most significant of Peru's civilizations who created some of the finest and most intriguing works of art: the Moche and the Nazca.

The Moche

The Moche conquered the territory from the Piura River in the north of Peru to the Huarmey in the south. They were a bloodthirsty lot: there are many representations on their ceramics of prisoners and battles, but the lack of defensive buildings within the Moche empire suggests that once they conquered a race there was peace. Judging from the structures they left behind, they organized their empire in quite a complex way. In the north they ruled through local puppet lords leaving very few large buildings of their own while in the south they ruled directly, building monumental administrative centres in each valley. The Moche state lasted about 1000 years, but their legacies lasted longer still: they were great craftsmen in metallurgy, in architecture but most importantly in clay.

Moche ceramics One of the great highlights of pre-Hispanic Andean art is Moche portrait pots, the naturalism of which is breathtaking. The high points are the portraits of men: looking on the finest of these is like looking into the eyes of a still-breathing Moche noble. However, Moche artists could represent many other things: from buildings to demons, from human pregnancy to a llama

El Señor de Sipán – a hoard missed by the Spaniards

As well as producing portrait pots, the Moche also decorated their ceramics with line drawings in a style rather like that of the ancient Greeks. It's thought that these line drawings illustrate about 25 different stories from the mythology of the Moche. In one scene captives are paraded before an important person, then killed with their fresh spurting blood being caught in a cup. The cup is then handed to the VIP, who wears quite unmistakable clothing. Archaeologists call this person the Warrior Priest. He was the subject of one of the most amazing archaeological finds of the century.

In 1987, the body of a Warrior Priest was discovered, encrusted and surrounded by his unmistakable ornaments of office. *El Señor de Sipán* (Lord of Sipán), as he's been called, had evaded the greed of the Spaniards. Before his body was found, he'd been known only through representations on thousand-year-old pottery. The story of the discovery is fascinating in itself. A local man, Ernil Bernal, and his friends dug a small tunnel into an adobe pyramid of Huaca Rajada. After a night of pillaging the tomb, they were looking for a way out. Bernal's walking stick went into the roof above him. He pulled it out, and the roof began to give way. First some dust fell on him, then some clods of earth. And then, suddenly, a torrent of gold collapsed through the roof and he was buried in treasure. Sadly, it was a week before the curator of the local museum was told of the find, and by then much of value had been lost, ultimately to find its way into the hands of rich collectors in the USA. Only 123 objects from the tombs were ever returned to Peru.

with her young, and in the fired clay you can read things like happiness, serenity, surprise and even disease and disfigurement: there is a pot of a woman with leishmaniasis (a disease that rots the nose and lips) and a pot of a man with a cleft palate.

The Moche also made pornographic ceramics, quite astounding in their graphic representation of various sexual acts, small copies of which can be found in just about all the tourist markets of Peru. Scholars are divided as to why the Moche took such pains to represent such diversity of sexual acts (including bestiality and sex with skeletons), and theories range from the suggestion that these are a celebration of life to the idea that they may be religious artefacts.

Moche buildings The Moche's main temple was the huge **Huaca del Sol** (Sun Temple) complex which, in its time, was the largest adobe structure in the Americas. It was massive. What remains is a mere fragment of what was built because of the greed of the Spaniards who developed a novel way of pillaging these old tombs. Tunnels were dug under the structure and then a nearby river diverted to wash away the adobe. With the temple dissolved, gold and treasure could be either picked from the ruins or fished out of the river.

The Nazca

The barren desert pampa by the Nazca river was the workplace of German mathematician, Maria Reiche, for many decades. The whole pampa is crisscrossed by a multitude of lines, patterns, polygons and designs, discovered when the area was first surveyed from the air in 1926. There is a hummingbird that is five times the length of a jumbo jet, an enormous monkey with a whirl of a tail, a killer whale and a bird the size of a house. How? Why?

'How' is the easy question. The dry dusty surface is a natural blackboard – the dark surface conceals a light sandy base, and clearing the dark surface reveals the lighter sand underneath. By removing the dark surface, the Nazca created their patterns, and the desert is so stable that these have lasted through the centuries.

'Why' is more difficult. Theories range from the frankly bonkers (Erich von Däniken in his book, *Chariots of the Gods,* said that the Nazca lines are runways for extraterrestrial spacecraft) to the sensible (Maria Reiche thought that there were astronomical and calendrical reasons for the lines). The current favourite comes from the observation that many of the lines are orientated towards water sources, suggesting that they are likely to be processional routes designed to be walked upon as part of the ritual worship of water.

Nazca pottery The Nazca did not leave only their perplexing lines behind them. They also created some very fine polychrome pottery, drawing on pots with a palette of 13 slip colours, sometimes using the same icons as appear in the lines. The pots themselves are beautiful in their combination of colours and, in a similar way to the Moche portrait pots, appeal to today's aesthetic tastes.

THE INCAS

TIAHUANACO-HUARI (AD700 TO 1000)

The coast of Peru was again united at the end of the first millennium. Two related but distinct peoples dominated the Andes: the Tiahuanaco (or Tiwanaku) and the Huari (or Wari). The two were united by an icon that has been called the Gateway God, the Staff God or Viracocha.

Legendary Tiahuanaco

Tiahuanaco has been the site of legend for centuries. In some Inca myths, it was the place of giants, and Viracocha came here to make humanity out of mud. For today's mystics it's still a place of enduring mystery: HS Bellamy in *Built before the Flood* insisted that Tiahuanaco was built thousands of years ago and destroyed when one of earth's moons (he thought we had more than one) hit the surface of

The **Gateway God** (or Staff God), fundamental icon of the Huari and the Tiahuanaco people. The figure was carved on the Gateway of the Sun, a monumental doorway that's still standing at the extensive site of Tiahuanaco, now in Bolivia.

the earth. In early 1998 John Bashford-Snell, accompanied by a team from the Explorers' Club of New York, began searching in the area around Titicaca for Plato's lost city of Atlantis. More recently it was suggested that Tiahuanaco was the capital of a sophisticated worldwide civilization that was destroyed over 10,000 years ago.

The site of Tiahuanaco

Tiahuanaco is on the south side of Lake Titicaca, in Bolivia. It was first settled from 400BC, but it wasn't until about AD500 that stone buildings and high pyramids were constructed.

The whole site is very reminiscent of the Inca (with its giant blocks linked together without mortar), but it was built by people who flourished just under 1000 years before their rise. Old accounts say that Pachacutec (see p87) modelled Cusco on this site, which was already ancient by the time of the Incas.

The empire of Tiahuanaco Like the Inca empire, at its peak Tiahuanaco spread its wings over vast tracts of what is now Chile and Bolivia. The

Tiahuanaco traded with peoples as far to the south as the oasis of San Pedro de Atacama and the peoples of the Azapa valley, both of which are now in Chile. In cemeteries in these areas, amongst the dead buried in the local style, there are the graves of people buried surrounded by Tiahuanaco finery: wood carvings, gold, textiles. These artefacts are sufficiently small and light to be portable over long distances, and it's likely that they were carried by llama caravans across the desert, sent from Tiahuanaco to reward local agents of the Tiahuanaco empire, or perhaps local regents who ruled in the name of the faraway capital.

Closer to home, the Tiahuanaco ruled more directly. The major colony was a very large site called Omo in the Moquegua valley. Omo was occupied quite early on before it was suddenly abandoned, only to be re-inhabited later. This odd pattern might be explained by the fact that the Tiahuanaco felt threatened by the sudden establishment of the Huari citadel of Cerro Baul, just 20km away.

Tiahuanaco life   Like most great Andean peoples, the Tiahuanaco were skilled farmers. They developed a way of preparing the land that produced twice the yield of crops as the techniques of today. They built ridged fields: a field in which trenches are dug and the earth excavated is piled in a ridge between the channels, which are then filled with water. Tiahuanaco ridged fields have imported rock bases and have high quality imported soil on top, indicating that much work was involved in their construction. They are more fertile than other fields, but they're difficult to build and maintain. When the Tiahuanaco culture declined, these field systems declined and were ultimately replaced by the terraced hillsides of the Inca, but the land around Titicaca has never again been as productive as it was in the days of the Tiahuanaco.

In AD562 there was a great drought in the whole of Peru, which lasted thirty years. We know this from analyzing samples taken from glaciers, samples that indicate the weather patterns of Peru throughout the centuries. This drought was a contributory factor to the decline of the Moche – about this time the Huaca del Sol was abandoned. (Moche civilization was dealt a double blow by the drought killing crops and then the advance of sand dunes burying the ancient capital.) However, the Tiahuanaco survived and even thrived; an icon of the Gateway God has been found painted on a Moche pyramid, indicating that the Tiahuanaco cult stretched as far to the north as the river Piura.

The demise of the Tiahuanaco   Eventually the great civilization of Tiahuanaco suffered the fate of all peoples, and by AD1000 the fields lay fallow, the distribution of high-grade Tiahuanaco pottery had stopped, and the empire had fragmented. Why this happened isn't known – like so many things in Andean pre-history it is a mystery – but the creators of the earliest great Andean stone city lived on, spiritually in the myths of the Incas, and physically in the silent remains of their architecture.

The Huari

The Huari and Tiahuanaco knew of each other but it seems they didn't like each other. Near the river Moquegua the Huari built the fort of Cerro Baul within a short distance of the Tiahuanaco settlement of Omo, in what looks like a directly confrontational act. Nevertheless there's no doubt that the Huari were influenced by them: the Gateway God and other Tiahuanaco icons appear painted in many pieces of Huari pottery and tapestry. However, the way the Huari depicted the Gateway God illustrates that there were differences between the two cultures: the Tiahuanaco representations of the god has sun rays emanating from behind his head, while those of the Huari can be more abstract and often appear with different accoutrements, for example, sometimes bearing cobs of maize, not wielding rods of power.

Who the Huari were is one of these things about which scholars can't agree. Some say that they were an empire that expanded by force, but there is little evidence of military conquest about the time of their expansion. Others say that their style and icons were present in client states because of the influences of trade. Still others suggest the icon was dispersed throughout Peru because the Gateway God was a religious symbol of their shared Peruvian religion like the fanged cat of the Chavín.

The heritage of the Huari In a similar way to the Tiahuanaco, it's likely that the Huari survived so long and were so successful because of their agricultural technology: in their case a system of irrigation that involved long canals, high-altitude water sources and extensive irrigated terraces (probably derived from the Huarpa see p80). This was a labour-intensive technique but it was fruitful so they survived the days of drought. The Incas later adopted their methods.

THE DAYS BEFORE THE INCA (AD1000 TO 1450)

The Chimú (Chimor) culture from the northern coast dominated the period before the rise of the Incas. Other civilizations also flourished, such as the Aymara kingdoms that stepped into the void left by the decline of Tiahuanaco (the Aymara still thrive today).

Around Cusco, the Killke replaced the Huari and were probably descended from the Huari who lived in a settlement called Pikillacta, and on the south coast the Ica carried on the ceramic and textile traditions of the Nazca and the Paracas. To the north of the Rímac, where Lima is now, the Chancay thrived. The Rímac itself was inhabited by the Ichma.

The Chimú

The great rival of the Inca Empire was the northern empire of Chimú. At its height, this nation encompassed two-thirds of the Peruvian coast, stretching from Tumbes in the north to just above Lima in the south. It was not conquered by the Incas until AD1470, and when the Spanish arrived there were still people alive who remembered the old traditions.

The Chimú were not the only people on the north coast. At first, it seems they lived peacefully with their neighbours, irrigating the barren desert with extensive canal systems, but in about AD1100 there was a great flood caused by El Niño that altered the water system. No amount of careful rebuilding could repair the canals, so the Chimú began to take other peoples' agricultural land by conquest.

Chimú and Sican One of their more significant northern neighbours were the Sican, who lived near the site of the modern city of Lambayeque. The Chimú conquered the Sican in about AD1370.

Chimú stirrup-spout vessel

The Sican had an ancient history and are responsible for the production of much beautiful art, one of their main sites called Batán Grande yielding up thousands of golden artefacts. (Interestingly, the Sican manufactured a type of money in the form of small copper axes, which they buried with their dead.)

The origin myths of the Chimú and Sican are remarkably similar, and consequently there have been attempts to link these with archaeological discoveries. Sadly it's not really possible. In both traditions, society was begun by a man who arrived from the sea saying that he had been sent to take control. In the Sican tradition this man was called Naymlap. On his death, his court and 12 children spread the story that he had sprouted wings and flown away, and then each founded one of the 12 cities of the Sican people. For the Chimú, the man was called Taycanamu, and he settled in the lower Moche valley. When he died, his children did not found cities but extended the territory of his people by conquest, including, in the end, the Sican.

Chan-Chan The centre of the culture was the great Chimú city, Chan-Chan which covers 6 sq km and consists of 12 great palaces or *ciudadelas* built by communal (*mit'a*) labour (see p90). Ciudadelas are enclosures surrounded by a large wall, inside which there are labyrinths of storage rooms, a large platform (which doubles as a burial place) and audience rooms called *audiencias*. The outsides of the audiencias are decorated with adobe friezes of the sea, and they are often U-shaped – an architectural feature dating back to the Initial Period (see p76).

The ciudadelas were probably a ruler's residence and, when he died, his tomb. It's likely that as with the Incas (see p92), a ruler's estate was preserved for his living relatives and his successors had to make their own way in the world. Chan-Chan has been responsible for some of the greatest treasure found in Peru, and at one stage the Spanish formed a mining company to exploit these ruins. Chimú metalwork is some of the most sophisticated in ancient Peru, and if the Chimú were such craftsmen imagine what wonders the Incas must have produced.

Conquest of the Chimú The last Chimú ruler was Minchancamon. According to oral history, he was single-handedly responsible for the extension of the Chimú Empire from the river Chillón to the river Tumbes in the far north. According to archaeology, which has dated the Chimú settlements in these regions, this is unlikely; more probably he took the credit for the victories of his

THE INCAS

forefathers. When he was conquered by the Inca he was taken to Cusco with his best artisans, a puppet monarch was left to rule in his place and the Chimú empire was broken up. Loyal Inca settlers took over Chimú land, and the Chimú themselves were exiled to other places within the Incas' territory. So ended the last great empire before the Incas.

Days of the Inca

PIECING TOGETHER THE JIGSAW

The Incas did not have writing, so a caste of oral historians (*amautas*) arose to keep alive the legends and stories of the past. Much of the information that these people carried died with them but some was recorded by early Spanish writers. Fitting together these oral histories with the facts that can be deduced from archaeology is one way we can get a picture of what life was like under the Incas.

Oral history is inevitably unreliable: the Incas simply air-brushed awkward or embarrassing facts from their past. However, the nearer to the Spanish conquest you get, the clearer the picture becomes because there are other sources of information. The conquistadors wrote accounts, which they published on their return to Europe, and some of the Incas left their side of the story; a mestizo called Garcilaso de la Vega wrote an early history of Peru, and an account dictated by the rebel Inca Titu Cusi himself (see p105) has survived the years.

There are many other documents too, and new discoveries are still being made. The historians, Luis Miguel Glave, María Remy and John Rowe recently uncovered in the library of a Cusco monastery some papers that cast light on the mystery of Machu Picchu (see p279). Our knowledge of what life was like under the Incas, and what happened during their fall has been pieced together like a jigsaw.

THE ORIGINS OF THE INCAS

Myth

There are two different myths about the creation of the Incas. According to the first, the primordial Inca called Manco Capac emerged from the depths of Lake Titicaca and travelled underground with his brothers and their sister-wives to a place near Cusco called Pacaritambo. There they all emerged from the ground and made their way to the Cusco valley. Manco's three brothers were either turned to stone or grew wings and flew away, while Manco himself pressed on. When he arrived in the valley, he thrust his golden staff into the fertile soil and it disappeared. This he took as a sign from his father, the Sun, that the valley was good and there he stayed, naming the place Qosqo, which meant 'navel of the earth'. There, too, he built the first *Coricancha* (Sun Temple).

The second myth is also set near Lake Titicaca. In Tiahuanaco, the creator god, Viracocha, ruled over a shadowy people whose name has been forgotten (see p82). They angered him so he arose from the waters of the lake and turned them all to stone, replacing them with the sun, the moon and with humanity. These new people were sent out from Titicaca to the four corners of the earth, and the Incas were sent to Cusco.

Archaeology

The myths might be true when they say that the Incas aren't native to the Cusco region: there's archaeological evidence that a people called the Killke inhabited the area before the Incas (see p130) and were displaced by them. But there's also a lot of archaeological evidence suggesting that the Incas were a local people whose ceramics and architecture evolved from the arts of local populations like the Killke.

ORAL HISTORY

Inca is properly the title of the monarch (often called the Sapa Inca) and according to the chronicler Bernabe Cobo, writing 100 years after the conquest, the first eight Incas were Manco Capac, Cinchi Roca, Lloque Yupanqui, Mayta Capac, Capac Yupanqui, Inca Roca, Yahuar Huaca and Viracocha Inca. Little is known about any of them apart from Viracocha Inca. Stories exist about him because he was the father of one of the great folk heroes of Inca history, Pachacutec.

Pachacutec (c1438-1463)

Viracocha Inca's bitter enemy was the Canchas, a tribe who attacked Cusco. He and his anointed heir, Urco, fled but his younger son, Pachacutec, remained to destroy the Canchas. It was said that such was the support for him that even the stones of the field grew legs to fight on his side. Once his victory was complete he allowed his father back to Cusco, but usurped the throne for himself and exiled his brother, erasing him from the roll of history.

Pachacutec rebuilt Cusco and transformed it from a much more meagre settlement into a stone city based on the ruins he'd seen at Tiahuanaco. He also ordered Sacsayhuaman to be built (although the size of this place makes one suspect that it was the product of more than one Inca's rule) and he began the expansion of the Inca Empire. Pachacutec was an important figure in Inca history, but it may be that he usurped not only the throne but also the glories of his forefathers. The stories about his taking power differ; some leave out Urco, some credit Viracocha Inca with a much more dynamic rule – but also such great feats are attributed to him that doubt is cast on his historicity. Was he superhuman or a composite man?

Tupac Yupanqui (or Topa Inca: c1463-1493)

Pachacutec may have shared the latter days of his rule with his son, Tupac Yupanqui, as there may have been a greater and a lesser Inca ruling at the same time (see 'Clans' p89). When Pachacutec died, Tupac Yupanqui succeeded him.

THE INCAS

The Inca and his wife. An attendant holds a feather sunshade. This is one of a series of somewhat fanciful engravings by the 19th century traveller, Paul Marcoy.

He was a great conqueror and has been called the Alexander the Great of the Americas. He expanded the empire so that the Incas ruled a territory that ran from Ecuador to the river Maule in Chile, extending from the shores of the Pacific into modern-day Argentina. This was an empire that stretched the same distance as Cyprus is from London or Minneapolis from New York.

One of Tupac Yupanqui's greatest achievements was the conquest of Chimú, the desert empire that at one stage rivalled the Inca's own in size and sophistication (see p84). Sadly the Incas themselves left very little information about this conquest, even though it must have been a significant undertaking – an example, perhaps, of the Incas airbrushing their rivals from the record of history. The oral history we do have comes from accounts collected by the Spanish from old Chimú people who remembered the days before the coming of the Incas.

Tupac Yupanqui didn't do quite as well in the east. The Incas never extended their empire far into the Amazon, finding the heat, humidity and disease too much for their mountain troops.

Huayna Capac (c1493-1525)

Huayna Capac was Tupac Yupanqui's chosen successor, but he almost never made it to be Inca when his brother challenged the succession. However, Huayna Capac managed to beat off his sibling and took over the empire.

He started his rule by campaigning in the south, in Chile. After a year, he moved to the north of the empire where he spent the rest of his life fighting. He died shortly before the arrival of the first Europeans on Peru's shores, and was the last in the line of the great independent Incas.

CLASS AND CLANS

The Inca was the sovereign, the head of the state religion and the son of the Sun. He was a general too, and he led his forces into battle. He was the distillation of all power, the focus of all respect and the icon of his people. The state was governed by the Inca, supported by his nobles who were called *orejones* (big ears) by the Spanish because they extended their earlobes as a mark of rank. Positions of greatest responsibility were reserved for Incas true by blood, people of the same royal family or tribe as the Inca. In time the empire grew too large for these positions to be filled solely by his relatives so the Inca created a caste of Incas by privilege from the people who lived around Cusco in the Sacred Valley of the river Urubamba and allowed them to hold office.

Clans An important facet of Inca society was its division into two clans: *Hanan* and *Hurín*, which roughly mean upper and lower. You can see the physical expression of this division in the way that the Incas divided their cities into two parts: in Machu Picchu, for example, and in old Cusco.

Scholars disagree over the significance of this division. Some think it was simply tribal town planning, a way of making sure that there was a fundamental rift within Inca society, which reduced any risk of united opposition to central rule – on the principle of divide and rule. Others believe that these were two great clan groups that divided the whole of Inca society from top to bottom, even to the extent of having a greater and lesser Inca ruling at the same time. The monarch, drawn from the Hanan, was called the Sapa Inca.

INCA GOVERNMENT

Administration

At its height, the Inca Empire – Tahuantinsuyu – was 5500km (3400 miles) long, longer than the full extent of the Roman Empire. Tahuantinsuyu means place of the four quarters (*suyu*). The four suyu were: Collasuyu (to the far south), Cuntisuyu (to the south-west), Chinchaysuyu (the northern quarter), and Antisuyu (generally to the east: the forested lower slopes of the Andes). The word Andes is a derivation of this Quechua word Antisuyu. Four principal roads led from the centre of Cusco to these provinces.

Tahuantinsuyu was profoundly hierarchical – the Inca himself at the top, with his *orejones* below him, and below them men who were in charge of successively smaller clan groups called *ayllus*.

Land and labour

The lands of each ayllu were divided into three parts: the produce of one part went to the community, the priests had the rights to a second part and the produce of the last third was the state's. This maintained the state religion, the administration and fed the people. The members of the ayllu were also subject to a tax called *mit'a*, payable in food, cloth or labour. Mit'a labour built canals, walls, road and cities, and Sacsayhuaman, for example, the great fortress temple that overlooks Cusco.

When the Spanish came they greedily incorporated this system of taxation to their own ends, stating that a vast proportion of each Indian's yearly labour was to be for the benefit of the Spaniard who owned the encomienda on which the Indian lived. The Spanish argued that they were simply continuing the ancient system but changing the beneficiary from heathen to Christian.

August – a time of planting
FELIPE HUAMÁN POMA DE AYALA (c1590)

This was, of course, complete cant. In the days of the Incas, the people could expect to benefit from mit'a labour by being fed from the state's storehouses (*qollqa*) in times of famine, or being protected by a fort (*pucará*) in times of war. The burden of mit'a labour was relieved by the benefit of shared wealth and responsibility, but in the days of the Spanish mit'a labour was nothing more than exploitation.

The system wasn't bad for all the Indians, and the native middlemen, called *caciques* (originally a Caribbean word) or *curacas* (the Quechua word), generally did rather well. Some Incas went so far as to become Hispanicized, most importantly Don Cristóbal Paullu Inca, Atahualpa's brother. Paullu was baptized, took a Spanish name, built a church in Cusco (see p138) and led armies against the independent Inca state of Vilcabamba (see p105).

The system of ayllus survives to this day, and campesino society is founded on the notion of reciprocal obligations. If you need a roof on your house, your neighbours are obliged to come and help but in return you must help them with their harvest, say, next year. The ayllu structure is a pan-Andean thing, with the Aymara who live in Bolivia and northern Chile having the same basic attitude to communal work.

Expansion

The Incas were well versed in conquest by many means, from ethnic cleansing and resettlement, to indoctrination, to the menace of total war; but they preferred to conquer by threat rather than use of force.

When the Incas conquered a new nation they sent a group of loyal settlers (*mitimaes*) to the occupied territories. By planting loyal citizens the Inca could ensure a concentration of local support as the isolated settlers banded together in a hostile country.

In the meantime the leaders and chiefs of the newly conquered people were taken to Cusco, educated and indoctrinated into Inca civilization. The idols of the conquered were brought to Cusco, too, and were placed in minor shrines in the Coricancha (see p134). Should there be a revolt, despite all these precautions, the idols were brought out, befouled and thrown into the sewers, and the Incas would attack with ruthless violence.

HOW THEY RAN THE EMPIRE

Record keeping

The Incas never invented writing. Yet without writing, they managed to govern a vast territory and make provision to feed and provide work for the population who lived there. They had to keep records to be able to achieve this – records of how much food they had in storage, of how many people there were in this village, of how long it would take to get from that place to the next on the road. To record this information, the Incas used a system of knots on strings, called *quipus*. The secrets of reading quipus were entrusted to a class called the *quipucamayoc*, but the basic principles of quipu reading are still known.

The Incas counted in base ten, as we do, and they placed knots in different places on the string to indicate whether they were counting one unit, ten units, a hundred units and so on.

Quipucamayoc (record keeper)
FELIPE HUAMÁN POMA DE AYALA (c1590)

THE INCAS

Different coloured strings signified different things, so a roll of strings with knots could contain a large amount of information about provisions, populations and wealth. Many of these rolls of knotted string survive and you can see them in museums today.

Some people think that this wasn't the only form of record keeping that the Incas devised and that there's a lost form of communication hidden in Inca cloth. Many of the designs you'll see woven into Quechua fabrics today have significance: this one represents a condor, that one represents a llama. The theory suggests that in the days of the Incas similar cloth designs were a system of communication.

Inca roads

The Incas had a famous system of roads that led to every corner of the empire. It was said that the Inca in Cusco could breakfast on fresh sea-fish every morning, so efficient were the roads and the system of relay-runners (*chasquis*) that ran on them.

The road network was extensive; there were two main north–south trunk roads, one following the cordillera, one the coast, with numerous east–west link roads. Within this framework there were many smaller roads leading to sacred or important places: The Inca Trail to Machu Picchu is one of these. In total there were about 33,000km (20,000 miles) of roads covering the empire, enough to circle the earth two and a half times.

Travel was permitted only on official business, and the average campesino was not allowed to travel unless, for example, he was required for mit'a labour. Guardians of the roads were appointed to check on traffic, and overseers of royal bridges looked after the many twine suspension bridges traversing the deep canyons that fracture the Andes. Messages were carried by runners in relays, and there were *tambos* (inns, or way-stations) where travellers could rest and expect to find food and a place to sleep for the night.

Many roads still exist, and if you visit Chile's Atacama desert to the east of Chañaral, for example, or the nearby Parque Nacional Tres Cruces, you'll still see the faint outlines of implausibly straight roads heading off into the dust and heat, leading now to nowhere.

SPIRITUAL LIFE OF THE INCAS

The Incas worshipped a wide variety of gods. The main deities were Inti the sun, thunder, lightning, the rainbow, the Pleiades, Viracocha (the creator) and Pachamama (the earth-mother).

The Inca – Son of the Sun

The Inca was the son of the Sun, and therefore was a living emanation of a god. Religion and the state were so closely entwined that our separation of the two would have been incomprehensible to the Incas. As a living god the Inca was the head of the state religion but he was more than just a figurehead. His religious standing was the wellspring from which he drew his political power.

He wasn't an abstract figure. He was linked to everyday life by a complicated system of festivals and ceremonies. For example, no one was allowed to sow seed until they had been told that the Inca had broken the ground in Cusco (the information was sent out from Cusco by chasquis). Some of these festivals, such as Inti Raymi are still celebrated.

The Inca's power after death

The Inca's importance didn't end with his death. His estate was maintained (a system called *panaca*), and at every important ceremony his mummified body was brought out and placed on a sacred dais (*usno*) to participate with the living Inca and all the other dead ones. The dead were ritually fed and given drink, which was burnt on an altar beside them, before they were returned to the darkness of their living palaces.

A special class of people looked after his lands and preserved his wealth. Machu Picchu itself may have been such an estate, once owned by Pachacutec, and maintained for the benefit of his mummy. This system of fossilizing an Inca's possessions forced each new Inca to forge his own way and create his own heritage from newly conquered lands. It was a spur to conquest.

Priests and spiritual places

The state religion had a caste of priests, the chief of which was the *Villac Umu*. He was a very powerful man in the empire: he acted as a military adviser in the days of the Spanish conquest. The centre of religion was Cusco, the capital of the state. The centre of the centre was the Coricancha, the Sun Temple, from which sacred lines (*ceques*) radiated to sacred places (*huacas*), rather like the physical roads that ran from the main square to the four suyus. Modern scholars think that this is no accident, and that the huacas and ceques were orientated along the same sacred axes as the geographical quarters.

Despite the centre being in Cusco, religion wasn't centralized and each place had its own spirits and huacas that were worshipped. Some huacas were carved stones, such as the Yurac-Rumi, a carved white stone near Vitcos (see p242), or Qenko near Cusco (see p158). Others were simply geographical features like waterfalls or springs, and some were shrines such as the Intihuatana at Machu Picchu (see p288). Still others were supposed to be the fossilized remains of the magnificent dead, the hill overlooking Cusco's airport being those of one of Manco Capac's brothers. As the Inca Empire expanded, it absorbed new gods, spirits and huacas, some of which – like Pachacamac on the coast – became major shrines for the Incas themselves.

The Spanish destroyed huacas when they found them, and prohibited their worship, claiming that they were possessed by the devil. Intihuatanas were smashed, and places like the Yurac-Rumi were exorcized. It didn't work. To this day the Quechua find such places sacred, believing mountains, for example, to be inhabited by spirits called *apus*. Old huacas are still worshipped, and ceremonies like Qoyllur Riti (see p49) incorporate elements of the old religion into Christianity.

THE INCAS

Sacred women

Women were very important to Inca spirituality. One of the major deities was the female Pachamama (who inevitably got confused with the Virgin Mary); and the Inca's wife, the *coya* (who, as with the Pharaohs of ancient Egypt, was also his sister) was a person of high status and nobility.

Women were tightly bound into religious and profane life. There were convents of Inca nuns (*acllas*), drawn from the most beautiful maidens in the empire. They were headed by mother superiors (*mamaconas*), and their mission in life was to serve the Inca. They wove his fabric and looked after him, brewing his sacred *chicha* (maize beer) and preparing his food. The most beautiful acllas were awarded to high-status men as rewards for distinguished acts, whilst other acllas confined themselves to a life in his service. Some, indeed, confined themselves to a death in his service on the rare occasions when a situation demanded human sacrifice.

The Coya, the Inca's wife
FELIPE HUAMÁN POMA DE AYALA (c1590)

INCA CULTURE

Architecture

The Incas are of course most famous for their architecture. They built in a number of different styles, all of which seem to be characteristically Inca. Some of these characteristics are in fact Andean rather than Inca, such as mortarless walls derived from the Tiahuanaco, the trapezoidal arch (first seen in Kotosh) and terracing (derived from the Huari). Others are strikingly Inca, such as the way that their architecture incorporates a natural form, perhaps as a rock outcrop or a hillside, and enhances it with the structures that are built around it. Machu Picchu itself is a classic and perfect example of this, situated as it is astride a ridge and emphasizing the outcrop that is the Intihuatana, and surrounded by the terracing that forms and reflects the shape of the living rock.

Types of Inca building One type of Inca building is the imposing stone fortress-like Sacsayhuaman (see p156), whose walls are made from blocks the size of large cars, locked together without mortar but immovable because of the perfect fit.

Another type is the regular fine-bricked buildings such as Coricancha (see p134), whose delicate brickwork was reserved for the highest status buildings. Again these walls have no mortar, just accurately carved blocks in walls that taper inwards as they get higher to resist earth movements. In the famous circular wall in Coricancha you can see that these bricks aren't really rectangular blocks but are carved so their inside faces fit together in a three-dimensional jigsaw.

The Incas also built using simpler techniques. A method of fitting rough stone together with adobe (mud) was called *pirka*, and some pirka structures

still remain. The most basic construction technique was to build a simple adobe wall on a field-
stone foundation, but most of these haven't survived the passage of time.

How did they do it? It isn't known how the
Incas managed to achieve such a snug fit in their
ceremonial structures using the few tools they had
– river stones and small bronze crowbars (they
hadn't discovered iron).

There are many theories. One suggests that
after one row of stones was laid it was dusted
with a small film of fine sand, and when a new
course was placed on top and removed, marks in
the sand would indicate where the base layer
needed to be carved. The top layer was then hoist-
ed up on wooden props, the lower level was
carved, and then the new course was lowered into

Inca stonemasons
FELIPE HUAMÁN POMA DE AYALA (c1590)

its newly made slots. However, this theory doesn't explain how the Incas managed to get their vertical joints as good as their horizontal ones. Another plausible theory suggests that the Incas used a tool a little like a builder's scribe to
score a guideline on the rock to be cut.

Predictably, this question has attracted the usual outlandish theories: it's been
seriously suggested that the Incas achieved their masterful masonry by melting
the rocks, focusing the sun's rays into the corners using parabolic mirrors.

Textiles

It's difficult to overstate how important woven cloth was to the Incas. It was a
statement of rank, an object of value and even a medium of exchange. It's said

---

Inca technology in modern use
After the conquest, the highlands became depopulated as the Spanish
removed its inhabitants to purpose-built villages. The terraces and canals
fell into decline and the land has never again been as fertile as it was in
the days of the Incas. A project run by the Inca expert, Dr Ann Kendall, tried to
reverse that. Dr Kendall is an archaeologist who excavated in the Cusichaca valley
(see p186), paying close attention to the old Inca canals that transect these hills. She
realized that, using only ancient technology, these old watercourses could be repaired
and irrigate the dry terraces of the Cusichaca valley, thus increasing the area's agricultural productivity and benefiting the impoverished local community. So, in a practical spin-off from her archaeological excavations, she began to help the campesinos
to repair the old Inca water channels. The project worked, and the fertility of the area
increased massively.

Dr Kendall is now bringing these skills to other parts of Peru, breathing life into
the dead old water channels. If you'd like more information about this fascinating
blending of archaeology and development visit 🖳 www.cusichaca.org.

THE INCAS

that when the Spanish first arrived they were handed not gold and silver but fabric. What you wore was an indication of your rank. The acllas wove the finest fabric for the Inca, called *qompi,* some of which he gave away as an honour to the most worthy of his subjects. The tunics he wore were of magnificent patterning and were made from such varied fabric as vicuña wool and vampire-bat skin (see Fabrics, p62).

Soldiers had their own uniforms, and the reports of the first sight the Spanish had of the Incas describe the royal vanguard being dressed in black and white checked cloth. Everyday cloth was also made, called *awaska,* and was worn by the vast majority of people.

Ceramics

The Incas made pottery, but they never reached the aesthetic heights of their ancestors, the Moche and the Nazca. The characteristic Inca pot form is the large *urpu,* which has a fat belly, a curved base and long spout. It was generally a vessel for storage and transport of food: chicha, maize and chuño (freeze-dried potato).

It was carried slung over the back, tied to the body by a band of cloth that passed through the little eyes on the pot's side. Porters on the Inca Trail today still carry baggage in this way.

Metalwork

The melting down of Inca metalwork is one of the Spaniards' greatest crimes. Hardly any gold or silver escaped the furnaces; most of it reduced from dazzlingly-worked artefacts to lump-gold. A few objects remain but they're only things that were small enough to escape the flames of Spanish greed. We can only dream about what Inca metalwork must have been like, prompted by descriptions left by the conquistadors.

Inca gold

'In one cave they discovered twelve sentries of gold and silver, of the size and appearance of those of this country, extraordinarily realistic. There were pitchers half of pottery and half gold, with the gold so well set into the pottery that no drop of water escaped when they were filled, and beautifully made. A golden effigy was also discovered. This greatly distressed the Indians, for they said that it was a figure of the first lord who conquered this land. They found shoes made of gold, of the type that women wore, like half-boots. They found golden crayfish such as live in the sea, and many vases, on which were sculpted in relief all the birds and snakes that they knew, even down to spiders, caterpillars and other insects.'

Pedro Pizarro *Discovery and Conquest of the Kingdoms of Peru*, 1571.

(Opposite) Top: Quechua woman spinning wool in Cusco; the Quechua are the descendants of the Incas. **Bottom**: Giant mural in Cusco depicting the rise and swift fall of the Incas. (Photos © Alexander Stewart).

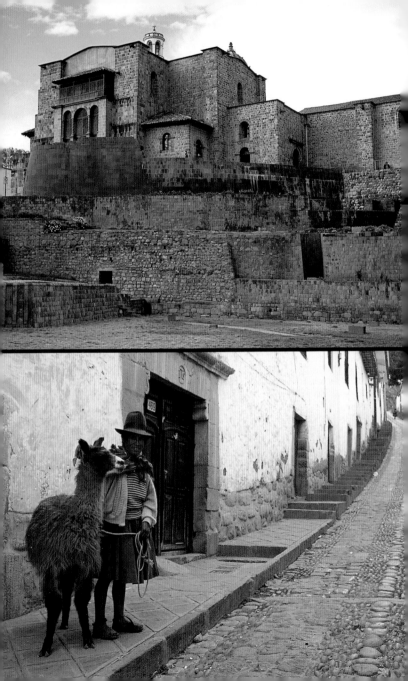

Hunting

Royal Hunts (*chacos*) were a great sacred event. Beaters encircled a large area and started to walk inwards; and inside the circle, the animals would be herded closer and closer together. Such was the scale of the hunt that it would take many days for the circle to tighten. When the beaters stood almost shoulder-to-shoulder, hunters entered the circle and killed or sheared the animals it contained: guanaco and vicuña (types of llama), puma, foxes, deer and bears. The hunt provided the locals with much meat and wool, and the nobles with sport.

Warfare

The Spaniards weren't very impressed with the Incas' weapons, and that's not surprising since the Incas hadn't progressed beyond the slings, clubs (*chambis* and *macanas*) and bronze-headed javelins that the Moche had used centuries before. At close quarters a Spaniard's lightning-fast rapier would usually make short work of an Inca armed only with a club or javelin. Despite its effectiveness the rapier wasn't the greatest advantage the Spaniards had over the Incas nor, given the amount of time it took to load and fire, was the arquebus (gun): it was the horse.

The Incas had never seen horses before and didn't know how to fight them. They must have felt rather like the Romans when faced with the elephants of

The Incas and Easter Island

Thor Heyerdahl, the Norwegian explorer and writer, was convinced for many years that the ancient Peruvians colonized Easter Island, the tiny speck of land 3700km west of Peru in the Pacific Ocean. He based his theory on a number of things: a wall on Easter Island which bears a striking resemblance to Inca masonry; the fact that the dominant tribe of Easter Island had elongated ears like the Inca Orejones (see p89); and the discovery of the sweet potato on Easter Island, a plant that's a species native to South America. Heyerdahl also pointed out that the predominant currents in the Pacific Ocean lead from Peru to Easter Island, a fact that, he said, makes the colonization of Easter Island from Peru likely. (Heyerdahl spectacularly proved that it is possible to float from Peru to Easter Island on a raft when in 1948 he did just that aboard his reed raft, *Kon Tiki*.)

It's a seductive idea, and it's backed up by oral history. On the coast of Peru, there's a myth that a king, called Kon Tiki, defeated in battle, sailed off into the sunset and was never seen again. There's a complementary myth that both Easter Island and its near neighbour, the Marquesas Islands, were colonized by a man from a country far away to the east who arrived by sea, and this man is called Tiki in some myths.

Sadly for Heyerdahl, his theories have never been accepted by the academic community, not least because there's no evidence of any Peruvian language, ceramics or textiles on these islands. Still, it's an intriguing possibility.

THE INCAS

(**Opposite**) **Top**: The Coricancha in Cusco (see pp134-5) was the Incas' Temple of the Sun. The Dominicans grafted their monastery, Santo Domingo, onto its foundations. **Bottom**: The alpaca, a close relative of the llama, is used for its wool. It looks similar to a llama but is a little smaller and has shorter ears. (Photos © Alexander Stewart).

Hannibal. The Spanish were, of course, excellent fighters, renowned in Europe for their prowess in war but it's unlikely that this alone would have been sufficient to take the Inca Empire.

Just the sight of an armoured Spaniard on the back of his beast, thundering towards the massed ranks of Inca warriors would have sent fear into the hearts of the bravest. Only by avoiding confrontations on flat ground were the Incas successful against the invaders. The native Americans who mastered the horse themselves, such as the Mapuches of southern Chile and the Apaches of North America, managed to check the Spanish advance.

How, then, were the Incas so successful in building their empire before the arrival of the Europeans? This is one of those questions to which there's no easy answer, but it's likely that the efficient road network was the key, allowing reinforcements to be brought up to support an Inca fighting column in times of need. The Incas could then overwhelm their adversaries by sheer force of numbers.

This fits with the fact that the Incas found it extremely difficult to subdue the peoples in the extreme north and south of their empire. The Chronicles tell how hard pressed the Incas were in the north, against local tribes who protected themselves with strings of forts, and in the south, the Incas never managed to conquer the Mapuche. Their lines of communication were stretched too far, and they couldn't bring up their support easily – they had literally reached the end of the road, even for their extremely efficient infrastructure.

The fall of the Incas

On 24 September 1532 Francisco Pizarro marched into the lands of the Inca Empire with 62 horsemen and 106 infantry. How he managed to subdue and rape the greatest empire of its day is a fascinating story of greed and cunning.

PLAGUE AND CIVIL WAR

Some years before Pizarro marched out, the old Inca Huayna Capac had retired to Quito, the northern city of the Inca Empire. Huayna Capac was in the north subduing local tribes. One of his legitimate sons, Huáscar, had remained in the imperial capital Cusco. The bastard son, Atahualpa, was with Huayna Capac in Quito.

Generally, these were times of peace, the empire was secure and life was luxurious. But it was not to last. Disaster struck in the form of a plague of biblical proportions that spread over the land, and Huayna Capac himself died as did his heir, Ninan Cuyuchi. Modern historians think that the plague was smallpox, or some other disease brought to the New World by the Europeans, freshly arrived in the hemisphere. The vanguard of conquest, it killed off the Inca, his heir and many of his court and brought the country to civil war.

Huáscar coveted the throne, as did his natural brother Atahualpa. Huáscar had the support of the Cusco nobility and the trappings of traditional empire.

Atahualpa was in the north, with the seasoned, battle-hardened generals of the Ecuadorian campaign. Civil war erupted. After a long, bitter struggle Atahualpa was the victor.

And so the scene was set for the arrival of Pizarro and his Spanish adventurers. Had they arrived two years before or two years later they would have discovered a stronger, united empire with armies well able to push them back into the sea. As it is, when they arrived they were lucky enough to march into a country ravaged by disease and broken by civil war.

Pizarro and Almagro set sail
FELIPE HUAMÁN POMA DE AYALA (c1590)

PIZARRO AND ALMAGRO

Pizarro was born in Extremadura in rural Spain. He knew hardship in his youth: he was a swineherd in the poorest part of a country still recovering from centuries-long occupation by the Moors. He was illiterate, a poor horseman but a Machiavellian judge of human character and a ruthless military genius.

By middle age he found himself a prosperous burgher in the new Spanish colony of Panama. This would have been enough for many: he had climbed far from his lowly beginnings. But it wasn't enough. He wanted more.

The search for El Dorado

Rumours reached Panama of a great, rich country to the south, a country where there were vast treasures of gold and hoards of silver. There had been attempts to reach it – one man had got as far as a river called the Biru (one explanation for the country's name), but had to turn back. Pizarro and his partner, Diego de Almagro, decided to fit out an expedition and go and see for themselves. News was breaking of how dashing Cortés had defeated the infidel Aztecs and secured Mexico for Spain, and these stories confirmed the possibility that there was another great kingdom filled with riches hidden in the undiscovered lands to the south.

First expeditions

Pizarro's and Almagro's first expeditions weren't successful. It's true that they met an ocean-going raft, filled with Inca cloth, which indicated that there was some truth in the rumours of developed lands, but Pizarro and his men became near-shipwrecked on a desert island in the bitter winter of 1527.

The conquest of Peru almost foundered at that point, and would have done had Pizarro not drawn a line in the sand with his sword and challenged his men to cross the line to greatness and riches. Thirteen crossed, and thirteen became the richest and most powerful men in all the Americas. Of that thirteen, how

THE INCAS

many died in their beds? Pizarro was murdered. Almagro was murdered. All but one of Pizarro's brothers met gruesome ends. Such is the price of greed.

In 1528 Pizarro returned to Spain to beg the indulgence of the crown. He got it, and with it the title of Governor and Captain-General of Peru. He secured for Almagro the title of Commandant of Tumbes, a little port on the coast. Almagro was to prove unhappy with this. He agreed to continue with the venture only if he was given all the land beyond Pizarro's claim. Pizarro then returned to Peru at the head of a small army. They landed on the coast at Tumbes, and found a ruined town, a result of the civil war that had been raging in the old Inca Empire.

FIRST CONTACT

Pizarro and his men marched up into the hills. They were impressed with what they saw: well-maintained roads, stone towns, orderly people, warehouses filled with food. One contemporary Spaniard wrote of: 'herds of sheep, large fields, and many irrigation channels, green and so beautiful, and the land appeared so cheerful that there was nothing to compare it with...it was undoubtedly the best and richest in the world'. This was obviously no land of barbarians. They, on the other hand, could not earn such praise. When they saw food they ate it and when they saw women, they took them.

News of the strange new arrivals reached the Inca's ear. Atahualpa was resting near Cajamarca taking his time over his triumphal return to Cusco, seeking to heal the country of the wounds inflicted by a fratricidal civil war. He heard mention from his chasquis that a group of men, accompanied by strange beasts a little like llamas, had landed on the coast and were walking on the roads without imperial permission. They were breaching all of the Incas' laws: stealing from imperial storehouses and even taking acllas, the sacred nuns, for their pleasure.

The Inca was with an army, numbered in tens of thousands. These weren't just any old soldiers; they were used to battle and were strong, fit and fierce. The Inca could have wiped away the Spanish with a flick of his wrist. Why he didn't is a fascinating question that has been asked and asked again over the years.

Fatally, the Inca allowed the Spaniards to advance. They came to Cajamarca, and were stunned when they saw the hills alight with the campfires of the Inca's army, and they were afraid. A Spaniard described the sight:

'The Indians' camp looked like a very beautiful city … So many tents were visible that we were truly filled with great apprehension. We never thought that Indians could maintain such a proud estate nor have so many tents in good order'.

The Spanish sent emissaries to the Inca, asking him to come and meet them in the main square of the town, to talk. That night, they laid a trap.

THE TRAP

The main square had one exit only and was surrounded by buildings. The small cannon that the Spaniards possessed was set up on a high point. At a certain sign, it was to be fired and the Spanish cavalry was to pour out of its hiding places around the square and attack the natives, who had never seen horses or guns. This would give the Spanish a chance. Despite the plan, and despite their horses and their guns, the Spaniards spent a fearful night.

The next day it looked as if the Inca wasn't going to come. The Spaniards posted as lookouts could see his camp and could see that there was no movement. Things got even tenser in the Spanish camp. Then, in the afternoon, the Inca and his army moved. The chroniclers described the scene: the Incas wore gold and silver crowns, dressed in fine clothing and sang 'graceful' songs. The townspeople swept the road before the procession, which was led by a squadron of men in chequered tunics. Seventy thousand warriors followed. The Spanish urinated out of pure terror.

Atahualpa made his way into the main square. The Spaniards' priest, Vicente de Valverde, approached the monarch as he sat on his litter, and said 'I have come to teach you the word of God'. Atahualpa seized the priest's breviary, and leafed through it, admiring the writing. He then, so the story goes, put it to his ear, then threw it to the ground in irritation. The priest cried out, cursing the Indian devils and letting slip the dogs of war.

It was a massacre. The Indians who bore the Inca's litter were his nobles and not his fighting men. They were amongst the first to fall. The cavalry butchered the rest of the Inca's escort, riding them down through the small, orderly streets or slaughtering them where they stood, dumb-founded by these strange charging half-beasts. It did not last long. A chronicler describes Pizarro's reaching Atuhualpa's litter and grabbing at the unarmed Inca 'with great bravery'. Atahualpa was captured. As John Hemming has said in *The Conquest of the Incas*, the conquest of Peru began with a great checkmate.

THE GREAT CHECKMATE

Atahualpa's troops, still for the most part massed outside the town gates, didn't mount a rescue attempt. The Inca sent word that they were to disband. Why?

Atahualpa had attempted a bargain for his life. He expected to be killed, and when he saw the Spaniards' lust for precious metal offered to fill a room with gold and two more rooms with silver for good measure in exchange for his life. (The Spanish could speak to him because they'd trained up an interpreter whom they'd captured from the ocean-going raft, see p99).

The Spanish agreed to the bargain, and as a gesture of good faith, Atahualpa sent word that his army should disband. Power in the Inca state was so distilled in the Inca himself, that without him at their head the people could not act. He was a god, a king, and a general. When he ordered something, they obeyed. So when he ordered that they should not attack the Spanish, they did not. There has seldom been a more crucial and catastrophic misjudgment by one man in the

The death of Atahualpa
FELIPE HUAMÁN POMA DE AYALA (c1590)

history of his race, or a less trustworthy set of people in whom a captive has placed his faith. The Spaniards were after the Inca's whole country, nothing less, and by ordering his people not to destroy them he destroyed his country.

Messengers were sent to the four suyus of the empire, and told to bring back gold and silver. In time the llama trains arrived – first little by little, then in small bands, then in floods. The room began to fill with gold.

A king's murder

The Spaniards became jumpy. What would happen when the room was full? Wouldn't the Inca go off and raise an army to return and annihilate every last foreigner in his land? They couldn't let him go. Happily enough for them, there were reports that a large Indian army was massing a couple of days' march from Cajarmarca.

Charges were laid against Atahualpa that he was planning a rebellion, and he was tried, found guilty and sentenced to death by burning. As an Inca, it was crucially important to him that his body should survive intact so it could be mummified and partake of future rituals, as tradition dictated. Burning was literally a fate worse than death. The Spanish told him that he could avoid the fire by converting to Christianity. So this he did.

Atahualpa, the last undisputed Inca, was garroted on 26 July 1533. In a particularly cynical piece of treachery, even for the Spanish, they burnt his body anyway. He was buried a Christian, and they say that Pizarro, in an act of superhuman hypocrisy, cried at his funeral.

The first puppet Inca

Pizarro realized the importance of maintaining a puppet monarch, through whom he could exercise power with the minimum of force. He therefore selected an Inca to succeed Atahualpa from one of the princelings in Atahualpa's retinue; he chose Huáscar's brother, Tupac Huallpa (Huáscar had died mysteriously, probably murdered on Atahualpa's orders, during the time of Atahualpa's imprisonment.) This was a masterstroke. Pizarro set himself and the Spanish up as protectors of Huáscar's line, and thus bought themselves support from the defeated side in the recent civil war.

Then the Spaniards began the march on Cusco.

THE MARCH ON CUSCO

The march on Cusco was long and hard, and each step of the way the Spanish were fearful of their own shadows and of an Inca army waiting to bar their way.

THE INCAS

The army that awaited them consisted of the remains of the army of the north, the army of Quito. However, as the Spanish marched they found friends: many tribes, only recently come under the Incas' yoke, gave them support and encouragement and the Huáscar faction inevitably preferred the foreigners to the northern army. So the Spanish weren't as entirely bereft of support as their more vainglorious accounts would have us believe, and on their march on Cusco they picked up supplies, willing helpers and auxiliaries.

About halfway to Cusco the young Tupac Huallpa died, probably of natural causes but there were many in Atahualpa's camp who wished him dead. Pizarro exploited the situation by playing off those who wanted the successor to be of Atahualpa's line against those who preferred Huáscar's children. When the Spaniards were nearing Cusco, Manco Inca, a young prince of Huáscar's line, came forward. With Pizarro's approval he was made Inca.

A desperate defence

The army of Quito did oppose the march on Cusco – but they had neither the weapons nor the tactics to oppose the full force of the Spanish cavalry. Every encounter save one resulted in a crushing rout of the Incas. The glorious exception was partly brought on by the arrogance of a dashing Spanish conquistador, Hernando de Soto.

De Soto wanted to be the first into Cusco, wanted the glory and the money, and he was leading the advance guard of the Spanish column. He came to the Apurímac river. The Indians had burnt the bridge, but the Spanish were lucky enough to find the river at low water and they forded it. As they were making their way up the other side, the horizon blackened with Inca soldiers. The Spanish tried to form up into a defensive line, but the Incas had let loose the mountainside at them, and stones, rocks and boulders crashed into their unprotected ranks, followed by a tidal wave of warriors.

The Spanish made for the top, but their horses were exhausted and five conquistadors fell from the saddle. Once off their horses, they were quickly despatched by the Incas that surrounded them. The remaining Spaniards then retreated and camped for the night, a night that they feared would be their last. However, with the morning light came reinforcements presciently sent forward by Pizarro, and the disheartened Incas faded into the morning mist.

CUSCO – CAPITAL OF THE EMPIRE

The Spanish rode into Cusco, and set up Manco Inca as their puppet. They took control of the city in an arrogant re-founding ceremony on 23 March 1534, and ruled the empire for a couple of years, in relative harmony; Manco was satisfied because he had status, the Spanish were satisfied because they had power. Many conquistadors went home and published accounts of the expedition, but others stayed on and were awarded plots of land, encomiendas, from which they could derive an income. All Spaniards had to live in Cusco, however, to establish a firm, secure and defensible concentration of men.

THE INCAS

The northern part of the empire, of course, had yet to be subdued, and the Quito army still posed a threat to the Spanish, but it was just a matter of time before that fell. The Spaniards now had a power base, access to the sea, and the loyalty of many of the subjects of the old empire. The Inca generals, Rumñavi, Zope-Zopahua and Quisquis deserve more of a mention than I can give them in these pages, but they were all conquered by 1535.

SOW THE WIND

That could have been the end of the story but it was just the start of another chapter. The first seed of discontent that was sowed related to Diego de Almagro, the short-changed partner of Pizarro. In 1535 he rather grumpily set off to inspect the territory he'd been awarded, and he discovered northern Chile, a vast tract of land as barren as the Sahara. Almagro was to come back, a cloud on his brow and envy in his heart at the riches of Cusco.

That was to prove a problem but a more immediate problem was caused by Francisco Pizarro's brothers. Francisco Pizarro had gone to the coast to found Lima, and the city of Cusco was left under the control of hotheaded and vulgar Juan and Gonzalo Pizarro. They began to insult Manco Inca and abuse his subjects.

REAP THE WHIRLWIND

At Easter in 1536, the announcement was made to the citizens of Cusco that Manco Inca had rebelled and headed for the hills. The conquistadors did what conquistadors do best – they rode out to meet the rebellion head-on. In the valley of Yucay, they came across it: 100,000 to 200,000 Inca soldiers bent on their death. The Spaniards only just made it back to Cusco alive.

The siege of Cusco

And so began the siege of Cusco. These were grim times for the Spanish, all 180 of them, only a half of whom had horses. On an early foray the Mayor had his head cut off. On 6 May the Incas entered Cusco and beat back the Spanish who holed up in buildings, so the Incas set fire to the city.

Manco Inca himself was directing the siege from Sacsayhuaman (see p156), a site that overlooks Cusco. The Spanish realized that dislodging him from this fortress-temple was the only solution. They rode out, around the obstacles that had been placed to trip up their horses, and took possession of the Rodadero. There they faced the massive, three-tiered walls of Sacsayhuaman, which in those days were topped by three castles.

It was a long, savage fight. Juan Pizarro was hit on the head by a sling-shot and killed, but Gonzalo Pizarro and the Spanish, fighting with a desperation borne of terror and a courage that was their wont, took the citadel. They say that in the days that followed condors feasted on the piles of the dead Incas lying around the walls of Sacsayhuaman. The arms of the city of Cusco, granted in 1540, show a castle surrounded by condors that represents this terrible day.

Vilcabamba – the last refuge of the Incas

Manco Inca escaped. He was pursued, and retreated – from Pisac, from Ollantaytambo, and then deep into the jungle where he founded a new city called Vilcabamba. It was here that he carved out a new Inca state, a mere rump of the glories of the past but a state where there were no Spanish.

Manco Inca was attracted to Vilcabamba by its inaccessibility. This, after all, is a region choked with cloud forest, a land of vertical terrain, wild rivers, hazardous bogs and rain. To the Incas this area was known as Antisuyo, one of the four quarters of their once-mighty empire and the only one that had yet to be conquered by the Spanish.

Manco Inca founded his new city in 1538, one year after his decision to retreat from Ollantaytambo (see p164). His first attempts at establishing a new capital proved decidedly ineffectual: Vitcos, on the hill of Rosaspata between the Río Vilcabamba and the Andenes stream, was too exposed and vulnerable as was proved when Diego de Almagro's General Orgóñez stormed it. Only the Spaniards' lust for gold saved Manco: while they ransacked the palace, he managed to lose his pursuers and disappear into the jungle.

Manco only escaped with the help of 20 of the fastest runners from the Lucana tribe, who spirited him away. He had to leave almost everything behind, including his son Titu Cusi, who was taken to Cusco and placed in the house of a noble. (Cusi describes being treated well by his captor, Pedro de Oñate, so well that Manco sent Oñate a message thanking him for his conduct). At this point Manco must have been at his lowest ebb, as he realized his remaining people needed somewhere more secure to hide from the Spaniards. And so the site of Vilcabamba was found, a small enclave hidden beneath an almost impenetrable cloak of rainforest, at the northern end of a wide, low valley.

Yet as it transpired even this secluded hideaway proved insufficient, for just two years later Vilcabamba was attacked by Francisco Pizarro's half-brother Gonzalo and 300 Spanish soldiers. Once again, however, Manco managed to flee in time and the Spanish, though they caused chaos in Vilcabamba, were unable to find him.

After two unsuccessful attempts at catching the Inca, the Spanish authorities decided to embark upon less aggressive means to flush him out and switched to diplomacy. But Manco was well used to Spanish duplicity and gave these initiatives short shrift. Following his brutal death (see p242) in 1541, however, his successor, Sayri Tupac, proved to be more receptive to the Spaniards' friendly overtures, and in 1557 Tupac was lured out of his forest redoubt with sizeable rewards of property and money and went on to live a life of comfort in Cusco.

Titu Cusi

But if the Spanish thought this was the end of resistance in Vilcabamba, they were mistaken. Instead, the native empire continued much as it had done before, overcoming the loss of their leader by the simple expedient of replacing him with somebody else.

That somebody was Titu Cusi, the half-brother of Sayri Tupac. Captured at the battle of Vitcos and educated by the Spanish in Cusco, Titu Cusi was a wise and capable ruler. He was also one of the great chroniclers of the last years of the Inca empire, towards the end of his life dictating his memoirs which were later made into a book, *Relación*.

His reign coincided with a period of relative peace and prosperity for the inhabitants of Vilcabamba, thanks in no small part to his skill as a negotiator and peacemaker, keeping the Spaniards off his territory by the simple method of ensuring that they never had a pretext to invade.

Guerrilla raids on Spanish encomiendas and churches were discontinued under his rule, and by forbidding Spanish settlement in his territory, he thus prevented any arguments occurring between his people and the Spaniards that could escalate into something more serious. He also allowed two Spanish missionaries into Vilcabamba to preach to his people and was himself baptized into the Christian faith (though the traditional pagan rituals continued unabated).

Titu Cusi's policy of appeasement was vindicated on 24 August 1566 with the signing of a peace treaty with the Spaniards that allowed him to remain as ruler in Vilcabamba. But while Titu Cusi had opted for peaceful coexistence, his successor, Tupac Amaru, a legitimate son of Manco Inca, preferred confrontation.

Not long after his accession the Spanish priests in Vilcabamba were killed in retaliation for the death of Titu Cusi (see p254), the borders of his kingdom were closed and all correspondence between the two sides came to an abrupt end.

The end of Vilcabamba

For the Spanish and their brutally efficient viceroy, Francisco de Toledo, the final straw came with the murder of one of their envoys to Vilcabamba, Atilano de Anaya, in 1572. An army of 250 Spaniards, along with 2000 friendly natives, was hastily mustered and on 14 April Toledo officially declared war on the state of Vilcabamba.

The very next day an élite advance party set out on the long march from Cusco, and were soon occupying the strategically important bridge over the Urubamba at Chuquichaca (in modern-day Chaullay).

As was so often the case throughout the conquest, resistance to Spanish rule was extinguished with more of a whimper than a bang. Tupac Amaru had at his disposal only 1000 fighting men, nearly all of whom were still using the same weapons – stones, slings and axes – as their forefathers two centuries before. The advancing army met with only one concerted defence on their march, and by the time Hurtado de Arbieto arrived to plant the Spanish flag in the middle of the plaza at Vilcabamba, on 24 June 1572, most of the inhabitants had already fled, having razed the city by fire before they departed.

Over the course of the next two months they were rounded up. Tupac Amaru had sought refuge in the jungle, taking with him the Punchao, the Sacred Idol of the Sun, the icon that in happier days had stood at the heart of the Coricancha in Cusco; the Inca himself was the last to be caught. Tupac Amaru preferred to trust in his Spanish pursuers rather than in the jungle tribes that were his native bodyguards. It was trust that was yet again to prove misplaced, and he was publicly executed in Cusco's Plaza de Armas after a sham trial.

His last words, likely testament to the tortures that had been inflicted on him, amounted to a betrayal of his Inca past. He said:

'Lords, you are here from all the four suyus. Be it known to you that I am a Christian, they have baptized me and I wish to die under the law of God. And I have to die. All that I and my ancestors the Incas told you up to now – that you should worship the sun Punchao and the huacas, idols, stones, rivers, mountains and vilcas – is completely false. When we told you that we were entering in to speak to the sun that it advised you to do what we told you, and that it spoke, this was false. It did not speak, we alone did; for it is an object of gold and cannot speak.'

Punchao, a gold figure the size of a small boy, was recovered by the Spanish but has never been seen again.

REAP ANOTHER WHIRLWIND

The other seed that was sown, that of Almagro's discontent, also grew and blossomed. Almagro returned from his gruelling Chilean venture in 1537, disappointed at the thin pickings of the place. He marched on Cusco, and took it, but his victory was short lived, as the Pizarrists would not let go that easily. In 1538 when the Almagrists controlled the sierra and Pizarrists controlled the coast, confrontation was inevitable, and the matter was finally settled at the battle of Las Salinas in April.

Diego de Almagro was captured, put on trial and executed. He had his revenge from beyond the grave. On 26 June 1541 Francisco Pizarro was murdered by supporters of the dead Almagro. One story says that with his dying breath, Pizarro drew the sign of the cross on the floor with his blood. Another story says that his murderers crushed his hands as he was trying to make absolution and cried that he would have to confess his sins in Hell.

So died the conqueror of Peru, murderer of Atahualpa and scourge of the Incas.

❑ **Epitaph**
'OLD MARTIN: So fell Peru. We gave her greed, hunger and the Cross: three gifts for the civilised life. The family groups that sang on the terraces are gone. In their place slaves shuffle underground and they don't sing there. Peru is a silent country, frozen in avarice. So fell Spain, gorged with gold; distended; now dying'.
Peter Shaffer *Royal Hunt of the Sun*, Act 2 Scene 12.

THE INCAS

PART 4: LIMA

Lima

At the centre of the city lies the decaying hulk of a great colonial shipwreck. In flaking baroque these relics gaze, stained and weary, over the tin and concrete and electric wires.
Matthew Parris, *Inca Kola*, 1990

'Lima the Horrible' was the rallying cry of a band of 1950s Peruvian intellectuals, and after a day or two in this smog-smothered city you may well end up agreeing with them. Certainly the noise, pollution and chaos, added to the need to be on constant alert against muggings, make Peru's capital a stressful place. But it would be harsh to write it off completely, and while it's unlikely anyone would come to Peru just to see Lima, there's enough here to keep you entertained as you prepare to head up to Cusco and Machu Picchu.

Cloaked in the thick, grey *garúa* (sea fog) that engulfs the city for most of the year are still some fine colonial buildings, informative, well laid-out museums and excellent seafood restaurants. The Limeños themselves are a good advertisement for their city – most are wonderfully welcoming.

HISTORY

Origins
People have lived here at the mouth of the Rímac river for the past 7000 years. When you fly into Jorge Chávez airport, you'll see from the aeroplane window some of the large adobe pyramids that these early Limeños built, now surrounded by Lima's urban sprawl. These date from about 3000BC, long before the arrival of the Spanish, long before even the Incas. They were built in the U-shaped style that's characteristic of the temples on this part of the Peruvian coast (see p77).

By the 15th century when the Incas arrived, the local shrine and oracle called Pachacamac was already ancient, having been established about 900 years earlier. The Incas absorbed it into their religion, building an *acllahuasi* (convent) at the site. They then occupied the district, and by the time the Spanish arrived there were about 400 temples along the river supported by a network of peaceful communities.

The days of conquest
In 1535 the city of Lima was founded on the banks of the Rímac by Francisco Pizarro, shortly after he'd captured Cusco. He wanted to build his capital close to the sea because this provided the Spaniards with contact to the motherland, and here was a good harbour with a reliable water supply. The city was called *Ciudad de los Reyes* (City of the Kings) after the Magi and the kings of Spain

but the name didn't stick, and by the late 16th century the place was known as Lima, a corruption of Rímac.

Only a year after it was founded, the city was almost destroyed and the Spaniards pitched into the ocean during the revolt of Manco Inca (see p104). The Inca general, Quizo Yupanqui, besieged Lima but was destroyed by the power of the Spanish cavalry riding on flat ground. The failure to take Lima meant that the Incas could not cut the Spanish off from their lifeline to the sea, and the whole Inca rebellion was doomed.

Capital of Spanish Peru

The viceroy of Spanish South America lived in Lima, and the city attracted the trappings of power. It became a rich place. The University of San Marcos, the continent's oldest, was founded in 1551, and in 1569 the city became the seat of the Spanish Inquisition. An account survives of the entry of a new viceroy into the city in the 18th century that illustrates the wealth of the municipality. It describes streets hung with tapestries, local officials decked out in crimson velvet and brocade, and celebrations involving days of bullfights and banquets. This evidence of riches attracted the attentions of less welcome visitors, and Sir Francis Drake was the first of many privateers (pirates) to raid Lima when he attacked the port in 1579. The city walls were built as a result.

In 1746 there was a catastrophic earthquake, one of the many from which Peru has suffered. Most of the glorious old colonial buildings were reduced to dust; 16,000 people died from the quake and its ensuing plagues. A vivid eye-witness account runs: 'Monday 31st [three days later] there was a suffocating smell coming, not only from the countless corpses, but also from the dead horses, dogs and donkeys. The bodies were taken in cartloads to the cemetery where they were buried in large trenches.'

Capital of independent Peru

San Martín liberated Lima from the Spanish in 1821. He was criticized for delaying but said that he felt that the Limeños didn't want to be liberated: they were so plump with the opulence of Spain. San Martín waited until the locals discovered that there was to be no help from the mother country, at which they turned their loyalty to him. The viceroy escaped to the mountains with an army (see p42).

Charles Darwin visited in 1830 on his voyage aboard *The Beagle*, and provided a description of Lima post-independence: 'The city of Lima is now in a wretched state of decay: the streets are nearly unpaved, and heaps of filth are piled up in all directions; where the black gallinazos [vultures], tame as poultry, pick up bits of carrion. The houses have generally an upper story [sic], built, on account of the earthquakes, of plastered woodwork; but some of the old ones, which are now used by several families, are immensely large, and would rival in suites of apartments the most magnificent in any place. Lima, the City of the Kings, must formerly have been a splendid town.' (*The Voyage of the Beagle*).

The city walls were torn down in 1870 as Lima expanded. Although the land was needed for houses, the demolition of the walls was a mistake because in 1881 the city was occupied by the Chileans during the War of the Pacific (see p43). They didn't leave for two years.

More recent times

In 1920 there was a huge influx of poor, unskilled labour and the city's population grew to 170,000. President Leguía worked hard to rejuvenate the city, constructing sewers and building open places such as Plaza San Martín, but the sheer number of people here has been a problem ever since. The population is now over 8 million.

Many live in *pueblos jóvenes* (shanty towns) which aren't as bad as others in South America but are still pretty dismal places; unemployment and underemployment are rife. You'll no doubt be driven around by university graduates who work as *taxistas* because it's the only work there is, and for many from the pueblos jóvenes, the only work is on the street.

As with other capitals, there is another side to Lima, a face decorated with the wealth and opulence of the wealthy neighbourhoods of San Isidro and Miraflores, inhabited by people who can afford to shop for groceries in Miami.

WHAT TO SEE

You'll probably want to spend as little time in Lima as possible while you sort out your transport to Cusco, but there's lots you could see and do here. Some of it you may not consider seeing unless you are really interested in pre-Hispanic South American ceramics or 18th-century colonial Spanish church architecture, so what follows is a short guide to the best of Lima's sights tailored for the person heading out to Machu Picchu.

Lima Centro

● **Plaza de Armas** Plaza de Armas is a nobly proportioned plaza built on the site of an ancient Inca square. Behind high metal railings, the **Palacio de Gobierno** (Government Palace: irregular opening hours, free) takes up the whole of one side of the plaza, and red-and-purple-uniformed guards parade in the courtyard every morning, usually at 8am. On the right of this building is the **Cathedral** (variable opening hours Monday to Friday but usually 9am-4.30pm, Saturday 10am-4.30pm, entrance s/6, s/4 students), the construction of which first began in 1535. It's been rebuilt a number of times since, and was completely flattened in the 1746 earthquake. The structure you see dates from 1758. Francisco Pizarro's remains lie to the right of the entrance, surrounded by colourful mosaics. Set between the Government Palace and the cathedral is the **Archbishop's Palace**, with its delicate carved wooden balcony.

On the opposite side of the square, running away from the Rímac is **Jirón de la Unión**, a pedestrian precinct lined with cheap shops and fried chicken restaurants.

● **Palacio de Torre Tagle** Now occupied by the Foreign Ministry, this 18th-century mansion is one of Lima's colonial pearls. You can poke your head into the patio during office hours and relish the fine balcony and intricate carvings.

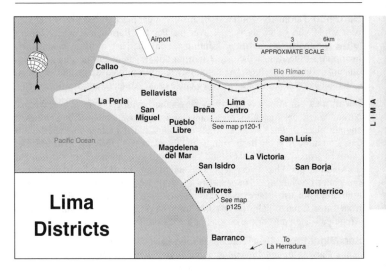

There's a 16th-century carriage in the main courtyard with a built-in commode.

● **Church of San Francisco** (cnr Lampa and Ancash, 9.30am-5.30pm, entrance s/6) One of the few large buildings to survive Lima's earthquakes, this church was consecrated in 1673. It's a very pretty building, but the main attractions are the **catacombs** of the monastery, still piled with the bones of 70,000 of the city's dead.

● **La Merced** (cnr Jirón de la Unión and Miró Quesada, 8am-noon, 4-8pm, free). There's been a church here since Lima's first mass was celebrated on this spot. It's such an important place that the Virgin of La Merced, the patroness of the religious order that lives here, has been made a marshal in the Peruvian military. The building itself has a façade of dauntingly ornate baroque, a frontage worthy of its importance, constructed from white Panamanian granite which made its way to Lima as ballast in cargo galleons. It's been rebuilt several times.

Other districts

Callao La Puenta (the Point) is refreshingly exposed to the sea breeze and can make a pleasant change from the claustrophobic atmosphere of Lima Centro.

Nearby there's **Castle of Real Felipe** (open daily, 8am-12 noon, 1-6pm, s/5, s/3 students), a squat, solid piece of military architecture, completed in 1767. Inside you'll find the **Military Museum** (same hours, no further charge) and around the corner is the **Naval Museum** (Av Jorge Chávez 121, Monday to Friday 9am-5pm, Saturday and Sunday 9am-4pm, entrance s/5, s/3 students). Both of these museums yield an interesting insight into the minds of the Peruvian military, and a lot of space is devoted to explaining why they lost the War of the Pacific to Chile (see p43).

Barranco Definitely worth a visit, this is a great place to relax over a chilled beer while you watch the sunset over the Pacific. Barranco is where Lima's artists and musicians gather, and during the day the pace of life is more gentle here than in the rest of the city. Courting couples frequent the Puente de los Suspiros (Bridge of Sighs). At night, this is a place for dancing and drinking. Catch a bus from Av Tacna in Lima Centro or Av Arequipa in Miraflores.

Miraflores Miraflores is Lima's modern suburb with good views over the sea, North American franchise restaurants and high-rise hotels. It's a pleasant enough place if you like these kinds of things, but it's rather characterless. It gets a bit more lively in the evenings, and the place has a thriving night-life. The central Parque Kennedy (also called 7 de Junio – the name changes often but it's the same park) has a very good weekend **art and craft market** at lunchtime, especially on Sundays. The standard of work for sale is, on the whole, very high, not your usual tacky watercolours; it's expensive though. To reach here from Lima Centro, jump on any bus from Av Tacna that's heading down Av Arequipa (listen out for the conductor's cries of 'Todo Arequipa').

San Miguel San Miguel contains the zoo (☎ 464 4282, usually 9am-5pm, s/6) in the **Parque de las Leyendas**. Even if you don't like zoos, this is a better place to catch up on your Peruvian wildlife than the **Natural History Museum** (Arenales 1256, Jesús María; Mon-Fri 9am-4pm, Sat 9am-5pm, Sun 9am-1pm, s/2.50, s/1.50 students) – at least the animals are alive. There's also an ancient adobe pyramid in the grounds.

Recommended museums
● **Museo de la Nación** (☎ 476 9875; Av Javier Prado Este 2465, San Borja) open Tuesday to Sunday, 9am-5pm, entrance s/8, students s/4, children s/2. A splendid museum (inside an ugly, concrete monstrosity next to a busy main road) that's as well laid out as it is informative. It's an ideal place to put in context all the ancient things you're going to see in Peru, and includes scale models of many of the Inca sights around Cusco. They also have folk-dancing exhibitions on Sundays at 5pm. To get here, catch a bus to Javier Prado from Av Tacna in Lima Centro, or from Av Arequipa in Miraflores, and a second along Javier Prado to the museum.
● **Museo Nacional de Antropología y Arqueología** (☎ 463 5070, Plaza Bolívar, Pueblo Libre) open Tuesday to Saturday 9am-5pm, Sunday and holidays 9am-4pm, entrance s/10. This is a bit of a prim maiden aunt compared to the flashy Museo de la Nación, but it's a good place: it contains the original objects of which the Nación only has copies. Look for the icons of Chavín (see p78): the Raimondi Stela (if you look at it upside down the image reads completely differently, see p79) and the Tello Obelisk (a sculpture of a male and female cayman), and the Paracas mummies looking rather shocked at having been dug up after centuries under the sands. The model of Machu Picchu will clarify the layout of the original when you get there. On the corner of the square you can quench your thirst at the friendly café. From Centro, catch a bus to Av

Brasil from Tacna, jump out at block 22 and go west along Av Vivanca. The bus to Av Brazil from Miraflores leaves from Av Pardo.

● **Museo de Oro del Perú** The Gold Museum (☎ 345 1292, 💻 www.muse oroperu.com.pe; Calle Alonso de Molina 1100, Monterrico) is open daily, 11.30am-7pm, entrance s/30, children s/15. This private collection contains a staggering display of pre-Hispanic gold (though many of the gold pieces on display are copies, as many as 98% according to some reports), Paracas textiles and ceramics including Moche erotic pots.

It's wise to have some idea about Peru's pre-history before you come here – go to the Museo de la Nación first as the Museo de Oro won't teach you much: everything is just stuffed in cupboards or laid on tables without explanation, but this may be corrected by the refurbishment underway at the time of writing (the museum remains open). There's also an excellent bookshop, and a large display of military objects connected with important people from South American history. From Lima Centro catch a bus to Av Angamos in Miraflores and from there to Monterrico.

● **Museo de Arte** (☎ 423 4732, 💻 www.museoarte.perucultural.org.pe; Paseo Colón 125) open Thursday to Tuesday 10am-5pm, entrance s/10, s/5 students, s/3 children. A handsome repository of Peruvian art, exhibiting a panoramic collection spanning 3000 years of cultural history, from pre-Columbian ceramics and post-conquest masterpieces of the Cusco School, to the portraits and landscapes of the republican period, to the cream of indigenous contemporary art. There are also regular temporary exhibitions, and a museum shop and café.

● **Museo del Tribunal de la Santa Inquisición** (Plaza Bolívar, Calle Junín 548, open Monday to Friday 9am-1pm and 2.30-5pm, entry free). The headquarters of the South American Spanish Inquisition. The tribunal room is beautiful with its carved wooden ceiling, and the dungeons show the unbelievable tortures that went on downstairs.

Huaca Pucllana

This pre-Columbian archaeological site (daily except Tuesday, 9am-5pm, entrance free) on the corner of Borgoño and Tarapaca covers about six hectares in the midst of a residential part of Miraflores. It dates back to AD500 and was one of the most important ceremonial and administrative centres of the Lima culture (AD200-700). A large adobe pyramid, which originally stood 23m high, dominates the site even though it has been badly eroded by the weather over the years. Extensive excavations are still being carried out and you can get a guided tour in Spanish and a bite to eat at the excellent restaurant overlooking the complex (see p126). Lying cheek-by-jowl with city buildings, it couldn't be a better counterpoint to the bustle of modern Lima.

Pachacamac

Thirty kilometres south of Lima is the ancient shrine and oracle of Pachacamac (Monday to Friday 9am-5pm, s/6, s/3 students); you can get here on one of the buses which leave every couple of hours from Av Abancay or Av Grau in Centro (look for Lurín-Pachacamac, s/2; 1hr 20mins). The pyramids are on the whole

LIMA

badly preserved, and to the untrained eye tend to look like piles of dry mud but some, like the acllahuasi (see p109), have been reconstructed.

The Spaniards would have looted Pachacamac to collect Atahualpa's ransom (see p101) but it had been stripped by the priests before they arrived. There's a description of what the main shrine looked like in those times, written by the conquistador, Miguel de Estete: 'Its locked door was closely studded with a variety of objects – corals, turquoises, crystals and other things. This was eventually opened, and we were certain that the interior would be as curious as the door. But it was quite the contrary. It certainly seemed to be the devil's chamber, for he always lives in filthy places… It was very dark and did not smell very pleasant'.

PRACTICAL INFORMATION
Arrival
A note of caution Lima has a crime problem, and you need to be careful – see p63.

By air There's a cambio in the arrivals terminal, a glass box of a building, and ATMs (for both soles and dollars) in the departures area. To get to the departures area, go through the doors at the end of the arrivals' hall, try to brush away the touts you will inevitably attract, turn left into the next-door building. The cambio is on the right and the ATMs a little further on.

The centre of town is to the east of the airport. Most people stay in either **Lima Centro** or **Miraflores**, and to take you there the taxistas will ask for twice as much as you should be paying – they quote around US$20 (s/65) to take you the 12km to Lima Centro but you should pay only about US$5-10 (s/15-35). A taxi to Miraflores should cost about US$3-5 (s/10-15) more. Walk through the car park and hail a cab from the road and it's even cheaper, for taxi drivers have to pay a fee every time they enter the airport.

If you book a hotel in advance they may offer to collect you from the airport for around US$10. A good alternative to catching a taxi is the Urbanito bus (s/10 to the centre, s/15 to Miraflores, s/20 to Barranco), which will take you to the hotel you request. Their desk is next to the regulated taxi counter. It's not a great

idea to get a local city bus into town if new to Lima and laden down with bags (see p63).

Incidentally, you may be accosted at the airport by people falsely claiming to work for the tourist board. They're mostly harmless, and indeed they can be positively helpful on occasions, though if you agree to take one of their taxis expect to pay double the going rate.

By bus Many buses come in near to the Hotel Sheraton near the Parque Universitario, very near Lima Centro, but there isn't a central bus terminal in Lima, so the place at which you'll arrive will depend on which company you're travelling with and from where. It's best to take a taxi from the terminus to your hotel, as bus stops are a magnet for thieves.

Getting around
Taxi One car in seven in Lima is a taxi, and most of these are currently unregulated: they're just private cars displaying a 'Taxi' sticker. But this is changing. If you see a cab, with a number painted on the side of the door it's been registered with the authorities. Yellow cabs (usually flimsy Daewoo Ticos) with numbers on the door are one stage further on; they're regulated. Both are less likely to try to cheat you.

Central Lima to Miraflores costs around s/8, to Barranco s/10 (s/4-5 from

Miraflores) and to the airport s/10-15 (s/20-25 from Miraflores). The journey from the town centre (or Miraflores) to the Museo de la Nación should be s/6 and to the Museo de Oro s/10.

Bus The bus network in Lima is a mess. Apparently it all used to be better: buses that ran on particular routes were painted the same colour and there were timetables but nowadays the colours mean nothing and there's no real timetable. They do have their route number and destination written on their front and sides; your hotel will tell you which bus you need to get and from where. **Beware of pickpockets and bag-slashers**.

The main bus thoroughfares in Lima Centro are Av Alfonso Ugarte and Av Tacna, and in Miraflores it's Av Arequipa. The fare is s/1.20 to anywhere in town, or s/2 for outlying districts such as Barranco or Pachacamac from Monday to Saturday. On Sunday the fares are fractionally higher.

The bus marked 'Faucett/Aeropuerto' goes to the airport. Although it's cheaper than taking a taxi, it's also much slower, less reliable and not as safe.

Tours Condor Travel (☎ 442 3000, 💻 www.condortravel.com.pe), Blondet 249, San Isidro, specializes in top-end tours of Lima's major museums and attractions. **Lima Vision** (☎ 447 0482, 📄 446 9969 💻 www.peruvision.com), Jr Chiclayo 444, Miraflores, offer half-day tours of the museums and the city for US$20-35, and a separate half-day tour out to Pachacamac for US$35. **Expediciones Viento Sur** (☎ 429 1414), Av Grau, La Punta, Callao, do cruises around the bay of Lima out towards San Lorenzo Island for US$35. (Abimael Guzman (see p45) is imprisoned on San Lorenzo Island). **Inka Wasi** (☎ 447 8096, 💻 info@inkawasitravel.com), Jr Tarata 265, Miraflores, organizes city tours and general expeditions, and can book flights and buses on

your behalf. **Peru Expeditions** (☎ 445 7874, 💻 www.peru-expeditions.com), Arequipa 5241, Office 504, Miraflores, runs 4WD trips around Lima and beyond. There are many other companies.

Car rental Alamo (☎ 444 7000), Benavides 1180, Miraflores; **Avis** (☎ 434 1111, 💻 www.avis.com), Av Javier Prado Este 5233, Miraflores and at the airport; **Budget** (☎ 442 8703, 📄 441 4174), Canaval y Moreyra 569, Miraflores, and at the airport (☎ 575 1674); **Dollar** (☎ 444 3050, 444 4920), Cantuarias 341, Miraflores, and at the airport (☎ 575 1719); **Hertz** (☎ 445 5716, 💻 www.hertz.com.pe), Av Cantuarias 160, Miraflores and at the airport; **Localiza** (☎ 242 3939), Av Benavides 735, Miraflores (☎ 242 3939); **National** (☎ 433 3750, 💻 www.nationalcar.com), Av Espana 543, Lima. Prices are variable but range from US$30 to US$50 a day.

Orientation [see map, p111]
Lima is built on a flat plain above a large arc of a bay. It's a big place with many different neighbourhoods; the distances between them are too great for walking.

Lima Centro is the ancient centre of the city on the banks of the Rímac, a good few miles inland from the sea. Plaza de Armas is here, as is the cathedral, the statues of Bolívar and San Martín, a pedestrian zone and many cheap hotels. To the south-west, close by, is the more residential district of **Breña**. To the north are the poorer suburbs. To the south-east is the industrial-commercial area of **La Victoria** and the suburbs of **San Luís** and **San Borja** where the Museo de la Nación is (see p112). Further out is the plusher **Monterrico** and the Museo de Oro del Perú (see p113).

Driving west from Lima Centro, you'll come to **Bellavista**, the sea and **Callao**, the port of Lima. There's a fort, a good view of the sea and some excellent cheap *cevicherías* (seafood restaurants selling the dish ceviche). Callao is really not as dangerous as some guidebooks make out, although it's wiser to be out of here by night.

Down the coast from Callao you'll pass through **San Miguel** where the zoo is; **Magdalena del Mar**, the posh embassy district of **San Isidro**; residential **Miraflores** with its more expensive hotels and North American airs, and bohemian **Barranco** with bars and night-life. You'll end up climbing El Morro, the hill which provides a first-class view of the coast and the city. Beyond El Morro is **La Herradura** – the name means 'horseshoe' because that's what the bay looks like.

Unless otherwise noted, addresses in this chapter are for Lima Centro.

Banks and cambios
The following banks have branches all over Lima: **BCP** (Visa), Jr Lampa 499 in the city centre, and Av Pardo 425 and Av Larco at Pasaje Tarata in Miraflores; **Banco de Comercio** (Visa), Jr Lampa 560 in the city centre, and Av Pardo 272 and Av Larco 265 in Miraflores; **Banco Latino** (MasterCard), Av Paseo de la Republica 3505; **Telebanco** (Visa), Jr de la Unión 790; **Banco Mercantil** (AMEX), Carabaya and Ucayali, **Banco Wiese** (Mastercard), Av Diagonal 176 on Parque Kennedy and Av Pardo 697 in Miraflores; **Citibank** (Citicorp), Av 28 de Julio 886 and Av Emilio Cavenecia 175 in Miraflores and Ribeira Naearrete 857, San Isidro.

For cambios try **Boulevard Tarata** at 248 Miraflores (☎ 444 3381), and many others, for example **Interbank**, Jr de la Unión 600 in the centre and Av Pardo 413, Av Larco 690 and Larcomar in Miraflores, which is quick and gives good rates. **Travex SA**, Av Santa Cruz 621, Miraflores, replaces lost or stolen American Express cheques. **Western**

Unión (☎ 422 0014), is at Av Larco 826, Miraflores, although its main office is at Av Petit Thouars 3595, San Isidro.

Books and newspapers (English)
For books in English try **Ibero Librerías**, Benavides 500, Miraflores; the **British Cultural Library** (☎ 221 7550), Av Arequipa 3495, San Isidro; or **El Virrey** (☎ 427 5080), Pasaje Nicolás de Rivera El Viejo 107-115, Lima centre. The **SAE** (see box p118) has a book exchange for members. Day-old English-language newspapers (costing around s/7) are available from street-sellers in Miraflores on the Ovalo, and in front of Café Haiti and the El Pacífico building, and at **Mallaco's** on Av Larco 175.

Communications
● **Telephone and fax** The code for Lima is ☎ 01. **Telefónica del Perú** (☎ 433 1616) is at Jr Carabaya 933, Plaza San Martín, but it's expensive and you'd be better off direct dialling from a pay phone in the street. Or, cheaper still, you can phone over the Internet. Check out **Cybersandeg** at 853 de la Unión near Plaza San Martín; they're welcoming and the staff will help you if you are unsure what to do.

● **Post** The main **post office** (*correo*), is on the block on the north-west corner of Plaza de Armas, on Jr Camaná 195, open Monday to Friday 7.30am-7pm, Saturday 7.30am-4pm, Sunday 8am-4pm. There's a poste restante here. In Miraflores, there's a post office at Petit Thouars 5201, Angamos Oeste. For **American Express** client mail go to Lima Tours (☎ 222 2525, 🖹 222 5700), Pardo y Aliaga 698, San Isidro. The **SAE** also holds mail for members. For an express service try **DHL**, Los Castaños 225, San Isidro; **UPS**, Av del Ejército 2107, San Isidro; or **Federal Express**, Av Jorge Chávez 475, Miraflores.

● **Email** All Internet cafés charge between s/3 and s/5 per hour. In Lima

❏ **Embassies and consulates**
Argentina (☎ 433 5704), Pablo Bermúdez 143, 2nd Floor; **Austria** (☎ 442 0503, 442 1807), Av Central 643, 5th Floor, San Isidro; **Australia** (☎ 222 8281), Víctor Belaúnde 398, San Isidro; **Belgium** (☎ 241 7566), Angamos Oeste 392, Miraflores; **Bolivia** (☎ 422 8231), Los Castaños 235, San Isidro; **Brazil** (☎ 421 5650), José Pardo 850, Miraflores; **Canada** (☎ 444 4015), Jr F Gerdes (or Libertad) 130, Miraflores; **Chile** (☎ 221 2818), Javier Prado Oeste 790, San Isidro; **Colombia** (☎ 441 0954), Av Jorge Basadre 1580, San Isidro; **Ecuador** (☎ 461 8217), Las Palmeras 356, San Isidro; **France** (☎ 215 8400), Arequipa 3415, San Isidro; **Germany** (☎ 212 5016), Arequipa 4202, Miraflores; **Ireland** (☎ 446 3878), Angamos Oeste 340, Miraflores; **Israel** (☎ 433 4431), Natalio Sánchez 125, 6th Floor; **Italy** (☎ 463 2727), Gregorio Escobedo 298, Jesús María; **Japan** (☎ 218 1462), Av San Felipe 356, Jesús María; **Netherlands** (☎ 476 1069), Av Principal 190, Santa Catalina; **New Zealand** (☎ 221 2833), Av Camino Real 390, San Isidro; **Spain** (☎ 212 2155), Jorge Basadre 498, San Isidro; **Sweden** (☎ 442 8905), C La Santa María 130, San Isidro; **United Kingdom** (☎ 617 3000), José Larco 1301, 22nd Floor, Miraflores; **USA** (☎ 434 3000), Av Encalada 17, Surco.

Centro there's **Carabaya@net**, Jr Carabaya 376 (2nd floor), or the **Internet café** underneath Hostal Hostal España, or you can try **Cybersandeg** (see opposite). In Miraflores there's the massive **Studio 2** at the corner of Prado and Ovalo, and **Cyberclub** at 455 Schell. The **SAE** (see box p118) allows members to use its computers to send and receive email.

Emergencies and medical services
● **Ambulance** Alerta Médica (☎ 225 4040); Cruz Roja (☎ 265 8783, 222 0222), or take a taxi.
● **Doctor** Dr Alejandro Rivera (☎ 471 2238) at Instituto Médico Lince, León Velarde 221, speaks English.
　　Dr Jorge Bazán (☎ 9735 2668) at Backpackers Medical Care (☎ 9735 2668, 🖳 backpackersmc@yahoo.com), speaks English and will visit hostels for consultations.
● **Hospitals** Anglo-American (☎ 221 3656), Alfredo Salazar, Cda 3, San Isidro; Maison de Santé (☎ 467 0753), Chorrillos. Clínica Internacional (☎ 433 4306), cnr Washington 1471 and 9 de Diciembre. Instituto Médico Lince (☎ 471 2238), Leon Velarde 221, Lince.

● **Pharmacy** Botica Inglés, Jr Cailloma 336, is well stocked. Superfarma (☎ 440 9000), Amendariz 215, Miraflores.
● **Rabies** Specialist anti-rabies centre (☎ 425 6313), Jr Austria 1300, Breña.
● **Vaccinations** International Health Department (☎ 517 1845) at the airport, is open 24 hours. The International Vaccination Centre (☎ 264 6889), Av del Ejército 1756, San Isidro, is open Monday to Friday 8am-3pm and on Saturday from 8am to 2pm.

Laundry
There are laundries all over Lima Centro, and in addition most hotels will do laundry for a price. In Miraflores, try **Servirap**, Schell 601 (which charges US$2.5 per kilo); **Presto**, Av Benavides 433; or the slightly more expensive **Lavandería 40 minutos** (☎ 446 5928), Espinar 154, Miraflores.

Maps
● **Lima** Maps of the city can be bought at kiosks and tourist shops, but there's a full map with an index of streets in the back of the *Páginas Amarillas* (Yellow Pages) which you'll find at your hotel.

LIMA

☐ **South American Explorers Club (SAE)**
This useful club for travellers in South America provides a wide range of assistance to members – everything from storing equipment to helping to find a trekking partner; from reconfirming flights to holding mail, faxes and email. There's a good library of books in English, and maps and reports, the latter written by other travellers, on just about every corner of Peru. The people who run the place are a fount of helpful information on everything from train times to more complex issues such as the current political situation in the highlands. There's a comfortable lounge where you can escape Lima's bustle, and the place contains what is probably the only Arsenal football club shirt in the whole of the continent.
    SAE (☎ 445 3306, ☒ limaclub@saexplorers.org, www.saexplorers.org) is at Calle Piura 135 in Miraflores. They're open Monday to Friday, 9.30am-5pm (to 8pm on Wednesday), and on Saturday, 9.30am to 1pm. Membership costs US$50 per year (US$80 for couples) and you can sign up there and then. There's a branch in Cusco, now at Choquechaca 188, ☎ 84-245484, ☒ cuscoclub@saexplorers.org). There are also other branches in Quito, Ecuador, and in the USA (☎ 607-277 0488, ☒ explorers@saexplorers.org), 26 Indian Creek Rd, Ithaca, New York.

● **Hiking maps** The **Instituto Geográfico Nacional** (☎ 475 9960, 475 3090, ▤ 475 9810), Av Aramburú 1198, Surquillo (take a taxi there), open Monday to Friday 8am-12 noon, 1-5.30pm sells good 1:100,000 maps of the hikes in this book, road maps of the entire country (1:2,000,000) and a four sheet topographical set at 1:1,000,000. You can also pick these up at the **SAE** (see box above).

Police

Police emergency number ☎ 105. Tourist police (☎ 424 2053), Jr de la Unión, are useful if you have had anything stolen or need advice. English-speaking officers are usually available.

Tourist information

The official tourist information office (☎ 427 6080) is one block west of Plaza de Armas at Paseo de los Escribanos 145, though they proved to be less than helpful whenever I called in. Your best bet is to visit **iPerú** (☎ 421 1627, iperulima@promperu.gob.pe, Mon-Fri 8.30am -6.30pm), which has offices at the airport (open 24 hours), Av Jorge Basadre 610,

San Isidro and in the Larcomar shopping complex in Miraflores (☎ 445 9400, Mon-Fri 12 noon-8pm). Alternatively, try **Info Peru** (☎ 424 7963, infoperu@ qnet.com.pe, Mon-Fri 9.30am-6pm, Sat 9.30am-2pm), Jr de la Unión 1066, Belén. Privately owned, the offices are genuinely helpful, the staff knowledgeable and English-speaking, and there's a refreshing lack of any hard-sell tactics too. You'll find another information office on Parque Kennedy in Miraflores.

There are lots of other places offering tourist information but they're generally trying to sell you something.

Visa extension

Dirección General de Migraciones y Naturalización (DIGEMIN) (☎ 330 4020), Av España 700-734, Breña. They charge s/12 for every extension, which is usually granted on the same day.

Where to stay

The districts of Lima Centro and Miraflores have the highest concentration of hotels and services for tourists. Of the two, Lima Centro is dirtier, noisier and has a greater crime problem but is more central and cheaper. In the following list I have also included a couple of hotels in the exclusive district of San Isidro, home to many of the consulates and big businesses. Note that the more expensive hotels add 28% tax to their rates; the cheapest budget ones often have no signs outside and look just like private residential houses – a way of dodging red tape and the taxman.

Incidentally, if you're staying in Lima's lower-budget accommodation, here are two bathroom tips that will improve your holiday no end: firstly, throw your toilet paper in the bin provided rather than down the toilet, or you'll block it; and secondly, if you're struggling to get hot water in the shower, try turning the tap just slightly rather than all the way.

Note: the following abbreviations are used here: **com = room with common bathroom; att = bathroom attached; sgl/dbl/tpl = single/double/triple**.

Lima Centro (budget accommodation)

The first mention has to be *Hostal España* (☎ 427 9196/428 5546, ☐ www .hotelespanaperu.com), Azángaro 105, close to the Church of San Francisco. Top of the list of places to stay in some guidebooks, this has inevitably become gringo central. It's a rambling old building with an interior courtyard; it has lockers, an Internet café, an information service and a rooftop restaurant that doubles as a kind of mini-zoo. Beds in the dorm cost US$3, singles/doubles are US$6/9 and there are even a few triples at US$12 each. If this is full, there's *Hostal Europa* (☎ 427 3351), Ancash 376, just up the road which costs a little less at US$5/7 (sgl/dbl) and offers a similar package but not to the same standard. Around the corner at Azángaro 127 is the clean, modern, though a bit soulless *Hostal San Francisco* (☎ 426 2735, ☐ hostal_san_francisco@terramail.com

.pe), which is a bit pricier at US$8 for a dorm bed (att).

I prefer *Pensión Ibarra* (☎ 427 8603/427 1035, ☐ pension_Ibarra@ ekno.com), Av Tacna 359, 14th and 15th floors, Flat Nos 1402 and 1502, a place where your mother would be happy for you to stay. There's no sign outside, and it's in a tower block, but it's safe, has a fridge and cooker and good views. The women who run it are helpful and do laundry, and if you book ahead they'll even pick you up from the airport. Rooms cost US$7/10 (sgl/dbl, com), though the singles are a little grubby. If tower blocks turn you off, try *Hotel La Casona* (☎ 426 6552, ☐ casonahotel@ latinmail.com), Moquega 289, a wonderful old tiled building. The beds are a bit soft and the rooms a bit tatty, but it's well priced at US$4 per room (sgl/dbl), or US$6 with attached bathroom. It is, however, less secure than other hotels.

Hostal Iquique (☎ 433 4724, ☐ 423 3699, ☐ hiiquique@terra.com.pe), Jr Iquique 758, Breña, is recommended as it's safe, very helpful, friendly and light and clean – though the ground floor rooms smell musty. It costs US$7/10 (sgl/dbl, com) and US$10/14 (sgl/dbl, att), and there are discounts if you're a member of the SAE (see box opposite).

If you're after the **lowest prices**, there's a road of cheap hotels in Pasaje Teodoro Peñaloza (off Nicolás de Pierola), charging US$3 a night (single, com). Don't expect much, and be careful. Around the corner, there's *Hostal Atenas* (☎ 330 5149), Nicolás de Pierola 370, which is US$3/5 (sgl/dbl, com), gringo-free, pretty clean with a lovely painted lobby, and a little less sleazy than the others around here; while just to the north of Jr Lisson is *Hostal Monaco* (☎ 330 3861), Washington 949 – the same kind of thing without the interior decoration at US$3/4 (sgl/dbl, com).

The best-value hotel in this price range, however, is the wonderful *Hostal*

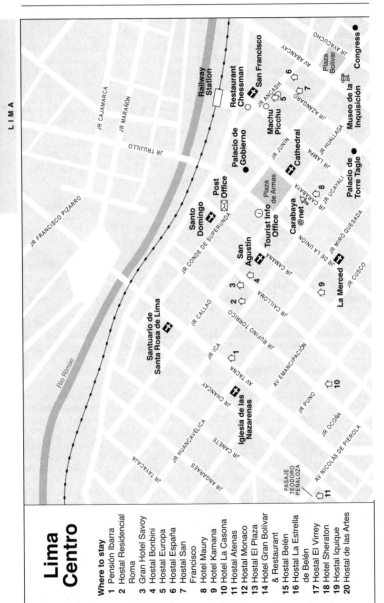

Lima Centro

Where to stay

1 Pensión Ibarra
2 Hostal Residencial Roma
3 Gran Hotel Savoy
4 Hostal Bonbini
5 Hostal Europa
6 Hostal España
7 Hostal San Francisco
8 Hotel Maury
9 Hotel Kamana
10 Hotel La Casona
11 Hostal Atenas
12 Hostal Monaco
13 Hostal El Plaza
14 Hotel Gran Bolívar & Restaurant
15 Hostal Belén
16 Hostal La Estrella de Belén
17 Hostal El Virrey
18 Hotel Sheraton
19 Hostal Iquique
20 Hostal de las Artes

LIMA

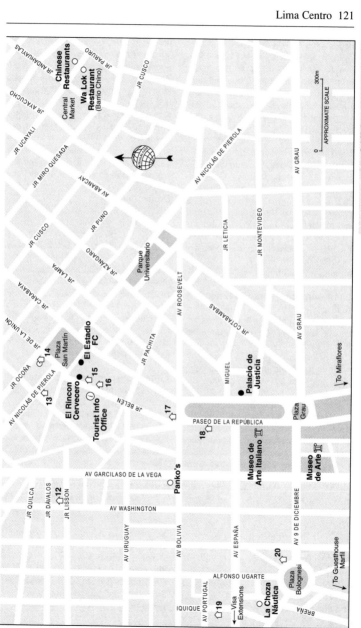

LIMA

APPROXIMATE SCALE

0   300m

Chinese Restaurants

Wa Lok Restaurant (Barrio Chino)

Central Market

JR PARURO

JR ANDAHUAYLAS

JR AYACUCHO

JR UCAYALI

JR MIRO QUESADA

JR CUSCO

AV ABANCAY

JR PUNO

JR AZANGARO

Parque Universitario

AV NICOLAS DE PIEROLA

JR LAMPA

JR CARABAYA

JR DE LA UNION

JR OCOÑA

Plaza San Martin

El Estadio FC

El Rincon Cervecero

Tourist Info Office

AV NICOLAS DE PIEROLA

JR BELEN

JR PACHITA

AV ROOSEVELT

JR LETICIA

JR MONTEVIDEO

JR COYBABAMBAS

MIGUEL

Palacio de Justicia

Plaza Grau

AV GRAU

To Miraflores

PASEO DE LA REPÚBLICA

Museo de Arte Italiano

Museo de Arte

AV GARCILASO DE LA VEGA

Panko's

JR QUILCA

JR DAVALOS

JR LISSON

AV WASHINGTON

AV URUGUAY

AV BOLIVIA

AV ESPAÑA

AV 9 DE DICIEMBRE

To Guesthouse Marfil

ALFONSO UGARTE

AV PORTUGAL

IQUIQUE

Visa Extensions

La Choza Nautica

Plaza Bolognesi

BREÑA

13 14 15 16 17 18 19 20 12

de las Artes (☎ 433 0031, 🖳 www.artes welcome.tripod.com) at Jr Chota 1469, just to the north of Plaza Bolognesi. From the beautiful tiled lobby and high glass ceiling to the comfy rooms, this Dutch-owned place oozes class, and is very affordable too at US$8/14 (sgl/dbl, com), US$11/17 (sgl/dbl, att). They will also pick you up from the airport for US$12. Not far behind in terms of quality, though unfortunately in an inconvenient location to the south of Centro in Pueblo Libre, is *Guest House Marfil* (☎ 463 3161, 🖳 yma25@yahoo.com) at Parque Ayacucho 126, between the third and fourth blocks of Av Bolívar. Rooms cost just US$8 per person per night, English is spoken, kitchen and laundry facilities are provided and the owners even offer Spanish classes.

Lima Centro (mid-range hotels) A similar type of place to Hostal Iquique, though in a building with more character, is the good *Hostal Residencial Roma* (☎/🖷 427 7572, 🖳 www.itete .com.pe/resroma), Jr Ica 326. The people who run the Roma are helpful and polyglot, and charge US$10/15 (sgl/dbl, com), US$13/20 (sgl/dbl, att, cable TV extra), which is a little too much.

Hostal Belén (☎ 427 8995, 🖳 arco bel@terra.com.pe), Jr Unión/Belén 1049, is also in a sprawling old building, and has clean lavatories and soft beds in rooms that some people will find poky. The communal areas are light and airy, and there's a wonderful old marble staircase. It costs US$6/12/18 (sgl/dbl/tpl, all com). Next door is the not very friendly *Hostal La Estrella de Belén* (☎ 428 6462), Jr Unión/Belén 1051. It is, nevertheless, clean and modern and charges US$12/15/24 (sgl/dbl/tpl, att).

At the more expensive end is the recommended, business-orientated *Hotel Kamana* (☎ 426 7204, 🖳 www .hotelkamana.com), Jr Camaná 547, used by tour companies. It's well-run if a

little antiseptic; sgl/dbls cost US$32/37. *Hostal El Virrey* (☎ 426 8305, 🖳 www.perutravelnet.com/elvirrey), Av F Roosevelt 115 – don't confuse it with Hostal los Virreyes – is also good at US$/20/25-35 (sgl/dbl, att), and you're getting the same views as you get at the Sheraton. You could try *Gran Hotel Savoy* (☎ 428 3520, 🖳 www.hotel-savoyperu.com), Jr Cailloma 224, where a stay in a genuine 1950s hotel room will cost you US$30/45 (sgl/dbl, att, includes breakfast), or the smart and stylish *Hostal Bonbini* (☎ 427 6477, 🖷 427 3027), opposite at Jr Cailloma 209, where their spacious rooms go for US$30/40 (sgl/dbl, att with cable TV). *Hostal El Plaza* (☎ 428 6274, 🖳 hplaza @ddm.co.pe), Nicolás de Piérola 850, is better decorated than its neighbours and charges US$25/30 (sgl/dbl, att), and finally, the newly renovated, *Hotel Maury* (☎ 428 8188, 🖳 hotmaury @amauta.rcp.net.pe), Jr Ucayali 201, teeters on the expensive bracket at US$48/59/108 (sgl/dbl/suite), but is smart and popular.

Lima Centro (expensive hotels) If you're going to splurge on an expensive hotel don't stay in Lima Centro, go to Miraflores. If you must be based here the best hotel is the Lima *Sheraton* (☎ 315 5000/5022, 🖷 315 5024, 🖳 reservas@ sheraton.com.pe), Paseo de la República 170, where you can stay in a standard Sheraton room tinged with Lima shabbiness for US$170/190 (sgl/dbl, att).

Hotel Gran Bolívar (☎ 426 7438, 428 7672/3, 🖷 428 7671, 🖳 bolivar@ terra.com.pe), Jr de La Unión 958, just off Plaza San Martín, has a beautiful 1920s lobby – check out the glass ceiling – and it's much more classy than the Sheraton; it's considerably cheaper at US$102/115 (sgl/dbl, att, breakfast), but the rooms are disappointing and there seems to be a shortage of staff.

Miraflores and San Isidro (budget accommodation) There are a few youth hostels in Miraflores. *Albergue Juvenil* (Youth Hostel; ☎ 446 5488, 📄 444 8187, 💻 www.limahostell.com.pe), Av Casimiro Ulloa 328, Miraflores, is the best known and longest established, with clean, spacious rooms, lockers, and a travel agency, though the staff can be a little trying at times; dorm beds cost US$11, double rooms US$26 (discount for members). More friendly is *Hiker's House* (☎ 445 9763, 💻 hikers@hikershouse.com), in a very central location at Calle Frederíco Recavarren 427, to the north of Av Benavides; rates are the same as at the youth hostel. Also charging the same is *Albergue Juvenil Kusi Wasi* (☎ 444 1983, 💻 kusiwasi@terra.com.pe), at Av José Pardo 991, with two-, three- and four-bed rooms, hot water round the clock and kitchen and laundry facilities; rates include breakfast. *Friend's House* (☎ 446 6248, 💻 friendshouse_peru@yahoo .com.mx), Jirón Manco Capac 368, is an established backpacker haunt that charges US$6/14 (dorm/dbl). The oddly named *Flying Dog Backpackers* (☎ 445 6745, 💻 www.flyingdog.esmartweb.com), Diez Canseco 117, is also very popular with backpackers with dorm beds costing US$5 per person including breakfast. Similarly good value at US$6 per person is the cut-price *Albergue Juvenil Malka* (☎ 222 5589, 💻 hostelmalka@terra .com.pe), at Los Lirios 165; it's friendly and comfortable enough, but unfortunately rather inconveniently located in San Isidro, though it is close to Av Arequipa from where you can catch buses to Miraflores and Lima Centro. *Pensión Yolanda* (☎ 445 7565, 💻 pensionyolan da@hotmail.com), Domingo Elias 230, is a little overpriced at US$12/22 (sgl/dbl,

com, breakfast), but friendly, quiet and safe. *Hospedaje Tahuantinsuyo* (☎ 445 3776), San Fernando 494, in a well-preserved colonial house minutes from the attractions of Larcomar, is better value at US$12/25 (dbl, com/dbl, att) and breakfast is included.

One venue a little further afield that's worth mentioning is *The Point* (☎ 247 7997, 💻 www.thepointhostel.com), Junín 300, to the south of Miraflores in Barranco. It's a spacious, sea-front house with a laidback atmosphere that attracts globetrotters; dorm beds cost US$8.

Miraflores and San Isidro (mid-range hotels) Most of these hotels have cable TV, fan and phone in the room. At the lower end of the scale is *Hostal Bellavista de Miraflores* (☎ 445 7834, 💻 www.hostalbellavista.com), Jr Bellavista 215, Miraflores, centrally located with a pleasant courtyard at US$40/45 (sgl/dbl, com, breakfast, att extra). *Hostal el Carmelo* (☎ 446 0575, 💻 carmelo@ amautoa.rcp.net.pe), Bolognesi 749, Miraflores, is trying hard, and has a good location close to the sea-front Parque al Amor. Singles/doubles (att) with breakfast are US$35/45 but you can probably bargain them down.

Hostal Lucerna (☎ 445 7321, 📄 446 6050, 💻 hostallucerna@terra.com.pe), Las Dalias 276, Miraflores, is a good, clean hotel with a lovely garden and costs US$45/53 (sgl/dbl, att). The recommended *Suites Eucalyptus* (☎ 445 8594, 📄 444 3071, 💻 www.tsi.com.pe/eucalip tus), San Martín 511, is more imaginative, with studies of famous artworks in the rooms. There's no garden here. Rates start at US$33/41 (sgl/dbl, all att). One of the best at this price range is *Hostal El Patio* (☎ 444 2107, 💻 hostalelpatio@q

KEY TO MAP OPPOSITE

Miraflores – Where to stay

LIMA

net.com.pe), Diez Canseco 341A. This friendly place has an attractive courtyard and good-value rooms for US$30/35/40 (sgl/dbl/suite, att, breakfast).

At the top end of this price bracket is *Hostal Señorial* (☎ 445 9724), José Gonzales 567, Miraflores, a colonial house with a lovely courtyard, good rooms and parking, and a gym, Jacuzzi and sauna. They charge US$40/50/60 (sgl/dbl/tpl, att, breakfast included).

Worth considering is *Hotel las Palmas* (☎ 444 6033, ▤ 444 6036, ▭ www.macrostudio.net/laspalmas), Bellavista 320, Miraflores. It's central, adequate and the rooms are inexpensive at US$20/28 (sgl/dbl, att) but it lacks charm.

Hotel San Antonio Abad (☎ 447 6766, ▤ 446 4208, ▭ www.hotelsanan tonioabad.com), Ramón Ribeyro 301, Miraflores, is recommended. Run by a helpful, polyglot manager (he even speaks Japanese), this is a good, safe, clean place costing US$50/60 (sg/dbl, att, breakfast).

Miraflores and San Isidro (Expensive hotels) Probably the finest hotel in Miraflores is the *Marriott* (☎ 217 7000, ▭ www.marriotthotels .com), which has a superb waterside location at Malecón de la Reserva 615, opposite the Larcomar complex. The rooms are stylish and packed with mod cons, but come at a price – US$175/ 190/225 (sgl/dbl/suite). Another flashy

number is *Hotel Las Americas* (☎ 241 2820, 444 7272, ▭ www.hoteleslas americas.com), Benavides 415, a five-star hotel with everything you'd expect for US$180-330 plus tax. If you haven't got that sort of money, you could try their other establishment the *Residencial Las Americas* (☎ 242 6600, ▭ www .hoteleslasamericas.com), Bellavista 216. Suites here begin at US$70 plus tax. The striking marble, glass and granite *Miraflores Park Hotel* (☎ 242 3000, ▭ www.mira-park.com), Malecón de la Reserva 1035, enjoys fine ocean views, not least from its rooftop pool, and has all the amenities you'd expect for its US$265/340 (sgl&dbl/suite) price tag. In an elegant, converted mansion, *Hotel Antigua Miraflores* (☎ 241 6116, info@ peru-hotels-inns.com), Av Grau 350, has three grades of rooms, starting at US$64/ 74 (sgl/dbl) and rising to US$89/104 (sgl/dbl) for the most opulent.

Finally, located out in San Isidro are a couple more good hotels; *Swissôtel* (☎ 421 4400, ▤ 421 4422, ▭ reservations. lima@swissotel.com), Via Central 150, Centro Empresarial Real, charges from US$195 a night.

Better though, is the stunningly renovated *Country Club* (☎ 611 9000, ▭ www.hotelcountry.com), Los Eucaliptos 590, a 1927 building with a beautiful lobby beneath a stained-glass dome and rooms redolent of colonial charm at US$250 (sgl & dbl).

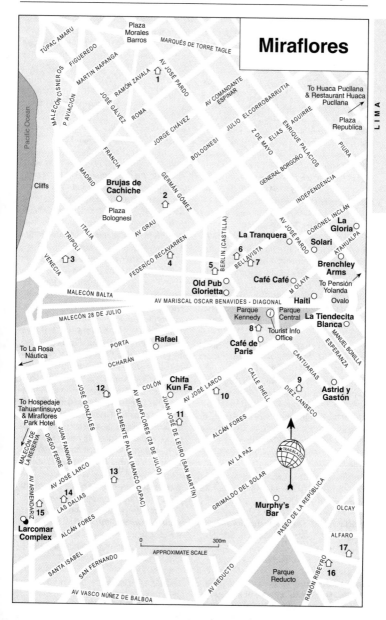

Miraflores

TÚPAC AMARU

Plaza
Morales
Barros

MARQUÉS DE TORRE TAGLE

To Huaca Pucllana
& Restaurant Huaca
Pucllana

Plaza
Republica

LIMA

FIGUEREDO

MARTIN NAPANGA

RAMÓN ZAVALA

JOSÉ GÁLVEZ

ROMA

AV JOSÉ PARDO

1

AV COMANDANTE
ESPINAR

JORGE CHÁVEZ

BOLOGNESI

AV EL CORRO

BARRUTIA

JULIO

2 DE MAYO

Z DE ELIAS

ENRIQUE PALACIOS

AGUIRRE

GENERAL BORGOÑO

PIURA

MALECÓN CISNEROS

PAVIACION

JOSÉ GÁLVEZ

FRANCIA

MADRID

INDEPENDENCIA

Pacific Ocean

Cliffs

ITALIA

TRIPOLI

VENECIA

3

GERMÁN GÓMEZ

**Brujas de
Cachiche**

2

Plaza
Bolognesi

AV GRAU

FEDERICO RECAVARREN

4

5

BERLIN (CASTILLA)

BELLAVISTA

6

7

La Tranquera ○

AV JOSÉ PARDO

CORONEL INCLÁN

ATAHUALPA

**La
Gloria** ○

Solari ○

**Brenchley
Arms** ○

Café Café ○

M OLAYA

To Pensión
Yolanda

**Old Pub
Glorietta** ○

AV MARISCAL OSCAR BENAVIDES - DIAGONAL

MALECÓN BALTA

MALECÓN 28 DE JULIO

Parque
Kennedy ⓘ Parque
Central

Haiti ○

Ovalo

**La Tiendecita
Blanca** ○

MANUEL BONILLA

ESPERANZA

To La Rosa
Náutica

PORTA

OCHARÁN

Rafael ○

8

Tourist Info
Office

**Café de
Paris** ○

CANTUARIAS

To Hospedaje
Tahuantinsuyo
& Miraflores
Park Hotel

JOSÉ GONZALES

COLÓN

12

**Chifa
Kun Fa**

AV JOSÉ LARCO

10

9

DIEZ CANSECO

**Astrid y
Gastón** ○

11

JUAN JOSÉ DE LEURO (SAN MARTÍN)

CALLE SHELL

ALCÁN FORES

JUAN FANNING

DIEGO FERRE

AV MIRAFLORES (28 DE JULIO)

CLEMENTE PALMA (MANCO CAPAC)

AV LA PAZ

MALECÓN DE
LA RESERVA

AV JOSÉ LARCO

13

GRIMALDO DEL SOLAR

PASEO DE LA REPÚBLICA

AV ARMENDARIZ

14

LAS DALIAS

15

**Larcomar
Complex**

ALCÁN FORES

SANTA ISABEL

SAN FERNANDO

**Murphy's
Bar** ○

OLCAY

ALFARO

17

16

RAMÓN RIBEYRO

Parque
Reducto

AV VASCO NÚÑEZ DE BALBOA

AV REDUCTO

0   300m
APPROXIMATE SCALE

★ TRAILBLAZER

Where to eat and drink

Lima caters for every palate and pocket. You may not be here for long, but there's no reason to suffer at mealtimes.

Budget food There are lots of cheap eating places in **Lima Centro**. The *restaurant without a name* under Hostal Europa (see p119) is fine for breakfasts; try the Americano (egg, bread, jam, tea/coffee, juice) at s/4.50. Just along the road are some good places for lunch: *Bar-Restaurant Machu Picchu* (Ancash 312), which seems overpriced until you see the size of the portions, and *Restaurant Chessman* (Ancash 273). At Av Breña 204-209 you'll find a good cevichería, *La Choza Náutica*.

There's a string of cevicherías by La Puenta in **Callao**. It'd be a shame to pick any one of them out; they're all excellent, and the fish is so light it almost floats off the plate but try *Chifa Marina*. There are other good cheap cevicherías by the fish market on the south of the bay near the Playa Aqua Dulce, underneath El Morro.

In **Miraflores** you can still get a good s/3.50 lunch in the restaurants in the side roads around Larco and Benavides: try the *causa rellena* (spiced potato cake) if you see it. In **Barranco** you can get an excellent traditional dinner in the restaurants under the Puente de Sospiros; walk down towards the sea, they're on your left. Try the *jalea* (fried whitebait) or the *chupe de camarones* (prawn chowder). If you're brave have *anticucho* (calf's heart kebabs), which are surprisingly tender and taste a little like roast liver.

Mid-priced restaurants One of the best mid-priced restaurants is *Mi Perú*, Plaza Butters, cnr Calle Lima, Barranco, which serves exceptional seafood at a reasonable price. For a traditional meal with a song, try *Brisas del Titicaca*, Jr Walkuski 168, or *Manos Morenas*, Av

Pedro de Osma 409, Barranco. Shows generally start at about 10pm.

There's decent, if a little overpriced, international food (sea bass, filet mignon) with a Peruvian touch in a relaxing dining-room, at *La Ermita*, Bajada de Baños 340, Barranco. If you're a confirmed carnivore and fancy a challenge, try to get through the *parilladas* (mixed grill) at *La Carreta,* Av Rivera Navarrete 740, San Isidro.

In **Miraflores** visit *Mango's*, Larcomar complex, for good food and a seaview, *La Tranquera*, Pardo 285, an Argentine grill-house doing great steaks, *La Tiendecita Blanca*, Larco 111, for Swiss-style pastries or *Solari*, Pardo 216, where you can enjoy international cuisine in a giant glass building within earshot of an artificial waterfall.

There are **pizza restaurants** around Parque Kennedy by the Diagonal, particularly on Berlin (Castilla); most are overpriced, boring and safe, but *Glorietta*, at Diagonal 181, stands out above the rest as a relaxed, open-fronted Italian eatery. *McDonald's* and *Burger King* are also on Parque Kennedy.

Finally, don't forget Lima's **Chinese restaurants**. Lima has the largest Chinese community in South America, and the Chinese food (*chifa*) here is said to be the finest on the continent. The best place to head for Oriental fare is *Wa Lok*, at Jirón Paruro 864-878, or Angamos Oeste 700-720. Alternatively, try *Capon*, to the east of Jr Abancay, or *Chifa Kun Fa* at San Martín 459, Av Larco.

Expensive restaurants Though it's not cheap, the restaurant at Hotel Gran Bolívar (see p122) is good value; for a lot less than other, flashier restaurants in the city, you can sample some of the best cuisine in Lima. The food at *Brujas de Cachiche*, Bolognesi 460, Miraflores, who specialize in traditional dishes, is excellent – try ceviche here if you're not going to risk it anywhere else. Another of these top-rate restaurants is the famous *La Rosa Náutica* at Costa Verde, on the end of the pier off the beach below Miraflores. Its location is unrivalled in the whole of Lima, and the food, especially the crab, shrimp and shellfish, is sensational.

Restaurant Huaca Pucllana, at General Borgoño, 8th Block, also boasts a fancy location, overlooking the floodlit ruins of the pre-Inca pyramid of the same name. It serves first-rate contemporary Peruvian dishes.

For fantastic international and fusion cuisine, you can't do much better than tuck into the well-presented food at *Astrid y Gastón*, Cantuarias 175, Miraflores or *Rafael*, at San Martín 300, Miraflores, which both expertly draw on European and Latin American traditions. *La Gloria*, Atahualpa 201, also offers exceptional fare (the risotto in black calamari ink and the lobster are beyond compare), while *Valentino*, Manuel Bañón 215, San Isidro, is fêted for its blend of Italian and Peruvian influences.

Remember that expensive restaurants add up to 28% tax to the price of your meal.

Cafés *Café Café*, Matir Olaya 250, Miraflores, and in the Larcomar complex, serves large portions of well-cooked, unchallenging dishes (lomo cordon bleu and milanesa) in a jazzy café with good music, and claims to have over a hundred blends of coffee. If you're after a Gallic-style café there's the French-run *Café de Paris* (Jr Diez Canseco 180, Miraflores – near Larco, just south of Parque Kennedy), where the brasserie food is good. *Haiti*, just off the Ovalo at Diagonal 160, Miraflores, is a great spot to unwind over a drink and a pastry while the world goes by and *Panko's*, at Garcilaso de la Vega 1296, is a fine bakery with tasty pastries and cakes. A good place to watch the sun set over the Pacific is *La Posada del Mirador*, Calle Ermita

104, Barranco. Cross the Puente de los Suspiros from the plaza, turn left and walk towards the viewpoint. Pick up some *picarones* (doughnuts with honey) from one of the small cafés on the way.

Bars and nightlife In **Lima Centro**, two good bars popular with ex-pats are *El Rincón Cervecero*, Jr de la Unión 1045, and the football-mad *El Estadio F.C.* at Jr Nicolás de Piérola 926; if you're desperate for a fix of European football, this is the place to come. If neither of these appeals, go to Sentarosa, immediately to the west of Plaza de Armas, which has a number of cosmopolitan bars; they're all overpriced, but they do have the advantage of being within staggering distance of the cheaper hostels. For a nostalgic glimpse at Lima's glamorous past, visit the bar in the Hotel Gran Bolívar (see p122) and sample the definitive Pisco Sour.

In **Miraflores** there's a proliferation of ex-pat bars that are busy most nights and generally have a good atmosphere. Try the *Brenchley Arms*, Atahualpa 176, which serves English pub grub, the *Old Pub*, San Ramón 295, or *Murphy's Bar*, Calle Schell 627. But the best place to go bar crawling is Barranco; *La Noche*, Bolognesi 307, *Sargento Pimienta*, Bolognesi 755, and *Deja Vu*, Grau 294, are all lively, perennially popular venues – and within a short stumble of each other.

If you want live music, *La Estación*, Av Pedro de Osma 112, Barranco, usually has a Latin singer accompanied on a guitar.

For dancing, there's *Break Club* at 1551 Arequipa (Thurs to Sat only). There are also a number of discos in the Diagonal in Miraflores. Hip Limeños head to the bars and discos in the Larcomar complex at Malecón de la Reserva 610 on the sea-front for their late-night drinking and dancing.

❏ **Airline offices in Lima**
AeroCondor (☎ 441 1354), Juan de Arona 781; **Aerolíneas Argentinas** (☎ 444 0810), José Pardo 805, 3rd Floor, Miraflores; **Air France** (☎ 444 9285), Av José Pardo 601, Miraflores; **Air New Zealand** (☎ 444 4441), Alijovín 472, Miraflores; **Alitalia** (☎ 447 3899), Martir Oláya 129 off 1703, Miraflores; **American Airlines** (☎ 211 7000), Canaval y Moreyra 390, San Isidro; **Continental** (☎ 221 4340), Víctor Andrés Belaúnde 147, V Principal 110, Office 101, San Isidro; **Iberia** (☎ 421 4616), Av Camino Real No 390, Central Tower, 9th Floor, Office 902, San Isidro; **KLM** (☎ 421 9500), Calderón 185, San Isidro; **Lan Chile** (☎ 213 8300), Av Pardo 513, Miraflores; **Lan Peru** (☎ 213 8200), Av Pardo 513, Miraflores; **Lloyd Aereo Boliviana** (☎ 241 5510), José Pardo 231, 1st and 7th Floors, Miraflores; **Lufthansa** (☎ 442 4455), Av Jorge Basadre 1330, San Isidro; **Qantas** (☎ 242 6631), Bolognesi 599; **Taca** (☎ 213 7000), Espinar 331, Miraflores; **Tans** (☎ 213 6000), Arequipa 5200, Miraflores; **Varig** (☎ 442 4361), Camino Real 456, Office 803-804, San Isidro.

Lima airport: General enquiries (☎ 575 1434, 575 0912), national flights (☎ 574 5529), international flights (☎ 575 1712).

Shopping

Centro Artesenal, Camino Real 485, San Isidro, is a rather bland Peruvian crafts market. For a more challenging experience and a larger choice, go to the massive **artesanía** market between 600 and 1000 on Av de la Marina out towards Pueblo Libre. A taxi here from Lima Centro will cost around s/6. There's also a weekend arts market in **Parque Kennedy** in Miraflores and a mix of swanky boutiques, craft shops and fashion outlets at the **Larcomar** complex at Malecón de la Reserva 610, also in Miraflores.

There are dozens of overpriced shops to the west of Plaza de Armas; most of the stuff on offer is rather naff, but if you're at the end of your holiday it's your last chance to purchase that life-sized cuddly llama you've been promising yourself.

Moving on

By air to Cusco Lima to Cusco takes about an hour and a one-way ticket costs US$69 upwards. Currently, Lan Peru (three flights per day) and Tans (twice daily) make the journey. There is a s/15 departure tax on domestic flights.

Overland to Cusco Travelling overland by bus (or by bus and train) is by far the more scenic way to get to Cusco, even if it does take a lot longer. There are two main routes, via **the highlands** and via **Arequipa**. The most travelled route is via Arequipa because it's shorter and the roads are better; in the rainy season the highland roads can become completely washed away.

For details of bus companies, see box opposite.

Highland routes The **northern** route goes from Lima inland to La Oroya, turns south-east to Huancayo and Ayacucho, and then heads to Abancay and Cusco. There's no direct **bus** – you take one from Lima to Huancayo and then change. It takes about 50 hours and costs about US$30. There is a railway from Lima to Huancayo but at the time of writing no trains were running on it.

The **southern** route follows the coast, visiting Pisco before heading inland to Ayacucho and then passing through Abancay to reach Cusco. This takes about 30 hours and costs about US$25. Catch the bus from Lima to

---

❏ Bus companies
There are many companies, including:
● **Cruz del Sur** (☎ 424 1005, 💻 www.cruzdelsur.com.pe), Jr Quilca 531, and Javier Prado Este 1109, the biggest company, recommended for most destinations; the more luxurious, more expensive services leave from the terminal on Javier Prado Este.
● **Carhuamayo** (☎ 426 0785), Montevideo 766 and Av 28 de Julio 1758, have a 'direct' service (via Arequipa), to Cusco.
● **Civa** (☎ 332 5236, 💻 www.civa.com.pe), cnr 28 de Julio and Paseo de la República 575, good for the Lima–Arequipa–Cusco route.
● **Molina** (☎ 428 4852), Ayacucho 1141-1145, operates services to Ayacucho and Cusco.
● **Ormeño** (☎ 427 5679, 💻 www.ascina.com/ormeno), Carlos Zavala Loayza 177, and Javier Pardo Este 1059, a big bus company covering all areas of the country.
● **Tepsa** (☎ 427 5642), Lampa 1237, good for northerly destinations.
● **León de Huanuco** (☎ 424 3893), Av 28 de Julio 1520, Victoria, specialize in travel to Ica, Nazca and all points south.
● **Empresa Paz S.A.** (☎ 428 5095), Montevideo 106, also cover routes to Ica, Nazca and all points south.

Ayacucho where you change to the Abancay or Cusco bus. There is a **third route** via Nazca and Abancay; for years this was shut because of banditry, and although it has now reopened, few companies use this road even though it is the quickest at about 24 hours. The Molina bus company at Jr Ayacucho 114 (see above) runs a service on this route.

All these routes were closed to travellers for many years, but are now opening up again. Don't, as I did, read Mario Vargas Llosa's novel *Death in the Andes* on the bus to Cusco, as it starts with a description of two French tourists taking the highland bus and getting held up and murdered by the Sendero Luminoso.

Arequipa route The other way to travel to Cusco is via Arequipa. It looks like a terrible detour on the map, but in fact it's one of the quickest overland routes at about 30 hours for the entire trip. Anyway, Arequipa is a very pretty city and you might be able to fit in a climb up the volcano El Misti or a trek down the Colca Canyon. There are direct buses from Lima to Arequipa. To get

from Arequipa to Cusco, you can take a bus or the train.
● **Lima to Arequipa (bus)** Direct buses on this route cost US$10 for a standard service, and US$28 for a luxury bus; the journey time is about 16 hours.
● **Arequipa to Cusco (bus)** The bus can either go via Juliaca (a reasonable road) or straight to Sicuani (a less good/terrible road); both take about 12 to 15 hours and cost around US$12-15. Travelling by night is not really recommended because you'll miss the view.
● **Arequipa to Cusco (train)** The privatization of Peru's rail network means all the routes and schedules were subject to change and some routes were discontinued. The Arequipa–Puno route was suspended in June 2002, although Perurail operates trains for pre-booked groups of more than 40 people. For more details, check the situation with the SAE or at 💻 www.perurail.com.

See p301 for details of current timetables and prices.

Cusco
(Qosqo, Cuzco)

What remains with you is the sense of a great outrage, magnificent but unforgivable. The Spaniards tore down the Inca temples and grafted splendid churches and mansions onto their foundations. This is one of the most beautiful monuments to bigotry and sheer stupid brutality in the whole world. **Christopher Isherwood**, *The Condor and the Cows*, 1948.

Cusco was the capital of the Incas, the cultural and religious focus of the empire. Today it's the focus for almost all visitors to Peru but it's much more than a tourist town. With a population of almost 300,000 it's a large commercial centre and the administrative capital of Cusco department.

Cusco is 3360m (11,000ft) above sea level, and the air is thin here. When you first arrive, don't do anything too energetic: take a couple of days to acclimatize.

HISTORY

It's difficult to know much for certain about Cusco's origins because there is no written record of Peruvian history before the arrival of the Spanish, and there are very few recorded oral histories of the times before the rise of the Incas.

The Huari and the Killke

What *is* known is that before the Incas the great culture known as Huari dominated the Cusco valley. The area around Cusco and the sacred valley of the Urubamba were part of the highland frontier of the Huari state. The Huari declined and withdrew to their capital west of Cusco. The local people, the Killke, were left to their own devices, building hilltop defences throughout the area.

One place where the Killke did not build their forts was in the Cusco valley itself. This makes archaeologists think that it wasn't necessary to build fortifications around Cusco, suggesting that by about the 12th century there were settlements in Cusco already stable, secure and strong enough to deter attacks from outsiders. The Incas had taken them over by about the 13th century.

The capital of the Incas

Cusco in the days of its glory as the capital of the Incas must have been a magnificent sight. The seat of the god-king, the Inca, it was a city constructed to reflect the might of the empire. Walls were sheathed in gold, something which was imposing enough to impress even the Spanish thugs sent by Pizarro to gather loot for Atahualpa's ransom (see p101). One was sufficiently moved to write to the king: 'The city is the greatest and finest seen in either this country or anywhere in the Indies. We can assure Your Majesty that it is so beautiful and has such fine buildings that it would be worthy of notice even in Spain.'

Cusco was impressive not only because it was built from fine dressed stone and covered in precious metals. It had also been built with an understanding of the infrastructure a city needs and boasted channels providing running water and sewerage making it cleaner and more healthy than any European city. Such cleanliness did not survive the conquest, and another Spaniard wrote: 'now there are large piles of garbage on the banks [of the river Huatanay]. It is full of dung and filth. It was not like this in the days of the Incas, when it was clean and the water ran over stones. The Incas sometimes went there to bathe with their women.'

The city was not only the seat of political power, but also the cultural and religious centre of the empire. The cardinal roads to each *suyu* of the Inca empire led out from the main square, and sacred religious lines from spiritual places converged on the Coricancha. All roads led to Cusco, and the *ceques* pointed towards Cusco.

Construction and destruction

Despite the vast amount of work that clearly went into Cusco's construction, legend has it that the city was built on the orders of one man alone: the Inca Pachacutec (see p87). He tore down Cusco's old humble buildings shortly after seizing power and ordered them to be replaced with a stone city. Some say that Pachacutec designed Cusco to look like a puma, a sacred animal of the Incas. The river Tullumayo formed the spine of the puma, the river Huatanay the belly, and the fortress or temple mound of Sacsayhuaman made the puma's head.

But the Cusco of Pachacutec has been lost to us although you can still make out the puma, and we see only a pale imitation of past splendours. The magnificent gold was torn off by the greedy hands of the Spanish, and in the siege of Cusco the whole city was burnt when rebel Incas put it to the torch in a desperate attempt to smoke out the Spanish invaders (see p104).

Cusco after the conquest

After the conquistadors secured Peru for the king of Spain, they needed to found a capital. They were dependent on the sea for communications and reinforcements so Cusco was not a suitable place to set up government. Francisco Pizarro therefore founded his capital on the coast, in 1535. From this point, Cusco's influence began to wane.

The town itself was largely rebuilt by the Spanish on old Inca foundations, re-using the snug Inca stonework pillaged from many sites including the massive Sacsayhuaman. The Spanish work is less strong than that of the Incas, as shown by the occasional serious earthquake that shakes colonial buildings to the ground leaving their Inca foundations standing. The monastery of Santo Domingo (which is built over Coricancha) has pictures showing that exactly this happened in the 1950 earthquake.

Throughout the following centuries Cusco was overshadowed by Lima, but it did enjoy brief flashes of its former importance. It was the centre of rebellion in 1780 when José Gabriel Condorcanqui, also called Tupac Amaru II, rose against the Spanish, and again in 1825 when Bolívar himself arrived and set up camp. The royal oath of independence was sworn by Peru's first Prefect, Garmarra, before the cathedral's *Señor de los Tremblores* (see opposite), and in the 17th and 18th centuries, the city's artists distinguished themselves in creating the famous Cusco School of painting.

With the rebirth of interest in the ancient civilizations of Peru, the discovery of Machu Picchu in 1911 and the development of the subsequent tourist trade Cusco re-emerged as one of Peru's principal cities.

WHAT TO SEE

Plaza de Armas

Just as it is today, the main square was a focal point for the people of Cusco in the time of the Incas, but it used to be twice as big. Plaza de Armas was once called Aucaypata ('the square of war or weeping') and was a ceremonial area enclosed on three sides by the imposing mansions of the Inca. The other side of the river Huatanay, which ran down one side of Aucaypata in a stone ditch, was Cusipata ('the joyful square') where Plaza Regocijo and its surrounding buildings now stand. Cusipata was the square of celebration, and a Spaniard described being there on a feast day when so much chicha (corn beer) was drunk that the drainage ditch overflowed with pure urine; to this day, the gutters and flagstones of Plaza de Armas are regularly awash on festival days.

☐ Boleto Turístico Único (BTU) – Visitor's Ticket

To visit many of Cusco's museums and archaeological sites you'll have to buy the Boleto Turístico Único (BTU or Visitor's Ticket), which costs s/70 (approx US$21; half price for students with a valid ISIC card) and must be paid for in soles. It is valid for 10 days and is sold at the **Oficina Ejecutiva del Comité** (OFEC; Monday to Saturday 8am-5pm and Sunday 8am-2pm) on the corner of Garcilaso and Plaza Regocijo, at the Centro Artesanal by Huanchac Station, or at any of the sites included in the ticket. The ticket allows only one entrance to each of the 16 sites it covers – tiresome if you want to go back. Note that the ticket does not cover the Coricancha-Santo Domingo complex, merely the small (and rather dull) museum in the grounds whose entrance is on Av El Sol. The BTU Visitor's Ticket allows you entry to these sites:

Sacsayhuaman	Pachacutec Monument
Pikillacta	Popular Art Museum
Tipón	Municipal Museum of Contemporary Art
Ollantaytambo	Regional History Museum
Pisac	Chinchero ruins
Qenko	Santa Catalina Museum
Puca Pucara	Centre of Native Dance
Tambo Machay	Coricancha Museum (not the complex)

Religious sites ticket

There is a separate ticket for the Cathedral, the Church at San Blas and the Museum of Religious Art, which costs s/15 at OFEC and the locations mentioned above.

❏ The Virgin saves the Spanish

During the siege of Cusco, the Spanish were at one stage cornered in the Suntur Huasi or round house (where the Triunfo church is now). The roof of this building was thatched, and the Incas aimed a hail of red-hot stones from their slings at the straw until the roof caught fire.

What happened next depends on who you want to believe. The Spanish said that they were protected by divine intervention. The Virgin Mary appeared, joined by Saint James (the patron saint of the Spanish Army) and sprinkled water on the flames to douse the fire, and save the Spaniards. The Incas, on the other hand, remarked that the Spanish had positioned some of their auxiliaries on the roof to beat out the fire.

Mary douses the flames
FELIPE HUAMÁN POMA DE AYALA (c1590)

Cathedral

(Monday to Wednesday and Friday to Saturday 10-11.30am and 2-5.30pm, Thursday 12-6pm, Sunday 2-6pm, entrance through the church of Jesús María is s/10 or with a Religious Sites Ticket.) Built between 1556 and 1669 in the Renaissance style, the cathedral nestles between the church of **Jesús María** (1733) on its right and on its left **El Triunfo** (1536), the site of Cusco's first church and the resting place of the historian, El Inca Garcilaso de la Vega. All three buildings are currently undergoing restoration, and for this reason certain sections may be closed off, and paintings removed when you visit. The cathedral is probably built on the site of Inca Viracocha's palace, and the next-door Triunfo is built on the site of the Suntur Huasi, where the Spaniards hid during the siege of Cusco.

The floor plan of the cathedral is a Latin cross with added processional aisles and ambulatories. It's filled with wonders, from the carvings of alder and cedarwood by Martín Torres and Melchor Huamán (don't miss the minute detail on the choir), to the sacristy, filled with portraits of past bishops of Cusco. The blackened crucifix, generally kept halfway down on the right, is the *Señor de los Tremblores* (Lord of the Earthquakes, currently in the Triunfo), which was paraded around Cusco to stop the 1650 quake. It worked and this example of particularly Andean religiosity is commemorated in a painting that currently stands facing the entrance to the Triunfo.

There's also a very famous painting in here of the Last Supper, by Marcos Zapata, at which Christ and his disciples are shown feasting on cuy (guinea pig). However, during the current building renovations it's occasionally covered or put into storage.

CUSCO & AROUND

Loyala captures Tupac Amaru
FELIPE HUAMÁN POMA DE AYALA (c1590)

The Compañía (Jesuits' Church)

(No set opening hours; admission free). This is the other massive church on Plaza de Armas. The Jesuits wanted it to be more imposing than the cathedral but the Pope intervened to stop them just before they finished. The two buildings are so very similar it's a close-run thing, though in *Deep Rivers* the writer José María Arguedas came down with the Jesuits: 'Instead of being overpowering, it made me rejoice. I felt like singing in the doorway...the Cathedral was too big.'

Work began in 1578, but the structure was practically demolished by the 1650 earthquake, and the church wasn't finished until 1668. It is a single nave design and was built on the palace of the Inca Huayna Capac, described by chronicler Pedro Sancho as the greatest of the Incas' palaces on the square with its red and white gateway ornamented with precious metal.

One of its most interesting paintings, which hangs by the door, represents the marriage of Martín García de Loyola to Ñusta (Princess) Beatriz. Loyola was the nephew of the Jesuits' founder, St Ignatius, but he was also the gallant captain who hunted down the last Inca, Tupac Amaru. Beatriz was of royal Inca blood, and the marriage of the two was highly significant for the Jesuits because it associated them with this symbolic union of Spain and Peru, so Loyola's and Beatriz's noble forbears look on approvingly at the union.

Other sights around Plaza de Armas

● **Museum of Natural History** (Monday to Friday 9.30am-12 noon and 3-6pm, s/1). The museum is housed in a little building to the right of the Compañía. It's not very informative but is worth a visit if only to see the horrors it contains: a two-headed alpaca, a two-headed guinea pig, a six-legged goat and a frog the size of two clenched fists.

● **Inca walls** The wall on the north-western side of the plaza is probably the remains of the Inca Pachacutec's palace, and the northern corner of the square is the site of the palace of the Inca Sinchi Roca.

Coricancha (Temple of the Sun) and Santo Domingo

(About 500m south-east of Plaza de Armas; open Monday to Saturday 8.30am-5.30pm, Sunday 2-4pm s/6, s/4 students – not on the Visitor Ticket). The Coricancha was the centre of Inca religion. It was lavishly decorated, even by the standards of ancient Cusco. The Inca historian Garcilaso de la Vega, writing 50 years after the fall of the Inca Empire, described the interior: 'In the walls of the rooms giving on to the cloister, four tabernacles were hollowed out in each of the outside walls... They had mouldings round the edges and in the hollows of the tabernacles, and as these mouldings were worked in the stone they were inlaid with gold plates not only at the top and sides, but also the floors of the tabernacles. The edges of the mouldings were encrusted with fine stones, emeralds and turquoises, for diamonds and rubies were unknown there. The Inca sat in these tabernacles when there were festivals in honour of the Sun.' The Spaniards stole the lot.

The Corincancha consisted of a number of chapels dedicated to different deities: the Rainbow, Thunder and, of course, the Sun himself. The kidnapped idols of subdued tribes were kept hostage in the temple and if the tribe stepped out of line the idols were ridiculed and then destroyed.

Outside the temple was the garden, in which the Incas displayed some of the most astounding of their goldwork. Garcilaso describes what it contained: 'That garden, which now serves the monastery with vegetables, was in Inca times a garden of gold and silver such as existed in the royal palaces. It contained many herbs and flowers of various kinds, small plants, large trees, animals great and small, tame and wild, and creeping things such as snakes and lizards, and snails, butterflies and birds, each placed in an imitation of its natural surroundings.' He goes on to describe a field of golden maize and statues of men, women and children. Most, of course, did not escape the greedy Spanish furnaces.

After the Spaniards' triumphant entry into Cusco, Coricancha was given to Juan Pizarro but he didn't have long to enjoy it. He was mortally wounded at the siege of Sacsayhuaman and on his deathbed gave it to the Dominicans (the priest, Vincente Valverde, who accompanied the Pizarros was a Dominican), who built the monastery of Santo Domingo in its stead as a symbolic gesture of Christianity's superiority over the native religion. In 1950, however, an earthquake flattened the monastery, leaving the fantastic Inca masonry unmoved.

The monastery of Santo Domingo is worth a visit too, with a splendid carving of Santo Domingo by Melchor Huamán and the graves of the rebel Incas Sayri Tupac and Tupac Amaru and of Juan Pizarro himself. There is an underground Coricancha **museum** in the grounds (entrance via Av El Sol, Visitor's Ticket, 9am-5.30pm).

West and south of Plaza de Armas

This is the area south of Plateros, and north of Av El Sol behind the Portales de Comercio and Confiturías.

● **La Merced** (daily except Sundays, 9am-12 noon, 3-5pm s/3.5, s/2 students). Built in 1534 and then rebuilt after the 1650 earthquake, La Merced rivals the cathedral in its riches and has particularly beautiful cloisters. It faces the old Indian market, which allowed the clergy inside the church to preach to the milling crowds outside. Both Almagros are buried here, as is Gonzalo Pizarro. This is another monument that was undergoing restoration at the time of writing.

● **San Francisco Church** (Monday to Friday 6.30-8am, 6-8pm, s/3.5). Austere and with rather bloodthirsty decoration, this church and monastery, dating from the 16th and 17th centuries, dominates the square outside. There are two bone-filled crypts within the church.

● **Santa Clara Church** (free) The church isn't often open, but if you're lucky enough to get inside you'll find wall-to-ceiling angled mirrors which multiply a hundredfold the candlelight. When I visited, a woman was singing in a mournful, high-pitched, mesmeric wail which made the whole place feel like another world.

● **Regional History Museum and House of Garcilaso** (Monday to Saturday, 8am-5pm, entrance by Visitor's Ticket). The museum has an overview of Peruvian history with some interesting exhibits such as a Nazca mummy, and a collection of paintings of the Cusco School. Look for St Michael armed with a gun. The house itself was rebuilt by the famous Peruvian architect, Víctor Pimentel, after it almost collapsed in the 1986 earthquake.

● **Market** Bustling, smelly, noisy, and filled with fat women in large hats carving dripping hunks of meat or spooning multi-coloured beans from huge sacks. All the world's goods are here, such as living frogs and skinned dead ones being sold amongst the piles of fresh fruit. A must – but be careful of your wallet and watch out for bag slashers.

● **Santa Teresa** (unpredictable opening hours, free) A pleasant church with illustrations of Saint Teresa's life inside, but the outside of the building gets used as a public toilet, so hold your nose. The square in front of the church is pretty, and the wall bordering Calle Saphi is a marvellous example of polygonal field-stone masonry.

East of Plaza de Armas

This is the arc of streets south of Triunfo and north of Av El Sol, behind the Compañía.

● **Calle Loreto** Another famous Inca alley, leading off Plaza de Armas, the left-hand wall of which used to be the Acllahuasi (see p94).

● **Banco Wiese**, Calle Maruri (free, open when the bank is). The bank occupies the palace of Tupac Inca Yupanqui, with its wonderful Inca walls. There's a little museum inside telling you about the history of the building and exhibiting some of the artefacts found here.

● **Religious Art Museum and Archbishop's Palace** (Monday to Saturday 8am-5.30pm, Sunday 2-5.30pm, s/5 or free with Religious Sites Ticket). This building is in **Hatun Rumiyoc**, an alley which was originally the side of the palace of the Inca Roca. The wall contains the famous twelve-angled stone that you can see on every bottle of Cusqueña beer and which has become an enduring symbol of the city. The museum has a fine collection of religious paintings from the Cusco School and the colonial building founded on Inca remains is impressive. A small street runs along the back wall of the palace, featuring more outstanding Inca stonework and hidden in the intricately shaped blocks is the outline of a puma.

● **Convent and Museum of Santa Catalina** (Saturday to Thursday, 9am-5.30pm, Friday 8am-4pm, Visitor's Ticket). The museum is small and uninspiring, filled with some religious art and a couple of fairly interesting models. However, the proportions of the interior of the building are quite beautiful, especially by the stairs up to the first floor internal balcony.

❏ CUSCO – WALKING TOURS
West

Start your tour in **Plaza de Armas**, and face south-west. Walk down the small alley (Medio) towards Plaza Regocijo. To your right is the **Town Hall**, and the road which leads uphill (north or right) from the square leads to the church of Santa Teresa (see opposite), while on the other side of the square (downhill, left and south) there's the **Regional History Museum** (see opposite) in the reconstructed house of Garcilaso de la Vega. Head south-west down Garcilaso, the street that leads away from the square directly opposite the road on which you entered the square.

Walk one block further down here and you'll reach Plaza San Francisco, with the **Monastery of San Francisco** on the opposite side (see p135). The bottom corner of this square (south) is Santa Clara leading to the convent of the same name (see opposite), and ultimately the **market** and **railway station** for Machu Picchu. Be careful around here as the area is notorious for muggings and bag slashings.

Return to Plaza de Armas along Santa Clara.

South and east

Start in **Plaza de Armas** and face La Compañía. Walk south-east (downhill) through **Calle Loreto** (see opposite), and turn left at the end when you arrive in Maruri. Visit the **Banco Wiese**, and turn right at the end of the block down Romeritos until you reach a little square where the **Hotel Libertador** is situated. In front of you, slightly to your right, is the **Coricancha and Santo Domingo monastery** (see p134).

From Coricancha, go back up Romeritos to Maruri, then turn right and then left again up San Agustin. The fourth road on your right is **Hatun Rumiyoc** (see opposite), and on the corner is the **Religious Art Museum**.

Turning right, and walking down Hatun Rumiyoc will take you up to **San Blas**, and walking the other way back towards Plaza de Armas leads past the road in which there's the **Convent and Museum of Santa Catalina** (see opposite).

North

Stand in **Plaza de Armas** and face Sacsayhuaman. Walk up the little alley of Procuradores (also known as Gringo Alley or Pizza St) to the north-west. At the end, turn right, then left again and climb up Coricalle. At the end of Coricalle turn right, and you'll soon be on a large paved road.

Walk to the right uphill on the road, and you'll pass the church of **San Cristóbal** (see p138) on your left. Just before the church, turn right and walk downhill, down Resbalosa, savouring the view down towards Cusco. Turn left at the junction of Resbalosa and Waynapata, and continue along to Punacurco (which means 'puma's spine', a reference to the fact that the street plan of Cusco was originally designed to resemble a puma). Soon you'll arrive at a small square, the sides of which are graced by the **House of the Serpents**, **Cabrera's House** and the **Seminary of San Antonio Abad**, now a hotel (see p138).

If you turn right, heading back towards Plaza de Armas, you'll walk down a street called Cordoba del Tucumán, past **Museo Inka** (see p138) and end up back on the plaza.

CUSCO & AROUND

● **San Blas** (Monday to Saturday 10am-6pm, Sunday 2-6pm, entrance s/5 or free with Religious Sites Ticket) is a simple adobe church, but it contains a breathtaking carved cedarwood pulpit. At the top stands St Paul, his foot resting on a human skull, believed to belong to the craftsman who made the pulpit. The area around is the ancient district of Cusco's artisans.

North of Plaza de Armas

This covers the arc of streets between Plateros and Triunfo, under the shadow of Sacsayhuaman.

● **San Cristóbal Church** (free, no set opening times) stands proudly high above Cusco, its grounds enclosed by a massive Inca wall that is possibly the remains of the palace of the first Inca, Manco Capac. The church was built by the quisling, Inca Paullu, as a demonstration of his Christian faith.

● **Museo Inka (Archaeology)** and **Admiral's Palace**. This is on the corner of Ataud and Tucumán (Monday to Friday 8am-5pm, Saturday 9am-4pm, s/10). The museum's collection is well displayed and informative with leaflets in English. They also have some Inca gold though you might have to ask to see it, and some paintings. A particularly gory *Execution of Atahualpa* shows his head being cut off (it wasn't, he was garrotted and then partly burnt). Look out too for the reconstructed burial chamber, or Mallkiwasi. The impressive buildings belonged to Admiral Don Francisco Maldonado. It was badly damaged by an earthquake in 1650 but rebuilt and remains an imposing colonial building.

● **House of the Serpents** Legend has it that this house on Plazoleta de las Nazarenas was owned by the man who stole the golden disc of the Sun from the Coricancha, then gambled it away playing cards. It's called the House of the Serpents because of the carved snakes on its stones, and such ornamentation indicates it's a Spanish construction not an Inca one.

● **Museo de Arte Precolombino/Cabrera's House** Cabrera founded Ica on the coast and also Córdoba in Argentina, and his house on Plazoleta de las Nazarenas is an interesting colonial mansion with his coat of arms on the façade, its large salons and spacious interior patio graced with arches. The house has recently been converted into the **Museo de Arte Precolombino** (**MAP**; daily 9am-11pm, s/16), dedicated to the artistic achievements of the ancient cultures of Peru. The museum houses a fascinating collection of pieces from the Moche, Chimú, Paracas, Nazca and Inca cultures, including carvings, ceramics, gold- and silver- work, all of which are expertly lit and accompanied by English and Spanish text.

● **Seminary of San Antonio Abad** This is now Hotel Monasterio (see p148), which makes it easy to visit if you put on your clean clothes and are prepared to pay their prices for a beer. The open courtyards are spoilt by glassed-in cloisters, but it's a splendid building.

PRACTICAL INFORMATION
Arrival

Take a couple of days to acclimatize when you first arrive. Acclimatization is easier if you don't overeat and avoid smoking and alcohol.

A note of caution Cusco has a bad but deserved reputation for robbery. The area around San Pedro station and the market can be a hot spot, as is the San Blas district. Be careful when you walk around, especially when arriving and leaving. See p63 for more details.

By air The airport is about a five-minute taxi ride (2km) from Plaza de Armas. A taxi to the plaza will cost about s/10 from the airport car park, and s/6 from the road outside, because there is a fee *taxistas* (taxi drivers) have to pay to get into the compound. Walking to the plaza would take you about 40 minutes, but I wouldn't recommend it (see 'A note of caution' opposite).

By rail The train from Puno arrives at **Huanchac station**, which is at the south-eastern end of Av El Sol, 20 minutes' walk from the centre of town. The train from Machu Picchu and Ollantaytambo arrives at **San Pedro station** (also called Machu Picchu station) which is just by the church of San Pedro, 10 minutes' walk from the south-west of the plaza.

By bus Long-distance buses will bring you to the bus terminal, which is close to the statue of Pachacutec to the south-east of town, near the airport. Take a taxi to the centre – it'll cost about s/10.

Getting around
Taxis in Cusco are much better than they were in the past; they should charge a flat fare of s/2 for a trip anywhere in the centre (except to the airport), or s/3 after 9pm, though if they see you've just arrived, they might just forget this. You can flag them down on almost any street, or find them around Plaza de Armas. There have, however, been reports of taxi drivers robbing people; the safest thing would be to arrange a taxi through your hotel so that they know who you're going off with. A reliable firm with licensed drivers is Aló Cusco (☎ 222222). Other forms of transport are the communal **colectivos** which are cheaper if much less comfortable than taxis.

If you're on a bigger budget you may want to hire a **car**. Try **Avis** (☎ 248800) at Av El Sol 808, ⌨ avis-cusco@terra.com.pe, with cars from US$25 per day, or **Localiza** (☎ 242285/263448, ⌨ localiz@mail.cosapidata.com.pe), Av El Sol 1089. You've got to be over 25 to drive a hire car, and the daily rates vary from company to company. Fuel's extra.

Orientation
Central Cusco is small and set out almost on a grid, with Plaza de Armas pretty much in the middle. If you stand by the fountain in the plaza and look up at the figure of Jesus (north), the hill to Jesus' right is the hill of Sacsayhuaman (north-west). Between Sacsayhuaman and the plaza is a district of steep streets and cheap hotels. Between Jesus and you is the cathedral and the district of San Blas, while behind you (east and south) is the Compañía and Av El Sol which leads to Huanchac station, the indoor souvenir market (see p152) and the airport. Jesus is looking almost to the south-west, towards the market and San Pedro station.

Wandering around Cusco, you'll notice a rainbow flag hanging from houses, shops and bars. It looks very much like the gay and lesbian banner but the flag's actually the emblem of the Quechua and is a different design, though only slightly, bearing as it does an extra blue line.

Banks and cambios
Most banks are on Av El Sol. Long queues are common and counters close at 1pm, opening again between 4pm and 6pm, but you can withdraw US dollars or soles from ATMs around the clock. You'll find more ATMs around Plaza de Armas and about town generally.

BCP (Visa), Av El Sol 189; **Interbank** (Visa), Av El Sol 380; **Banco Continental** (Visa), Av El Sol 366; **Banco Latino** (Mastercard), Av El Sol 395; **Banco Wiese**, Calle Maruri 315, charges the lowest commission when changing travellers' cheques but is slow.

There are **cambios** all over Cusco, and it's difficult to pick out any one over the other. Those on the western side of Plaza de Armas tend to charge slightly higher commission than those on Av El Sol. **Multitours**, Av El Sol 314 (☎ 236946), exchange Visa, Thomas Cook

❏ Tour agencies

Over the last few years the Peruvian government has been bringing in rules to regulate access to the Inca Trail. The rules are designed to reduce the environmental impact of thousands of trekkers and are now strictly enforced, so it's important that you're familiar with them; for details refer to the 'Inca Trail Regulations' box on p182. It's now prohibited to trek in the Machu Picchu Historical Sanctuary without a licensed guide and a trekking permit, both of which you'll have to get via an approved and licensed tour agency. The rules apply to most of the trails in this book, but not the Vilcambamba, Choquequirao or Santa Teresa treks; theoretically you can also hike the first parts of the Mollepata walk or the Chilca walk, as long as you don't end up at Machu Picchu.

The UGM (Unidad Gestión Machu Picchu) is the government authority responsible for granting licences to agencies, allowing them to lead tours within the Sanctuary. At the time of writing there were over 150 licensed agencies, all of which are listed on p306. If past history's anything to go by, this number's likely to change, so before you hand over any money, ask to see the company's paperwork.

The prices for hiking the Inca Trails run from about US$240 to whatever you're willing to pay. Realistically, you should expect to pay US$270-350. Some operators say their prices are 'estimates': don't fall for that. Get a fixed price.

The licence supposedly ensures that an agency has good equipment, offers adequate standards of service and employs properly qualified guides. But the cheaper deals aren't necessarily the best value, particularly on treks not covered by the regulations. Cut-price operators might bus you in and out of an area, leaving you with half-a-dozen other groups and an ill-informed guide who hardly speaks Spanish, let alone English. They also have a reputation for not clearing away their litter, not caring a fig about the environment, and treating their porters appallingly. And their equipment's likely to be dodgy. And the food's likely to be terrible. And transfers are probably not included in the price.

The days of just pitching up in Cusco and walking the Inca Trail are gone. At the very slowest times of year, you might be lucky and find a place within a week, but on the whole, you'll have to reserve your place weeks in advance; some agencies even advise booking at least three months in advance for treks in the high season (June to August), particularly if you're inflexible about dates. Most people, therefore, will have made their reservations for the Inca Trail long before they arrive in Cusco, and will have already given the tour company their passport details, and paid a deposit.

Those that do arrive on spec shouldn't expect to find spaces for the Inca Trail, but will be able to make arrangements to do the Santa Teresa trek (which actually finishes at Machu Picchu), or the Vilcambamba and Choquequirao treks at short notice. Many agencies also offer walks around the Ausangate circuit and the Lares valley, white-water rafting, mountain biking and trips down into the jungle in the Manu National Park.

and AMEX travellers' cheques. **DHL/Western Unión** (☎ 224167) is at Av El Sol 627A and Maruri 310 (☎ 248028).

Save up your **small-denomination notes and coins** before leaving Cusco: the towns and villages in the mountains seem to suffer from even more of a shortage of small change than the rest of Peru.

Bookshops

Many of the tourist shops on Portal de Comercio and Portal de Confiturías sell books; the best is **Special Book Service** (SBS) Av El Sol 781, opposite the post office, and **Librería Jerusalén**, Heladeros 143. **Los Andes**, Portal Comercio 125, also specializes in them.

Tour agencies (cont'd)

At the upper end of the price scale charging upwards of US$350 are the exclusive **Condor Travel** (☎ 225961, 🖥 www.condortravel.com.pe), Calle Saphi 848A; the long-established **Explorandes**, (☎ 238380; 🖥 www.explorandes.com), Av Garcilaso 316-A; the accomplished newcomer **Inka Natura** (☎ 243408, 🖥 www.inkanatura .com), Calle Ricardo Palma J-1, Urb Santa Monica; the old-handers **Inca Explorers** (☎ 241070, 🖥 www.incaexplorers.com), Calle Ruinas 427; and the frequently recommended **Peruvian Andean Treks** (☎ 225701, 🖥 www.andeantreks.com), Av Pardo 705, who also specialize in local mountaineering.

Mid-priced agencies (around US$300-350), which also offer a high standard of service, include the proficiently run **Andean Life** (☎ 221491, 🖥 www.andean life.com) at Plateros 372; the small but highly professional **Peru Treks and Adventure** (☎ 805863, 🖥 www.perutreks.com) at Calle Garcilaso 265, Office 11, 2nd Floor, who are also heavily involved in community projects and plough half their profits into schemes aimed at benefiting local people; upmarket **Q'ente** (☎ 238245, 🖥 www.qente.com), Calle Garcilaso 210; and **SAS Travel** (☎ 243050, 🖺 225757, 🖥 www.sastravelperu.com), on Calle del Medio 123 and Portal de Panes 167, Plaza de Armas (☎ 237292), a well-organized outfit that tries to limit group sizes to less than eight people. **United Mice** (☎ 221139, 🖥 www.unitedmice.com), Calle Plateros 351, have long been popular for inexpensive tours, but they've recently hiked their rates up to $350; they are still worth checking out though.

At the least costly end of the market (less than US$300) is the cheap and cheerful **Wayki Trek**, (☎ 224092, 🖥 www.waykitrek.net), Procuradores 351, a recommended agency and one of the few to run trips to Vilcabamaba. The popular **Liz's Explorer** (☎ 246619, 🖥 www.lizexplorer.com), Calle del Medio 114B operates a competent budget service.

For the jungle, **Manu Expeditions** (☎ 226671, 🖺 236706, 🖥 www.manuexpe ditions.com), Urb Magisterio, 2nd Floor G-5, run by the expert ornithologist Barry Walker, have a good reputation, as do the excellent **Pantiacolla Tours** (☎ 238323, 🖥 www.pantiacolla.com), Plateros 360, who promote environmental and social initiatives within the Manu reserve.

For horse-riding around the archaeological sites near Cusco choose **The Corcel Ranch** (☎ 245878, ask for Hernán), Procuradores 351; it's s/20 for a trip that takes about four hours. For adventurous mountain bikers or those looking to access the jungle region of the northern Urubamba or Pongo de Mainique, **Eco Trek Peru** (☎ 253653, 🖥 www.ecotrekperu.com), Choquechaca 229, is a reputable and environmentally friendly agency.

Disabled travellers should contact **Apumayo Expeditions** (☎ 246018, 🖥 www .apumayo.com), Calle Garcilaso 265, Interior Office 3, who run special tours to Machu Picchu and Tambopata, and specialize in white-water rafting trips.

Communications

● **Telephone and fax** Cusco's telephone code is ☎ 84. There are public pay phones everywhere, and it's easy to ring abroad with a Telefónica phonecard that can be bought from most of the small shops lining Plaza de Armas. Alternatively, you can get someone else to do it for you at **Telser** (☎ 242424; they also send and receive faxes), Calle de Medio 117, or the central **Telefónica del Perú** on Av El Sol 382. Remember that you can also phone via the Internet from some Internet cafés.

● **Post** For letters, the **correo** (daily 7.30am-8pm, ☎ 224212), is at Av El Sol

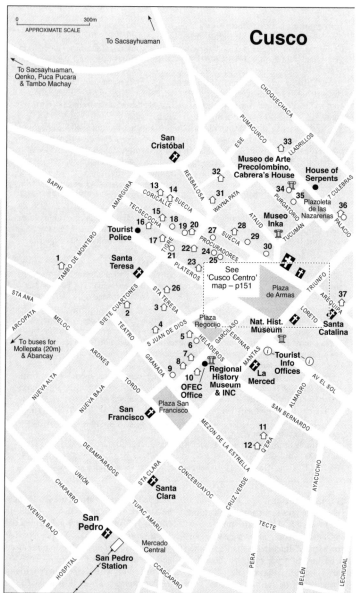

0   300m
APPROXIMATE SCALE

Cusco

To Sacsayhuaman

To Sacsayhuaman,
Qenko, Puca Pucara
& Tambo Machay

CHOQUECHACA

PUMACURCO

ESE

LLADRILLOS

33

San
Cristóbal

Museo de Arte
Precolombino,
Cabrera's House

House of
Serpents

7 CULEBRAS

34

35

SAPHI

RESBALOSA

32

PURGATORIO

Plazoleta
de las
Nazarenas

36

PALACIO

13   14

CORICALLE

SUECIA

31

WAYNA PATA

ATAUD

Museo
Inka

AMARGURA

TECSECOCHA

15

18

Tourist
Police

16

19 20

27

28

SUECIA

29

TUCUMÁN

TORE

17

22

PROCURADORES

24

30

TIGRE

21

25

Santa
Teresa

23

PLATEROS

See
'Cusco Centro'
map – p151

TRIUNFO

37

STA ANA

ARCOPATA

MELOC

SIETE CUARTONES

STA TERESA

26

Plaza
de Armas

LORETO

AREQUIPA

Santa
Catalina

To buses for
Mollepata (20m)
& Abancay

ARDNES

TEATRO

2

3

S JUAN DE DIOS

4

Plaza
Regocijo

GARCILASO

ESPINAR

Nat. Hist.
Museum

NUEVA ALTA

GRANADA

TORDO

5

6

7

HELADEROS

MANTAS

Tourist
Info
Offices

NUEVA BAJA

8

9

10

OFEC
Office

Regional
History
Museum
& INC

La
Merced

ALMAGRO

AV EL SOL

San
Francisco

Plaza San
Francisco

MEZON DE LA ESTRELLA

SAN BERNARDO

DESAMPARADOS

UNIÓN

CHAPARRO

Santa
Clara

STA CLARA

CONCEBIDAYOC

11

12

QERA

AYACUCHO

CRUZ VERDE

San
Pedro

TUPAC AMARU

TECTE

AVENIDA BAJO

HOSPITAL

San Pedro
Station

Mercado
Central

CCASCAPARO

PERA

BELEN

LECHUGAL

CUSCO & AROUND

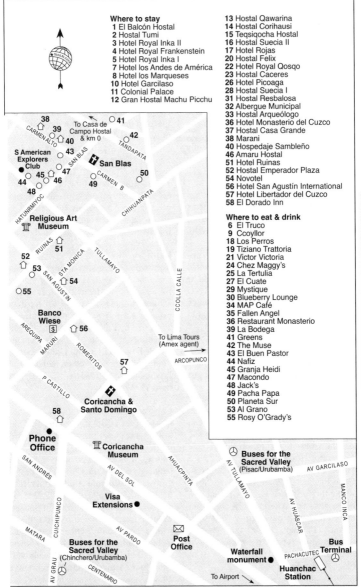

Where to stay
1 El Balcón Hostal
2 Hostal Tumi
3 Hotel Royal Inka II
4 Hotel Royal Frankenstein
5 Hotel Royal Inka I
7 Hotel los Andes de América
8 Hotel los Marqueses
10 Hotel Garcilaso
11 Colonial Palace
12 Gran Hostal Machu Picchu
13 Hostal Qawarina
14 Hostal Corihausi
15 Teqsiqocha Hostal
16 Hostal Suecia II
17 Hotel Rojas
20 Hostal Felix
22 Hotel Royal Qosqo
23 Hostal Caceres
26 Hotel Picoaga
28 Hostal Suecia I
31 Hostal Resbalosa
32 Albergue Municipal
33 Hostal Arqueólogo
36 Hotel Monasterio del Cuzco
37 Hostal Casa Grande
38 Marani
40 Hospedaje Sambleño
46 Amaru Hostal
51 Hotel Ruinas
52 Hostal Emperador Plaza
54 Novotel
56 Hotel San Agustín International
57 Hotel Libertador del Cuzco
58 El Dorado Inn

Where to eat & drink
6 El Truco
9 Ccoyllor
18 Los Perros
19 Tiziano Trattoria
21 Victor Victoria
24 Chez Maggy's
25 La Tertulia
27 El Cuate
29 Mystique
30 Blueberry Lounge
34 MAP Café
35 Fallen Angel
36 Restaurant Monasterio
39 La Bodega
41 Greens
42 The Muse
43 El Buen Pastor
44 Nafiz
45 Granja Heidi
47 Macondo
48 Jack's
49 Pacha Papa
50 Planeta Sur
53 Al Grano
55 Rosy O'Grady's

CUSCO & AROUND

800, six blocks downhill from Plaza de Armas. **DHL**, Av Sol 627, is useful if you are sending packages overseas.

● **Email** You won't have any trouble finding an Internet café – they're everywhere and they all charge about s/2 per hour. All of them are pretty good and many have scanners, webcams and CD burners. Four to recommend are: **Mundo Net** (Santa Teresa 344), which has fast, reliable machines; **Telser** (Calle del Medio 117), which is also reliable; the friendly **Internet Station** (Tecsecocha 422); and **Trotamundos** (Portal Comercio 177), which is also a very pleasant café.

Emergencies and medical services
Fire ☎ 103; **Police**: ☎ 105; **Tourist Police**: ☎ 249654 (24 hours), Saphi 510, and an office on Plaza de Armas at Portal Carrizos 250, near the Compañía (9am-6pm), very helpful; **Hospitals**: Regional ☎ 231131, IPSS ☎ 221581, Lorena ☎ 226511; **Tourist Medical Assistance** ☎ 222644/621838 (24 hours). **Pharmacy** (☎ 245351), Calle Helaredos 109 (24 hours), and Inka Farma (☎ 242601), Av El Sol 174 (24 hours).

Equipment rental
Camping equipment can be hired at most of the tour agencies on Plateros and Procuradores, but do check the quality because some of it is pretty ropy. Butane and butane-propane gas cylinders can also be obtained at these places, or at one of the tourist shops on Portal de Comercio. However, the best place for all of this is **Soqllaq'asa** (☎ 252560), Calle Plateros 365, on the second floor, where they will also buy equipment you no longer need. Alternatively, check out the outdoor and travel equipment shop **Tatoo**, at Plazoleta de las Nazarenas 201.

For **shoe repair**, try Elmer at 270 Matara, down the hill to the south-east of Plaza de San Francisco.

Hiking provisions
There's a good supermarket on the corner of Almagro and Av El Sol, another at Plateros 346, and the market opposite San Pedro station.

Film and camera shops
It would be much wiser to take your films home to be developed but if you can't wait, there is a string of film shops that also do developing on the first block of Av El Sol down from Plaza de Armas, on the west side of the road, such as Sandy Color, as well as around the plaza itself. Nishiyama, at Triunfo 346 and Mantas 109, is one of the better developers and slightly more expensive because of it. If you have to buy film, check the use-by date and avoid those that look as if they might have been kept in the sun.

Laundry
You won't have any trouble finding someone willing to take in your laundry for a small consideration. Prices start at s/2 per kilo, but rise to s/3.5-4 for extra services such as collection and delivery, as offered by **Lavaclín** at Suecia 400 and **Splendor** at Suecia 326. Also recommended is **Pacífico on Choquechaca**. There are scores of other laundries on Procuradores and Plateros. Most are open 7.30am-8pm.

Language courses
Classes cost US$5-10 per hour for one-to-one sessions, but you'll get better rates if you learn in a group or book courses of more than 20 hours. Of all the language schools in Cusco, the best is probably **Academia Latinoamericana de Español** (☎ 690293, 🖹 225235, 🖳 www.latinschools.com) at Av El Sol 580, which can also arrange for you to stay with a host family. Other possibilities include **Amauta** (☎ 241422, 🖳 www.amautaspanishschool.com), Suecia 480, 2nd Floor; **Amigos Spanish School** (☎ 242292, 🖳 www.spanishcusco.com),

Zaguán del Cielo B-23; **Cusco Spanish School** (☎ 226928, 🖳 www.cuscospanishschool.com, Calle Garcilaso 265, 2nd Floor; **Excel** (☎ 235298, 🖳 www.excel-spanishlanguageprograms-peru.org), Calle Cruz Verde 336; **San Blas Spanish School** (☎ 247898, 🖳 www.spanishschoolperu.com), Tandapata 688.

Tourist information

There is one very helpful tourist office in the arrivals hall of the airport, and one less helpful and reliable one at Portal Mantas 117 (☎ 252974/263176) in the arcade next to the Merced. They both hand out free maps and provide information, as does the **iPeru** office (☎ 252974, 🖳 iperucusco@promperu.gob.pe) at Av El Sol 103. The **SAE** (☎ 245484, 🖳 www.saexplorers.org), two blocks from Plaza de Armas at Choquechaca 188 Apt. 4, is also a veritable treasure trove of information, and members receive discounts at many of the hotels, sights and entertainments in Cusco (including 10% off drinks at the Cross Keys, see p154).

Visa extension

Ministerio del Interior, Av El Sol 620 (☎ 222741), open Monday to Friday, 9am-1pm, 3-6pm.

Embassies and consulates

Belgium (☎ 221146/098), Av El Sol 954 (under the Savoy Hotel); **France** (☎ 233610), Av Micaela Bastidas 101, Diagonal, 4th Floor, Huanchac; **Germany** (☎ 235459), San Augustín 307; **Holland** (☎ 264103), Av Pardo 854; **Ireland** (☎ 243514), Santa Catalina Ancha 360; **Italy** (☎ 224398), Av Garcilaso 700, Huanchac; **UK** (☎ 239974), Barry Walker (landlord, Cross Keys Pub), find him at the pub or Av Pardo 895; **USA** (☎ 224112), Instituto Cultural Peruano Norte Americano (ICPNA), Calle Tullumayo 127.

Where to stay

Hot water is a problem in Cusco, whatever the people at the hotel may tell you. Water supply is unpredictable and has been known to vanish completely at certain times of the day. Try to talk to someone already staying in the hotel to get an idea of whether you are going to get a shower for your money or not. As for the cost of your room, Cusco prices are highly negotiable and depend on the usual laws of supply and demand. If you find yourself in Cusco in low season, you'll be able to find plenty of bargains.

An organization has been set up to help find rooms for visitors with a traditional Cusqueño family. Contact **Asociación de Micro y Pequeñas Empresas de Establecimientos de Hospedaje** (Small Business Association of Family Lodgings), Portal de Panes 123, Office 109 (☎ 242710, 🖳 ititoss@terra.com.pe).

Note: the following abbreviations are used here: **com = room with common bathroom; att = bathroom attached, sgl/dbl/tpl = single/double/triple.**

Budget accommodation The best place to find cheap hotels is in the hilly streets that lead from Plaza de Armas up to Sacsayhuaman. Recommended is *Hostal Resbalosa* (☎ 224839/240461), Calle Resbalosa 494, which has a bright friendly courtyard, beautiful 180° views over the town towards Mount Ausangate, and costs just s/15/23/35 (dorm/sgl/dbl com). Avoid the rooms around the entrance, which are older and noisier and bear in mind that taxis can only reach within about 100m of the hotel as it is set on a steep, cobbled, pedestrian-only street. Another good-value place is *Hotel Rojas* (☎ 228184), Tigre 129, with a pleasant green courtyard behind enormous front doors, s/25/35/45 (sgl/dbl/tpl

CUSCO & AROUND

Cusco area code: ☎ 84. If phoning from outside Peru dial ☎ +51-84.

com), s/50/70 (sgl/dbl att). Try to get the top floor rooms, which have a view.

Worth looking at are *Hotel Royal Qosqo* (☎ 226221), Tecsecocha 2, which is well maintained and costs s/15/30/40 (sgl/dbl/tpl, com), s/35/60 (sgl/dbl, att), and *Hostal Felix* (☎ 241949), Tecsecocha 171, a real gringo dive s/20 (dbl, com) – as is *Hostal Tumi*, Siete Cuartones 245, s/15/25 (sgl/dbl, com), s/25/30 (sgl/dbl, att). Also worth considering is *Hostal Caceres* (☎ 232616/228012), Plateros 368, an old house with blue creaking woodwork and a friendly welcome; s/20/30/40 (sgl/dbl/tpl, com), and one double with attached bathroom for s/50.

In other areas, there are the highly recommended *Gran Hostal Machu Picchu* (☎ 231111), Calle Quera 282, with its two colonial courtyards and talkative parrots ('¡Hola gringo!'), s/40/70/100 (sgl/ dbl/tpl, com), or at the other end of town in San Blas the recommended *Hospedaje Sambleño* (☎ 262979, 📠 221452), Carmen Alto 114, which has cable TV in the lobby and is a bargain at s/20 per person for a room with attached lavatory, though prices are bound to go up. There are many other little hospedajes tucked away around here in Calle Tarapata.

South of San Blas there is the friendly *Hostal Casa Grande* (☎ 264156, 📠 243784), Santa Catalina Ancha 353, a slightly shabby old house that's nonetheless recommended and good value at s/15/30/45 (sgl/dbl/tpl, com), or s/30/40 (sgl/dbl, att).

Other places worth looking at are the two Hostals Suecia run by the same people who are friendly and popular with foreigners. *Hostal Suecia I* (☎ 233282, 📠 hsuecia1@hotmail.com), at Calle Suecia 332 offers plain rooms around a courtyard for s/23/35 (sgl/dbl, com). *Hostal Suecia II* (☎ 239757), set in a colonial-style building at Tecescocha 465 costs s/20/30 (sgl/dbl, com), and has some rooms with attached bathroom for s/30/50 (sgl/dbl).

Also recommended is the youth hostel: *Albergue Municipal* (☎ 252506, 📠 albergue@municusco.gob.pe), Kiskapata 240, which is spanking clean, has a café and good views from a sunny concrete balcony. It costs s/25 a person with a discount for members and is a great place to stay if you're in a group. The dorms have bunk beds for four to eight people.

Finally, *Hotel Royal Frankenstein* (☎ 236999), at San Juan de Dios 260, deserves a mention for sheer weirdness if nothing else. With a sales pitch that advertises 'Cold dark gloomy rooms' with 'spiders on request' it's a wonder they receive any guests at all. To be fair they're selling themselves a bit short and it's not that bad, with cooking and laundry facilities for guests to use but it is rather overpriced at US$10 for a dorm bed, US$17/20 sgl/dbl.

Incidentally, there are cheap hotels around both train stations (the *El Imperio* by San Pedro has been recommended), but they are a little out of the way and in unsavoury areas.

Mid-range hotels Hotels in this category are spread throughout Cusco, and usually set their rates in US dollars, but be careful to check whether the price includes taxes and service. Budget hotels tend to forget about taxes and service, and expensive hotels slap the extra percentage on top but you can never be sure with the mid-range places.

A little expensive for what you get but with great character is the recommended *Hotel los Marqueses* (☎ 232512, 📠 marqueseshotel@hotmail .com), Calle Garcilaso 256, an old house with ancient carved doors, antique chairs, old paintings in the lobby and a very pretty courtyard. They charge US$25/35 (sgl/dbl, att, breakfast).

Closer to Sacsayhuaman than the Albergue Municipal are two other recommended hotels which are on the same street as each other. The first is *Hostal Qawarina* (☎ 228130), Calle Suecia 575, which is efficient, clean, modern and friendly and offers free coca tea throughout the day, which can be taken in a communal living room area with exceptional views over the city. It has only six rooms and is good value for Cusco at US$18/28 (sgl/dbl, att, breakfast). Just down from Qawarina is *Hostal Corihausi* (☎ 232233, 🖳 www.cori hausi.com), Calle Suecia 561, Casilla Postal 157, which charges US$30/40/50 (sgl/dbl/tpl, att, breakfast). This larger, labyrinthine hotel is favoured by some adventure-tour companies and can get fully booked quickly. Try to get the room directly above reception which has the best view in all Cusco.

If you fancy something a little more central there's *Hostal Emperador Plaza* (☎ 261733/227412, 🖳 www.emperador @nexopera.com, emperador@terra.com .pe), Santa Catalina Ancha 377. It's as clean as a new pin, has cable TV in the rooms and costs from US$48/53/68 (sgl/dbl/tpl, breakfast); the balcony rooms are best. Also central but much older is the aptly named and rather splendid *Colonial Palace* (☎ 232151), Calle Q'era 270, US$18/25 (sgl/dbl, att, breakfast) and *Teqsiqocha Hostal* (☎ 248600), Calle Tecsecocha 474, where all the rooms are en suite and piping hot water is usually available on tap around the clock; this quiet little place is reasonably priced at US$20/25/32 sgl/dbl/tpl and deservedly growing in popularity.

Hostal Loreto (☎ 226352, 🖳 hlore to@terra.com.pe), Loreto 115, deserves a mention because some rooms have genuine Inca walls, but it's overpriced at US$25/40/50 (sgl/dbl/tpl, att, costs more in high season). If you want to stay in San Blas, try *Amaru Hostal* (☎/🖻 225933, 🖳 www.cusco.net/amaru), Cuesta San Blas 541, an old house with a green courtyard filled with geraniums in rusty cans. It's also a good meeting

place, has a book exchange and piano, and they charge US$8/12 (sgl/dbl, com), US$15/22 (sgl/dbl, att). Alternatively, try *Marani* (☎ 249462, 🖳 www.hostal marani.com), Carmen Alto 194, which oozes character and is run by a very knowledgeable couple who are heavily involved in the local community; they charge US$25 (dbl, att). For the chance to stay in part of the historian Garcilaso de la Vega's (see p53) colonial house, head to *Hotel Garcilaso* (☎ 233031, 🖳 hotelgarcilaso@hotmail.com), Garcilaso 233; the building is fantastic though the rooms are fairly modest for US$40/55/ 70 (sgl/dbl/tpl, att). *Hostal Arqueólogo* (☎ 232569, 🖻 235126, 🖳 reservation @hotelarqueologo.com), Pumacurco 408, featuring Inca stonework leading up to the entrance, is a favourite with the French. It's pleasant enough but at US$35/55/75 (sgl/dbl/tpl, com, breakfast) you can do better for the money. The same is true of *Hotel Virrey* (☎ 221771, 🖳 hvirrey@amauta.rep.net.pe), Portal Comercio 165, whose rooms at US$30/45 (sgl/dbl, att) are nice enough, but you're really paying for the wonderful views of Plaza de Armas. For those who want to get away from it all, *Casa de Campo Hostal* (☎ 244404, 🖻 243069, 🖳 www.telser.cm.pe/amauta), at the very northern end of Tandapata in San Blas at number 296B is just delightful. Built on a slope overlooking the town, the rooms and terrace are simply gorgeous, the location so peaceful, and they'll even throw in an airport pickup if you book in advance. Rooms start at US$25/40/55 (sgl/dbl/tpl), though bargaining is distinctly possible, and there's a 10% discount for SAE members.

The most impressive hotel in this category, however, is *El Balcón Hostal* (☎ 236738, 🖻 225352, 🖳 www.el-bal con-hostal-cusco.com), Tambo de Montero 222, housed in a restored pre-colonial house dating back to 1630. All 16 rooms are en suite, many with magnificent views of the city, and the staff are incredibly friendly, as is the office cat. It's a bit of a climb to get here, but it's worth every step: room prices are US$35/55/65 (sgl/dbl/tpl, breakfast).

Expensive hotels More than others, these hotels jack up their prices in high season and are willing to bargain when the rooms are empty. The prices quoted can go up by about 20% in June/July.

The two best hotels in Cusco are the Hotel Monasterio del Cuzco and the Hotel Libertador del Cuzco. *Hotel Monasterio del Cuzco* (☎ 241777, 🖳 www.orient-express.com), Calle Palacio 136, Plazoleta Nazarenas, is a sensitive conversion of the old Seminary of San Antonio Abad, and along with everything you'd expect from an international five-star hotel it also has a gilded chapel, a Michelin-starred chef and oxygen-enriched air in the rooms (US$25 additional fee). It's not cheap at US$265/275/305 (sgl/dbl/tpl, att, breakfast), but you can knock the prices down. *Hotel Libertador del Cuzco* (☎ 231961, 🖳 www.libertador.com.pe), Plazoleta Santo Domingo 259, is a converted colonial building, once a palace called the Casa de Los Cuatro Bustos. Again this hotel has the full five-star package but is a little more welcoming to dirty trekkers than the Monasterio. It costs US$236 (single or double, att, breakfast) and around US$300 for a suite.

The *Novotel* (☎ 228282, 🖳 reservations@novotelcusco.com.pe), San Agustín 239, born from the earthquake-damaged ruins of the home of the conquistador Miguel Sánchez Ponce, boasts an impressive glass-covered courtyard and four-star services. Rooms in the contemporary wing begin at US$180 but prices rise to US$230 for something in the more attractive colonial section.

Down from the first rank but still very good is *Hotel Ruinas* (☎ 260644/ 261136, 🖳 www.hotelruinas.com), Calle Ruinas

472. This well-sited place has character; the rooms with outside views are the best. It's well run and costs US$100/125/155 (sgl/dbl/tpl, att, breakfast). Also good is the relatively new *Picoaga Hotel* (☎ 227691, 🖳 www.picoagahotel.com), Santa Teresa 344, formerly the colonial home of the Marqués de Picoaga. It makes the most of its handsome colonnaded courtyard and rooms cost US$120/140/170 (sgl/dbl/tpl, att, breakfast).

Hotel San Agustín International (☎ 221169/231001, 🖳 www.hotelsan agustin.com.pe), Calle Maruri 390 deserves a mention because of its adobe-style interior decoration; it costs US$89/102/120 (sgl/dbl/tpl, att, breakfast). If you can't afford the San Augustín International, *El Dorado Inn* (☎ 231232/231135, 🖷 240993, 🖳 doratur@telser .com.pe), Av El Sol 395, has a similar quirky interior with aerial walkways. Rooms are US$90 (sgl/dbl, att, breakfast).

Hotel Royal Inka I (☎ 222284), Plaza Regocijo 299, US$54/78 (sgl/dbl, att, breakfast) is built on the foundations of Pachacutec's palace. It's slightly better than its more expensive sister, *Hotel Royal Inka II* (☎ 231067, 🖳 royalin ka@terra.com.pe), which is just up the road at Santa Teresa 335 and costs US$68/90 (sgl/dbl). Also good is the efficient *Hotel los Andes de América* (☎ 222253, 🖷 223058; 🖳 losandes@telser .com), Garcilaso 234-236, US$110/130/160 (sgl/dbl/tpl, att, breakfast).

Where to eat and drink

Cusco is overflowing with places to eat and drink, from cheap steaming anticucho barrows on the street to exclusive restaurants; from back-street bars with sticky plastic tablecloths to loud, brash clubs where the music hits you like a fist. If you're looking for food or drink, just wander around Calle Procuradores or Calle Plateros and you are bound to find something that takes your fancy. If you can't afford many of Cusco's culinary pleasures, there are any number of the usual **cheap** s/3 menu places, particularly on Pampa del Castillo, near the Coricancha, or south of Plaza de Armas on Mantas and around Plaza San Francisco, including my favourite, the *Ccoyllor* café at 291 Garcilaso.

The following is only a small selection of what's on offer:

Best food in Cusco The competition for this prestigious award has been rather blown away by the arrival of Cusco's first-ever Michelin-starred chef at *Restaurant Monasterio* (see opposite) in Hotel Monasterio. With food this exquisite being served in suitably sumptuous surroundings, you could be in any one of the finer restaurants in Europe – an illusion that the bill will do nothing to dispel.

Back in the real world, honourable mentions must go to the *Inka Grill* (see Best Peruvian); *Los Perros*, on Tecsecocha 238, for its magnificent salads and *wontons* to die for; and *Macondo*, at Cuesta San Blas 571 which is simply the coolest and campest restaurant in Cusco, and one run by one of its most flamboyant citizens. *El Truco*, Plaza Regocijo 261, is stylish and has good service and if you're lucky they'll put a flag on your table to remind you of your nationality. *La Retama*, Portal de Panes 123, can cook fish meunière and steak béarnaise (dinner for two s/115 with wine) but it's often booked up. Equally busy is the elegant *Tunupa*, Portal Confiturías 233, which has panoramic views of Plaza de Armas and serves first-rate international and contemporary Peruvian food as well as lavish buffets. The *MAP Café* in the Museo de Arte Precolombino (see p138), Plaza de las Nazarenas 231, is run by the same people in charge of the Inka Grill and the food is similarly delicious. Set in a beautiful courtyard of a restored colonial house, the restaurant serves a creative menu of first-rate Peruvian cuisine, although it isn't cheap (main course s/27-

60, wine s/66-120, cocktails s/10-25).

Don't forget by the way that expensive restaurants add 28% tax and service on to your bill.

Best Peruvian My favourite restaurant in Cusco is *Inka Grill*, on Plaza de Armas at Portal de Panes 115, which is more modern and imaginative than its competitors as regards food and décor. They try to give Peruvian dishes a contemporary twist, so you could have *pollo relleno prosciutto* (chicken stuffed with prosciutto ham), or a good (but very expensive at s/28) *ají de gallina*. A meal for two with wine will cost about s/170. A close second, however, and a little cheaper, is *Pacha Papa* on Plaza San Blas at No 120. With dishes ranging from commonplace roast *cuy* (guinea pig) to the more exotic *alpaca* steaks, a very pleasant evening can be had munching on the native wildlife; the outdoor seating is a bonus too. *Mystique*, Calle Suecia, is a venue like the Inka Grill where traditional food is brought into the 21st century; their alpaca and trout dishes are especially good. *Paititi*, Portal de Carrizos 270 (on Plaza de Armas) has decent Peruvian dishes and folk music; around s/50 for two people. *Mesón de Espaderos,* Espaderos 105, has a wider range which includes cuy, anticucho, trout, and fine *parilladas.* *Pachacútec*, Portal de Panes 105, is pretty much the same as the rest, but it does extend to ceviche. It has Inca walls inside. Crammed full of glitter and kitsch, the *Fallen Angel*, Plazoleta Nazarenas 221, is a flight of fancy by the same creative genius behind Macondo; tuck into sumptuous fare (the steaks are particularly good) off a table-cum-aquarium, a perspex-topped bath full of fish and coral.

Best pizza An honourable mention must go to the two homely little places on Tecsecocha, *Les Cyranos* and *Pizzería Urpi*, both of which are

CUSCO & AROUND

equipped with proper ovens which they use to churn out pizzas every bit as good as those you'd find in Italy. The tiny corner restaurant *Tiziano Trattoria* at Tecsecocha 418 is also worth a shout for its pleasing ambience. But the queen of pizzerias remains *Chez Maggy's*. With no fewer than three establishments on Procuradores (at Nos 344, 365 and 374), another on Plateros (No 348), and a further outpost in Aguas Calientes, Maggy's has come to dominate the city's pizza industry – though the bases are a bit crispy for me. They also run a delivery service (☎ 246316).

Best vegetarian For something very different try *Tercer Mundo*, 346A Matara, to the east of Plaza San Francisco; it has a limited but imaginative three-course menu (s/3) that changes daily (their banana tortillas are a treat). *Govinda*, Espaderos 128, is run by Hare Krishnas and serves filling set meals.

Best Mexican While their portions are sometimes on the small side, *El Cuate*, at Procuradores 385, has fought off the competition to snaffle this particular award, thanks to the helpfulness of the staff, the charmingly rustic interior and some mighty fine dishes, including a lava-hot stuffed pepper that will blow your socks off. Expect to pay about s/10-15 for a main course.

Best all-you-can-eat buffet breakfast Two candidates here: *Amaru* on Plateros 325 is proving very popular, not least because of its balcony seating and the variety of breakfasts on offer. A good place but the award for this particular category goes to *La Tertulia* at Procuradores 44, thanks to the classical music that accompanies every breakfast, the efficient service provided by its adorable waitresses and the superior quality of its scrambled eggs.

Best bakery Streets ahead of any rivals in Cusco, *El Buen Pastor*, at 579 Cuesta San Blas, has everything you could ask for from a bakery: great, great bread, fantastic *empanadas*, drool-inducing gateaux and low prices. What's more, this place is a charitable concern, helping to finance a home for girls from disadvantaged backgrounds.

Best place to hang out *Trotamundos*, Portal de Comercio 177 (overlooks Plaza de Armas), has a laid-back atmosphere, board games, internet, good breakfasts and real toast. If the views from the balconies overlooking the plaza are starting to bore, *Los Perros* on Tecsecocha, with its comfy armchairs, book exchange and six-year old *Rolling Stone* magazines is as good a place as any to wile away an afternoon. During the day, *Blueberry Lounge*, Portal de Carnes 236, is a tranquil place to hang out, but by night it becomes a hip bar and restaurant serving some excellent, Asian-influenced dishes. *Varayoc*, Espaderos 142, is a peaceful café where you can feel completely at ease as you enjoy a selection of pastries and fondues.

The Dutch-owned *La Bodega*, 146 Carmen Alto in San Blas, is another laid-back and friendly place with magazines and they do some great snacks too – their chicken sandwich was the best I tasted in the city. *The Muse*, Calle Tandapata 684, spills enticingly out onto the pavement above Plaza San Blas and serves fresh coffee and scrumptious snacks.

Best Chinese Sadly I found that none of the Chinese restaurants in Cusco could match their rivals in Lima, but if you're desperate for a plate of fried rice try *Chifa Sipan*, on Calle Quera 251, on the other side of the road from the Colonial Palace. There's a second, less good branch on Plateros, in the corner of Plaza de Armas.

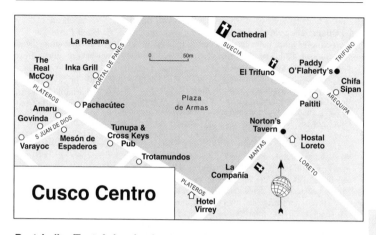

Cusco Centro

Best Indian/East Asian food The poor showing in the Chinese category is made up for by *Al Grano*, Santa Catalina 398, in this one. It serves delicious, reasonably priced Indian, Sri Lankan, Malay and Vietnamese dishes from a menu that changes daily, as well as good coffee and home-made pastries.

Best Middle Eastern food To be honest, the Peruvians have yet to master the art of Middle Eastern cooking, though there are a few places that are trying pretty hard: for example *Nafiz*, at Choquechaca 132 in San Blas, tries gamely at *falafel*. *Narguila*, on the bend of Tecsecocha, is more authentic and the waiter speaks Hebrew but *Victor Victoria*, nearby on Tigre, wins this category. Don't take my word for it – ask the vast number of Israelis who hang out here.

Best British *Greens*, round the back of the church at San Blas at Tandapata 700, used to win this award for its giant sofas, games, book exchange, English newspapers and library – and by virtue of there being no competition. Their generous Sunday lunch is just fine, though a bit pricey at s/30 and you do have to let them know you're coming at least one day in advance. However, the roast at the stylish yet relaxed *The Real McCoy* on Plateros 326 costs s/22, comes complete with sage and onion stuffing and gravy, and doesn't require advance booking, meaning that this newcomer clinches the award. They don't stop with Sunday lunch though, and serve fabulous big breakfasts, salads and sandwiches as well as Brit-classics such as toast and marmite, cauliflower cheese, Branston pickle and custard (though not necessarily all at once).

Best coffee There are many places that *claim* to brew the best coffee in Cusco, from the achingly trendy *Los Perros* on Tecsecocha (top of the best cappuccino category) to *Planeta Sur* in San Blas – winner of the award for most stylish coffee machine if nothing else. But for my money the best coffee in the city, or at least the best-value coffee, can be found at *Cross Keys*: OK, so you have to plunge the filter yourself, but two cups for s/3 is marvellous value.

Best juices A couple of swanky juice bars have opened up on Procuradores, and *Jack's* on the corner of Choquechaca and Cuesta San Blas pours a decent drink. (*Continued on p154*)

❏ Cusco shopping – a guide

As well as its other, more enduring claims to fame, Cusco enjoys a reputation as the souvenir capital of Peru. Souvenirs here are more varied and a good deal cheaper than elsewhere in the country.

The first place you should look — just to get an idea of prices if not actually to buy — is the **Centro Artesanal**. In May 2001 the street sellers who used to occupy the arcades between Plaza de Armas and Plaza Regocijo, and who imbued the centre of Cusco with so much colour and character, were removed by the city authorities overnight and banned from returning. Those who could afford the rent made their way to the mercado, a purpose-built but rather anaemic indoor market by Huanchac station at the southern end of Av El Sol. Few tourists actually bother to make it this far down Av El Sol – bad news for the vendors, but good news for those after a bargain and willing to haggle. Those vendors who couldn't afford to hire a kiosk at the indoor market have set up shop in other locations in the city, in particular the Plazoleta Nazarenas, above Plaza de Armas to the east.

Three other Cusqueñan markets you should know about: the plaza in San Blas is the venue for a cute little **Saturday craft fair**, while on Plateros 334 is the daily **Tesoros del Inca market**. On the way to the airport (catch a cab from the centre of town) is the **Centro Comercial el Molino**, commonly known as **Contrabandas**. As the name suggests, many of the vendors here deal in smuggled goods and designer rip-offs and as such the market does a good line in cheap cigarettes (half the normal price) and compact discs (s/9 a throw). The quality of the goods cannot be guaranteed, of course, nor should you expect a refund if things go wrong, so shop carefully. Watch your bags and wallets here too. Other places to buy traditional goods are the markets at Pisac (see p160) and Chinchero (p162).

San Blas is Cusco's artisan district and there are a number of workshops here worth visiting. **Taller Olave**, Plaza San Blas 651, **Taller Mérida**, Carmen Alto 133, and **Taller Mendivil** on the plaza have striking artefacts, sculptures, colonial religious images and icons, ceramics and earthenware.

Then there are Cusco's souvenir shops, most of which look the same, sell the same sort of stuff, and charge roughly the same amount for it too. The following, therefore, may not be a list of the best, but at least it contains some of the more interesting souvenir shops in Cusco.

● **General souvenirs** Four worth mentioning are: the **Galería Latina**, San Augustín 427, which is hugely expensive and a bit too flash for some but which has just about the best of everything, from antique blankets and carpets to cotton shirts and Panama hats, via Alpaca jumpers and gold jewellery.

Jatum Maqui, next to Los Perros at Tecsecocha 432, manages to be a good deal cheaper without suffering a commensurate drop in quality.

La Mamita, on Plaza de Armas at Portal de Carnes 244, has a small but exquisite selection of pottery (see opposite), jewellery, baskets and blankets.

Minka, San Blas 525-529, is a charitable concern which has been set up to help people with special needs.

● **Jewellery** **Carlos Chaquiras** at Triunfo 375 is perhaps the finest jewellers in Cusco, though there are a few around Plaza de Armas that aren't far behind. Of these, the best is probably **Ilaria**, Portal Carrizos 258.

Leo's Fancy at Procuradores 372 has some interesting necklaces, and there are some inexpensive beads-and-bangles places further up the alley.

(continued opposite)

Cusco shopping – a guide (cont'd)

No summary of Cusco's jewellery shops would be complete without mentioning **Magic Hands** on San Blas. The owner, a mystical sort of fellow, is very selective about whom he lets into his establishment: only those with auras of a benign colour, apparently, are permitted to enter. Pass this test and you'll find yourself in a dimly lit store contemplating some fine and highly individual necklaces and earrings, while the owner advises which particular pieces will be good for your chakras. It's all rather bizarre. (Those with the wrong shade of aura, incidentally, may find that walking up to the door with a big bag of money causes the owner to suffer from temporary colour blindness.)

● **Leather** Take a trip down San Agustín, below San Blas, and you'll come across three shops — **Sumac Tika** at No 216, **Miguel Ángel** at No 327 and **El Tumi** at No 345 — specializing in leatherwear, their stock including hats, shoes, wallets, belts and bags.

● **Alpaca and llama woollens** Alpaca III (🖥 www.alpaca111.com), Plaza Regocijo 202 and also at the Monasterio del Cuzco Hotel, Libertador Hotel and the Museo de Arte Precolombino, has good quality alpaca woollens in Frank Bough designs but note that there's a cheaper branch of the same shop in the departure lounge of the airport and **Etno Artesanía**, Triunfo 118, has more modern styles. **Alpacas Best**, Portal Confiturías 221 and Plaza Nazarenas 197-199, has a selection of handmade sweaters, jackets, coats and accessories.

The **Center for Traditional Textiles of Cusco**, Av El Sol 603A, is a non-profit organization set up to provide support to weaving communities and to keep textile traditions alive; some fine work is on sale here.

● **T-shirts** For something a bit different from the common-or-garden Peruvian football shirt, the ubiquitous Cusqueña and Inca Kola shirts or the awful 'I love Cusco' numbers, check out **Hecho en Cusco** at 340 Procuradores, with psychedelic handmade designs starting at about s/30 (bargaining possible).

● **Footwear** Not everybody's cup of tea it has to be said, but those brightly coloured shoes and boots made out of a combination of leather and thick woven cloth enjoy a small but intensely loyal following among travellers. Buy a pair at **Away**, Procuradores 361, which also has a fine collection of blankets for sale.

● **Ponchos and textiles** Trendas Museo, just down from the Cross Keys pub on Plaza de Armas, has the widest range of antique and new ponchos in Central Cusco. A little expensive but it's worth coming here to see some of the fabulous old blankets and ponchos they have in the store even if you don't want to buy. The **Tankar Gallery**, Calle Palacio 121, has a variety of traditional Andean tapestries and ceramics produced by local artists.

● **Ceramics and pottery** Maky at Carmen Alto 101 has a fine collection of tea sets, incense holders and other pottery decorated with pre-Hispanic and Inca motifs.

Slightly superior, and much more expensive too, is **La Mamita** on Plaza de Armas at Portal de Carnes 244, the stockists for Seminario Cerámicas of Urubamba (see p162).

● **Instruments** Half museum, half shop, **Takinuna** at Carmen Alto 110 has a wide variety of instruments both great and small, weird and wonderful — though it's difficult to distinguish between what is on sale and what is an exhibit.

Instrumentos Qosco at Cabracancha 455, the narrow alley to the south of the Religious Art Museum, is the place to head to for locally made guitars.

● **Andean music** Try **Flutes of Peru** at 230 Av El Sol, which has a fair selection of traditional and modern Peruvian music on tape ad CD, and the owner is both knowledgeable and helpful.

CUSCO & AROUND

(*Continued from p151*). None of the juice bars can compete in terms of price, atmosphere or taste with the juices on offer at the **market** in San Pedro. Around s/2 will get you glass after glass of your favourite fruity concoction.

Best hot chocolate This category was invented specifically to honour the Swiss-run *Granja Heidi*, at Cuesta San Blas 525, which serves up half-litre jugs of piping-hot, authentic chocolate for just s/2.5. If there were awards for best natural food (evening meals feature produce from the owner's farm), best yoghurt or best crêpes, they'd probably win those too.

Bars and clubs *Cross Keys*, Portal Confiturías 233, is almost a British pub (and is therefore your best bet for showing premier-league football) just as *Paddy O'Flaherty's* at Triunfo 124 and *Rosy O'Grady's* at Santa Catalina Ancha 360) are almost Irish pubs (the former being far superior although a fraction of the size), *Norton's Tavern* is almost a North American biker bar (but with a conspicuous absence of customers, though this may be because the entrance is hidden away in Hostal Loreto's courtyard) and *Km 0* at Tandapata 100, San Blas, is almost a Mediterranean cantina, complete with tasty tapas. *Los Perros* (see p150) remains the most popular watering hole, despite the art exhibitions on the wall. A possible rival, *Fallen Angel* (see p149), hosts outrageous parties and serves devilish cocktails.

You'll have no trouble finding a **club** in Cusco; the difficult part is trying to avoid them. Touts swarm around Plaza de Armas handing out flyers and free drink tokens, so it is now possible to spend an entire evening touring around the clubs without once paying for your drink. Happy hours also seem to cover most of the evening, typically from 6 to 7.30pm and then again from 9 to 10.30pm. The clubs themselves tend to be located on the corners of the plaza; while names change regularly, this seems to be a constant. The longest-running venue is *Mama Africa,* Portal Harinas 191, 2nd Fl, which plays something for everyone and is usually packed. So popular is this club that it has spawned *Mama Amerika*, Portal Belén 115, decorated in a jungle theme. It serves food, has any number of drink specials (happy 'hour' 3-10pm) and plays an eclectic mix of music. The similarly busy *Extrem*, Portal de Cranes 298, plays dance music, has a big screen for films and sport and a couple of bars that seem to give out an awful lot of free drinks. *Kamikase*, Plaza Regocijo 274, lies in a cavernous basement and plays rock music, hosts daily live acts, while *Golden Rock*, Calle Tecsecocha 436, plays exactly that and hosts live music on Fridays and Saturdays. For jazz, funk and Latin rhythms try *Tangible Myth*, San Juan de Dios 260, or for hardcore dance and techno, occasionally interrupted by hip hop and funk, head for the hip *Spoon*, Plateros 334. *Ukuku's* can boast the widest selection of music, including reggae, rock, techno, salsa, samba, blues, jazz and Huayno and is consistently popular, not least for its live acts every evening.

Other entertainment and things to do
Peliclub, at Tecsecocha 458, is a small independent **cinema** that shows some classic old movies (s/5, s/2 students). Just down the road is Sunset Café – part of the Hotel Royal Qosqo (Tecsecocha 2) – which shows three recent releases per day (s/2 per film), and many of the pubs and nightclubs (Cafetacuba on Portal de Panes 109, Mama Africa's, Ukuku's, Extrem) also show movies in the afternoon. If none of the films on offer grabs you, you can always visit the video store at Portal de Panes 123, where you can choose any video you want and watch it in the comfort of one of their private video booths (s/6).

If you fancy doing something a little more active, Mama Amerika (see opposite) has **salsa lessons** starting at 9pm, followed by **samba lessons** at 10pm.

Finally, if you've just back from the trail there's no better way to pamper yourself than to visit Siluet at Calle Quera 253, down an alley by the Chinese restaurant, a **health spa** with a sauna (s/25), Jacuzzi (s/12) and masseur/se (s/25). It's open every day from 10am to 10pm. You could also get a therapeutic massage at Yin Yang on Portal Espinar 144; Angel Hands at Heladeros 157; the Aquabella Spa and Sauna at San Agustin 371; and the Body Shop Spa at Procuradores 50.

MOVING ON
Air
The airport is five minutes by taxi from Plaza de Armas, whence you can fly to most major Peruvian towns. Airport departure tax is US$10 for international flights and US$3.50 for domestic flights.

Airlines include: **AeroCondor** (☎ 252774), at the airport; **American Airlines** (☎ 248282), Calle Saphi 848; **Lanperu/ Lanchile** (☎ 255552/3/4, 📠 255555, 💻 www.lan.com), Av El Sol 627B; **Lloyd Aéreo Boliviano** (☎ 222990, 📠 229220, 💻 www.labairlines.com), Santa Catalina Angosta 160; **TACA** (☎ 249921, 💻 www.taca.com), Av El Sol 602B; **TANS** (☎ 242727, 📠 251000 and Lima 213 6000, 💻 www.tansperu.com .pe), San Augustín 315-317.

There are seven flights daily to Lima. The cheapest leaves early in the morning and costs around US$69. Later flights cost US$10-20 more. Views out of the right-hand window of Salcantay, about 10 minutes after takeoff, are spectacular. The flight takes 50 minutes. You should try and catch as early a flight as possible since there is a higher risk of flights being delayed or cancelled later in the day.

The helicopter service to Aguas Calientes was suspended in 2001 because the vibrations from the choppers were beginning to damage the ruins at Ollantaytambo and threatening the ruins and ecosystems within the Machu Picchu Historical Sanctuary.

Bus
All long-distance buses leave from and arrive at the terminal (the *terminal terrestre*) near the airport. The route to Lima via Abancay and Ayacucho is now open again, and the run takes 22-24 hours and costs US$20-25. The alternative is to go via Arequipa, which takes 30 hours and costs US$20-30. Other destinations include Nazca (check with South American Explorers about whether this route is safe) which costs US$20, Abancay US$5, Juliaca US$6, 6 hours and Arequipa US$10-14, 11 hours. The bus offices are at the terminal, but you can get tickets at agencies on Av El Sol and in Plaza de Armas if you don't mind paying a commission.

Local buses leave from a variety of departure points but there's a stop near Clorindo Matto de Turner school on Av de la Cultura for the Sacred Valley (take a taxi there), or try Av Grau near Centenario. Tickets for the furthest destination in the Sacred Valley, Ollantaytambo, cost a few soles, and the journey takes half a day.

Rail
The station for the Puno line is **Huanchac** and the station for trains to Aguas Calientes (for Machu Picchu) is **San Pedro**. Tickets for the Puno line can be bought only at Huanchac. Tickets for Aguas Calientes can be bought from either, but you'll need to show your ID. Check the train timetable, the times when the stations are open to sell tickets and the ticket prices as everything changes often. Those wishing to get to Machu Picchu as cheaply as possible should heed the advice given on p301.

● **Buying tickets** The central reservation office of Perurail can be contacted

on ☎ 084-238722 or try 🖥 www.peru
rail.com. **Huanchac station** is open for
tickets from Monday to Friday 7am-
5pm, and Saturday to Sunday 7am-12
noon. **San Pedro station** is open for
tickets Monday to Friday 8am-3pm,
Sunday 8am-12.30pm. If you haven't
booked in advance, it's worth going
along an hour before the train leaves to
see if there are any tickets left.

For details of times and prices, see
pp301-2.

Around Cusco

RUINS NEAR CUSCO (DAY HIKE)

There are lots of small but interesting sites within walking distance of Cusco's
Plaza de Armas. You could probably cover many in half a day if you wanted to
but you'd miss so much; it's worth spending a little time exploring each one,
and anyway walking through the rolling grassland around Cusco is a pleasant
way to acclimatize to the altitude. Four of the five sights below are included in
the Cusco Visitor's Ticket (BTU; see box p132) – the fifth, Salapunco, is free
to enter anyway; or, if you don't have that, you can buy a separate ticket covering just these five sights for s/21 (s/10.50 students).

The 8km route described here is the most commonly walked day hike and
visits Sacsayhuaman, Qenko, Salapunco, Puca Pucara and Tambo Machay –
take a packed lunch. If you don't feel like a walk, you can always take a tour
(box pp140-1; s/20), take the bus (Pisac bus, s/3 – ask to be dropped off at
Tambo Machay), catch a taxi (US$6 for the trip from Cusco to Puca Pucara) or
hire a horse (s/20-25 per day). Horses are readily available at Sacsayhuaman;
just ask around. If your Spanish isn't good enough to do this, one of the tour
agencies will be able to sort it out.

Sadly there have been muggings in the ruins close to Cusco and some
attempted rapes (at Sacsayhuaman and Qenko). Leave valuables at the hotel and
don't go to these places on your own, or at dawn and dusk.

Sacsayhuaman

(Open daily, 7am to 5.30pm, Visitor's Ticket). It takes about 20 to 30 minutes
to walk to Sacsayhuaman from Plaza de Armas. There are several routes but the
easiest way is to go up one of the streets by the cathedral to Pumacurco, also
called Palacio and Herrajes, turn left and walk uphill. After some stairs you'll
reach a main, tarred road; at the top of the first bend is the ticket office (make
sure you have the right money as they very rarely have any change) and a path
leading up the hill along a small gully. Follow the stairs (you can go either way
around the large hillock that blocks the way) until you reach the massive stones
of Sacsayhuaman on your left.

No one knows for sure what Sacsayhuaman was. It was called 'the Fortress'
by the Spanish, but current research suggests that it was more likely to be a temple, and Inca tombs have been discovered in the area. Whether or not it was

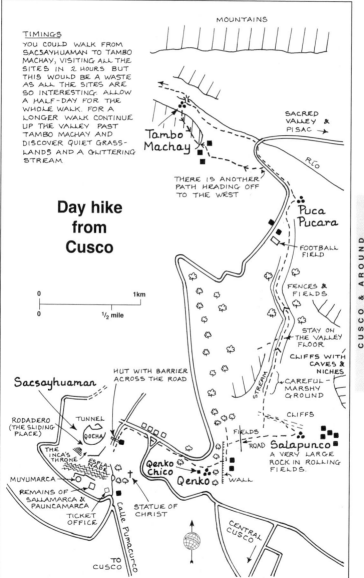

Day hike from Cusco

TIMINGS
YOU COULD WALK FROM SACSAYHUAMAN TO TAMBO MACHAY, VISITING ALL THE SITES IN 2 HOURS BUT THIS WOULD BE A WASTE AS ALL THE SITES ARE SO INTERESTING. ALLOW A HALF-DAY FOR THE WHOLE WALK. FOR A LONGER WALK CONTINUE UP THE VALLEY PAST TAMBO MACHAY AND DISCOVER QUIET GRASS-LANDS AND A GLITTERING STREAM

MOUNTAINS

Tambo Machay

SACRED VALLEY & PISAC →

RÍO

THERE IS ANOTHER PATH HEADING OFF TO THE WEST

Puca Pucara

FOOTBALL FIELD

FENCES & FIELDS

STAY ON THE VALLEY FLOOR

CLIFFS WITH CAVES & NICHES

CAREFUL - MARSHY GROUND

STREAM

CLIFFS

0 _____ 1km

0 _____ 1/2 mile

HUT WITH BARRIER ACROSS THE ROAD

Sacsayhuaman

RODADERO (THE SLIDING PLACE)

TUNNEL

QOCHA

THE INCA'S THRONE

ESPLA-NADE

MUYUMARCA

REMAINS OF SALLAMARCA & PAUNCAMARCA

TICKET OFFICE

Calle Pumacurco

Qenko Chico

Qenko

STATUE OF CHRIST

FIELDS

ROAD

WALL

Salapunco
A VERY LARGE ROCK IN ROLLING FIELDS.

CENTRAL CUSCO

TO CUSCO

CUSCO & AROUND

Sacsayhuaman

'This was the greatest and most superb of the edifices that the Incas raised to demonstrate their majesty and power. Its greatness is incredible to those who have not seen it; and those who have seen it, and studied it with attention, will be led not alone to imagine, but to believe, that it was reared by enchantment – by demons, and not by men, because of the number and size of the stones placed in the three walls, which are rather cliffs than walls, and which it is impossible to believe were cut out of quarries, since the Indians had neither iron nor steel wherewith to extract or shape them. And how they were brought together is a thing equally wonderful, since the Indians had neither carts nor oxen nor ropes, wherewith to drag them by main force. Nor were there level road over which to transport them, but, on the contrary, steep mountains and abrupt declivities, to be overcome by the simple force of men. ... It passes the power of imagination to conceive how so many and so great stones could be so accurately fitted together as scarcely to admit the insertion of the point of a knife between them'.

Garcilaso de la Vega *Comentarios reales que tratan del origen de los Incas* (1609).

designed to be a temple, it was certainly used as a fort by the armies of Manco Inca when they attempted to dislodge the Spaniards from Cusco (see p102), and the Spanish chronicler, Pedro Sancho, estimated that it was large enough to hold a garrison of 5000 Spanish soldiers. He went on to say that the widely travelled Spaniards he was with commented that they had 'never seen a building to compare with this fortress, nor a stronger castle'.

For maximum defensive strength the largest stones were set at the apices of the zigzags that form the wall. John Hemming has calculated that the largest stone stands 8.5m high and weighs 361 tons; even so, these massive blocks curve into one another as if squashed together like clay.

The structure was topped by three towers and riddled with tunnels in which the historian, Garcilaso de la Vega, remembers playing when he was a child. The towers were called Salla Marca, Paunca Marca and Muyu Marca. The concentric rings of foundations of the last remain, but the stones of the others were pillaged in the days when Cusqueños used Sacsayhuaman as an unofficial quarry. Some tunnels remain in the northern amphitheatre – bring a torch.

The mound opposite the zigzag walls is called the Inca's Throne or the *rodadero* (the slide). It was probably where a high-ranking person supervised sacred ceremonies, but nowadays the deep polished grooves in the rock are used by children as a slide. The green meadow between the Inca's Throne and the tiered walls is called the Esplanade.

Qenko

From Sacsayhuaman, the path leads to Qenko (7am-5.30pm, Visitor's Ticket), which is further to the east beyond the statue of Christ. If you stand in the Esplanade and look away from Cusco you'll see a path heading uphill towards a barrier (which you can't see from the Esplanade) with a hut beside it. Walk up there, turn right (east) beyond the hut and follow the road past some souvenir sellers into a small wood. The road turns to the left (north), and on your right there is the stone mound of Qenko Chico (little Qenko), at the bottom of which there is a wall containing a block carved with twenty-one angles. A little further on, by a car park on the right-hand side of the road, is the large, eroded limestone outcrop of Qenko.

Qenko – the name means 'zigzag' or 'labyrinth' – is a huaca (sacred site). Immediately below the car park at the front of the site there is a monolith called the Seated Puma which is enclosed by a niched wall of fine masonry.

There are carvings everywhere, but some are a little indistinct: a llama, a condor, and snakes have all been identified. Inside the rock are several large niches and what looks like a sculpted altar. One recent discovery is a structure that seems to cast a shadow rather like a puma's head when the sun rises on the winter solstice (21 June). You'll probably have already seen a photograph of this on the cover of *The Awakening of the Puma*, sold in every bookshop in Cusco.

Salapunco

At Qenko it's best to ask someone for directions but you should follow the road uphill for about 50 metres; just before it joins the main road there is a path off to the right through the trees towards a village.

Go down the path to a small gully, pass through a gap in the wall and turn left uphill along the side of the gully. Keep the village on your right and just past it you come to a crossroads. Take the diagonal path (east) across the fields to a large rocky outcrop ahead. This is Salapunco, aka Cusilluchagoc (always open, admission free), another carved limestone monolith riddled with passages and providing excellent views from the top. It isn't on the tour routes so is often deserted.

Puca Pucara

If you stand on the top of Salapunco and look away from Cusco, you can see directly below you a clear track. Follow the track to the left (west) for just a few minutes until you come to a junction with a smaller path coming from your left. Follow this path north and down to a small marshy depression and on through boggy ground as it traces the seasonal course of a small stream. After climbing for about half an hour you pass a small village with a football field on your left, and beyond it you should be able to see the road running parallel to you. Shortly after this the path joins the road, and then Puca Pucara (7am-5.30pm, Visitor's Ticket) appears 50 metres away on the right.

Puca Pucara was probably a hunting lodge on one of the Inca's private estates near Cusco. It was originally thought to be a military checkpoint or on a main Inca road. The name can be translated as 'red watchtower' or 'red fort'.

Tambo Machay

You can see the signpost to Tambo Machay from Puca Pucara. Return to the road, walk away from Cusco and turn left (west) at the corner following the signpost to Tambo Machay (7am-5.30pm, Visitor's Ticket). It is about 200 metres away. Alternatively, in order to stay off the tarmac, cross the road and pick up the faint path that climbs the hill north-west through a small hamlet to emerge above the site.

Tambo Machay (the name means 'inn cave') is known popularly as Los Baños del Inca (the Inca's Baths), and was probably a centre of water worship. The whole complex is an architectural frame for a spring which falls from one terrace to another, slips underground, then emerges again in two cascades.

Returning to Cusco

You can either retrace your steps, or catch a bus or taxi on the road by the turning to Tambo Machay.

THE SACRED VALLEY   [see map, p163]

The fertile valley of the Urubamba river, also called the Vilcanota, snakes its way through the old Inca province of Antisuyu, an area which the Incas valued greatly. There, beside this tributary of the Amazon, they built their retreats, palaces and sacred places: the fortress of Ollantaytambo (clinging to the steep sides of the river's gorge), Pisac with its Inca canal, 3km long, its imposing terraces and, of course, the once-lost Machu Picchu.

Urubamba means 'place of the bugs or spiders' but the area is called the Sacred Valley in all today's tourist literature, no doubt to attract visitors to its proliferation of ruins. Yet, some do suggest the valley is sacred because it was Cusco's granary, and others because it is connected with the sun and sky. (However, there's no question it was very important to the Incas, and previously unknown carvings were uncovered in the valley in March 2000). One Quechua legend says that after the sun sets in the evening it passes through the underworld beneath the Urubamba where it drinks the chill water to refresh itself before emerging at dawn. Another legend says that the Urubamba is the earthly mirror of the celestial river, the Milky Way, and that water flows from one into the other.

There are many good hikes around the Sacred Valley. Hilary Bradt's *Backpacking and Trekking in Peru and Bolivia* describes some splendid little walks, as does Charles Brod's *Apus & Incas*, although this book is hard to obtain. Regular buses run from Cusco to the towns in the Sacred Valley (see towns below and also p155), and there are many hotels out here where you can stay to escape Cusco's bustle.

Pisac

Viceroy Toledo, who supervised the crushing of the last Incas, built Spanish Pisac on an Inca settlement in the shadow of the great terraces of the Inca ruins known as the Citadel. Many tombs have been found here, and there is a rare Intihuatana – a sacred carving or 'hitching post of the sun', many of which had their tops broken off by the Spanish. The site is open 7am-5.30pm (Visitor's Ticket) and is definitely worth visiting. Guides charge US$5 for a tour of the ruins. It's a large, sprawl-

---

(**Opposite**) **Top**: Across Cusco's Plaza de Armas. (Photo © Alexander Stewart).
Bottom: Parade of the Señor de los Tremblores – see p133. (Photo © Henry Stedman).

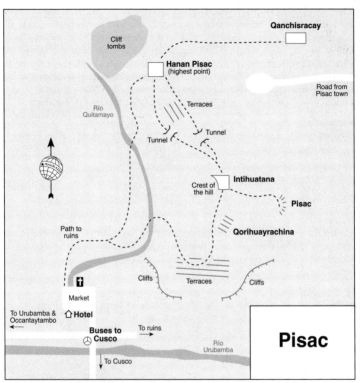

Pisac

ing site and you should allow a couple of hours to explore the terraces, water ducts, ruins and hidden chambers as well as to take in the stunning views of the valley, the patchwork fields, sheer cliffs and jagged ridges.

It's a fair climb up to the ruins (1-1½ hours), and if you're not yet acclimatized you'll need to take your time. The path begins behind (north of) the market, and forks after 10mins: the upper path (signposted 'subida', or 'ascent') is, misleadingly, the gentler, easier path, and follows the narrow Quitamayo stream up to the northernmost ruins of Hanan Pisac; the other, steeper path heads across the river and straight up the hill to the fortress and lookout post overlooking Pisac town. A taxi to the ruins from the town costs US$3 and takes 20 minutes. You can also hire horses in the town for US$3 per person to ride up.

There are markets in Pisac on Tuesday, Thursday and Sunday mornings at

(Opposite) Pisac Market. At this traditional market (Tuesday, Thursday and Sunday) you can buy anything from brightly-coloured textiles to multicoloured maize cobs.

which you can pick up well-made souvenirs. A shop on Plaza de Armas is worth mentioning because it sells fabrics produced by a weavers' collective, and all profits the shop makes go straight back to the weavers. If you're looking for a nibble, try the freshly baked flatbread produced in traditional clay ovens on Mariscal Castilla.

Pisac is 32km from Cusco. To get here catch a minibus (45 mins-1 hour, s/3.5, departs from Cusco roughly every 15 mins) from Calle Huáscar, Calle Puputi 208 or Inticahuarina in Cusco. A taxi costs about US$10 each way.

Chinchero

This village set amidst the Anta plains overlooking the Sacred Valley, is home to some Inca ruins and terraces (7am-5.30pm, Visitor's Ticket) and its 17th-century church, built on Inca foundations, has paintings from the Cusco School. The colourful Sunday market (crafts as well as local produce) is worth coming for, particularly since it attracts fewer tourists than the Pisac markets. Buses from Cusco leave early in the morning, usually from Calle Huáscar (s/2).

Urubamba

Urubamba is a largish town, and the centre of the bus network; this is where you change if you're travelling between Cusco and Ollantaytambo. It also has a local market and is the home of a number of the local weavers, ceramicists, pot-

CUSCO & AROUND

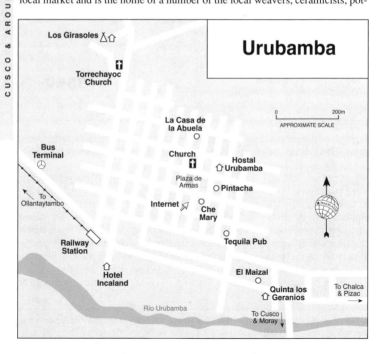

Urubamba

Los Girasoles

Torrechayoc Church

La Casa de la Abuela

Church

Hostal Urubamba

Plaza de Armas

Pintacha

Internet

Che Mary

Tequila Pub

Bus Terminal

To Ollantaytambo

Railway Station

Hotel Incaland

El Maizal

Quinta los Geranios

To Chalca & Pizac

Rio Urubamba

To Cusco & Moray

0   200m
APPROXIMATE SCALE

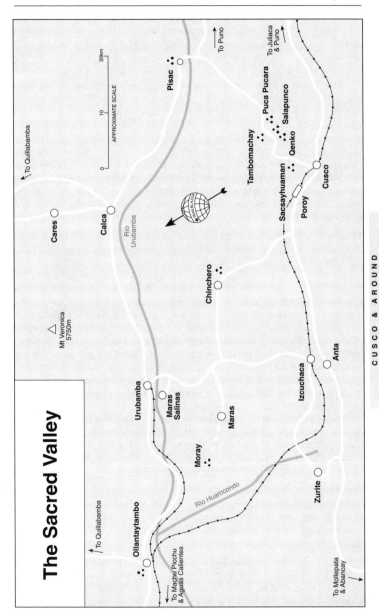

The Sacred Valley

To Quillabamba

To Quillabamba

Ollantaytambo

To Machu Picchu
& Aguas Calientes

Mt Veronica
5750m

Rio Huarocondo

Moray

Maras
Salinas

Maras

Urubamba

Zurite

Izcuchaca

Anta

To Mollepata
& Abancay

Cares

Calca

Rio
Urubamba

Chinchero

Sacsayhuaman

Poroy

Cusco

Tambomachay

Puca Pucara

Salapunco

Qenko

Pisac

To Puno

To Juliaca
& Puno

APPROXIMATE SCALE

0   10   20km

ters (Seminario Cerámicas at the Taller Workshop at Calle Berriozabal 111 are a particular favourite), sculptors and artists whose wares fill the souvenir shops in Cusco; you can spend a diverting morning wandering around their studios watching them at work and looking for bargains. Primarily, however, Urubamba is a good base from which to explore other parts of the Sacred Valley.

Moray (s/6, students s/3), probably an Inca experimental farm, where three natural depressions have been transformed into sets of concentric circular terraces of different sizes, lies two to three hours' walk from Urubamba (or you can catch a southbound bus, s/2 from Urubamba, and ask to be dropped off at the junction to Maras (s/2), from where you can hitch a lift to Moray 12km away). This strange place was probably used to study the effect of altitude on different plants; it's thought that the Incas may have cultivated more than 250 species of plants here.

You can walk 6km north-east from Moray (two hours) to the **Maras Salinas** (s/3), another bizarre site, where salty water from a hot spring up the valley is channelled into specially crafted pans, layered beige and white, and evaporated to produce salt.

Where to stay and eat There are plenty of hotels in Urubamba, which range from the expensive and rather flash English-owned *Hotel Incaland* on Av Ferrocarril (☎ 201126, 🖥 www.incalandperu.com) with room rates starting at US$70/80 sgl/dbl in the high season, to the mid-priced *Los Girasoles* (☎ 201390) on the outskirts of town beyond the Torrechayoc Church. Los Girasoles has camping sites, dormitory beds as well as doubles and singles; it's a touch overpriced at US$8 for a dormitory bed, or US$10/20 sgl/dbl, though you can't fault either the pastoral setting, the facilities (including a pizzeria, bar/leisure room and a permanent supply of hot water) or the spacious grounds. Otherwise, try *Quinta los Geranios* (☎ 201093), Cabo Conchatupa, which has clean new rooms for US$10/20/30 (sgl/dbl/tpl), a garden and an open-air restaurant. There are some cheaper places too, such as *Hostal Urubamba* (☎ 201062) on Jirón Bolognesi, one block east of Plaza de Armas, which charges s/10/20 (sgl/dbl, com) or s/20/30 (sgl/dbl, att).

For food *La Casa de la Abuela*, Bolívar 272, two blocks from Plaza de Armas, serves good fresh trout with baskets of roasted potatoes and *El Maizal*, Cabo Conchatupa, has a buffet of modern Peruvian dishes. For nightlife, try *Tequila Pub* on Av Mariscal Castilla, the inviting *Pintacha* on Bolognesi 523 or the cosy *Che Mary*, cnr Comercio and Grau.

Transport Urubamba is a 2½-hour minibus ride from Cusco (from Calle Huáscar or Inticahuarina, s/3). It's 1½ hours from Pisac and about 50 minutes from Ollantaytambo (s/1.5). There's also a tourist train service between Urubamba and Aguas Calientes (see p302 for details).

Ollantaytambo

At the end of its flat, verdant plain, the Urubamba river flows faster and enters a gorge which leads down from the Andes to the Amazon. It was in this beautiful, strategic spot, 68 kilometres from Cusco, that the Inca Pachacutec built his fortress of Ollantaytambo. It's a lovely place, green and relaxed, enclosed in

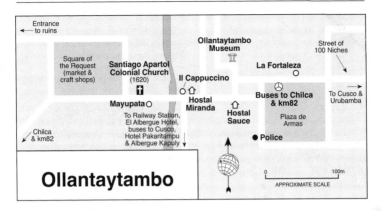

Ollantaytambo

hills that hide some of the most impressive ruins in the valley. Stay here if the strains of Cusco are getting you down, or if you want to explore the Sacred Valley or Machu Picchu from closer than Cusco itself.

The fortress temple Myth has it that the name comes from an Inca captain, Ollanta, who fell in love with Pachacutec's daughter. Pachacutec forbade them to marry, at which Ollanta rebelled. Pachacutec himself was killed in the ensuing battle, and Ollanta almost defeated the army of the empire but was betrayed. The new Inca took pity on him because of his great prowess in war and allowed him to marry the princess.

It was to the forbidding fortress temple (7am-6pm, Visitor's Ticket), high above the valley floor, that Manco Inca retreated when he was being pursued by the Spanish (p105), and from here that he defeated a raiding party of 70 Spaniards sent to seize him, forcing them to retreat after days of heavy fighting. It was the first time the Spanish had been worsted in open combat against the Incas. It was to be the last time too; a few months later Manco, realizing Ollantaytambo was too near to Cusco to be secure, opted to retreat over the mountains to Vilcabamba.

The steep terraces seem to bar your route up to the fortress, and walls rise from the near-vertical cliff faces – you can see why the Spanish failed to capture this place. More than 200 steps climb through the terraces from the open yard at the bottom to the main complex. At the top of the stairs lies the unfinished Sun Temple, consisting of six massive mortarless monoliths of pink porphyry, perfectly slotted together and stained with orange lichen. The double doorjambs you'll see here are rare in Inca buildings and indicate that this was a very important site. From the top you can see the quarry, Cachicata, 3.5km southwest of the site at the foot of Yana Urco (Black Mountain), where a huge rockfall provided loose stones of enormous size. A handful of giant blocks, known poetically as *piedras cansadas* ('tired stones'), litter the valley floor, lying where they were presumably abandoned while being transported from the quarry.

Ollantaytambo Museum
A burnished plaque on the museum in Ollantaytambo records its opening by none other than HRH Princess Anne. Many people wonder what she was doing out here. The answer is that Catcco, the organization that runs the museum, was set up as a joint project by the Cusichaca Trust (see p87), the University of Cusco, local community groups, and the British Embassy. It's an attempt to harness the tourist dollar to benefit the local people of Ollantaytambo directly, in a way that helps people come away with a greater understanding of campesino life and history. It's a very good museum, and is well worth a visit. It's open Tuesday to Sunday 10am-1pm and 2-4pm; entrance costs s/5, although two students can get in for the price of one. For a fascinating, detailed examination of the Inca stonework here, read *Inca Architecture and Construction at Ollantaytambo* by Jean-Pierre Protzen (1993).

Old town Below on the valley floor lies the old town of Ollantaytambo – one of the best surviving examples of Inca urban planning. The Incas built their towns in blocks called *canchas,* and one cancha housed several families. In most of Peru these canchas have long since been knocked down and the ancient Inca streets built over, but both remain here. Look out for more double door-jambs which show that this town itself was as important as the ruins that cling to the hills above. This place is one of the most photogenic in the entire Andes.

Where to stay and eat At the top end of the range, the modern *Hotel Pakaritampu* (☎ 204020) on the road just up from the station is comfortable and friendly, but pricey at US$99/104/134 (sgl/dbl/tpl, att, breakfast). *Hostal Sauce* (☎ 204044) has the best location, overlooking the Inca ruins and close to the main plaza. The rooms are as comfortable as they should be for US$69/79/105 (sgl/dbl/tpl, att, breakfast) although the service is brusque. There's also the excellent North American-owned *El Albergue* (☎ 204014), Casilla 784 Cusco (entrance on the platform of the station), which charges US$20/30 (sgl/dbl, breakfast), the more basic, cut-price *Albergue Kapuly* immediately on your left as you leave the station (US$10/20, sgl/dbl, att, breakfast) and the cheaper but very good *Hostal Miranda* (☎ 204091; s/20/30 sgl/dbl, but haggle). *La Fortaleza* is a good restaurant with branches on the north side of Plaza de Armas and on Plaza Ruinas, and the food at the Miranda is very tasty and they serve enormous portions. *Mayupata*, on Jr Convención by the bridge, serves good local food (menu US$7). For coffee and breakfasts try *Il Cappuccino*, just before the bridge.

Transport **From Cusco** you can get here by the expensive tourist train (about two hours, see pp301-2) or by colectivo or minibus. The railway station is about a 10- to 15-minute walk from the town centre. Colectivos and minibuses from Cusco leave from Calle Huáscar or in the side street of Inticahuarina. You will have to change in Urubamba. **From Ollantaytambo**, buses and colectivos to Urubamba, Chilca and Km82 leave from the main square, while direct buses to

Cusco (s/5) leave from the train station, where they meet the train coming from Aguas Calientes; as such, you may have to fight for a seat with those alighting from the train, though they try to lay on sufficient buses. You may be better off taking a colectivo to Urubamba and changing there.

Aguas Calientes
Also known as Pueblo Machu Picchu, this village is very much the end of the line now that the track that used to run on to Quillabamba has been destroyed. Really just a dormitory town for the ruins themselves, it's an ugly rash in the pristine forest of the Sanctuary. The town is named after some hot springs a few minutes' walk to the north, a series of rather tacky communal baths which are open 5am-8.30pm and cost s/6 to visit.

The trail up the mountain Putucusi starts here. Follow the railway track 250m west of the station to pick up a steeply ascending path. Parts of the trail have ladder rungs fixed in place and in others you may have to scramble. After rain the path can be slippery and treacherous. If you have difficulty locating the start of the trail ask at Gringo Bill's.

Also here, rather surprisingly for this remote place, is a first-class restaurant and the best hotel in the whole valley.

Where to stay The top hotel is *Machu Picchu Pueblo Hotel* (☎ 211122, 🖃 211124); reservations in Lima (☎ 422 6574, 🖃 422 4701, 🖳 www.inkaterra .com.pe), a beautiful place with bungalows set in the enclosing forest. Singles/doubles with attached bathroom cost US$155/173 plus tax, and not

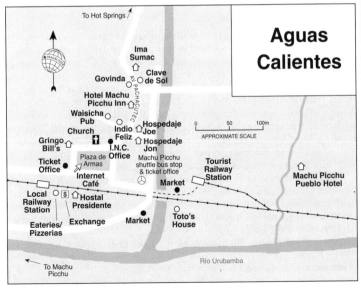

including breakfast. Slightly less expensive is the smart, recommended *Hotel Machu Picchu Inn* (☎ 211011, 📧 mapiinn@terra.com.pe, US$92, sgl & dbl) at Pachacutec 101, and the good-value *Hostal Presidente* (☎ 211034, 📧 presidente@terra.com.pe, US$50/60/70, sgl/dbl/tpl), hidden amidst the hostels and cheap eateries by the train tracks.

Other accommodation includes *Gringo Bill's* (☎ 211046, 📧 gringobill@yahoo.com), at Pasaje Colla Raymi 104, just off the plaza. Though the eponymous Bill no longer runs the show, the place still maintains its high standards; though room rates seem excessive at US$30/40 sgl/dbl, not including breakfast, there's a 10% discount if you stay for more than one night.

For cheaper accommodation, head up the hill towards the hot springs; this street, Av Pachacutec, is dotted with places to stay including the efficient and comfortable *Ima Sumac* (☎ 211021; US$20/25 sgl/dbl). Cheaper still, in an alley off Pachacutec are *Hospedaje Joe* and *Hospedaje Jon*, where rooms can cost as little as s/7 per person per night.

Where to eat The best restaurant is the French-run *Indio Feliz,* Calle Lloque Yupanqui Lt 4. If you walk up Av Pachacutec from the plaza it's on the left just after the school. Dishes here include freshly baked quiche lorraine and Urubamba trout smothered in melted butter. Prices are quite reasonable (three-course menu US$10-15) and portions large. *Toto's House*, overlooking the river at the eastern end of the village on Imperio de los Incas, offers an 'all-you-can-eat' buffet for US$10, while *Govinda*, on Pachacutec, serves well-priced vegetarian food. Cusco's Chez Maggy has a branch at Pachacutec 156, called *Clave de Sol*, selling decent pizzas. For live music in a good atmosphere try *Waisicha Pub* on Calle Lloque Yupanqui.

Transport The village boasts two **train stations**: the modern one, surrounded by wire fencing and policed by armed guards, serves the expensive tourist trains (the bridge to the platform was damaged in 2004, so trains couldn't pull up at the platform), while local trains (including the local train that has two Backpacker carriages attached and leaves at 5.45am) set off from the stretch of tracks running beneath the police station, to the south of the main square. There's no indication that this is a station, for it's little more than a rail track with pizza restaurants either side. All train tickets must be bought from the booth (8.30am-6pm) to the east of the police station. See pp301-2 for details and timetables of the train service. This is also where the train from La Hidroeléctrica, at the end of the Santa Teresa trek, comes in.

The **bus for Machu Picchu** leaves from the bus 'station' (just a patch of concrete where the train tracks pass over a small stream) every half hour from 6.30am to 1pm. You can buy tickets for the 20-minute journey at a concrete office near where the bus leaves (US$4.50 one way). Alternatively, **walking** up the path takes 1½-2 hours.

See p293 for more information on transport from Aguas Calientes and Machu Picchu.

PART 6: MINIMUM IMPACT

Minimum impact trekking

There are problems on the Inca Trail. Some are unavoidable: people are attracted to the spot because of its solitude, and when they arrive they turn it from an unvisited oasis to a tourist attraction. Some of the problems, however, can be avoided, such as those of litter and erosion, of pollution and destruction of the ancient Inca sites.

A lot of the damage done by tourists flows from selfish thoughtlessness. They forget that they're not the only people who'll walk in these hills: others, too, will be tempted to light a little cooking fire or camp in the ruins – a knock-on effect that endangers the environment. We who have the privilege of walking in this place must also accept the responsibility of helping to preserve it, at the very least by removing our rubbish.

ENVIRONMENTAL IMPACT

Continue to contaminate your bed, and you will one night suffocate in your own waste. **Chief Seattle**, taken from *Chief Seattle's Testimony* (Pax Christi and Friends of the Earth, 1976).

We are not entering a wilderness when we come to the Machu Picchu Historical Sanctuary. People, plants and animals have been living here for centuries in harmony. The influx of tourists threatens to ruin this delicate balance and we are part of the problem. By following a few rules, however, we can be part of the solution.

Pack it in, pack it out
If you've carried something into the Sanctuary, carry it out again. Some suggest burying litter but this isn't a solution as there are too many people walking these trails. Put your used packets and empty tins in a large plastic bag and dispose of them in Cusco. The rubbish bins along the trail are usually full to overflowing so it would be helpful if you took away some of the litter left by other people, too.

● **Is it OK if it's biodegradable?** Not really. Of course, things like an apple core will rot away in no time but orange peel takes six months to biodegrade, and clothes will take 15 years.

● **Lavatory paper** Lavatory paper is a vexed subject. Some people keep a lighter in a bag with their loo paper to burn the stuff. I find it difficult to get it to catch light so I pack it out along with everything else I've brought in. Put one plastic bag inside another (in case of ruptures), put the used paper inside and seal the top with a piece of wire. When you get to a lavatory (there are five on the trail) you can just flush the paper away. It might be biodegradable but if you leave it on the ground it will flutter around for a long time, a sordid reminder of your passing. Pack out tampons and sanitary towels, too.

Bury your excrement
Bring a little trowel to bury excrement. Make sure you do it *well* away from the trail.

Don't pollute water
Don't relieve yourself within 20m/70ft of a stream or other water supply. People have ignored this rule, and as a result giardia (see p180) has infected the streams in the Sanctuary.

Don't pollute streams with soap. Some people bring a collapsible plastic bucket to collect water to wash in from a stream. Dirty water should be poured away at least 20m/70ft from the water source.

Avoid using detergent to clean pans; use a wire scrubber in swiftly flowing water. If you must use detergent, wash up in a collapsible bucket away from the stream. I think 'biodegradable camping detergents' are a con, because all detergents are biodegradable – the problems only start when they've biodegraded.

Erosion
Inca roads were designed for llama hooves and bare human feet, and there wasn't much traffic in those days as no one could travel without a permit. Today the old stones bear the weight of thousands of tramping boots and running porters, and the old paths have become deeply scored into the mountainside.

There have been efforts to deal with the problem, and the section up to Abra de Huarmihuanusca (Dead Woman Pass) was paved in 1997. However, you can help things get better by sticking to the paths and camping only where you're supposed to. Trekking poles have also been banned, unless you cover the sharp metal tip with a rubber bung.

Camp-fires
It's a park rule that you're not allowed to have a camp-fire, so don't. This is because the wood you're burning is not unlimited and also there's the danger of camp-fires getting out of control: there were large fires in 1988, 1994 and 1997 that were probably caused by careless tourists or their porters.

Camping in the ruins
Inca ruins that have stood for hundreds of years are being damaged by selfish hikers who want the experience of sleeping in them, and think that it won't do any harm. But it does. Just peek over the other side of Sayacmarca and you'll see a pyramid of turds and a field of paper dropped by people who think that they're the only ones who've ever camped here.

Litter's not the only problem. Camp-fires can cause damage to the ancient walls, and careless campers knock off stones. And there's the more intangible way that people stake ownership with their sweaty bodies and nylon tents to the ruins that should belong to everyone.

Machu Picchu cable car
Some threats to the Sanctuary are caused by the desire to improve the locals' standard of living and attract more tourists. The most important is the cable car. First mooted in 1998, then shelved in 2001, and then proposed once more in 2002 only to be shelved a second time, this would have taken up to 400 tourists an hour from the valley floor up to Machu Picchu. I've great doubts about it, both because it could increase the number of tourists tramping around the old stones, and also because it'd detract from the wonderful isolation of the site. Others disagree with me, notably John Hemming, the author of *The Conquest of the Incas*, who points out that it couldn't be much worse than the current set-up: a dreadful road from the valley floor, trafficked by knackered old buses belching filthy black smoke into the pristine mountain air.

Obey the park ruling and don't camp in the ruins, tempting as it might be. Wardens occasionally patrol the ruins to catch people camping illegally.

Don't pick flowers or disturb animals

You will be walking in a UNESCO natural World Heritage Site. It's a sanctuary where plant- and wild-life are supposed to exist without human interference, so don't pick the plants and leave any animals you see in peace.

The authorities may also be responsible for damage to the place, sometimes by accident, at other times on purpose. An example of accidental, well-meaning damage happened at Intipata (see p198). The site was regularly cleared of encroaching plant life until it was discovered that it was a haven for a rare orchid.

ECONOMIC IMPACT

If tourists were more aware of the power of their money and the responsibility that goes with it, they could do a lot of good.

The power you have to do good

Some locals are as guilty of not looking after the Sanctuary as the tourists and authorities. The villains are often cheap tour operators, who drop litter and exploit their porters: porters are often paid very little for the back-breaking work of carrying your bags, and may not be provided with either food or shelter (see Porter Welfare, p172).

● **Pay a fair price for a fair service** If you take a cheap tour, the misery of the porters and the filth that's dropped on the ground is your responsibility – you're the one who's saving the price of a trip to the cinema by not giving these people a living wage. Don't encourage this situation. Go for the more up-market tours where the porters are more realistically paid and more effort is made to ensure that litter is removed.

There's nothing worse than the shameful sight of a Westerner bargaining with a porter over what is to him the price of a newspaper and to the porter a square meal. Of course you may need to bargain and you shouldn't allow your-

Porter welfare

Over 5000 indigenous Andean men, mostly subsistence farmers, work the Inca Trail as porters. Many more work the other trails as arrieros. Porters and arrieros need fair wages, decent meals and warm, dry overnight accommodation, but in the past they have often been exploited, and have had to put up with inadequate equipment and very low wages. Fortunately this situation is changing. The Porters' Law passed in 2001 demands a wage of s/35 per day for the four-day classic Inca Trail, and limits loads to 25kg. Organizations dedicated to porter welfare are also campaigning for better working conditions. However, a few agencies continue to operate unscrupulously, and those offering the classic Inca Trail trek for less than US$240 are very unlikely to have the porters' best interests at heart. The minimum wage has proved to be unenforceable and the typical rate is currently around s/20-25 per day. Porters' loads are weighed and checked at fixed points along the trail, but some agencies have abused the system by getting guides and assistants to carry packs through the checkpoint, only to hand them back to porters on the other side.

As a trekker, there are a number of things you can do to help. Tell your agency that porter welfare is important to you and it makes a difference when you choose an operator. Ask how much the porters are paid and enquire about the standard of their equipment. Do they have waterproof clothing? Do they all sleep in tents and have access to sleeping bags and mats? Once on the trek, get to know your porters, share some coca leaves and pick up a smattering of Quechua. At the end of the trek make sure that you tip your porters properly. You could thank them individually and give tips to them directly; this will stop a collective tip being unfairly distributed by a selfish guide.

If you encounter agencies taking advantage of their porters or witness abuse bring it to the attention of the guide. He might not be that responsive, so on your return to Cusco, make an official complaint at the agency office, and submit a report to the South American Explorers Club (see box p118), the Inka Porter Project, who keep logbooks of incidents in their Cusco office, or Andean Travel Web (see below). Your observations will force agencies to recognize that in order to continue to do business they must respect and look after their porters.

Inka Porter Project – Proteadores Inka Ñan

This organization, at Dept 4, Choquechaca 188, Cusco (☎ 246829, 🖳 www.peru web.org/porters), is dedicated to improving the working conditions of porters and muleteers. It provides English lessons to better employment prospects, training workshops, an equipment-loan programme, and a drop-in centre in Ollantaytambo where porters can discuss work-related issues. It's also the base for courses in environmental training, health, first aid and sanitation. You can get its quarterly newsletter, *El Ch'aski*, in many cafés and pubs in Cusco, or read it online.

Andean Travel Web

This website, 🖳 www.andeantravelweb.com, runs community projects and is dedicated to raising awareness of porter welfare, as well as being a fantastic source of information about Cusco, its environs and all the region's treks. When in Cusco you can donate clothing or school equipment at their office (Calle Garcilaso 265, Office 13, 2nd Floor). The office overheads are all paid for by Peru Treks and Adventure (see box p141), so any cash donations go directly to the communities.

self to get ripped off, but find out from other hikers what the current fair price is, and pay accordingly.

The power you have to do bad

Well-meaning trekkers have created a begging culture amongst the children who live along the trail. In the busier villages, you'll be swamped with little hands and engulfed by children's voices piping: '*Dame dulce*', '*Dame regalo*' (give me a sweetie/candy, a present). Because of their success with other tourists, little kids now associate gringos with an unlimited supply of money and sweets.

What you do about it is a matter for you. It's hard to resist the plaintive faces and grubby hands. I think that giving makes the situation worse: if they've done something helpful, reward them. Otherwise, sing them a song or make them laugh and they'll begin to see you more as a person, and less as an animated gum-ball machine.

CULTURAL IMPACT

Many campesinos get a pretty odd idea of life outside Peru as all they see of the world is well-dressed, apparently rich, tourists. Explain to them what the cost of living is like back home – how much does a loaf of bread cost, or a pint of milk – and how many hours you worked to earn the money to come to their country. Help them put your holiday into perspective and realize that we're not all millionaires.

Consider the feelings of local people

Some tourists leave their basic tact at home and forget that the locals they meet on holiday can be offended just as easily as they can themselves. It's often simple things caused by thoughtlessness that can really irritate.

● **Photographs** Ask permission before you take a photo and if your subject doesn't want you to take one, don't. Some children dress up and look deliberately cute, and then charge money when you ask to photograph them. Don't rip them off, but if you pay too much it becomes demeaning when they earn the same amount in ten seconds as their parents earn in ten hours.

● **Camping** If you're planning to camp somewhere near a village, ask permission: making contact can also help with safety.

● **Clothing** Although it matters less in Peru than in Islamic countries, wearing inappropriate clothing can still offend.

In churches you should show proper respect by covering normally exposed skin. Don't bathe naked in mountain streams where you could be spotted.

● **Don't flaunt your wealth** However poor you may be by Western standards, your wealth is way above the wildest dreams of most campesinos so don't flaunt it. Never leave valuable items such as cameras or watches lying about.

● **Be polite** Some campesinos can be offended if they offer you a place to stay the night and you refuse and set up your tent in their fields instead. Not surprisingly, they can also get offended if they offer you food and you turn it down and cook your own. Wouldn't you be? Be aware of this, and try not to step on any toes. Some campesinos are over-friendly in a way that's not helpful; they might point you in a direction you know is wrong, or proffer unwanted help. Keep your patience and just decline pleasantly.

● **Always keep your sense of humour** If things aren't working out as you want don't lose your temper. It's more likely that the person you're talking to does not understand what you want than that they're being deliberately obstructive. A smile costs nothing.

Return hospitality
You'll probably encounter hospitality that will make you swell up with guilt, as someone who can afford nothing gives you much and won't accept repayment. If you find yourself in this position, don't force money on people who don't want it as they have their pride just as you do. Share your food with them, and try and give them something of yourself in return: try and speak Quechua, listen to them (some shepherds are just lonely), and tell them about your home or how much you like their country. Campesinos are as proud and patriotic as anyone.

Safe trekking

SAFETY IN THE HILLS

If you're properly prepared for your trek, you should have no problems, just a wonderful time.

Weather
The weather in the Machu Picchu Historical Sanctuary is very changeable. Expect rain and carry warm clothing, even if the sun's out and it's a beautiful day, because while the valleys are bathed in beautiful sunshine the high passes may be enveloped in cloud. For more information about the climate see p20.

Getting lost
In good weather most of the trails described in this book are clear and easy to follow. I don't believe it's possible to get lost on the stretch from Huayllabamba to Machu Picchu, as it's a heavily beaten path and there'll be many other people walking at the same time as you. In bad weather, however, there are points on the more remote trails where the path will disappear, and there are sections of the Mollepata, Santa Teresa and Vilcabamba treks, and to a lesser degree the Choquequirao trek, that are difficult in any weather.

Therefore a **compass** is absolutely essential if you're walking the longer trails. Some people bring a handheld GPS (Global Positioning System), but they really aren't worth it unless you're taking the Vilcabamba trail or heading off into the wilderness.

Tell people where you're going

Before you leave on your trek, it's wise to inform someone at home and to tell your hotel manager or a fellow traveller where you're going and when you plan to be back; they should be aware of what to do if you don't get back, and how long to wait before raising the alarm.

Dogs

Dogs can be dangerous if they're carrying rabies and a nuisance when you're hiking. They'll often bark as you pass, but they seldom attack. If they look threatening, throw stones at them – this is what the locals do. The mere act of bending down to pick one up often scares them off.

A note of caution

Sadly there are some theft problems on the Inca Trail, and you'll hear some scare stories from other travellers but only believe one-tenth of what you hear. Remember many thousands of hikers walk these trails each year without meeting any trouble at all.

You can easily reduce the risk of being a target by travelling in groups, by stuffing your valuables deep down into your rucksack when you walk and by not leaving anything tempting outside your tent when you zip-up for the night. The SAE (see box p118) in Cusco is a good source of information as to the current situation.

Villages on these trails are usually trouble free, but when you camp near one it's best to ask a local family for permission, partly out of politeness but also to come under their protection.

HEALTH IN THE HILLS

Walking in the Sanctuary is invigorating. It's generally a very healthy place, the blustering winds blow the cobwebs away and the sun warms your heart. When you come down from the high altitude, you'll feel like Superman. Nevertheless, you should be aware of illnesses associated with altitude above 3000m/ 10,000ft.

AMS – acute mountain sickness

AMS and the medical conditions, High Altitude Pulmonary Oedema (HAPO or HAPE) and High Altitude Cerebral Oedema (HACO or HACE), that can result from it are all entirely preventable if certain precautions are taken.

The important thing to remember is that **it is the speed of ascent not the altitude itself that causes AMS**. The body takes several days to adapt to an increase in altitude. The higher you go above sea-level, the lower the barometric pressure, resulting in less oxygen reaching your lungs with each breath you take. At 2500m/8202ft it's about 25% lower but up to this altitude the effects are rarely felt; at 5000m/16,400ft the pressure is almost 50% lower.

AMS is uncomfortable but not dangerous unless it's a severe case. You'll feel a headache and nausea. In bad cases you may start vomiting. It's a bit like having a hangover, and it usually passes after one to three days. You can take painkillers (but not sleeping tablets) and acetazelomide (see below), but the best thing to do is rest, and if it gets worse, descend.

HAPO and HACO are very serious, and potentially life-threatening. You should know both how to recognize them and what to do if you suspect someone's got either of them, but if you take care you're very unlikely to come across either. **HAPO** occurs when the lungs get waterlogged. Symptoms include not being able to breathe properly and finding it more difficult to exert yourself than usual. It tends to progress from AMS, but it's not common in trekkers. The pulse increases, fluid is coughed up, there's fever, and your extremities go blue (compare fingernail beds with a healthy person). Sometimes there's also chest tightness, and the lungs sound crackly. Once the person descends, recovery is usually quick and complete.

HACO is a build-up of fluid in the brain. Anyone who gets it will suffer from loss of balance, severe lassitude and will eventually fall into a coma. There may also be an altered mental state – hallucinations, weakness or numbness on one side of the body, and an inability to talk or make sense. Headache, nausea and vomiting are also symptoms. Death occurs quickly if the person remains at altitude, and even if you get them down, there can be long-term neurological damage.

All are caused by the body's response to the lower oxygen pressure in the air, and all can be largely treated by descending promptly.

● **Headache** Headache is an important warning sign of trouble. If you have a headache follow Dr Peter Hackett's headache rule: rest, don't ascend, eat snacks, drink plenty of fluids, take mild pain medicine. If it's not going away or you suspect altitude sickness, don't ascend. If you suffer from severe shortness of breath at rest (you don't get your breath back after 15 minutes) or if you have any of the symptoms listed in the boxed text on p177 **descend immediately** – even if it's the middle of the night.

● **Ataxia** Ataxia is altered balance and muscular coordination. You can test for it by drawing a 2m (6ft) line on the ground and walking heel-to-toe along it. If you can't walk in a straight line, fear the worst and descend.

● **Acetazelomide** Acetazelomide (Diamox) is a drug that can prevent and treat AMS (not HAPO or HACO). It's a diuretic so will make you urinate more, and it makes your fingertips tingle. It's widely available in Peru. The dose is 125mg twice a day, usually taken before you go to sleep. You can stop taking it after a couple of days at altitude. Some doctors recommend taking the same dose as a treatment for AMS, though by far the best thing is to descend. Don't take acetazelomide if you're allergic to sulpha drugs.

● **Coca leaf** Coca leaf (see p51) has been used for centuries to reduce the effects of AMS. You chew it in a quid in your mouth, with a little *llibita* (a catalyst made of lime and potash). Some say it works; all it did for me was turn my shirt green when I spat out the juice and missed the ground.

SERIOUS AMS SYMPTOMS – IMMEDIATE DESCENT!

- **Persistent, severe headache**
- **Persistent vomiting**
- **Ataxia** – loss of co-ordination, inability to walk in a straight line, making the sufferer look drunk.
- **Losing consciousness** – inability to stay awake or understand instructions.
- **Liquid sounds in the lungs**
- **Very persistent, sometimes watery, cough**
- **Difficulty breathing**
- **Rapid breathing or feeling breathless at rest**
- **Coughing blood, pink phlegm or lots of clear fluid**
- **Severe lethargy**
- **Marked blueness of face and lips**
- **High resting heartbeat – over 130 beats per minute**
- **Mild symptoms rapidly getting worse**

Injury

An elementary knowledge of First Aid is always useful. In an emergency, the basics are ABC: first check the casualty's **airway's clear**, then check **breathing** and **circulation**.

- **A Airway** Make sure the mouth is clear and the tongue is not obstructing the airway. Clean out vomit or anything else that's in the way.
- **B Breathing** Check the casualty's breathing by putting your ear close to his mouth.
- **C Circulation** Check the heart's beating by feeling for a pulse on the wrist, groin or neck, or by feeling the chest. If there's no pulse, start cardiac massage. Remember to stanch any wounds that are bleeding profusely (if it's arterial blood – red and spurting – press heavily on the bleeding point for 10 minutes, then apply a crepe bandage. Raise the wounded area above the level of the heart).

If the injury is serious and you need trained medical help you'll have to get the casualty out because there are no doctors on the remoter regions of this trail. Strap up suspected broken bones, try to keep the person as immobile and as warm as possible, and ask the locals for help.

Animal bites

- **Rabid animals** If you get bitten by a dog, bat or other similar animal, there's a risk of contracting **rabies**, so wash out the wound with copious amounts of soap and water. Use a stiff brush if you have one, and get into the corners of the wound even if it hurts, then disinfect. Seek medical help as quickly as possible – there's a rabies centre in Lima (see p117). Rabies can kill you and since it may lie dormant for months; you must get advice even if you feel fine.
- **Snakes** You are very unlikely to get bitten by a snake. If you do, don't try sucking the venom out or cutting into the wound. Keep still, wash the wound

MINIMUM IMPACT TREKKING

and surrounding skin with water to remove any excess venom. It's reassuring to know that many snakes aren't venomous, and many snake bites don't result in venom being injected. Remove any rings, watches or other constrictions because the bitten area may swell.

If you can, capture and kill the snake so it can be identified but make sure it's dead. I read somewhere the story of a paratrooper who was bitten by a snake. His colleagues did all the right things to the victim, caught the snake so that it could be identified by the doctor, beat it to death and stuffed it in a sack. The victim and sack were evacuated by air but in the plane, the 'dead' snake escaped from its sack and bit the pilot.

If a limb's been bitten, splint it, but don't apply a tourniquet unless you know what you're doing. Many limbs are lost through inexpertly applied tourniquets. It's vital not to panic, **keep calm**, reassure yourself that even if you're bitten you're unlikely to die. Gene Savoy, the explorer of Vilcabamba, was bitten by a venomous snake and didn't die from the bite.

Extreme heat and cold
● **Hypothermia** A person gets hypothermic when they are extremely cold, and this can kill them. If someone's hypothermic, they'll stumble, be confused, act oddly and be extremely cold to the touch. They may not notice they are ill, so if someone's acting like this warm them up. The best way to do this is to share bodily warmth, as James Bond said in *The Spy Who Loved Me*: strip the victim naked, get undressed yourself and jump into a sleeping bag together.

● **Sunburn and sun-stroke** The tropical sun in the high Andes burns quickly. **Sunburn** can be avoided by covering exposed skin (wear a long-sleeved cotton or linen shirt rather than a T-shirt) and putting sunblock on your face – especially your nose and ears. Always wear a hat.

When a person's temperature has been driven up dangerously high by the sun (usually above 40°C or 104°F), they've got **sun-stroke**. A sun-stroke patient will be confused and possibly delirious. Breathing and pulse rate will be rapid (over 30 breaths a minute and a pulse of over 100 beats a minute). Reduce temperature by fanning, gradually cooling them by sponging frequently with a cool damp cloth. If the person loses consciousness you must get them to a doctor quickly.

Not dangerous but irritating
● **Blisters** If you feel skin rubbing, put a piece of moleskin on it or some of the second skin (Compeed) you can buy in pharmacies. If you've got a blister you can burst it with a sterilized needle (hold it in a flame for a few seconds) then cover it with a sterile dressing. Alternatively cover the unbroken blister with a build-up of moleskin.

● **Cracked skin and lips** Carry moisturizing cream and lip balm. Some people find the skin painfully pulling back from their nails and cracking – it grows back when you descend to lower altitudes.

Cook it, peel it, wash it or forget it

Many of the bugs that travellers pick up come from dirty water or food that's been prepared by someone with dirty hands. The key to avoiding these diseases is hygiene, but that's not something you're going to have complete control over. If you are doubtful about something you're offered to eat – if it's had flies on it, if it's not piping hot, if it's raw – leave it. The travellers' golden rule is if you can't cook it, peel it, wash it (in purified water) then forget it. Sadly that means that you should avoid ceviche (it's raw fish), which is a shame because it's a wonderful dish. I'm not encouraging you to go against sensible medical advice but it's worth saying that if you leave Peru without eating ceviche, you're missing out. If you do try it, perhaps wait until after you've been trekking.

Water purification

When you're hiking, you should purify your water unless you're getting it from a spring right at the top of a valley, as humans and livestock upstream from you are probably polluting it. There are a number of ways of doing this. You can use iodine tablets or drops, a water filter, or you can do it by boiling.

● **Iodine tablets** If you use tablets, use iodine not chlorine, as bugs like giardia aren't killed by chlorination. However, you shouldn't use iodine at all if you've got a thyroid problem, and it's not good for anyone to use it for long periods of time. It makes the water taste disgusting but you can add Vitamin C tablets or flavoured fruit powders to neutralize the taste. There are a number of brands on the market in the West (eg Potable Aqua and MicroPur). One tablet purifies a litre of water in about ten minutes.

● **Iodine drops** Using a 2% solution (Tincture of Iodine), the dose is 5 drops per litre of clean water which must then stand for 20-30 minutes. If the water is cloudy double the dose. You need a dropper to dispense the correct dose. Wrap the bottle and dropper in more than one plastic bag. An iodine leak in the centre of a pack can be a very messy business.

● **Water filter** This is a portable device that chemically or mechanically removes impurities from water, but they're expensive, and mechanical filters don't clean the water thoroughly enough to be much use.

● **Boiling** Current research shows that water need be brought only to the boil (even at altitude) to kill the bugs in it so drinks made from boiling water are generally safe.

Diseases from other people's filth

● **Diarrhoea** Despite the best precautions, just about everyone gets the 'Inca Two Step' in Peru. It's nothing to worry about. Don't plug yourself up immediately with Imodium: if your body wants to get rid of the contents of your bowels, let it. Drink lots of (uncontaminated) fluids: take a little weak soup or flat soft drinks, have some camomile tea with sugar and if you have re-hydrating powders, use them now. Only block yourself up if you have to travel or are becoming seriously dehydrated; avoid travelling if you can because it's best to rest for a couple of days. Be reassured that most of these attacks pass. However, if you're not better after two to three days, or if you get worse, you should try to see a doctor as you could have one of the following:

● **Dysentery** Dysentery is caused by drinking infected water or eating contaminated foods. It feels like diarrhoea with stomach cramps, and you may have blood in your faeces. Dysentery is treatable, but amoebic dysentery can cause difficulties if it's not caught.

● **Giardiasis** Giardiasis (giardia) is caused by eating or drinking giardia parasites that live in dirty water and food. The symptoms are foul-smelling belches and wind and a distended belly. The symptoms often go away on their own, but you could still be spreading the disease for months afterwards, so it's best to get it treated by a doctor.

● **Cholera** Transmitted in a similar way, cholera is rare in travellers. It mostly afflicts people who live in poor conditions where there's little fresh water; it's easily treatable.

Things not to worry about

I'm writing this last bit, not because you're in the least likely to come across any of these diseases, but to give you something to read on the bus.

● **Chagas disease** This is a rare, insect-borne disease transmitted by the bite of the assassin bug. The colourfully named insect lives in the walls and roof of rustic huts, and comes out at night to feed on you. When it bites your skin, it tramples its faeces into the puncture hole and with the faeces go the germ that causes the disease. The bite hurts, so you'll know you've been bitten. If you're unlucky enough to be infected, the bite will swell and become inflamed. If this happens, get a blood test because the symptoms don't begin to appear properly for some years, by which time they're difficult to treat. Interesting fact about Chagas disease: Charles Darwin probably died from it, aged 73.

● **Leishmaniasis** This disease is transmitted by sand-flies, and causes ulcers, most of which heal painlessly – but some don't. Interesting fact about leishmaniasis: this is the disease you can see afflicting some of the subjects of Moche pots who look like Boris Karloff. Obviously the people portrayed in the pots suffered from the unhealing kind of ulcer.

● **Oroya (verruga) fever** This is another rare disease, caused by the bite of the phlebotomus sand-fly which lives only on Andean slopes between 800m and 2600m (2625ft and 8525ft). It's easily treatable with antibiotics, but if not caught will cause death by breaking down your red blood cells. The symptoms are bone and muscle pain, and anaemia. Interesting fact about Oroya fever: it's extremely rare, but everyone who gets a touch of fever thinks they've got it.

PART 7: TRAIL GUIDE & MAPS

Using this guide

ROUTE DESCRIPTIONS

In the route descriptions that follow, directions are given as a compass point and an indication of whether to go right or left. An example might read: 'turn north (R)' which means north is to your right, or 'turn left (W)' which means left is a westerly direction.

Direction

On all the trails except three you can walk in the opposite direction to the one given here. The exceptions are that you're not allowed to start at Machu Picchu and walk to Huayllabamba or to Chachabamba (Km104), and it wouldn't be sensible to do the Chilca Circuit in reverse because you'd have to pay the Inca Trail fee without actually walking it. The Choquequirao trek is done as a there-and-back hike along the same route by most people although it's possible to link it with other treks (see p276).

ROUTE MAPS

(See pp22-3 for Route Planning map)

Scale and walking times

These maps are drawn to an approximate scale of 1:50,000 (20mm to one kilometre). Remember that much of the walking is uphill and down, and the mere length of a trail is no indication of how long it's going to take you. Walking time is more important. In the margin of the maps, you'll see the time it takes to get from one '▲' to the next '▲'. Timings usually run in both directions and are approximate: some people are going to walk much faster, and some slower than I did. If you've got a mule or porter to carry your kit, you'll take only about a half to three quarters of the time given.

Note that **the time given refers only to time spent actually walking**, so you will need to add more time to allow for rest stops. This will obviously vary from person to person but as a rough guide add 20-30% to allow for stops.

Up or down?

The trail is shown as a dotted line. Many of the trails are up or down. One arrow indicates a steep slope; two arrows indicate a very steep slope. The arrow points towards the higher part of the trail. If, for example, you were walking from A (at 900m) to B (at 1100m) and the trail between the two were short and very steep, it would be shown like this: A - - - >> - - - B.

THE INCA TRAIL REGULATIONS IN A NUTSHELL

(See also pp11-12 and box pp140-1); note that these regulations are subject to change; before booking check the latest information with the SAE (see box p118), or on the Internet at the excellent 💻 www.andeantravel web.com). The **key points** of the regulations are as follows: a maximum of 500 people are allowed to start the Inca Trail each day. This daily limit covers the classic Km88 route, its various offshoots (Km82 and Km77), those joining it at Huayllabamba (including the Mollepata and Silque Valley treks), and the shorter Km104 trek. It also includes the guides, cooks and porters associated with each group, meaning that only around 200 tourists actually begin the trails each day (approximately 180 who will trek through Huayllabamba and 20 who set out from Km104). All of which means that there is fierce competition for permits, so **you need to make a reservation long before you do your trek**. You can walk from Mollepata or Chilca to Huayllabamba without a licensed guide or tour group. However, once you get to Huayllabamba you won't be able to get any further unless you've made arrangements to join an organized group there. Many agencies offer this service, but charge the full trek price even though you join the tour at the start of its second day. You should also note that no group may start a trek on the classic Inca Trail during February (see p20).

To book your **permit**, you must provide the tour agency with your name and passport details, and pay the entrance fee. Permits are non-transferable and non-refundable and it's impossible to change the date of the trek departure once it's been booked. Bear in mind that tour agencies have to book all the permits for a trekking group in one go and cannot make changes afterwards. As a result agents like to wait as long as possible for groups to fill up, which is more profitable for them (see p12).

The **entrance fee** for the classic Inca Trail is s/192 (around US$60) for adults and half-price for children under 15 and students under 28 with a valid International Student Identity Card (ISIC); this card must be presented at the time of booking. The fee must be paid by anyone trekking to Machu Picchu via Huayllabamba, whether starting from Km88, Km82, Chilca, Mollepata or anywhere else. The entrance fee for the shorter trek from Km104 is US$25/15 adults/children under 15 and students. The fee for all routes includes the US$20 one-day entrance charge to Machu Picchu.

All companies offering the Inca Trail trek must have an **official license,** To get one they must prove they provide professional, licensed guides, good camping equipment, radio equipment and first-aid supplies including oxygen. Licences are reviewed every February. Tour groups can have no more than 16 persons, and must include two guides if larger than 8 (or 7 for the shorter Km104 trek).

See box pp140-1 for information on **arranging treks in Cusco** and p306 for a list of licensed Cusco tour agencies.

Regulations have also been imposed to improve working conditions for **porters**, whose permits are paid for by the tour agency (see box p172).

Trekkers must carry their **passport** (a photocopy will not do) on the trail and will be required to present it along with their trek permit and ISIC card (where relevant) at the checkpoints at Km82 or Km88, Huayllabamba and the Trekkers' Hotel.

The following have been **banned from the trail**: plastic bottles (although evidence along the trail suggests that this is not yet being enforced properly); pets and pack animals (though llamas may go as far as Huayllabamba); and walking poles unless the tips are covered by a rubber bung to minimize damage to Inca paths.

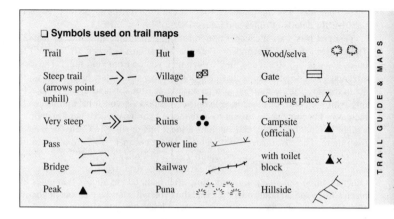

❏ **Symbols used on trail maps**

Trail	— — —	Hut	■	Wood/selva	🌳 🌳
Steep trail (arrows point uphill)	⟩—	Village	⊠⊠	Gate	▱
		Church	+	Camping place	△
Very steep	⟩⟩—	Ruins	∴	Campsite (official)	▲
Pass	⌣	Power line	⌄⌄		
Bridge	⥤	Railway	⊢+++	with toilet block	▲ ×
Peak	▲	Puna	𖠿 𖠿 𖠿	Hillside	⋰

Altitudes
The altitudes in this book were taken from GPS and altimeter readings and have an average margin of error of +/- 150m.

Place names
Quechua words can be spelt in a number of ways. In this section of the guide, places are spelt in the Hispanic way, because it's more familiar and because that's the spelling used on most maps.

Some places have more than one name: for example, Ancascocha is Silque on some maps, Patallacta is sometimes called Llactapata, and Paucarcancha often goes under the name of Inca Raccay ('raccay' means 'ruin' in Quechua, so 'Inca Raccay' indicates any Inca ruins). Where there's a potential cause for confusion I've given all the names.

Practicalities

FOOD AND WATER

Many of the smaller streams shown on the maps are seasonal and may be dry when you walk, so you should carry more water than you think you need. Note that there's **nowhere to buy food on these trails**: you (or your porters) need to carry everything you're going to eat.

GETTING TO THE TRAILHEADS

The **trains** from Cusco to Machu Picchu leave regularly each day from San Pedro station (see p155), though the cheapest tourist service is now more than

US$40 one way. The train stops en route at Chilca and Kms 82, 88 and 104. See pp301-2 for details of times and prices.

Tourist buses are a cheaper option for those travelling to Chilca or Km82. Tickets from the travel agents on Plaza de Armas cost between s/12 and s/17; buses leave at 6-6.30am, and they'll even pick you up from your hotel. The disadvantage of taking these is that they don't arrive at the start of the trail until about midday; furthermore, if you're starting at Km82, because you're travelling with a bus full of other travellers the likelihood is you'll be walking with them too. For this reason, if you have the time I strongly recommend spending a night in Ollantaytambo, and catching a **local bus** or truck to Chilca or Km82 from there. The advantages are threefold: it's far cheaper (s/4.5 from Cusco to Ollantaytambo by local bus, and another s/1.5 to Chilca or Km82); you arrive at the start of your trek much earlier (the first truck or bus leaves Ollantaytambo's main square some time after 6am, taking about 30 minutes to reach Chilca and an hour to Km82); and thus you will start way before anybody else. Ollantaytambo has much to recommend it too (see p164).

Buses to Mollepata leave from Cusco's Calle Arcopata at 5am. There is sometimes a later one, though not everyday. Buses to Abancay from the same place can drop you at the bottom of a track that leads up to Mollepata. See p218 for details of why these aren't such a good idea. Both buses charge s/5-8. The situation changes often, so ask at your hotel for the latest information (don't trust what they tell you at the tourist information office because they often get it wrong).

For details of how to get to the start of the Vilcabamba Trail at Huancacalle, see p240; for information on Cachora, the trailhead of the Choquequirao trek see p266.

❏ **Walking times on trail maps**
Note that on all of the trail maps in this book the times shown alongside each map refer only to **time spent actually walking**. When planning your walking for the day you should add about 20-30% to allow for rest stops.

The classic Inca Trail

Starting through the eucalyptus forest on the banks of the Urubamba river, the trail quickly turns into a steep series of climbs and descents. There are three passes to go over, the highest being 4200m (13,750ft) and it takes three to four days to reach Machu Picchu.

KM88 → HUAYLLABAMBA   [MAP 1, p187]

Km88 to Patallacta

The train stops very briefly at **Km88** – watch the kilometre markers by the side of the railway or ask someone to tell you when it's near so you can be prepared to gather your kit and make your way to the doors. Jump off, pass along the tracks in the direction the train's been going (W) and follow a little path down to the river, where you'll find a **bridge** and a **park warden's booth**. Your permits and passports will be checked here. Km88 is sometimes known by its Quechua name, Corihuayrachina.

Across the bridge, you can go either left (E) or right (W). To the right there's a detour to the seldom-visited ruins of **Huayna Quente** and **Machu Quente** (see p186), a 20-minute walk away. The path actually continues all the way to Chachabamba, a pleasant and much quieter alternative to the other Inca trails (see box on p206).

The main trail goes off to the left (E), following the southern banks of the Urubamba through a eucalyptus forest. After three-quarters of an hour you'll reach the valley of the **Cusichaca river** and the extensive ruins of **Patallacta** (see p188) where you can *camp*. (On some maps Patallacta is shown as Llactapata).

The small round tower on the ridge by the river is called **Pulpituyoc**, which means 'containing a pulpit'. The Incas built only round walls when a building was particularly significant, so this was an important place.

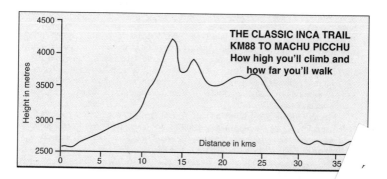

THE CLASSIC INCA TRAIL
KM88 TO MACHU PICCHU
How high you'll climb and
how far you'll walk

Patallacta to Huayllabamba

Passing by the foot of Patallacta, the trail continues south before crossing over the Cusichaca and climbing up the opposite slope for 10-15 minutes. It's a bit steep here, a foretaste of the rest of the trail. It settles on the eastern bank, and you begin to follow the Cusichaca towards Huayllabamba.

The path climbs gently but steadily for an hour, passing first beneath cliffs covered in bromeliads and then through gentler terrain. Ignore the lesser tracks leading down to the river, one of which crosses a bridge to a small settlement on the far, western bank. Continue on the eastern bank to some huts, where you can buy soft drinks. From this point there are good views back down the valley to Mt Veronica, visible as a pyramid in the middle of the valley. Beyond the huts the path arrives at a second bridge. Cross the Cusichaca here to the small settlement called Hatun Chaca, where you can also buy soft drinks or chicha. Half an hour after Hatun Chaca, cross another bridge over a tributary of the Cusichaca, the Llulluchayoc, at the outskirts of **Huayllabamba**, a sprawling village built above Inca terraces.

Huayllabamba is the largest village that you'll pass through, and it's the last place where you can buy basic supplies before the Trekkers' Hotel at Huinay

Huayna Quente and Machu Quente

The people who lived by the Urubamba before the coming of the Incas never ventured further downriver than the site of Huayna Quente and Machu Quente, and no sign of their settlements has been found beyond these sites. This all changed after the Inca Pachacutec conquered this region (see p87), and the Incas drove roads along both the north and the south banks of the Urubamba river, deep into the Amazon rainforest. Details of a walk along the southern trail of the Urubamba can be found on p237.

Huayna Quente and Machu Quente were two sites along the southern road, and like most of the sites on the Inca Trail were some sort of combination of a *tambo* (an inn or waystation), a gateway, a religious site and an agricultural station. **Huayna Quente** was the more important and built in a different style from the sites further upstream of Patallacta (see p188) and Huillca Raccay (see p202). Reached by a glorious Inca path leading off the main riverside track, Huayna Quente in some ways resembles Machu Picchu itself, intricately planned and built in fine stonework. Scholars think it dates from the end of Pachacutec's reign, or the beginning of the reign of his successor, Tupac Yupanqui (Topa Inca), in the second half of the fifteenth century. The high standard of the stonework suggests that it was primarily a small pilgrimage centre on a road to Machu Picchu. Its two stone baths were associated with the ritual worship of water, and its two sacred rocks and a sacred cavern were *huacas* (sacred spots). Like most of the Inca sites on the trail it was probably self-sufficient agriculturally – it might even have exported some maize – and it's surrounded by extensive terraces and canal systems. Thirty-four thousand square metres of terracing have been uncovered.

Machu Quente is much less interesting, and seems to have been a more utilitarian agricultural site. There is a large building that could have been a barracks, as well as a curious carved stone, reminiscent of the much larger Ñusta España at Huancacalle (see p244) by the bridge over the stream.

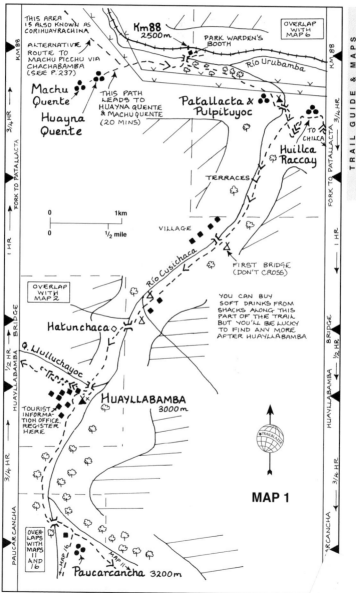

THIS AREA IS ALSO KNOWN AS CORIHUAYRACHINA

Km88 2500m

PARK WARDEN'S BOOTH

OVERLAP WITH MAP 6

ALTERNATIVE ROUTE TO MACHU PICCHU VIA CHACHABAMBA (SEE P.237)

Río Urubamba

Machu Quente

THIS PATH LEADS TO HUAYNA QUENTE & MACHU QUENTE (20 MINS)

Huayna Quente

Patallacta & Pulpituyoc

TO CHILCA

Huillca Raccay

TERRACES

0   1km
0   ½ mile

VILLAGE

Río Cusichaca

FIRST BRIDGE (DON'T CROSS)

OVERLAP WITH MAP 2

YOU CAN BUY SOFT DRINKS FROM SHACKS ALONG THIS PART OF THE TRAIL BUT YOU'LL BE LUCKY TO FIND ANY MORE AFTER HUAYLLABAMBA

Hatunchaca

Q. Llulluchayoc

HUAYLLABAMBA 3000m

TOURIST INFORMATION OFFICE. REGISTER HERE

TRAILBLAZER

MAP 1

OVERLAPS WITH MAPS 11 AND 16

Paucarcancha 3200m

KM 88

¾ HR   FORK TO PATALLACTA   1 HR

HUAYLLABAMBA BRIDGE   ½ HR

¾ HR   PAUCARCANCHA

KM 88

FORK TO PATALLACTA   1 HR   ¾ HR

HUAYLLABAMBA BRIDGE   ½ HR

ARCANCHA   ¾ HR

TRAIL GUIDE & MAPS

Patallacta and Pulpituyoc

Patallacta is one of the largest and most important sites in the whole area. It was first discovered by Hiram Bingham in 1911 and, while it was excavated when Bingham returned in 1915, most work on the area has been done since the late 1970s by Dr Ann Kendall and the Cusichaca Trust; you can see the results in the museum at Ollantaytambo.

Patallacta was primarily an agricultural station set amongst extensive terraced land that was used for growing maize, the staple of the Incas, and it supplied Machu Picchu and Ollantaytambo with part of their food. It's also near the high-altitude lands up the Cusichaca river where potatoes and other root crops were grown, produce that probably made its way through Patallacta for shipment to other parts of the district. In its buildings lived the labourers, both local and mit'a, that tended the fields and the soldiers who manned the hill fort of Huillca Raccay (see p202). It was probably built around 1450 as it's a classical Inca settlement, and it consists of 116 buildings and 5 baths, all laid out on a regular pattern. The main canal that fed the town's baths fell into disuse shortly after the Spanish conquest, which suggests that Patallacta was abandoned around 1540.

The other function of Patallacta was strategic. Inca roads run along both the north and the south banks of the Urubamba and up the Cusichaca, and Patallacta was built at this major road junction rather as Birmingham in England grew up at another major transport intersection. Built where it was, Patallacta could provide a reservoir of loyal Incas producing food for the region at this strategically important cross-roads.

Pulpituyoc is the religious or ceremonial complex of Patallacta, and consists of eleven buildings, two baths and a carved rock. Unlike Patallacta, Pulpituyoc was built on virgin ground, uninhabited before the arrival of the Incas. The exact nature of the religion or ceremonies carried out at Pulpituyoc remains a mystery.

Huayna. There are a number of *campsites* here with toilet blocks and cold running water. Huayllabamba used to have a reputation for theft but it is much improved and is one of few sites along the trail where you can camp within a community, chat with locals and even join a game of football on the local pitch (though it is exhausting work at this altitude). At the top of the village is the warden's office where you must register and where porters have their loads checked and weighed.

HUAYLLABAMBA → PACAMAYO CAMP   [MAP 2, opposite]

Huayllabamba to Llulluchapampa campsite

From the bridge over the Llulluchayoc the path leads uphill on the river's left-hand (SW) bank. It hairpins and gets very steep, and after a pretty exhausting hour you reach the **Yunkachimpa campsite** alongside the Río Chaupihuayjo (also shown as the Río Huayruro on some maps). The campsite itself is OK, but the surrounding area is badly littered and has in places been used as an *al fresco* toilet by inconsiderate trekkers.

Pass through the campsite and over a **bridge** across the river. Then head steeply uphill through a clearing and small campsite called Ayapata, before following the left-hand (SW) bank of the Llulluchayoc as it veers to the west.

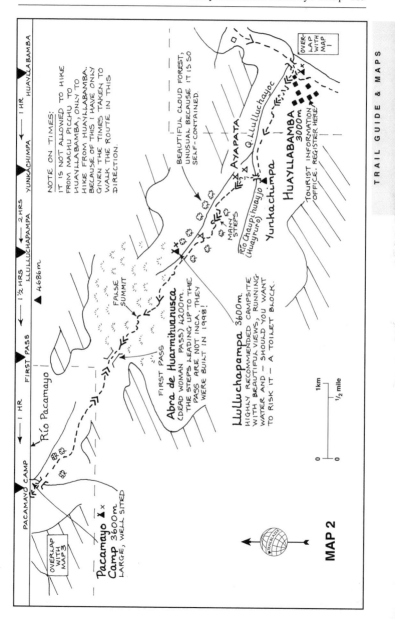

MAP 2

NOTE ON TIMES:

IT IS NOT ALLOWED TO HIKE FROM MACHU PICCHU TO HUAYLLABAMBA, ONLY TO HIKE FROM HUAYLLABAMBA. BECAUSE OF THIS I HAVE ONLY GIVEN THE TIMES TAKEN TO WALK THE ROUTE IN THIS DIRECTION.

Pacamayo Camp 3600m. LARGE, WELL SITED

Abra de Huarmihuañusca (DEAD WOMAN PASS) 4200m. THE STEPS LEADING UP TO THE PASS ARE NOT INCA, THEY WERE BUILT IN 1998!

Llulluchapampa 3800m. HIGHLY RECOMMENDED CAMPSITE WITH BEAUTIFUL VIEWS, RUNNING WATER AND — SHOULD YOU WANT TO RISK IT — A TOILET BLOCK.

BEAUTIFUL CLOUD FOREST, UNUSUAL BECAUSE IT IS SO SELF-CONTAINED.

Huayllabamba 3000m. TOURIST INFORMATION OFFICE, REGISTER HERE!

Lupins and snapdragons line the path and you soon enter a beautiful **cloud forest** or *polylepis* woodland, rare in the Andes because it's self-contained. The path climbs steeply up an exhaustingly large number of steps, following the river course up through the wood, at times going right down to the river, at times rising up the valley side away from it.

About an hour from Yunkachimpa there are another two *campsites*. The first is just inside the forest, but if you continue upward for another 20 minutes, just beyond the edge of the forest you'll reach another: **Llulluchapampa**. This is a much better place to camp, with running water and wonderful views down the valley, but the site is quite exposed and can get cold at night; after heavy rain it can also be a bit boggy. On the top tier of sites there's a toilet block just by the thatched shelter with a cross on top.

Llulluchapampa to Dead Woman Pass/Abra de Huarmihuanusca

You can see the first pass (4200m/13,775ft) – no one knows who the dead woman was though many guides claim the name arose because the pass looks like a dead woman – from Llulluchapampa. It looks deceptively close but in fact it's a gruelling 1½-hour walk.

The trail runs parallel to the river and climbs up into the hills above the river's spring, through windy puna, over paving slabs laid in 1998 to protect the mountain from erosion.

Dead Woman Pass to Pacamayo camp

Here begins the first of the three tiring descents you'll face on the trail. You'll experience considerable strain on your knees as you step down 800m/2624ft over about 1¼ miles.

At the bottom there's a very large *campsite*, nestling in some trees on the floor of the valley of the river Pacamayo. There are two toilet blocks here, and it's large so it's a favourite place for tours; guides must register at the warden's hut in the centre of the camp. It's a good idea to fill your water bottles at the stream here, as the water on the way to Sayac Marca can be unreliable and brackish.

PACAMAYO CAMP → THE THIRD PASS   [MAP 3, opposite]

Pacamayo camp to the second pass

From the Pacamayo camp the path climbs very steeply up a series of **steps**; you'll be glad to pause every now and then at viewpoints over the valley below. After about an hour, you reach the Inca ruins of **Runcu Raccay** (see p192), a circular structure with a rectangular outbuilding. This was probably a tambo, where chasquis rested, but some think it was a guard post or even, because of the circular walls, a ritual building, although the fairly basic build quality suggests otherwise. Camping is not permitted around the ruins.

The second pass (3950m/12,955ft), sometimes called Abra de Runcu Raccay, is another hour up, beyond a series of **false summits**. Just before the real pass, the path winds between two **lakes** where Andean gulls sometimes gather. Down by the lakes, there's a sign saying 'Deer Area', but you'll be very

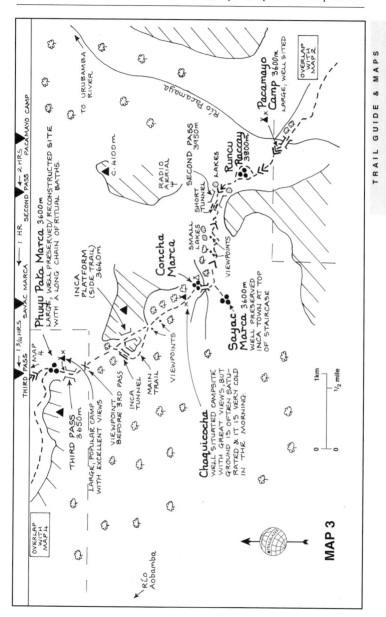

TRAIL GUIDE & MAPS

OVERLAP WITH MAP 2

To Urubamba River

Río Pacamayo

X Pacamayo Camp 3600m
LARGE, WELL SITED

Runcu Raccay 3800m

Second Pass 3950m

Lakes

Short Tunnel

Radio Aerial

c. 4100m

THIRD PASS ◄── 1¾ HRS. ──► SAYAC MARCA ◄── 1 HR. ──► SECOND PASS ◄── 2 HRS. ──► PACAMAYO CAMP

Phuyu Pata Marca 3600m
LARGE, WELL PRESERVED/RECONSTRUCTED SITE WITH A LONG CHAIN OF RITUAL BATHS.

Inca Platform (SIDE TRAIL) 3640m

Concha Marca

Small Lakes

Viewpoints

Sayac Marca 3600m
WELL PRESERVED INCA TOWN AT TOP OF STAIRCASE.

MAP 3

THIRD PASS 3650m

LARGE, POPULAR CAMP WITH EXCELLENT VIEWS

VIEWPOINT BEFORE 3RD PASS

MAIN TRAIL

INCA TUNNEL

VIEWPOINTS

Chaquicocha
WELL SITUATED CAMPSITE WITH GREAT VIEWS, BUT GROUND IS OFTEN SATURATED & IT IS VERY COLD IN THE MORNING.

OVERLAP WITH MAP 4

RÍO Aobamba

1km
½ mile
0

MAP
3

Runcu Raccay

The small, circular site of Runcu Raccay was discovered by Hiram Bingham when he was searching out the entrance roads to Machu Picchu. He considered it to be a fortress, dominating the highway. It was explored in more detail in 1940 by Dr Paul Fejos, who thought it was a tambo, a rest-place for passing travellers. In design it's a transitional building, a bridge between the practical styles of the Cusichaca river and the more elaborate designs of Machu Picchu and the Cedrobamba sites (Cedrobamba is the name given to the areas around Machu Picchu).

It's interesting that the ruins of the Inca Trail were excavated during two periods when the northern nations of the world were embarking on the two most murderous wars in history. Bingham's second expedition was digging quietly in these hills in 1915 while the fields of Flanders were soaked in blood, and Fejos was busy excavating these ruins in 1940.

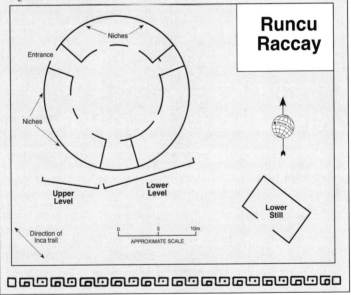

Runcu Raccay

lucky to see any these days. To protect this fragile ecosystem, camping is no longer allowed by the lakes or at the pass.

The second pass to Sayac Marca

From the second pass the trail heads generally westwards. It passes through a short tunnel, the first of two on the route, and begins to switchback steeply as it descends to a small viewpoint, after which it continues down more gently.

(**Opposite**) **Top**: Runcu Raccay. **Bottom**: Huinay Huayna (Photos © Alexander Stewart).

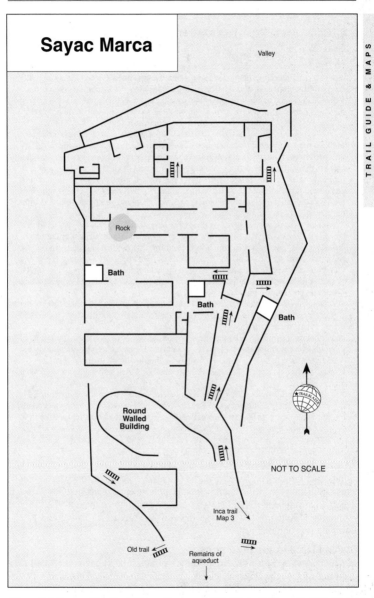

Sayac Marca

Valley

Rock

Bath

Bath

Bath

Round
Walled
Building

NOT TO SCALE

TRAILBLAZER

Inca trail
Map 3

Old trail

Remains of
aqueduct

(Opposite) Approaching Dead Woman Pass – see p190. (Photo © Alexander Stewart).

Sayac Marca (see p193) and Concha Marca

Sayac Marca was discovered by Hiram Bingham when he followed an Inca road across the hills from Machu Picchu, but the name Sayac Marca was coined by the Fejos expedition in the 1940s. Bingham's half-Spanish, half-Quechua name for these ruins, Cedrobamba (Cedar Plain), actually refers to the elongated spur on which all the sites close to Machu Picchu are built. Fejos changed the name to Inaccessible Town, a name that describes the position of the ruins perfectly, protected as they are on three sides by a precipice that descends to the dense jungle of the valley of the river Aobamba below.

The dramatic setting of Sayac Marca was no accident as it's built at a fork in the old Inca road. Today's Inca Trail follows one fork to Machu Picchu, but the other fork descends to the bottom of the Aobamba valley. From here it's been traced up the other side of the valley, where it passes through some ruins called Llactapata, and then descends to the Santa Teresa river. From the river it climbs again to more ruins, Ochopata, about 15km from Sayac Marca, and then it becomes lost in the jungle. This road is completely overgrown these days, and you shouldn't attempt to follow it without a map, compass and experience in jungle hiking.

There is some very impressive stonework here, indicating that this was an important place. Look for what Bingham called 'eye-bonders', holes drilled in corners of buildings and edges of walls, which were used for securing thatch roofs (you can see reconstructions of Inca roofs in Machu Picchu). Notice also the characteristic way that the Incas incorporated and emphasized the natural features on which they built – a large outcrop is the unadorned centrepiece of Sayac Marca, and the whole structure is built on and emphasizes a prow of rock.

Bingham thought that Sayac Marca was a fortified outpost of Machu Picchu, but Fejos wasn't so sure, saying that if the Incas wanted to build fortifications they could do a much more impressive job – he takes Sacsayhuaman as an example. Nevertheless it's unlikely that the site was a tambo (as were the nearby buildings of **Concha Marca** with their small terrace system): there isn't enough agricultural land for Sayac Marca to be a farming outpost, nor is the stonework impressive enough for it to be a religious centre. No one has come up with a conclusive answer as to what the ruins were.

While the function of Sayac Marca isn't clear, the date when it was constructed is more certain. The planning of the site is elaborate; the layout is flexible and responds to the terrain, which makes archaeologists think it was built after the classical period of Inca construction, and the ruins are dated to the last half of the 15th century.

To your right (N), you'll see some large algae-coated lakes and in front (W), clouds permitting, you'll see Sayac Marca perched on a rocky promontory above the cloud forest. The trail descends quite steeply again, and just before it makes a hairpin bend right, there's a staircase going up on the left (SW). About 50 metres (150ft) up this staircase lies **Sayac Marca** (see above and p193). Camping is prohibited here.

Sayac Marca to the third pass

In the shadow of Sayac Marca, tucked away in a little valley is the small Inca dwelling of **Concha Marca**, which was only uncovered in the early 1980s. There's a stream nearby, and it's a good place to fill up with water as there are no more streams until the third pass, but in the interests of health make sure you purify your water carefully because there used to be a small campsite here, and the stream could still be contaminated.

The section of trail from here to the third pass is very, very beautiful. The paving is for the most part original Inca, and the path crosses high stone embankments as it skirts deep precipices. You're enclosed in a cathedral of forest. If you find yourself walking this part of the trail in the mist, you'd be sensible to camp (itineraries permitting) and wait for the weather to clear: it's such a wonderful view, missing it would be a crime. There's a good *campsite* about 20 minutes' walk from Sayac Marca, called **Chaquicocha**, where there's a toilet block and plenty of space on the grassy knolls either side of the path. The higher ground is usually less boggy.

Just after Chaquicocha the path heads steeply uphill and passes two **viewpoints**. Near the second viewpoint a side trail leads off the main path to the right (N). This path returns to the main route about a kilometre (half a mile) further on. However, since it bypasses the main Inca tunnel it is very rarely used and has consequently become very overgrown. It leads to a remote and pleasant platform before descending again to the main trail.

The main trail skirts a spur, turning from the north-west to the north-east. It descends on finely engineered Inca paving and goes through an impressive 16m-long **Inca Tunnel** that exploits a fault in an otherwise sheer cliff face, before climbing again to the third pass (3650m/11,970ft). A little before the third pass you'll reach a spot from where you can see down to two different river valleys, the Urubamba and the Aobamba. It's a spectacular view. Just after this is a large *campsite*, right on the top of the pass. From here you can see Palcay (c.5600m/18,370ft) and Salcantay (6270m/20,565ft) to the south; Pumasillo (6000m/19,680ft) some 35km to the west; and Veronica (5750m/18,860ft) 15km to the north-west.

THE THIRD PASS → MACHU PICCHU   [MAP 4, p197]
Phuyu Pata Marca

The other side of the pass there's the most impressive Inca site yet: Phuyu Pata Marca. Once more, this name comes from the Fejos expedition, and it means 'Cloud-Level Town'. The name's well chosen: you'll often see banks of clouds billow over this pass and you may be engulfed in a field of seamless white. It was once a remote, magical place, but it's surrounded by a large *campsite* now, which makes it lose much of its mystery.

Look for the six 'Inca baths' that you'll walk through on your way to the ruins. Despite the name, these are probably not baths, or even public hydrants, which are what Bingham thought they were. More likely they are a feature of ritual worship of water, and there are similar structures at Huinay Huayna, Tambo Machay (see p159) and Machu Picchu itself. The stonework you'll see in Phuyu Pata Marca is by far the most impressive you've come across so far, but it will get even better.

Walk to the other side (W) of Phuyu Pata Marca from the baths and head to the lower terraces of the ruins. You'll see **descending stairs**, the start of the

Phuyu Pata Marca

Phuyu Pata Marca is another site that was discovered by Bingham but fully excavated by Fejos. When Bingham passed by, all he noted were the baths and the tops of some of the walls of the uppermost buildings; everything else was covered by the jungle. When Fejos set about digging he discovered a much larger and much more important site than Bingham had ever imagined existed, and in two months of work he managed only partially to clear the area. He discovered two plazas, four house groups and one intriguing house hidden in a terrace, discoverable only by a door in the terrace wall (it's to the east of the site near the lower road).

Phuyu Pata Marca, like Sayac Marca is built in a late Inca style, when the formalism of classical Inca planning had given way to a more fluid style. Archaeologists think that it was put up late in Pachacutec's reign or early in that of his successor, Tupac Yupanqui (Topa Inca), late in the 15th century. The stonework on the upper terrace is particularly fine, with a wall where the stones are almost perfectly slotted together. Towards the bottom of the site, to the north-west, there is a group of caves that have been enlarged and extended by the Incas. When they were discovered the roofs were blackened and the floors were covered with a thick layer of ash, but all this was recent and not related to the Incas. Only a few Inca remains were found, pottery of a plain type used for cooking.

Phuyu Pata Marca's function, like that of Sayac Marca, is unclear but the fountain or baths suggests that the site was associated with the ritual worship of water, and perhaps it was a place for ritual cleansing on the final leg to Machu Picchu. It could also, of course, have been a guard settlement, or a remote hunting lodge.

most impressive flight of steps on the entire Inca Trail. The Incas turned a 500m (1500ft) hillside into a staircase, etching each step out of the natural shape of the bedrock; one giant boulder has over 30 steps carved into it. The trail twists and turns its way down into dense cloud forest, making this one of the most delightful wooded sections on the trek. It's a lovely walk, but be careful of your knees, which will feel the strain by the end of the day. It will take about three hours to reach the Trekkers' Hotel.

There used to be another trail from Phuyu Pata Marca, which everyone took up until the Inca Staircase was discovered during the early 1980s. Now closed, the old trail left Phuyu Pata Marca from the west and contoured around the valley side, hugging the lie of the land. It was a couple of kilometres longer, but offered excellent views of Machu Picchu and Urubamba.

After about an hour on the Inca Staircase, you'll be able to see the tin roof of the Trekkers' Hotel: a monstrous wart in the virgin forest. This is where the trail is heading. After about 2½ hours, you'll reach a **pylon** just off the trail. A 30-minute shortcut to the hotel descends east (R) from just a few metres before this pylon, switch-backing steeply as it loses a lot of height. This short-cut isn't actually that much quicker and is a lot less pleasant than the normal route, which continues on under the wires to the Inca site of Intipata (see p198). The path emerges on one of the upper terraces; the trail back south to the hotel leads off from the bottom terrace.

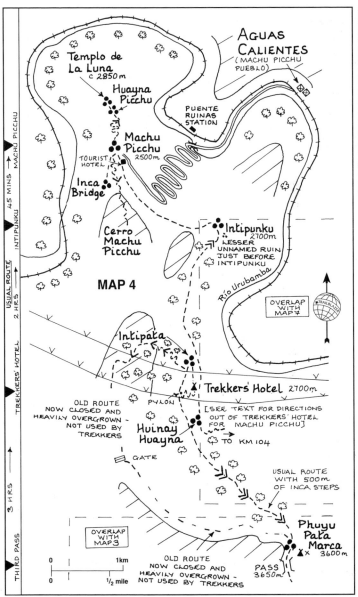

AGUAS CALIENTES
(MACHU PICCHU PUEBLO)

Templo de La Luna
c 2850 m

Huayna Picchu

PUENTE RUINAS STATION

Machu Picchu
2500 m

TOURIST HOTEL

Inca Bridge

Intipunku
2700m

LESSER UNNAMED RUIN JUST BEFORE INTIPUNKU

Cerro Machu Picchu

Río Urubamba

MAP 4

OVERLAP WITH MAP 7

Intipata

Trekkers' Hotel 2700m

PYLON

OLD ROUTE NOW CLOSED AND HEAVILY OVERGROWN - NOT USED BY TREKKERS

[SEE TEXT FOR DIRECTIONS OUT OF TREKKERS' HOTEL FOR MACHU PICCHU]

Huinay Huayna

TO KM 104

GATE

USUAL ROUTE WITH 500m OF INCA STEPS

OVERLAP WITH MAP 3

Phuyu Pata Marca
3600 m

PASS 3650m

OLD ROUTE NOW CLOSED AND HEAVILY OVERGROWN - NOT USED BY TREKKERS

MACHU PICCHU →

← INTIPUNKU 45 MINS

USUAL ROUTE 2 HRS

TREKKERS' HOTEL

3 HRS

THIRD PASS

0   1km
0   ½ mile

Trekkers' Hotel

The *Trekkers' Hotel* (not to be confused with the expensive, plush Tourists' Hotel, Machu Picchu Sanctuary Lodge (see p279), at Machu Picchu) isn't a pleasant place. It's all concrete-walled tin shacks, and the place has a bad reputation for theft. It's crowded, smelly and cramped, but it's the **last place where you're allowed to camp** before Machu Picchu – hence it's always full. The narrow tent pitches are pre-booked by the agencies, so there's not a lot of choice – it's generally a noisy and disturbed night wherever you go. There's a restaurant here (ridiculously overpriced at s/15 for a main course), some beds (s/20 a night) or you can sleep on the floor for s/5, and a number of wash blocks with cold running water. If you're prepared to stand in a long queue, there's a hot shower (s/10) in the main block of the hotel, which frequently runs cold. You'll also find a small shop and a mediocre museum full of stuffed animals. By the time you read this though, plans to demolish the hotel, an eyesore that won't be missed, may have been carried out, leaving just a campsite and a warden's office.

A 10-minute trail leaves from the southern end of the hotel to the ruins of **Huinay Huayna** (see p199), a glorious terraced complex with a flight of 10 baths and some very impressive stonework. If you do come here, don't leave anything valuable in your tent. The ruins close every evening at dusk.

Trekkers' Hotel to Machu Picchu

It takes two hours to trek to **Intipunku** (the gateway to the sun). Machu Picchu is 45 minutes further on. **You are not allowed to camp at Intipunku**. Although

Intipata

The site of Intipata is of interest to both historians and naturalists alike. For the latter, there is a very rare breed of orchid that is said to grow amongst the stones of the ancient Inca terraces. So concerned are the authorities to preserve this habitat for the flower following insensitive clearing and clumsy restoration work, that rumours currently abound that the site is to be left uncleared, thereby allowing the jungle to reclaim the land once more.

This would no doubt disappoint Dr Fejos, who in 1940 spent four months clearing over 40,000 square metres of the forest, discovering and mapping 48 of the site's terraces. Despite these four months Dr Fejos didn't feel he'd discovered everything and was sure that there were many more terraces. In his record of the expedition he describes Intipata, almost despairingly, as 'extending indefinitely to the south'. Like Phuyu Pata Marca, three of Intipata's terraces are hollow and hide what Fejos called 'terrace houses'.

The name Intipata was thought up by a member of his expedition, and means 'Sunny Slope'. Not only because of the number of terraces, but also because of the absence of plazas, religious structures or fortifications, there's little doubt that Intipata was primarily an agricultural settlement, but it probably had a strategic function as well. From Intipata you can see across to the lookout platform on the top of Cerro Machu Picchu, and down to the Inca site of Choquesuysuy. Messages could be transmitted to the mountain city of Machu Picchu from the floor of the Urubamba below through the lookout point on the top of Intipata. From the bottom of the terraces a path leads directly back to the Trekkers' Hotel.

the sky will have lightened by the time you reach Intipunku, you'll still be there in time to see the first rays of sun to break over the mountaintops on to the ruins. Remember to have your torch (flashlight) to hand as you'll be starting the walk in the dark.

The gate out of the Trekkers' Hotel opens at 5.30am and closes at 2.30pm. The only possibly difficult thing about this part of the trail is finding this gate; check before you go to bed to avoid a frantic search in the small hours of the morning. In the lower northern corner of the Trekkers' Hotel site you'll find

Huinay Huayna (Wiñya Wayna)

The name means 'forever young' in Quechua, and the place is named after a pink orchid of that name that grows here.

The similarities between Huinay Huayna and the nearby Intipata are startling, as both are sites where the Incas terraced the whole side of a mountain. Obviously they were both used for growing food, but Huinay Huayna was more important – there are more buildings, the stonework is of a higher quality and there is a magnificent sequence of 10 baths. All this suggests that the site was a religious centre, probably associated with the ritual worship of water, although some think it was a high-status hunting lodge where the Inca or his highest caste retainers might escape the trials of public life. The upper terrace, which incorporates some of the largest polygonal blocks in the whole area, contains some particularly fine masonry, and all over the site you'll find gabled houses, exterior pegs used for securing thatch and recessed niches. This, coupled with the flexible way the settlement was planned, suggests that it was built after the classical period of Inca architecture, in the latter part of the 15th century.

A window at the bottom of the site frames beautifully the nearby waterfall; some say this shows the Incas shared our aesthetic values of what makes a good view.

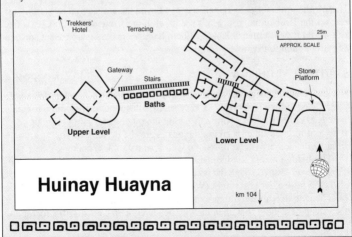

Huinay Huayna

three doorless privies and a path descending from them. Follow it down to an unimposing wooden gate, the Gateway to Machu Picchu – a gate which looks as though it leads to the rubbish bins not to one of the greatest archaeological sites on the planet.

Most trekkers crowd by the gate in the dark, hoping to get the earliest start to Machu Picchu when it opens. The result is a convoy of bobbing headlamps in the mad dash to reach Intipunku by sunrise. You may consider delaying your departure from the Trekkers' Hotel by 15-30 minutes to enjoy an emptier path and the very attractive final section of the Inca Trail in better light. After all, sunrise over Machu Picchu is often hazy or obscured by cloud, so chances are you won't miss much by arriving a little later, and you'll still get to enjoy the ruins before the tours and trainloads of day-trippers arrive.

The trail to Intipunku is mostly flat. It goes up and down a little, passes a couple of apparently impassable sheer rock faces, before climbing about 14 very steep steps to what you think is Intipunku. It's not. It's the remains of a watchtower commanding superb views south back to Intipata, Huinay Huayna, Phuyu Pata Marca and to Choquesuysuy at the start of the Purification Trail. Intipunku is just around the corner, up steps with a gentler gradient. This is an awe-inspiring approach, the architecture reinforcing your sense of anticipation. When you finally reach **Intipunku**, you look down across the wide bend of the Urubamba and can see, sheltering under the sugar-loaf mountain of Huayana Picchu, your journey's end, **Machu Picchu** (see Part 8, p277).

Variations on the classic trail

These variations add an extra half-day to a day to the classic trail by starting further up the Urubamba. You won't see much more from starting at Chilca than you would if you started at Km82, although it does make for a pleasant and gentle introduction to the trek.

STARTING AT CHILCA   [MAP 5, opposite]

You can reach Chilca by road or by train – the tour companies drive here. Chilca, also known as Km77, is a very small village, but there's more to it than there is to either Km88 or Km82. If taking the train, make sure you're prepared to get out in good time; if taking the bus, warn the driver that you wish to get off at Chilca, otherwise he'll assume your destination is Km82.

The **bridge** across the Urubamba is slightly to the west of where the train stops – travel south through the houses towards the river bank, and you'll see it. Cross the bridge, and turn right (W).

The path to Km82 continues west, following the southern bank of the river. It's a steep descent at first, then the trail heads through a **eucalyptus forest** dotted with bromeliads, chilca and wild pepper trees, before turning north-west.

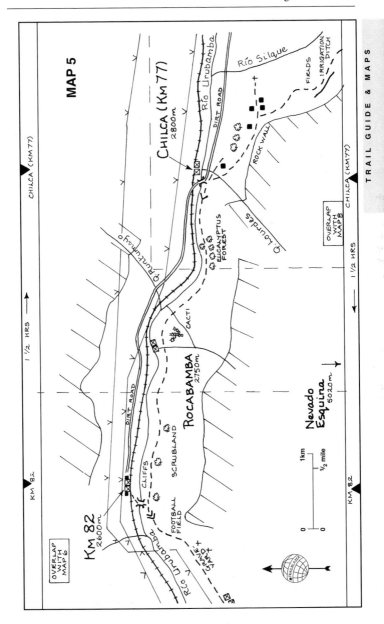

Shortly before you come to the village of **Rocabamba** where there's a stream, you'll walk through some interesting tree-like **cacti**. The trail and river then both turn west again, and pass through **scrub** before heading towards the Km82 bridge. See below for directions from Km82.

STARTING AT KM82   [MAP 6, opposite]

This is the end of the road for the tourist buses, which pull in at the 'car park' at the top of the town, and begin the trek from here. For train travellers, once again the train stops only briefly at **Km82**, so ask your fellow passengers where to get off and prepare yourself to jump. There are a couple of shops at Km82 with a few basic supplies, and the warden's kiosk where you have to register (showing your passport). Walk along the tracks (W), and down towards the river where you'll find a new bridge, which you should cross

On the south side of the Urubamba, turn right (W) and follow the trail as it climbs steeply up from the river. Soon it levels out and passes through a football field following the river's south-westerly course. You walk through a graveyard and a small village full of children who will fearlessly pester you for presents and sweets. Just where the river turns due west again, you'll come to the village of **Miskay**, where you can buy soft drinks.

At the end of the village you'll come to a place where there's a path heading south off the main trail; apparently going through someone's front garden. Turn left (S) here, heading towards a wall of rock where the trail veers to the right (SW) again.

Follow the path as it goes westward. It soon leads down one side of a deep gully to a stream and then up the other side. Shortly after this you come to the ruins of the Inca hillfort **Huillca Raccay** high above the mouth of the Cusichaca

Huillca Raccay
Huillca Raccay doesn't look like much, but is one of the most fascinating sites in the whole area, and one of the earliest, and it has been extensively excavated by Dr Ann Kendall. She's discovered that people lived here for many years before the arrival of the Incas, and that it was the first site that the Incas developed when they arrived. They built a fort here, called Chuncuchua by some, and Dr Kendall found a site nearby where the builders of the fort lived when they were working on its construction. Modern experiments and archaeological discoveries suggest that the fort itself was erected in just one season.

It's easy to see why the Incas built here. High up in this eyrie, Inca soldiers had an excellent view up and down the Urubamba river and controlled the mouth of the Cusichaca. And if the area had once been a centre of pre-Inca power, the building of an Inca fort was a visual statement of the arrival of the Inca Empire. Later, when Inca control was secure and Patallacta was built (see p188), Huillca Raccay could protect and control the agricultural settlements below it on the floor of the Urubamba valley.

It's quite a complicated site. Dr Kendall has discovered 37 buildings, including storage lofts, control buildings (gate-houses) and what are possibly barracks, as well as 70 pre-Inca buildings on the tableland behind.

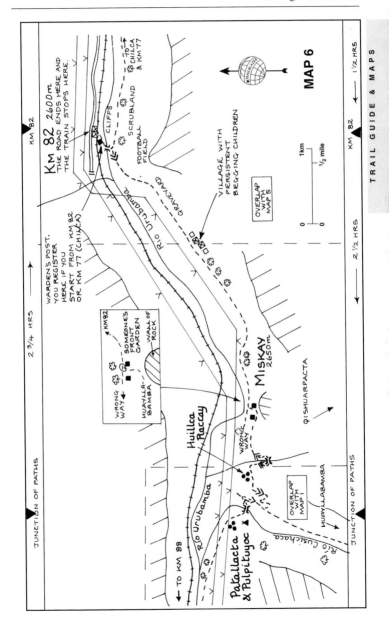

Beware of the Pishtaco

On your walk in the hills, if you come across a pale gringo wearing a dark robe – beware! He could be a vampire, or as they're known locally, a Pishtaco. These apparitions were first seen about the time of the conquest. They take the form of pale-skinned strangers, and carry with them a bag of dust, the powdered bones of their victims. They'll creep up on you when you're unaware, and blow this magic powder in your face, rendering you completely insensible. Then they'll drag you off to their lair, where they hang you upside down and let your fat drip into large bowls beneath your body. In the old days, it was said that this human fat was used to make church bells, now the story goes that it's used to power the space shuttle.

The anthropologist, Robert Randall, has pointed out the myth of Pishtacos has a basis in truth, albeit allegorical truth. These pale-skinned strangers who kidnapped locals and used their fat are a symbol of the conquering Spanish, who worked the Incas to the bone and used their sweat to grease the wheels of the Spanish Empire.

and the extensive site of **Patallacta**. Huillca Raccay is a very ancient site, and it's been inhabited since 500BC. The Incas, when they conquered the area, took over this place and built a fort here because it commands the entrance to the Cusichaca valley. You won't see much evidence of pre-Inca remains here today, however, though for some of the trail you'll be walking on a pre-Inca canal (the section of the path flanked by stones).

From here it's simple to descend to the **main trail from Km88 to Huayllabamba**, which follows the eastern bank of the Cusichaca river though there are lots of paths down through the bush and it's easy to think you've got lost as you weave between the broom and lupins. You'll be fine as long you continue generally west and downhill towards the Cusichaca. You'll soon come to a large, heavily beaten trail heading north–south. This is the path you want, turn left (S) and follow this trail to Huayllabamba. (**Route continues on p188**).

The shorter trails

These trails are useful for those who haven't got time to spare, or have come in February when the classic Inca Trail is closed. It's only a half-day's walk up a grassy hillside from Km104 to the Trekkers' Hotel and a couple of hours further to Machu Picchu along the classic Camino Sagrado del Inca. The tougher alternative route, along the river from Km104 to the Trekkers' Hotel, runs via Choquesuysuy and involves a steep climb up the Purification Trail. Either way, allow one day for the trek, and one day to see Machu Picchu.

In the past, trekkers on this route used to be able to spend the night in the dorms at the Trekkers' Hotel. However, the hostel may well be closed and demolished by the time you read this. Even if it's not, you are no longer permitted to stay here if starting from Km104. Instead you must press on to Machu

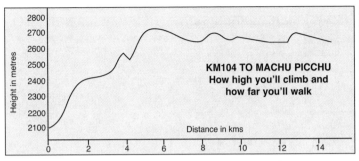

Picchu and then spend the night in Aguas Calientes. You then return to Machu Picchu the following morning for a full chance to explore the ruins.

KM104 → THE TREKKERS' HOTEL   [MAP 7, below]

The train pulls up at **Km104**, deep in the selva, 3½ hours after leaving Cusco. Km104 is low, my altimeter read 2100m (6888ft), and the heat can get oppressive down here on the valley floor.

The trail up to Huinay Huayna and the Trekkers' Hotel is mainly across the exposed flank of a mountain and in the summer there's **no shade** and the sun

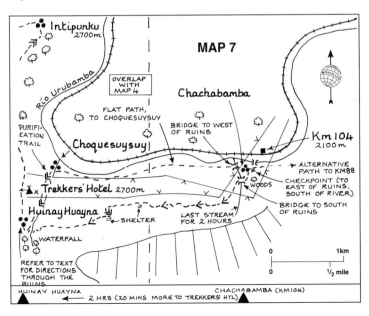

Chachabamba

Chachabamba sits on the old Inca road along the southern bank of the Urubamba river, most of which is lost in the undergrowth. The ruins have been cleared; they were built in a sophisticated style that's more reminiscent of Machu Picchu than of the earlier site of Patallacta. Archaeologists think it dates from the late 15th century.

There are both open and closed buildings (three-walled and four-walled), a boulder shrine, 14 baths – one of the largest sequence of baths on the Inca Trail – and a circular stone reservoir, all of which suggests that Chachabamba was an important religious site. This may have been combined with a gate-keeping function, with both Chachabamba and the site of Choquesuysuy lower down the Urubamba guarding this entrance to Machu Picchu.

Although the railway had already been built along the northern bank of the river just a short distance away, Chachabamba was not uncovered until 1940 when Dr Paul Fejos stumbled on it.

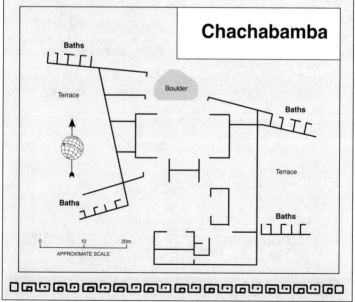

burns and dries you out. The weather is very changeable so bring **rain-gear**. You must take **water**, or you will have a very miserable couple of hours. Fortunately there is a small stream of sweet water at the beginning of the trail where you can fill your bottles. You are also under a little **time pressure** to get to the Trekkers' Hotel before the gate is locked at 2.30pm, and to reach Machu Picchu before the light starts to fade.

Choquesuysuy and the Purification Trail

Choquesuysuy is larger and more important than was first thought, and new terraces are still being dug out of the forest. Built on both sides of the Quebrada stream at Km107, the site comprises six complex house groups, a total of eighteen buildings and seven fountain baths, as well as some pretty terrific walls and terraces.

Undoubtedly built for some religious purpose, the Choquesuysuy complex also occupied a highly strategic position on the banks of the Urubamba, with paths leading both up to Huinay Huayna and along the valley to Machu Picchu. As such, the site must have had a secondary function as some sort of control post for people travelling up and down the valley. Though today the power station blocks the direct path along the valley to Machu Picchu, the trail up to Huinay Huayna is now open, though it's one heck of a steep climb – less than an hour down but 2-3 hours back up. The route has been dubbed the **Purification Trail**, picking up on the presumed function of Choquesuysuy as a place of ritual cleansing for those approaching Huinay Huayna.

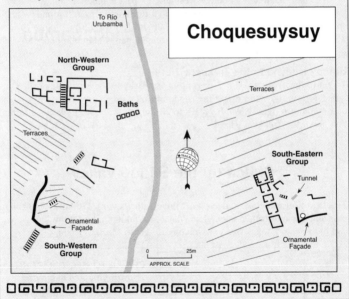

To Río Urubamba

Choquesuysuy

North-Western Group

Baths

Terraces

Terraces

South-Eastern Group

Tunnel

Ornamental Façade

South-Western Group

Ornamental Façade

0   25m
APPROX. SCALE

Km104 to Huinay Huayna

As at Km88, the train stops only briefly at Km104, so be prepared to jump out at a moment's notice. The trail leads down to the river to your left (S), but depending where you got off the train you might have to walk a little along the tracks to find the bridge and the warden's post across the river. Your permit and passport are checked here.

After crossing the river, the trail heads off to the right (W) towards the ruins of **Chachabamba** (see p206). From here you have two choices: either continue due west along the river to the ruins of **Choquesuysuy** (see p207), from where you can take a very steep path up to Huinay Huayna; or alternatively head due south away from the river behind the ruins, where the path begins to climb the mountain, entering some pleasant woods and crossing a stream. This is a good place to fill up with water. The path then heads westward and upward, leaving the woods for open grassland, soon passing under electricity pylons. The river itself is now far below you to your right (N). After 1.5km (just under a mile) you are treated to a sight of the wart that is the Trekkers' Hotel, with the Intipata in the distance behind it; a little further along the path you pass a shelter that's been built beside the trail. A little further still and you get your first view of **Huinay Huayna** (see p199), an island of stone enshrouded by the deep green of the surrounding forest. Down on the valley floor lies Choquesuysuy.

The path continues as before west and up, past another shelter, then undulates sharply before at last descending into a forest and shade. It rounds a small spur and then reaches a beautiful waterfall and forest. You pass close to Inca walls still lost in the green clutches of the jungle, before stumbling out into clear light at the foot of Huinay Huayna.

Huinay Huayna to the Trekkers' Hotel

To get to the Trekkers' Hotel, pass up the stairway to the urban area of the terraces, follow the stairs off to the right, and then ascend by the series of Inca baths, and turn right (NW). It's a 10- to 20-minute walk. See p198 for information about the Trekkers' Hotel.

Chilca up the Silque Valley

This beautiful walk takes you up the Silque valley, over a 4700m/15,740ft-high pass and down the other side to Huayllabamba, taking in fertile low-lying areas and high puna. It takes five to seven days to get to Machu Picchu.

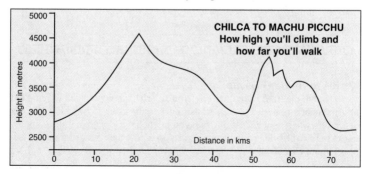

CHILCA TO MACHU PICCHU
How high you'll climb and
how far you'll walk

Height in metres

Distance in kms

CHILCA → HALFWAY UP   [MAP 8, below]

You can reach Chilca by road or by train – most independent travellers go by
train but the tour companies drive here. **Chilca** (also known as Km77) is a very
small village, but there's more to it than Km88 and Km82, including a rather
smart hotel on the edge of town, the ***Nustayoc Lodge***, which is popular with
tour groups. Make sure you're prepared to get out of the train in good time.

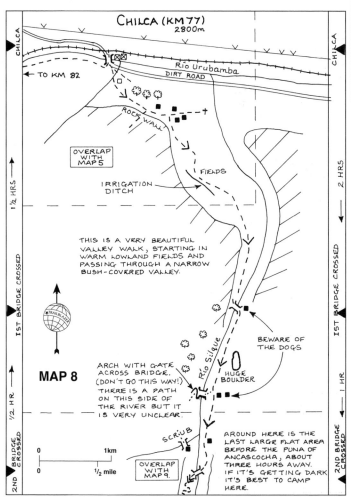

CHILCA (KM 77)
2800m

← TO KM 82

Río Urubamba
DIRT ROAD

ROCK WALL

OVERLAP
WITH
MAP 5

FIELDS

IRRIGATION
DITCH

THIS IS A VERY BEAUTIFUL
VALLEY WALK, STARTING IN
WARM LOWLAND FIELDS AND
PASSING THROUGH A NARROW
BUSH-COVERED VALLEY.

BEWARE OF
THE DOGS

ARCH WITH GATE
ACROSS BRIDGE.
(DON'T GO THIS WAY!)
THERE IS A PATH
ON THIS SIDE OF
THE RIVER BUT IT
IS VERY UNCLEAR.

MAP 8

Río Silque

HUGE
BOULDER

SCRUB

AROUND HERE IS THE
LAST LARGE FLAT AREA
BEFORE THE PUNA OF
ANCASCOCHA, ABOUT
THREE HOURS AWAY.
IF IT'S GETTING DARK
IT'S BEST TO CAMP
HERE.

0   1km
0   ½ mile

OVERLAP
WITH
MAP 9.

CHILCA

CHILCA

2 HRS

1½ HRS

1ST BRIDGE CROSSED

1ST BRIDGE CROSSED

½ HR.

1 HR

2ND BRIDGE CROSSED

2ND BRIDGE CROSSED

TRAIL GUIDE & MAPS

Once you get off the trail, look south-east and you'll see the valley of the river Silque. This is where you're heading.

The **bridge** across the Urubamba is slightly to the west of where the train stops. Travel south through the houses towards the river bank and you'll see it. Cross the bridge, and turn left (E), and you'll shortly come to a fork by a hut; take the right-hand, more southerly, fork. A little later the path hugs a rock wall and heads east, then the wall falls away near some huts, and the path forks again. Take the right (more southerly) fork, and continue up the valley away from the Urubamba. It's a pleasant walk along tractor ruts through the fields.

After about 25 minutes the valley begins to narrow and the path turns more to the south. After a further 50 minutes you come to a **bridge** over the river, guarded by a hut and ferocious dogs. You need to cross this bridge and get onto the left (E) side of the river. Carry on walking south past a couple more huts and, on your left, a field with a huge boulder at its centre. Ignore the next bridge you'll see across the river (with an arched gateway at its end) and, an hour after the bridge you crossed over, the path becomes steeper, passes another hut and reaches a third **bridge**. Cross this.

HALFWAY UP → PAST ANCASCOCHA   [MAP 9, opposite]

There's no flat place to camp for the next couple of hours, so if it's getting late you should *camp* around here. The path, now on the right-hand side of the river (W), climbs steeply through scrub and hairpins back and forth, before descending to the river again and passing over to the other side (E). It crosses the river five more times before settling for the west (right-hand) bank. This final **bridge** is just above the confluence of the Silque and another river.

Once on the western bank the path climbs steeply up the side of the valley – the floor's pretty flat and you can *camp* there. You'll pass an isolated farm set in mountain fields that almost everyone thinks is Ancascocha (a couple of hours further on) but this is actually **Sayllapata**. You'll know you've really arrived in **Ancascocha** because the village nestles in a flat area of puna at the confluence of three rivers. It's a fair-sized place; don't expect to be able to buy any provisions here but it's a good place to *camp* (make contact with the villagers first).

Ancascocha to the fork in the rivers

At the lower end of Ancascocha the path, valley and river all turn to the right (W), and you should cross the river near to some huts – there's a footbridge just by them. The path then ascends gently along the valley floor, and when the river forks you follow the left-hand (SW) river. The other one leads to some beautiful **waterfalls** (which you can see off to the west across the grassy puna), where it's also possible to *camp*.

> ❏ **Walking times on trail maps**
> Note that on all the trail maps in this book the times shown alongside each map refer only to **time spent actually walking**. Add about 20-30% to allow for rest stops.

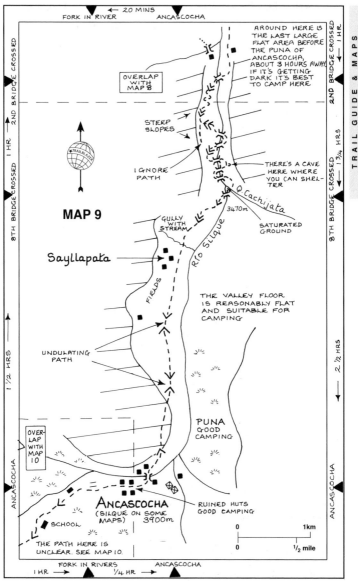

← 20 MINS
FORK IN RIVER — ANCASCOCHA

AROUND HERE IS THE LAST LARGE FLAT AREA BEFORE THE PUNA OF ANCASCOCHA, ABOUT 3 HOURS AWAY. IF IT'S GETTING DARK IT'S BEST TO CAMP HERE

2ND BRIDGE CROSSED ↑ 1 HR.

2ND BRIDGE CROSSED ↓ 1 HR.

OVERLAP WITH MAP 8

STEEP SLOPES

IGNORE PATH

THERE'S A CAVE HERE WHERE YOU CAN SHELTER

N ⊕ TRAILBLAZER

MAP 9

Q. Cachijata

8TH BRIDGE CROSSED ↑ 1 HR.

8TH BRIDGE CROSSED ↓ 1 3/4 HRS

3470m

GULLY WITH STREAM

SATURATED GROUND

Sayllapata

Río Silque

THE VALLEY FLOOR IS REASONABLY FLAT AND SUITABLE FOR CAMPING

FIELDS

UNDULATING PATH

2 1/2 HRS

1 1/2 HRS

PUNA GOOD CAMPING

OVERLAP WITH MAP 10

ANCASCOCHA

ANCASCOCHA

RUINED HUTS GOOD CAMPING

ANCASCOCHA (SILQUE ON SOME MAPS) 3900m

SCHOOL

THE PATH HERE IS UNCLEAR. SEE MAP 10.

0 — 1km
0 — 1/2 mile

1 HR → FORK IN RIVERS — 1/4 HR — ANCASCOCHA

PAST ANCASCOCHA → VALLEY TURN   [MAP 10, opposite]

The fork in the rivers to the pass (Puerto Huyanay)

From the fork in the rivers you head south-west. The path here is unclear, more a collection of braiding cattle-tracks, but as long as you keep ascending gently and going south-west, parallel to the river, you're doing fine. After a couple of hours you'll see in front of you a grassy spur that obscures your view – you need to walk up and across this. If the weather's clear, on the other side of the spur you'll see some glorious red mountains to your left and you cross a stream that runs from them. You can *camp* here. The path to the pass doesn't go towards the red mountains; it continues across the side of the scree-slope to the left of the waterfall that flows over a cliff ahead of you, feeding the lake below. The path heads in the direction of the waterfall but keeps above it. Soon you'll find yourself overlooking a corrie (cirque), with a small lake on its flat floor. A glacier is poised on the slopes of the mountain that's the other side (N) of the corrie to you. The floor of the corrie makes a lovely *campsite*.

To reach the pass (**Puerto Huyanay**) follow the path as it winds its way up to the head of the corrie – it gets steep and it switchbacks uphill. Just after the head of the corrie you walk across a large scree slope, following a little stream past some tiny lakes on your right. Continue south-west and in just over an hour from the corrie (around three hours from Ancascocha) you'll come to the pass (4700m/15,415ft), marked by an *apachita* (cairn – pile of stones) on a gently sloped puna hillock.

The pass to Inca Raccay

The pass and the area around it is all a bit flat and featureless and it's easy to get lost up here, especially when the visibility is bad. Use your compass to get the right general direction. The valley you want heads north/north-west from the pass, away from the glacier-clad red mountains to your left. (You need to aim for the far side (W) of the river as you walk downwards and westwards).

There are several trails mostly heading in the right direction but to be on the safe side follow the one that looks most worn, tend to bear left (W) and always

---

Inca Raccay

Inca Raccay is the first Inca ruin on the old direct road from Cusco to Machu Picchu, a road that rises from the plain of Anta up to the peaks of Salcantay, before descending along the Quesca river. The ruins don't look very impressive today, but they were originally a tambo – an inn providing food and shelter to travellers. Remains of watchtowers have also been discovered close by, so it's likely that Inca Raccay was also an outpost which could warn the people in the lush agricultural lands down near the Urubamba river of any danger that came over the pass.

The ruins were constructed to a standardized plan which makes them difficult to date but suggests that they were built before the virtuoso stonework of Machu Picchu and Cedrobamba (the buildings close to Machu Picchu); the first half of the 15th century seems likely. Originally there were seven houses, including three large, two-door buildings that contained the storage lofts (marcas) where provisions were kept.

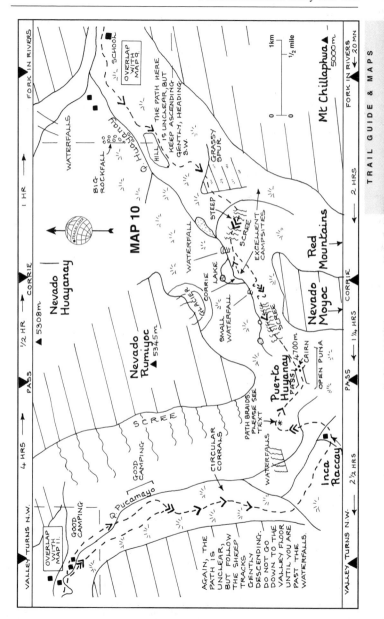

MAP 10

Nevado Huayanay ▲ 5308m.

Nevado Rumiyoc ▲ 5345m.

Mt Chillophua ▲ 5000m.

HILL: THE PATH HERE IS UNCLEAR, BUT KEEP ASCENDING GENTLY, HEADING S.W.

SCHOOL

OVERLAP WITH MAP 11

WATERFALLS

BIG ROCKFALL

Q. Huaruquy

GRASSY SPUR

STEEP

WATERFALL

EXCELLENT CAMPSITES

SCREE

Red Mountains

CORRIE LAKE

GLACIER CORRIE

SMALL WATERFALL

SCREE

Nevado Moyoc

CAIRN

OPEN PUNA

Puerto Huaynay PASS 4700m.

PATH BRAIDS PLEASE SEE TEXT

SCREE

GOOD CAMPING

CIRCULAR CORRALS

WATERFALLS

Inca Raccay

Q. Pucamayo

GOOD CAMPING

OVERLAP WITH MAP 11

AGAIN, THE PATH IS UNCLEAR, BUT FOLLOW THE SHEEP TRACKS GENTLY DESCENDING. DO NOT GO DOWN TO THE VALLEY FLOOR UNTIL YOU ARE PAST THE WATERFALLS.

1km
½ mile
0
0

VALLEY TURNS N.W. ◄ — 4 HRS — ► PASS ◄ — ½ HR — ► CORRIE ◄ — ½ HR — ► CORRIE ◄ — 1 HR — ► WATERFALLS ◄ ... FORK IN RIVERS

FORK IN RIVERS ◄ — 20 MN ► 2 HRS ◄ PASS ◄ — 1¼ HRS ► CORRIE ◄ — 1½ HRS ► VALLEY TURNS N.W. ◄ — 2½ HRS

go down. You'll know you've got it correct because you'll begin to head south and cross a stream to find what looks like a **derelict hut**, then cross another stream and head off to the north-west. The derelict hut is actually **Inca Raccay** – see p212.

Inca Raccay to the turn in the valley

Continuing downhill and north-west from the hut you'll descend gently and eventually ford another stream. When you can see a high three-tiered waterfall at the head of the valley behind you, make your way down to the valley floor over the next couple of kilometres (a mile or so). The path once again is not clear, and the intersecting cattle tracks are confusing. But you need to be on the valley floor by the time you reach the huddle of houses by the **westward bend** in the river. Stand at this turning point, look down the valley and you can see laid out below a much more tropical landscape, dotted with houses and fields and smudged by the smoke of a dozen cooking fires. This is a good place to *camp*.

TURN IN THE VALLEY → PAUCARCANCHA   [MAP 11, opposite]

The turn in the valley to Quesca

After the turn in the valley, the path switches from one bank to the other a couple of times. Another stream joins from the south and soon after a fast-flowing river joins from the east, followed by more rivers and streams until you find yourself walking in the middle of a huge network of waterways.

It is very, very easy to lose the path here: the best tactic is to join the southern (left-hand) side of the valley. If you can't ford the river there are a couple of rickety bridges you can use. The map opposite gives further details. If you're not sure of the path, just hug the riverbank until you arrive at the school at Quesca, about an hour downstream from the bend in the river and 3-4 hours below the pass. This is the largest village in the area, but it's not big. You can usually *camp* here if you get permission.

Quesca to Paucarcancha

Quesca to Paucarcancha is mostly a straightforward, uphill path keeping to the west bank of the widening river, but there's one difficult bit: shortly after you pass the ruins of a tambo called **Incasamana** (just off the trail to the right – north-east), there's a small gully carved out by a stream (coming from a hot

Incasamana

A half-day's walk from Inca Raccay along the Anta to Machu Picchu road is Incasamana, another tambo for passing travellers. Unlike Inca Raccay just by the pass, Incasamana is surrounded by land that was cultivated – over 300 square metres have been discovered, and storage lofts have been found here, too. Incasamana and Inca Raccay (see p212) were built along a similar standardized plan, probably around the same time in the early stages of the Incas' domination of the area (early 15th century). Nearby there's a hot spring and it's easy to imagine a weary Inca traveller soaking his bones in the water after crossing the high passes, knowing that he's only a couple of days' journey from Machu Picchu.

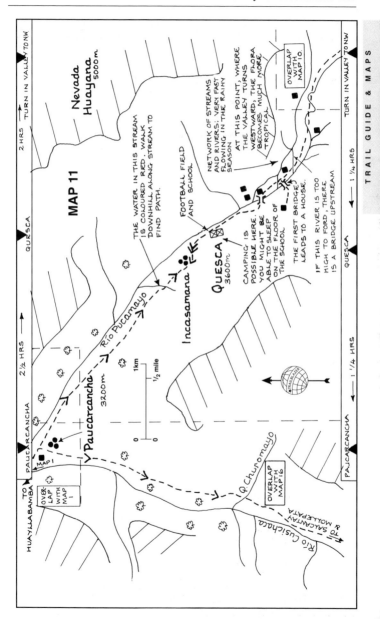

MAP 11

Nevada Huayana 5000 m.

2 HRS ► TURN IN VALLEY TO NW

▼ QUESCA

THE WATER IN THIS STREAM IS COLOURED RED. WALK DOWNHILL ALONG STREAM TO FIND PATH.

FOOTBALL FIELD AND SCHOOL

Río Pucamayo

Incasamana

QUESCA 3600 m.

CAMPING IS POSSIBLE HERE. YOU MIGHT BE ABLE TO SLEEP ON THE FLOOR OF THE SCHOOL

THE FIRST BRIDGE LEADS TO A HOUSE.

IF THIS RIVER IS TOO HIGH TO FORD, THERE IS A BRIDGE UPSTREAM.

NETWORK OF STREAMS AND RIVERS: VERY FAST FLOWING IN THE RAINY SEASON

AT THIS POINT, WHERE THE VALLEY TURNS WESTWARD, THE FLORA BECOMES MUCH MORE TROPICAL.

OVERLAP WITH MAP 10

TURN IN VALLEY TO NW

◄ 1 ¼ HRS QUESCA

◄ 2 ½ HRS PAUCARCANCHA

Río Pucamayo 3200 m.

1 km

½ mile

0

▼ Paucarcancha

MAP 1

TO HUAYLLABAMBA

OVERLAP WITH MAP 1

◄ 1 ¼ HRS PAUCARCANCHA

Q. Churomayo

OVERLAP WITH MAP 16

To SALCANTAY & MOLLEPATA

Río Cusichaca

Paucarcancha

Standing on the walls of this reconstructed Inca fort and looking down at the Cusichaca and Quesca rivers, you can see one of the reasons why the Incas chose to build it. Paucarcancha dominates both valleys, valleys along which Inca roads ran. These roads led over the Salcantay watershed to the Apurímac river, a source of danger to Inca stability since the days of the Cancha invasion. Paucarcancha was, therefore, a guarded entry point to Machu Picchu and the Urubamba from the Apurímac to the south.

The archaeologist, Dr Ann Kendall, discovered that a large non-Inca population lived in the areas around Paucarcancha and Huayllabamba. These people were the indigenous inhabitants of the area, and the Incas pretty much let them be but the imposing walls of Paucarcancha must have been a permanent reminder of who was really in control.

Paucarcancha is the first large Inca site that's been discovered on the old Anta to Machu Picchu road and is probably a gateway to the region. It was built quite late in comparison with the tambos of Inca Raccay and Incasamana, after the early constructions in the area around Patallacta, around the mid- to late 15th century. Within the complex are sixteen buildings, one of which looks a little like a barracks and could have held soldiers or perhaps mit'a workers. The people who lived in Paucarcancha had enough fields to grow all their food, and over 10,000 square metres of terracing have been discovered in the hills nearby. It's likely it also functioned as a tambo.

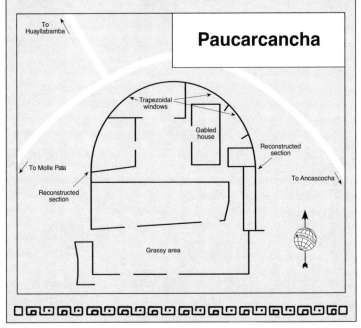

spring) that runs through red rock and is coloured red itself. Walk down the stream a little and you'll see the main path heading straight as an arrow through the now dense scrubland towards Paucarcancha. This is the path you want. Looking up on the skyline directly in front (NW) of you, you can see **Dead Woman Pass/Abra de Huarmihuanusca** (see p190), which is the first pass on the trail from Huayllabamba to Machu Picchu.

One and a half hours out of Quesca is the site of **Paucarcancha** (see p216). Paucarcancha is built at the junction of three valleys: the valley you've just walked down, the upper Cusichaca leading to Salcantay and Mollepata and the lower Cusichaca leading to Huayllabamba and the Urubamba river. Its position makes it a sensibly placed fort but it was probably a tambo as well.

OPTIONS FROM PAUCARCANCHA

From Paucarcancha, there are **three options**: the first is to turn left (S) and walk up the Cusichaca river towards Mollepata (see Map 16, p225); the second is to turn right (N) and walk for an hour towards Huayllabamba, then turn up the Llulluchayoc towards Machu Picchu along the classic Inca Trail (see Map 2, p189); the third option is to walk to Huayllabamba, then down the Cusichaca river to the Urubamba, where you could either pick up the train from Km88, Km82 or walk all the way back to Chilca and complete a circuit (see Map 1, p187).

The Mollepata trek

This hike takes six or seven days and is quite gruelling; the pass is at 4950m/16,235ft on the shoulder of the mountain Salcantay. However, it's a wonderful walk and takes you right from the watershed of the Apurímac to the Urubamba.

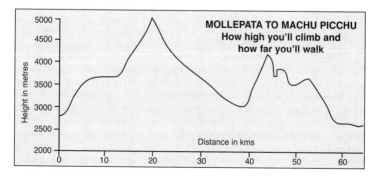

MOLLEPATA TO MACHU PICCHU
How high you'll climb and how far you'll walk

Height in metres

Distance in kms

MOLLEPATA → ABOVE MARCOCASA   [MAP 12, opposite]

Mollepata is a village at the end of a dirt track off the main Cusco to Abancay road. Described by E G Squier in 1877 as, 'a collection of wretched huts on a high shelf of the mountain with a tumbledown church, a drunken governor ... a place unsurpassed in evil repute by any in Peru', it has fortunately evolved into a pleasant mountain town overlooking the deep citrus-producing Apurímac valley.

The earlier buses from Cusco (5am and 1pm from opposite the western end of Calle Arcopata, s/6, 2¹/₂-3hours) will take you right into the village, but some of the later ones to Abancay will drop you only at the bottom of the dirt track, down by the Apurímac river in the heat among the biting insects. It's a good few kilometres from the main road to Mollepata, and you *could* walk it but I wouldn't recommend that unless you like desert hiking. You can usually hitch up from the main road to Mollepata, but you should pay the driver s/5 or so.

There are a couple of *hostals*, the better one (s/10 per night) being one block to the west of the main plaza, on the western side of a small plazoleta. On the same street, the reasonably priced **Restaurant Salkantay** is popular with locals and the food is fresh. There are a few small stores where you can buy some basic last-minute provisions. There are also arrieros for hire in Mollepata – the Pérez family and Victorino Sierro Partillo have been recommended and as a result they're a little more expensive than others: s/25-30 a day rather than the going rate of s/20-25, plus s/20 per mule. You also need to pay for their return trip, which from Huayllabamba should only be one day, and from Santa Teresa or La Hidroeléctrica two days. Uniquely, as far as I know, Mollepata also had a female arriero, Graciela Pinedo, who may still be there and lived near the Pérez family.

Mollepata to Marcocasa

The trail leaves from Mollepata's Plaza de Armas and takes the dirt road which goes all the way to Soray via the small settlement of Marcocasa (also known as Cruz Pata). Some tour agencies now drive up to Soray to start the trek from there. There's no public transport running from Mollepata to Soray, and the road is quiet and infrequently used but doesn't make for especially exciting trekking.

Take the concrete road that leaves from the plaza's north-west corner and follow it as it snakes through the houses. Ignore the dirt track branching left and continue until the concrete runs out at a T-junction after 200m. Turn right (NE) and follow the dirt road as it veers round to the left (NW) through a grove of eucalyptus.

As you leave the village, you're walking along the left (W) side of a valley that's heading roughly north-west. You can get off the road for a section by following a faint track dropping into the Pumachupán valley to the right of the road, which contours towards the head of the valley and climbs to Marcocasa, cutting between the bends and switchbacks of the road. It is difficult to pinpoint exactly where the track branches right, so check with your arriero. Don't drop too low into the valley as some trails simply lead to cultivated farm plots further below.

The road gains height gently towards the head of the valley, crossing a bridge and passing a pleasant glade, before it winds its way up to **Marcocasa**

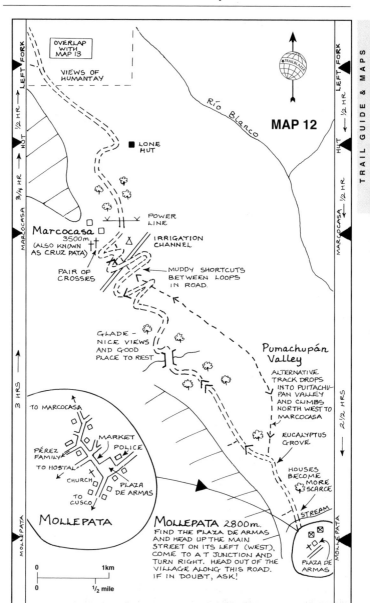

OVERLAP WITH MAP 13

VIEWS OF HUMANTAY

Río Blanco

MAP 12

LEFT FORK
½ HR.
HUT
MARCOCASA ¾ HR

LEFT FORK
½ HR.
HUT
½ HR.
MARCOCASA

LONE HUT

POWER LINE

Marcocasa 3500m.
(ALSO KNOWN AS CRUZ PATA)

IRRIGATION CHANNEL

PAIR OF CROSSES

MUDDY SHORTCUTS BETWEEN LOOPS IN ROAD.

GLADE - NICE VIEWS AND GOOD PLACE TO REST

Pumachupán Valley

ALTERNATIVE TRACK DROPS INTO PUITACHU- PAN VALLEY AND CLIMBS NORTH WEST TO MARCOCASA

3 HRS

EUCALYPTUS GROVE

2½ HRS

TO MARCOCASA

PÉREZ FAMILY
TO HOSTAL

MARKET
POLICE

CHURCH

PLAZA DE ARMAS

TO CUSCO

MOLLEPATA

HOUSES BECOME MORE SCARCE

STREAM

PLAZA DE ARMAS

MOLLEPATA

MOLLEPATA 2800m.
FIND THE PLAZA DE ARMAS AND HEAD UP THE MAIN STREET ON ITS LEFT (WEST). COME TO A T JUNCTION AND TURN RIGHT. HEAD OUT OF THE VILLAGE ALONG THIS ROAD. IF IN DOUBT, ASK!

0   1km
0   ½ mile

(3500m/11,480ft) on a series of hairpins. It takes about 2½-3 hours to reach the village from Mollepata. You can *camp* on a patch of ground about 100m to the right of the road, opposite two large blue crosses swaddled in different coloured cloths. Fill up your water bottles at a spring behind some houses at the back of the cleared area (to where the power lines lead), because the streams are seasonal and unreliable on the way to Soray. From Marcocasa there are expansive views of the snow-capped Huarohuirani (to the north behind the hill), the village of Qurawasi away in the distance to the west, and Mollepata off to the south.

ABOVE MARCOCASA → SORAY   [MAP 13, opposite]

Beyond Marcocasa the directions are simple – follow the dirt road all the way to Soray Pampa. It takes three to four hours to get there. Two hours after leaving Marcocasa the road passes the settlement of **Challacancha**: two huts and a small *campsite* to the right-hand side of the road. There are streams nearby but they're seasonal and not reliable.

From Challacancha it's around a further two hours to Soray; after 1-1½hrs the path passes through a **gate**, and after another 30 minutes or so it arrives on some high puna fields – Soray pampa. By now you will have excellent views of the bulk of Humantay and to its right as you look at it the sheer pyramid of Salcantay, whose name means 'Savage Mountain'.

The pampa is latticed with small concrete drainage canals and streams that you'll have to cross (though these disappear in dry years). Keep to the left (W) side of the pampa, close to the rockwall if you want to remain dry footed. At the far (N) end of the pampa stands **Soray** itself, on the other (N) side of a stream – often there's a simple bridge of tree trunks but you might have to use stepping-stones if this has been washed away. This is a good place to *camp*.

SORAY → INCA CHIRIASQ'UA   [MAP 14, p223]

You can hire arrieros (see p17) in Soray. One guy I've hired in the past was Antonio Huari Huillca, who was reasonable, reliable, friendly and had sound animals. No doubt his rates will rise as people request him.

Soray to Salcantay pampa

The trail heads up the valley to the north-east, to the right, and takes its northern (L) side until it crosses the Río Salcantay, a tributary of the Río Blanco. Pass through a **rustic gate** in a stone wall and begin a series of zigzags that ascend the other (E) side of the valley.

After about half an hour, you pass a second rudimentary **gate** set in another stone wall to enter Salcantay pampa. Mt Salcantay, the sacred mountain of the Incas is ahead of you. Descend to a stream and cross to the left-hand side where the path becomes boggy and the track indistinct. As long as you continue following the stream north-east, however, you'll be fine.

At the head of the valley is a massive wall of scree – the **terminal moraine** (end debris) of a glacier. The flat ground before the moraine is a great place to

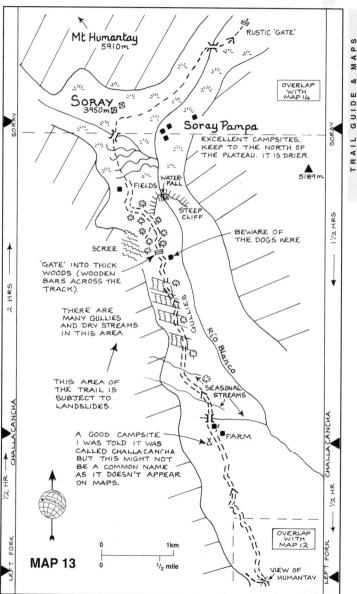

Mt Humantay
5910m

RUSTIC 'GATE'

OVERLAP WITH MAP 14

SORAY
3950m

Soray Pampa

EXCELLENT CAMPSITES.
KEEP TO THE NORTH OF
THE PLATEAU. IT IS DRIER.

SORAY

SORAY

5189m

1½ HRS

WATER-FALL

FIELDS

STEEP CLIFF

BEWARE OF
THE DOGS HERE

SCREE

'GATE' INTO THICK
WOODS (WOODEN
BARS ACROSS THE
TRACK).

THERE ARE
MANY GULLIES
AND DRY STREAMS
IN THIS AREA.

GULLIES

Río Blanco

2 HRS

THIS AREA OF
THE TRAIL IS
SUBJECT TO
LANDSLIDES.

SEASONAL
STREAMS

A GOOD CAMPSITE.
I WAS TOLD IT WAS
CALLED CHALLACANCHA
BUT THIS MIGHT NOT
BE A COMMON NAME
AS IT DOESN'T APPEAR
ON MAPS.

FARM.

CHALLACANCHA

CHALLACANCHA

½ HR

½ HR

TRAILBLAZER

0   1km
0   ½ mile

MAP 13

OVERLAP WITH MAP 12

LEFT FORK

LEFT FORK

VIEW OF
HUMANTAY

camp. The path splits here. The fork bearing left (NW) is the way for the Santa Teresa trek (see p226). To continue on the Mollepata trek take the right-hand fork (E), crossing back over the stream, towards the pass at Inca Chiriasq'ua.

Salcantay pampa to Inca Chiriasq'ua

To get to the pass at Inca Chiriasq'ua, follow the path which switchbacks steeply up the right-hand (E) hillside that faces the moraine. You'll soon reach a small, flat spot called Quera Machay (aka Isu Pata), which is another good place to *camp*. The path heads north from Quera Machay, then round to the right (E), steeply uphill. Don't go down to the lateral moraine of the glacier, keep the river between you and it. As you climb, the gully gets narrower and narrower, until the path seems to disappear when you reach the top. There's another stream here which you need to keep on your right – it's not the same as the one that runs down by the glacier. You'll know you've got it correct when you can look back over the wall of the lateral moraine and see two lakes.

From here, you should be able to see the pass at the top of a very, very steep path, surrounded by little ridges. Don't be tempted to cut out the pass and go over the watershed by the glacier – there are dangerous holes under the glacier and you could easily slip down into them. **Inca Chiriasq'ua** (4950m/16,235ft), which translates as 'the place where the Inca cools down', is the most knife-edged of passes I've ever seen – it's just a metre or so wide. You can look down into the great valley behind you and over into the wide valley ahead.

INCA CHIRIASQ'UA → PAMPA CAHUANA   [MAP 15, p224]

From the pass, head steeply downhill. Go over and have a look at the glacier on your left (N) which is the origin of the river Cusichaca. It's worth stopping and thinking that this is one of the origins of the Amazon, and the melt-water from this mountain flows to the Atlantic Ocean.

The trail from here to Paucarcancha is easy – you just follow the valley down – first east-north-east to Pampa Cahuana, then north-east.

Taking it step by step, the path first heads south-east across puna, then bends round to the north-east and descends quite steeply. Just before a ridge, about an hour and a half beyond the pass, there's a beautiful *campsite*, flat, green and protected from the wind but it's often occupied by tour companies. Down the other side of the ridge, the path crosses a plain of glacial outwash before settling on the northern (L) bank of the river. This area is flat and good for camping too, it's called the **Quebrada Sisay pampa**.

Keep on this side of the river, and skirt around two gullies with seasonal streams running in them. The land gets very steep. In a short while you'll see on the other side of the river a couple of **huts** and a large stream coming down from the south – there is a path on this side of the river too, but the main path's on the north. Just after the huts and stream, the valley turns north-east and looking down you can see an Inca canal, glistening in the sun (there's a better view from the southern path). This area's called **Pampa Cahuana**.

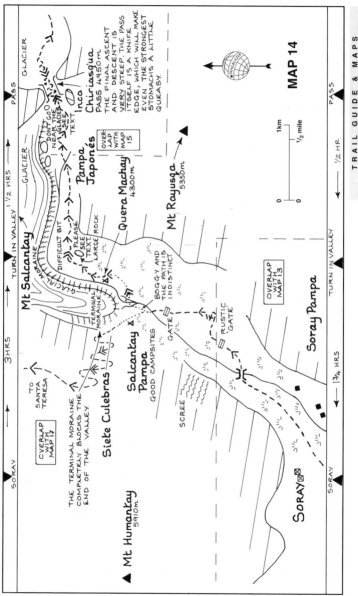

GLACIER

PASS

Inca
Chiriasq'ua
PASS 4950m.
THE FINAL ASCENT
AND DESCENT IS
VERY STEEP. THE PASS
ITSELF IS A KNIFE
EDGE, WHICH WILL MAKE
EVEN THE STRONGEST
STOMACHS A LITTLE
QUEASY.

MAP 14

GLACIER

TURN IN VALLEY 1½ HRS

DON'T GO
NEAR THE
GLACIER
SEE TEXT

Pampa
Japonés

OVER
LAP
WITH
MAP 15

½ HR.

PASS

Mt Solcantay

DIFFICULT BIT

GLACIAL
MORAINE

PLEASE
SEE
TEXT
LARGE
ROCK

Quera Machay
4300m.

Mt Rayusqa
5350m.

0   1km
0   ½ mile

TRAIL GUIDE & MAPS

3HRS

TERMINAL
MORAINE

BOGGY AND
THE PATH IS
INDISTINCT

OVERLAP
WITH
MAP 13

SOLCANTAY &
PAMPA
GOOD CAMPSITES

GATE

RUSTIC
GATE

TURN IN VALLEY

SORAY

TO
SANTA TERESA

OVERLAP
WITH
MAP 13

THE TERMINAL MORAINE
COMPLETELY BLOCKS THE
END OF THE VALLEY.

Siete Culebras

SCREE

Soray Pampa

1¾ HRS

SORAY

Mt Humantay
5910m.

SORAY ⊠

SORAY

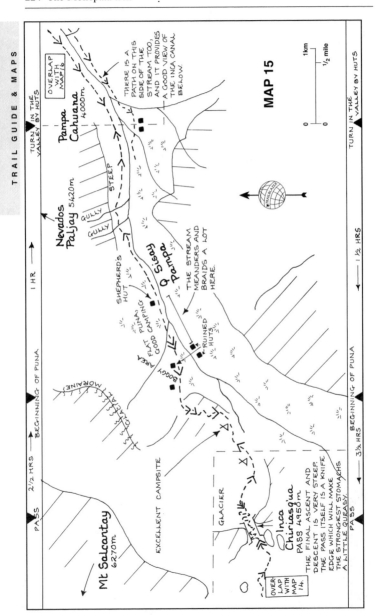

MAP 15

There is a path on this side of the stream too, and it provides a good view of the Inca canal below.

OVERLAP WITH MAP 16

TURN IN THE VALLEY BY HUTS

Pampa Cahuana 4000m

Nevados Paljay 5420m

STEEP

GULLY

GULLY

Q Sisay Pampa

The stream meanders and braids a lot here.

SHEPHERD'S HUT

FLAT PUNA GOOD CAMPING

RUINED HUTS

BOGGY AREA

GLACIER (MORAINE)

Mt Salcantay 6270m

EXCELLENT CAMPSITE

GLACIER

Inca Chiriasqua PASS 4950m

The final ascent and descent is very steep. The pass itself is a knife edge which will make the strongest stomachs a little queasy.

OVERLAP WITH MAP 14

PASS ◀ 2½ HRS ◀ BEGINNING OF PUNA

1 HR

TURN IN THE VALLEY BY HUTS

1½ HRS

BEGINNING OF PUNA ▶ 3½ HRS ▶ PASS

0   1km
0   ½ mile

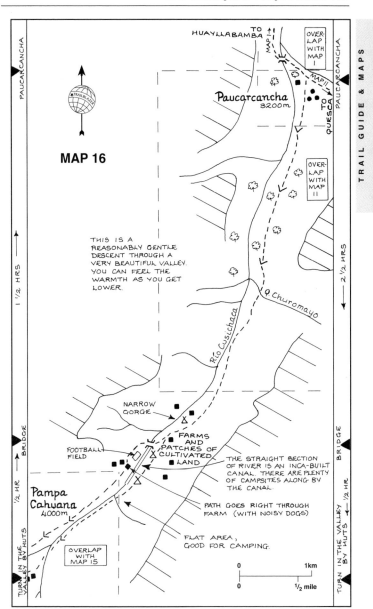

PAUCARCANCHA

TO HUAYLLABAMBA

OVER-LAP WITH MAP I

MAP I

OVERLAP WITH MAP I

MAP II

PAUCARCANCHA

Paucarcancha 3200m

TO QUESCA

MAP 16

OVER-LAP WITH MAP II

1 1/2 HRS

THIS IS A REASONABLY GENTLE DESCENT THROUGH A VERY BEAUTIFUL VALLEY. YOU CAN FEEL THE WARMTH AS YOU GET LOWER.

2 1/2 HRS

Q. Churomayo

Río Cusichaca

NARROW GORGE

BRIDGE

FOOTBALL FIELD

FARMS AND PATCHES OF CULTIVATED LAND

THE STRAIGHT SECTION OF RIVER IS AN INCA-BUILT CANAL. THERE ARE PLENTY OF CAMPSITES ALONG BY THE CANAL.

BRIDGE

1/2 HR

1/2 HR

Pampa Cahuana 4000m

PATH GOES RIGHT THROUGH FARM (WITH NOISY DOGS)

TURN IN THE VALLEY BY HUTS

OVERLAP WITH MAP 15

FLAT AREA, GOOD FOR CAMPING.

TURN IN THE VALLEY BY HUTS

0   1km

0   1/2 mile

PAMPA CAHUANA → PAUCARCANCHA [MAP 16, p225]

The path passes through the centre of a huddle of farms and a football pitch, and then crosses a **bridge** to the right-hand (E) bank of the river. You are crossing over an Inca canal. Then, after a narrow gorge, the river, valley and path all turn northwards. The valley descends gently, and the flora changes from high puna to scrub, bathed in warmth and flourishing with butterflies, insects, snapdragons and orchids. One and a half hours after the bridge you arrive at the ruins of **Paucarcancha** (see p216).

OPTIONS FROM PAUCARCANCHA

From Paucarcancha, you have **three options**: walk to Huayllabamba and complete the Inca Trail (see Map 1, p187); walk down the Cusichaca where you could either take a train out, walk to Chilca (see Map 6, p203), or walk west along the Urubamba to Chachabamba and Machu Picchu; turn up the valley you find on your right (E) and walk up to Puerto Huyanay (see Map 11, p215) and on to Chilca via the Silque valley.

The Santa Teresa trek

The Santa Teresa trek is the only 'back door' route to Machu Picchu (see overview map on pp22-3). It bypasses all the checkpoints, permits, expense and hassle thrown up by the Inca Trail regulations, which do not apply to it, and is therefore quickly growing in popularity with those short on time and money, and those who have fallen foul of the rules for the Inca Trail. The route itself had been closed since 1998 after a massive landslide (see box p231) destroyed much of the village of Santa Teresa and the nearby railway line, but the headaches caused by the regulations prompted the authorities to reopen it as an alternative route.

It is, however, a very different trek to the classic Inca Trail. There are no Inca ruins along the length of the route – except for one when you are in sight

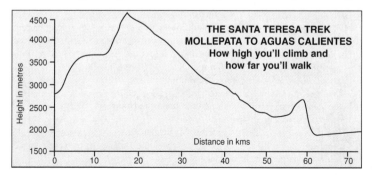

THE SANTA TERESA TREK
MOLLEPATA TO AGUAS CALIENTES
How high you'll climb and
how far you'll walk

of Machu Picchu. That said, the scenery is stunning and the diverse range of landscapes you'll pass through makes this is an extremely attractive route. You'll climb closer to the snowline and descend lower into subtropical forest than you would on the Inca Trail, meaning you'll probably encounter a greater variety of birds and flowers. The trek is also much quieter than its more famous counterpart, and rather than being surrounded by crowds of trekkers at the campsites, you'll have a chance to chat to locals living nearby. So it's not a bad alternative route to Machu Picchu at all, and a very pleasing trek regardless of the whole regulations issue.

Most agencies offer the Santa Teresa trek, but you can do it independently or with your own guide or arriero. The **dry season** (May to September) is the best time to go since the high pass can be blocked by snow during the wet.

The trek begins at Mollepata (for details on getting to the trailhead see p218) and typically takes four days; you'll probably want another day to enjoy Machu Picchu too. It's relatively taxing since it climbs from the watershed of the Apurímac (2800m/9185ft) to cross a 4700m/15,415ft pass below Mt Salcantay, drops back down into the thickly forested Santa Teresa valley (2300m/7545ft), crosses another pass at 2850m/9350ft and descends 600m/1970ft into the Aobamba valley to finish at the foot of Machu Picchu mountain.

MOLLEPATA → SALCANTAY PAMPA
[MAP 12, p219; MAP 13, p221; MAP 14, p223]

For information on the first section of the route, follow the start of the Mollepata trek (see p218).

SALCANTAY PAMPA → RAYAMPATA   [MAP 14, p223; MAP 17, p228]

At Salcantay pampa, the trail splits. The Mollepata track branches right (NE) around the moraine at the foot of Salcantay towards the Inca Chiriasq'ua pass and Huayllabamba. For the Santa Teresa trek you want to bear left (NW) around the left-hand side of the moraine towards the Salcantay pass.

The path begins to climb steeply up seven tight switchbacks, known as **Siete Culebras** (the Seven Serpents), and crests at a small knoll, where it begins to undulate north, parallel to the moraine, gradually gaining height.

Having scrambled through a boulder field, you snake across a level pampa to arrive at a small **lake**, Salcantaycocha, at its northern end. The track passes to the left (S) of the lake and climbs above it, over a succession of **ridges** and past a large boulder daubed with a red 'X'.

About 5-10 minutes' easy scrambling brings you to **Salcantay pass** (4700m/15,415ft), which is marked by a series of cairns (*apachitas*) up to 6ft tall, the more ghoulish of which include bones and skulls. It takes 3-3^1/$_2$hrs to get to the pass from Soray pampa.

The pass is part of the shoulder of Mt Salcantay, which rises to the east. If it's clear you should be able to see across the south face of the mountain to the Inca Chiriasq'ua pass in the distance.

TRAIL GUIDE & MAPS

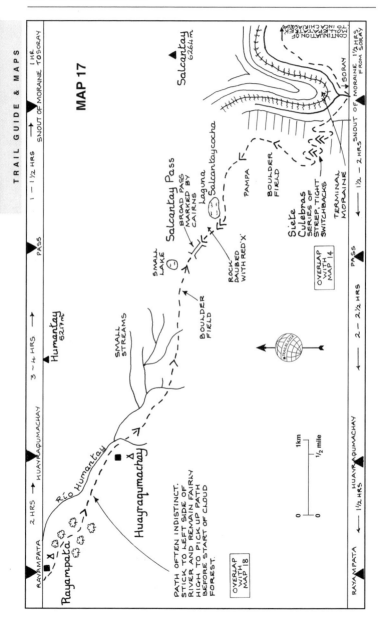

MAP 17

RAYAMPATA ← 2 HRS → HUAYRAQUMACHAY ← 3 – 4 HRS → Humantay ← 1 – 1½ HRS → PASS ← 1 – 1½ HRS → SNOUT OF MORAINE ← 1 HR → TOSORAY

Rayampata

Humantay 6217m

Río Humantay

Huayraqumachay

SMALL STREAMS

BOULDER FIELD

SMALL LAKE

Salcantay Pass

BROAD PASS MARKED BY CAIRNS

ROCK DAUBED WITH RED 'X'

Laguna Salcantaycocha

PAMPA

BOULDER FIELD

Siete Culebras SERIES OF STEEP, TIGHT SWITCHBACKS

TERMINAL MORAINE

Salcantay 6264 m.

CONTINUATION OF MOLLEPATA TREK TO INCA CHIRASCA

SORAY

← ½ – 2 HRS SNOUT OF MORAINE 1½ HRS FROM SORAY →

OVERLAP WITH MAP 14

PATH OFTEN INDISTINCT. STICK TO LEFT SIDE OF RIVER AND REMAIN FAIRLY HIGH TO PICK UP PATH BEFORE START OF CLOUD FOREST.

OVERLAP WITH MAP 18

1km
½ mile
0   0

RAYAMPATA ← 1½ HRS HUAYRAQUMACHAY → ← 2 – 2½ HRS → PASS ← ½ – 2 HRS SNOUT OF MORAINE

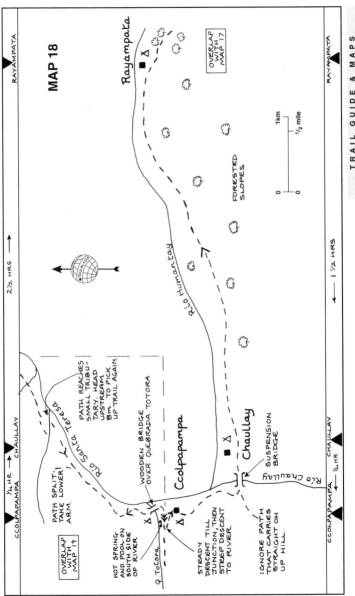

MAP 18

RAYAMPATA

2½ HRS →

Rayampata

OVERLAP WITH MAP 17

1km

½ mile

FORESTED SLOPES

Río Humantay

← 1½ HRS

RAYAMPATA

¼ HR → CHAULLAY

Río Santa Teresa

PATH REACHES SMALL TRIBU-TARY. HEAD UPSTREAM 8m. TO PICK UP TRAIL AGAIN

PATH SPLIT TAKE LOWER ARM.

CCOLPAPAMPA

WOODEN BRIDGE OVER QUEBRADA TOTORA

Ccolpapampa

Chaullay

SUSPENSION BRIDGE

Río Chaullay

HOT SPRING AND POOL ON SOUTH SIDE OF RIVER

Q. Totora

STEADY DESCENT TILL JUNCTION, THEN STEEP DESCENT TO RIVER.

IGNORE PATH THAT CARRIES STRAIGHT ON UP HILL.

OVERLAP WITH MAP 19

CCOLPAPAMPA

¼ HR → CHAULLAY

The Pass to Rayampata

Beyond Salcantay pass, the path descends steadily west, dropping past a small tarn and through a boulder field that chokes the narrow valley. As the valley broadens, the track frequently vanishes in muddy mires where a number of small streams cross the route. Stick to the left (W) side of the valley and you will pick up the track again lower down. In places simple stone walls span the width of the valley, but there are gaps or gates along them for you to get through. The bogs and streams eventually become the Río Humantay, which you follow on its left bank (W), crossing little tributaries as you go.

About two hours from the pass, you'll reach **Huayraqumachay** or 'Eye of the Wind', a couple of farm huts and a flat, raised patch of ground which makes a good *campsite*.

After Huayraqumachay the path can be hard to make out, but keep to the left (W) of the river and remain fairly high on the valley. You'll pass some giant boulders, and the valley sides will steepen as the puna gives way to scrub and then **cloud forest**, draped with moss and lichen. The path can get pretty muddy and churned up by mules during this forest section, but around an hour and a half after Huayraqumachay, you'll emerge and pass some gravestones marking the fringes of **Rayampata**, also shown as Arayan Niyoc on some maps. There are several huts to the right (NE) of the track and a few small terraces where you can *camp*. The families occasionally have soft drinks for sale. The views of the snow-capped range ahead are fantastic.

RAYAMPATA → CCOLPAPAMPA [MAP 18, p229]

The descent from Rayampata continues through thickly forested slopes. The skies are often clear first thing in the morning and an early start means that you'll be able to enjoy the outstanding views as well as the magnificent dawn chorus of forest birds. After an hour and a half you reach **Chaullay**, a very attractive little settlement at the junction of two valleys. Greener and cleaner than Rayampata, it would make an excellent *campsite* were it not for the clouds of mosquitoes; there are some other spots about 15 minutes further on if the biters are about.

Pass through the village and cross the Río Chaullay at the concrete **suspension bridge** (safer than the rickety wooden predecessor next to it), and turn right (N) on the far bank, ignoring the well-worn path that zigzags west up the side of the valley. Head downstream along the left (W) bank of the river to **Ccolpapampa**, a slightly larger community than Chaullay. There are several excellent level pitches here to *camp*.

To leave Ccolpapampa, walk across the grassy central square and continue down the valley. The path soon bends left (W) into the Quebrada Totora. At a fork below the lip of the valley, turn right (E), doubling back on yourself before weaving a steep descent down to the **wooden bridge** over the Totora river. A little upstream of the bridge, you can wallow in a hot spring, easily identified by the discoloured rocks and mineral deposits around it. Cross the bridge to a small *campsite* on the north bank.

CCOLPAPAMPA → LA PLAYA   [MAP 19, p232; Map 20, p233]

From the bridge, the trail leads along the left (W) side of the river, now the Río Santa Teresa, in a north-easterly direction. Where the path splits, take the lower arm (R) to make a slow descent through the cloud forest. Half an hour after entering the Santa Teresa valley the path reaches a small **tributary**. Head upstream along the tributary for about 8m before crossing it in order to pick up the trail on its far side. Soon you'll meet the thundering course of a 300m **waterfall**, which plunges from the cliff tops through the forest, crashing into the river in six large bounds. Traverse the falls on a series of rocks, watching your footing.

About 2km further on, you'll have to scramble over a landslide that has devastated the path and scarred the hillside. Cross a second stream on stepping stones and pass through a gate before descending to **Hatun Poccos**, a village of a few simple houses and some strips of farmed land. You can *camp* in a grassy clearing beside a small hut and thatched shelter.

The path continues on down the valley, and about one and a half hours after Hatun Poccos you'll get your first brief glimpse of Machu Picchu mountain before it disappears behind an intervening ridge as you descend.

About two and a half hours from Hatun Poccos the path meanders into **La Playa**, a relatively large community of farmers and arrieros. Walk across the football pitch by the local school to a cluster of houses by a stand of eucalyptus trees. You can *camp* here; there are standpipes for water by the houses, where you can also buy soft drinks and chicha. La Playa's modest town square, where basic goods and provisions are on sale at the market stalls and shops, is on the other side of the Santa Teresa river, ten minutes' walk away; take the track from the north-eastern corner of the football pitch and cross a makeshift bridge of iron struts, building supports and railway track and scramble up the opposite bank.

This is also where transport to the village of Santa Teresa (see box, below) departs, though you're unlikely to need to go there. On the other hand, you could catch a ride a short way along the road to Lucmabamba, from where the trail continues up the hillside.

Delivery trucks leave La Playa's town square around 6am and the bus usually goes at 10am.

Santa Teresa

Santa Teresa used to be a small, subtropical village connected to Aguas Calientes by a short train ride. The train was the main link to the outside world. But in 1998 both the village and the railway line were destroyed by an enormous landslide. Torrential El Niño rainstorms loosened the soil on the mountainside above, releasing a colossal landslip which swept over the town and railway line. Around 15 people died and over 350 families were left homeless. Almost 80% of the buildings in the old part of Santa Teresa were damaged or destroyed. The reconstruction and regeneration of Santa Teresa is under way, but it still has the air of a temporary settlement, comprised of makeshift wooden houses. The mangled railway line still hasn't been repaired.

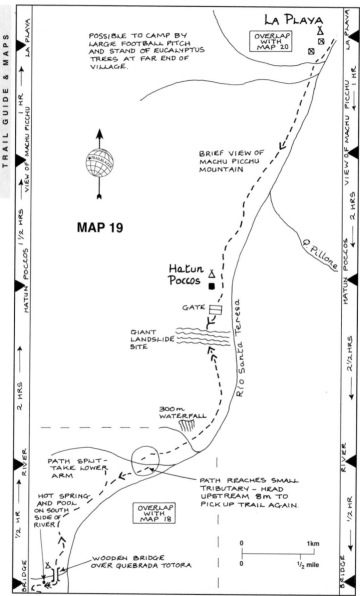

LA PLAYA

VIEW OF MACHU PICCHU 1 HR.

HATUN POCCOS 1½ HRS

2 HRS

RIVER

½ HR

BRIDGE

LA PLAYA

VIEW OF MACHU PICCHU 1 HR.

2 HRS

HATUN POCCOS 2½ HRS

RIVER

½ HR

BRIDGE

LA PLAYA

POSSIBLE TO CAMP BY LARGE FOOTBALL PITCH AND STAND OF EUCALYPTUS TREES AT FAR END OF VILLAGE.

OVERLAP WITH MAP 20

BRIEF VIEW OF MACHU PICCHU MOUNTAIN

MAP 19

Q. Pillone

Hatun Poccos

GATE

Rio Santa Teresa

GIANT LANDSLIDE SITE

300 m WATERFALL

PATH SPLIT – TAKE LOWER ARM

PATH REACHES SMALL TRIBUTARY – HEAD UPSTREAM 8m TO PICK UP TRAIL AGAIN.

HOT SPRING AND POOL ON SOUTH SIDE OF RIVER

OVERLAP WITH MAP 18

WOODEN BRIDGE OVER QUEBRADA TOTORA

0   1km

0   ½ mile

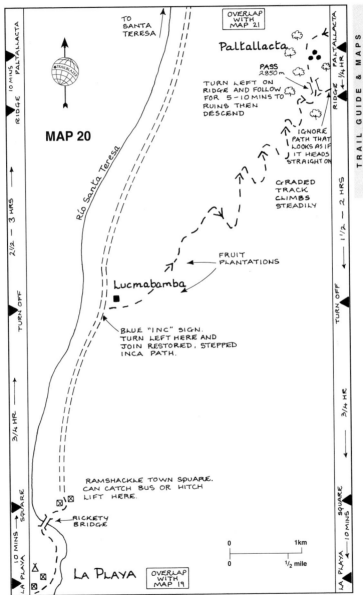

OVERLAP WITH MAP 21

TO SANTA TERESA

Paltallacta

PASS 2850 m

TURN LEFT ON RIDGE AND FOLLOW FOR 5-10 MINS TO RUINS THEN DESCEND

IGNORE PATH THAT LOOKS AS IF IT HEADS STRAIGHT ON

MAP 20

Río Santa Teresa

GRADED TRACK CLIMBS STEADILY

FRUIT PLANTATIONS

Lucmabamba

BLUE "INC" SIGN. TURN LEFT HERE AND JOIN RESTORED, STEPPED INCA PATH.

RAMSHACKLE TOWN SQUARE. CAN CATCH BUS OR HITCH LIFT HERE.

RICKETY BRIDGE

LA PLAYA

OVERLAP WITH MAP 19

0 1km
0 ½ mile

10 MINS PALTALLACTA · RIDGE

RIDGE PALTALLACTA ¼ HR

2½ – 3 HRS

1½ – 2 HRS

TURN OFF

TURN OFF

¾ HR

¾ HR

10 MINS · SQUARE

SQUARE · 10 MINS

LA PLAYA

LA PLAYA

TRAIL GUIDE & MAPS

Paltallacta (Llactapata)

The ruins of Paltallacta (also known as Llactapata) were initially uncovered by Hiram Bingham, who wrote, '...found some interesting ruins...The end of that day found us on top of a ridge between the valleys of the Aobamba and the Salcantay.' But his notes regarding its location were too vague for anyone to be able to retrace his steps, and slowly the forest closed back over the ruins. It wasn't until the early 1980s that Hugh Thomson relocated them, but the site is still to benefit from a full archaeological investigation.

It's now difficult to tell where the ruins begin and the vegetation ends. Bingham considered it 'a strategic spot', and it could have once been a sizeable site. It's thought that Paltallacta was built by one of Manco Inca's captains as a signalling post and watchtower over Machu Picchu's western flank – there is certainly a clear view of the city from here. But we're unlikely to know more until proper studies are carried out.

LA PLAYA → PALTALLACTA [MAP 20, p233]

Continue through La Playa and join the gravel road that runs above the river towards Santa Teresa. After 3km there is a large blue 'INC' sign on the right-hand side (E) of the road next to the small community of **Lucmabamba**. Turn right (E) here on to a grassy track and a short section of restored, broad Inca steps, which climb past coffee plantations and plots of lemon and passion-fruit trees. Continue ascending for $2^{1}/_{2}$-3hours around a number of spurs before entering dense forest and arriving at a ridge-pass (2850m/9350ft).

Ignore a broad, newly laid path heading east and follow the smaller, muddier track that curves left (N) and runs along the ridge for 5-10 minutes, before it drops down into the Aobamba valley. There are now tantalizing glimpses of Machu Picchu clinging to the ridgeline 5km ahead of you, shadowed by the unmistakable silhouette of Huayna Picchu.

The path runs down the hillside past the uncleared ruins of **Paltallacta** (also sometimes referred to as Llactapata), hidden under moss and leaves, and weighed down by a dense tangle of twisted tree roots.

PALTALLACTA → AGUAS CALIENTES [MAP 21, opposite]

Below the ruins is a clearing that has exceptional views of Machu Picchu and its surrounds. This would be an excellent *campsite* were it not for the lack of a reliable water source nearby; the next accommodation is at Aguas Calientes.

From the **clearing**, the descent begins in earnest for $1^{1}/_{2}$ hours, plunging 600m down a series of switchbacks to emerge at a **suspension bridge** across the Aobamba river. Once on the far side of the river, turn left (N) and follow the right-hand (E) side of the valley downstream towards the confluence of the Aobamba and Urubamba rivers. You'll see a huge stream of water spewing from a hole high on the cliff; it's part of the hydroelectric project (La Hidroeléctrica).

By now, you're on a gravel road heading towards La Hidroeléctrica and the small railway station next to it (you can cut off a corner on a faint path leading

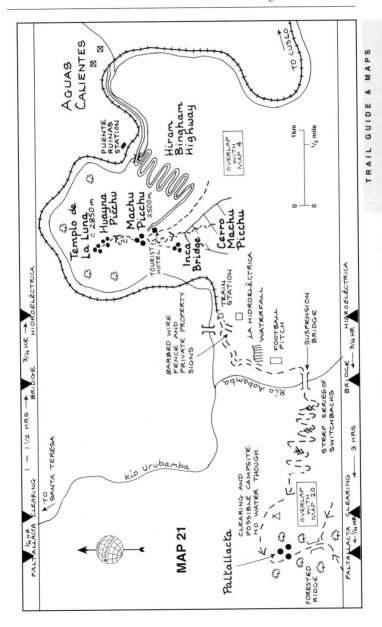

MAP 21

over a hillock into the Urubamba valley). Ignore the bridge over the Urubamba, and carry on to the station, which is signposted below some power-station out-buildings.

The platform, up a series of steps to the left of the road, is lined by shabby cantinas and stalls selling drinks and snacks. The ticket office is one of the last buildings on the right; it opens at around 3.30pm and the train to Aguas Calientes departs around 4pm.

It takes almost an hour for the train to trundle across the Urubamba, clatter past **Puente Ruinas** at the foot of Machu Picchu and gasp to a stop at **Aguas Calientes** (see p167) at the old station on Avenida Imperio de los Incas. Alternatively you can walk the 10km to Aguas Calientes in about 2-3 hours by following the railway tracks.

From Aguas Calientes, you can catch a shuttle bus up to Machu Picchu, something you'll most likely want to do first thing the following morning to get a full day at the site. For details on moving on from Machu Picchu and Aguas Calientes see p293.

Other trails near Machu Picchu

CHILCA CIRCUIT (5-6 DAYS)

(To follow this route description look at the Route Options map on pp22-3). A Chilca circuit would take you up the Silque valley, down the Cusichaca valley and back around to Chilca along the Urubamba river. It would take about five or six days. Remember that it's not a good idea to do this circuit anti-clockwise because you'd have to pay the Inca Trail fee twice.

THE FULL MOLLEPATA (2 WEEKS)

(See Route Options map on pp22-3). An extended Mollepata hike would take you from Mollepata, over the Salcantay pass, down the Cusichaca to the Urubamba, along to Chilca, then up the Silque valley. At the top of the Silque valley you'd turn right and head up to the pass of Puerto Huyanay. You'd then follow the Quesca valley and down to Paucarcancha and then Huayllabamba where you'd pick up the classic Inca Trail to Machu Picchu. This hike would take you about two weeks.

The Riverside Trail from Km88

An unusual and very pretty alternative to the classic Inca Trail is to follow the Urubamba valley all the way to Chachabamba. The permit for
this route costs the same as that for the Inca Trail, namely s/192 (US$60),
or s/96 (US$30) for students. The path begins across the bridge from the warden's
office (see Map 1, p187): while those following the classic Inca Trail turn left after
the bridge, the riverside path splits off to the right, heads due south away from the
river for 50m, then leads off west in the shadow of a large stone wall, and continues
west along the Río Urubamba for the next 15km (9 miles).

The walk is, as they say around these parts, 'muy tranquilo', which is its chief
attraction: I encountered precisely nobody after the first few hundred metres, and
heard nothing but the roar of the river, the occasional birdsong and the sound of my
own footfall for the next 15km. The walk's perfect if you want to avoid the crowds,
don't want any knee-jarring descents or steep climbs (the longest ascent lasts no more
than 15 minutes), or just want something different – a walk along forest- and grass-
clad slopes rather than over mountain passes. It's also shorter than the regular Km88
walk, taking two or three very easy, relaxing days.

There are some Inca ruins along the way too, including Machu and Huayna
Quente (see p186) – don't miss the wonderful little carved boulder by the bridge
beneath the former – and the impressive Torontoy complex on the northern banks of
the Urubamba. This is the Inca compound of Raccay Pata, more commonly known as
Torontoy after the canyon in which it is built. This site's age and purpose remain in
the realms of conjecture, though Ann Kendall has estimated from the fine, classical
stonework that it was probably built sometime during the latter part of the reign of
Pachacutec, or possibly the early years of his successor, Tupac Inca, during the hey-
day of the Inca Empire. Kendall has also suggested that at least one of its functions
was to serve as upmarket accommodation for the Inca or another member of the travelling élite – the Machu Picchu Pueblo Hotel of its day. A possible temple building
has also been identified within the compound. The rope and pulley contraption
(*oroya*) strung across the river has not been used since the footbridge at Km88 was
built so you'll have to make do with a distant view. If you do manage to get across,
look out for the incredible 44-angled stone in one of the walls – a marvel of masonry that puts even the 12-angled stone in Cusco in the shade.

There are other, lesser ruins lying unrestored in the forest, especially near the Río
Pacamayo. Unimpressive though they may be, some of the ruins here are circular in
design, suggesting pre-Inca occupation, which is highly unusual for this part of the
Urubamba.

The path is fairly well maintained and signposted, but because of the compara-
tive unpopularity of the trail it is sometimes a little overgrown. That said, it's very difficult to get lost, and the path never peters out altogether. Snakes, however, are a
potential hazard – I came across four while researching this walk, each one basking
in the sunshine on the path. But if you give them time to slither away and are careful
where you sit and tread, they shouldn't be a problem.

Campsites along the way include the warden's post by the Río Pacamayo, about
two hours from Km88, and by the ruins at Chachabamba, three hours further on.
From the latter you can either take the standard path up to the Trekkers' Hotel (see
p198), or continue along the river all the way to Choquesuysuy, from where the newly
established Purification Trail leads up to Huinay Huayna (see p207).

TRAIL GUIDE & MAPS

The Vilcabamba Trail

INTRODUCTION

This is a fascinating walk through the forest between the remote villages of **Huancacalle** and **Chaunquiri** via the ruins of Espíritu Pampa, believed to be the remains of Vilcabamba, the last city and capital of the Inca empire. The trail follows what is believed to be the same route taken by Manco Inca as he fled the Spanish in 1537, and also that taken by the Spaniards themselves in their two invasions of Vilcabamba in 1539 and 1572.

In common with the Inca Trail, the best time to attempt this walk is between **May and September**; outside this period the route is often impassable and you probably won't find a guide/arriero willing to take you. It involves approximately the same amount of walking time as the Inca Trail, namely four days. Unlike the Inca Trail, however, this is no walk in the (national) park. There are no designated campsites here, no rubbish bins, flush toilets or drink sellers. The path is extremely muddy and marshy in places. Depending on how many people have used it in the weeks before you, it may be very overgrown as well, and for some stretches you may find yourself having to hack your way through the forest – at times you'll feel like a true explorer.

The weather can play havoc with the trail: landslips that obliterate the path are common throughout the year, while bridges are often swept away by the raging rivers in the wet season – and in the Vilcabamba region it seems to be nearly always the wet season.

Having overcome all the obstacles and hazards, understandably you may anticipate something really spectacular at the end of the journey. Though the area covered by Vilcabamba La Vieja is large, the ruins don't stand up to such expectations; they bear little comparison with even the lesser monuments on the Inca Trail; nevertheless this trek has other attractions which make it a most

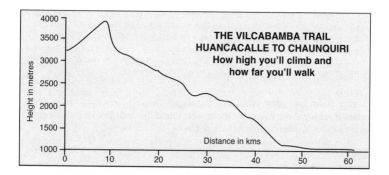

THE VILCABAMBA TRAIL
HUANCACALLE TO CHAUNQUIRI
How high you'll climb and
how far you'll walk

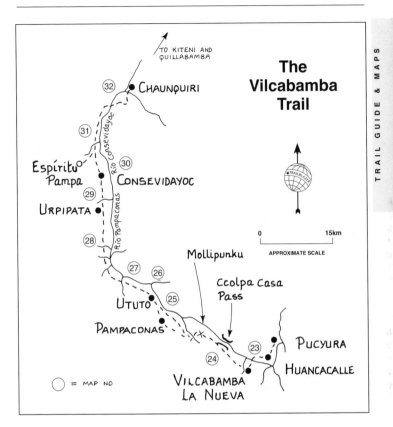

rewarding and memorable experience. The route itself is a gloriously beautiful hike through virtually every kind of vegetation zone found in Peru; as a crash course in the variegated ecology of this country, this trail is hard to beat. Then there are the ruins along the way, many of which are off the path and covered in vegetation. While none could be described as breathtaking, for those who feel that the ruins on the Inca Trail have been over-restored, and thus seem a touch artificial, here's a chance to see some in their pristine, untouched state. The path itself is also of Inca origin, and here and there you'll find the distinctive giant paving slabs. Nor must you forget the terrific sense of achievement one feels when reaching these ruins; for those who found the Inca Trail a bit of a cinch, this provides a much tougher challenge.

But perhaps the best feature of this trek is its remoteness. This is one walk where you can be sure (or 95% sure) that you won't meet other tourists. And for anybody who has found themselves shuffling along the Inca Trail in the high season as part of an endless human queue, it is another good reason to recommend this walk.

PREPARATIONS

There's no reason why anybody with a little stamina and a decent pair of calf muscles can't complete this trek, though some preparation is necessary.

You'll need a tent and food; there are no hotels or designated campsites but good camping spots have been marked on the maps in this section. Then you need to engage an **arriero**, which can be done in Huancacalle: see p244.

Other than a machete, which your arriero should have (check this before you leave), the walk needs no special **equipment**, though a bottle or two of insect repellent would come in useful, and keeping everything wrapped in plastic bags is even more necessary here than on other treks because of the extremely wet weather you're bound to encounter. This is a malarial area so don't forget your anti-malarials.

Finally, there is one more piece of preparation to be made before you head off to Vilcabamba: read about the place (see p32 for a list of books).

TIMING AND GETTING TO THE TRAILHEAD

This trail takes you from Huancacalle to Chaunquiri via Espíritu Pampa. To reach Huancacalle you need to take a bus from Cusco to Quillabamba (seven to nine hours), then another bus or a truck from Quillabamba to Huancacalle (four to five hours).

It takes around four days to walk from Huancacalle to Chaunquiri but the **timing of your walk** is very important. Since buses from Chaunquiri (at the end of the trek) tend to leave irregularly, most commonly after the weekly market on Saturdays and Sundays, you'd be well advised to aim to finish your walk at a weekend to avoid being stranded in the village. Remember to take into account the time it takes to travel to the Vilcabamba region, plus any time you may wish to spend before your trek in Quillabamba or Huancacalle, both of which are worth a day at least. Those in a hurry can jump out before Quillabamba at Chaullay and from there look for a bus or lift to Huancacalle: by bypassing Quillabamba it might just be possible to reach the start of the trail in one day from Cusco.

Taking all the above into consideration, however, it's best to allow at least a week for the whole trek, perhaps even as much as nine days.

❏ Chaullay

Chaullay was once the site of Chuquichaca, one of the Inca's famous rope bridges. As the main entrance into the Vilcabamba valley, the bridge became strategically crucial in the defence of the Inca's territory and was cut down if an invasion was anticipated. It was also here that the envoy Atilana de Anayo was murdered by Inca troops protecting the bridge, an event that led to the final invasion of Vilcabamba in 1572.

Cusco to Quillabamba

Buses to Quillabamba leave throughout the day (at 8am, 2pm and 7pm) from the Paso Santiago Terminal in the north-west of Cusco. It's a spectacular journey that takes you over the **Pass of the Eagle**, with awesome views of the Veronica range; don't take a night bus or you'll miss it all. The journey takes between 7-9 hours and costs s/15-18; Trans Tur seems one of the better companies. Ninety minutes before Quillabamba lies **Chaullay**, where those in a hurry can alight and try to catch a lift straight to Huancacalle.

Quillabamba

Built at the confluence of the Chuyapi and Urubamba (Vilcanota) rivers, **Quillabamba** is a friendly little jungle town with a large food market at its centre where you can buy provisions for the trek.

There's a variety of accommodation options in town. At the lower end of the scale is the cheap but clean ***Urusayhua Hostal*** (☎ 281426; s/10/15/20 sgl/dbl/tpl), Pasaje Lima 114, and the bright but basic ***Hostal Alto Urubamba*** (☎ 281131; s/15/23/30 sgl/dbl/tpl, com, or s/30/40/50, att) at 2 de Mayo 333.

(Continued on p244)

Quillabamba

Cibermaster Internet Café

Hostal Alto Urubamba

Church

Cibermaster Internet Café

Telephone Office

Don Carlos Hostal

Plaza de Armas

Post Office

Chemo's Panadería

BCP & money changers

Banco Continental

Venecia Pizzería

AV GRAU

Peña la Taverna

AV BOLOGNESI

Banco Continental

Quillabamba Hostal

Food Market

Plaza Grau

Hospital

SAN MARTIN

Chicken Restaurants

Urusayhua Hostal

Pharmacy

Buses to Huancacalle

LIMA

0   100m
APPROXIMATE SCALE

Fruit Market

Bus Station

THE VITCOS

The ruins of Vitcos lie between the Río Vilcabamba and Las Andenes stream and you can spend a delightful half day exploring these and neighbouring monuments. The caretaker of the ruins lives in Huancacalle in the house underneath the 'Welcome' sign, and officially you should register with him before setting off. The paths are clearly marked and it's difficult to get lost.

The trail begins across the two rivers from Sixpac Manco Hostal, from where it heads north via the ruins of an old Spanish mill up to the crest of the hill known as Rosaspata (3050m/10,004ft). At the northern end of the crest, overlooking the town of Pucyura, are the ruins of Vitcos, Manco's first capital in Vilcabamba, and another of Hiram Bingham's discoveries.

Manco established his palace here in 1537, before abandoning it just days later following a raid by Diego de Almagro's faithful commander, Orgóñez. Manco returned to Vitcos regularly, however, largely because its climate had more in common with the Inca's old home in Cusco (being only 600m lower than the former capital) than the sweaty humidity of the jungle. Indeed, Manco was eventually assassinated here in 1544 by a group of seven Spaniards to whom he had given refuge, supporters of the defeated Almagrist cause in the civil war against the Pizarrists (see p105). The fugitives hoped that the murder of Manco would curry favour with the conquering Pizarrists. The murder was recorded by his young son, Titu Cusi, one of the great chroniclers of post-conquest life and a future Inca himself:

'One day with much good fellowship they were playing at quoits with him: only them, my father, and me, who was then a little boy . . . Then just as my father was raising the quoit to throw, they all rushed upon him with knives, daggers and some swords ... he fell to the ground covered with wounds, and they left him for dead. I being a little boy, and seeing my father treated in this manner, wanted to rush over to help him. But they turned furiously on me and threw a lance which only just failed to kill me too.'

Manco survived for another three days, long enough to learn that his assailants had all been captured and suffered horrible deaths at the hands of his supporters. The heads of the seven renegades were still on display at Vitcos 21 years later.

Although Titu Cusi survived this assault he too met his death at Vitcos, after a violent illness. In the eyes of the Inca's followers this illness was the result of poisoning. The Spanish were once again implicated: Friar Diego Ortiz, one of the priests allowed into Vilcabamba as part of the peace treaty between Titu Cusi and the Spanish, was renowned for his knowledge of medicine, and relations between the Inca and his priest had been strained for some time prior to Titu Cusi's death. If anything, the poor friar's fate (see p254) was even more gruesome than that of the seven renegades who had killed Manco. Today the entire hill of Rosaspata is dotted with Inca foundations and ruins, though only those on the northern spur have been cleared of vegetation. The palace, however, is in the process of being restored and there is now a reconstructed upper level that includes residential buildings and storage facilities. On the lower level, the marble lintels abutting the plaza and, on the other side, a small, finely carved stone throne remain *in situ*; it's a pleasant spot for a rest.

From Vitcos, a second path heads south along the eastern slopes of the hill and down to a series of smart Inca terraces, or *andenes*, adorned here and there with gigantic carved boulders clearly the work of Inca craftsmen. Continue around Rosaspata and at the foot of its southern slopes (15-20 minutes) you'll find the ruins of the Inca temple of Ñusta España, also known as Yurac-Rumi ('White Stone'), an impressive set of elaborately carved stone chairs, large sacred rocks, foundations and water channels.

WALK (Map 22)

At the centre of Ñusta España lies a huge boulder over seven metres high and fifteen metres long. The smallness of the valley emphasizes the presence of the rock, which is carved with a series of small protrusions, steps, platforms and other decorations; this is a huaca, or sacred site. The stone work is outstanding and the light plays off every facet as the sun tracks around, illuminating different features as it goes. It is reminiscent of Qenko (see p158). According to one contemporary Spanish account 'There was a devil, captain of a legion of devils, inside the white stone called Yurac-Rumi,' and that devil was 'visible on various occasions'. Today sightings of the devil are rare, particularly since the temple was exorcized and burnt by Friar Diego Ortiz. The locals in Huancacalle tell of another former use for Yurac-Rumi. According to legend, in Inca times it was traditional for girls to urinate at the top of the pale grey channel running along the top of the boulder in order to prove their virtue: if the urine followed precisely the channel's course, so legend has it, then the girl had success-fully proved her virginity.

To return to Huancacalle, continue heading west from Ñusta España then down the steep hill to the river. The hike in and out takes around two hours, and you'll probably want to spend a couple of hours exploring the site too.

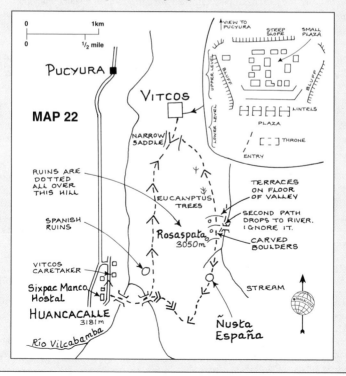

Quillabamba – places to stay (*continued from p241*) Smarter places include *Quillabamba Hostal* (☎ 281369; s/40/60/75 sgl/dbl/tpl) on Av Grau, which has its own pool, and the equally comfortable *Don Carlos Hostal* (☎ 281150; s/45/65/85 sgl/dbl/tpl), just to the west of Plaza de Armas, which has Internet facilities (s/5 per hour).

For food, try one of the *chicken restaurants* on San Martín, the bar-restaurant *Peña La Taverna* on Av Grau by Plaza Grau, or *Venecia Pizzería* on Plaza de Armas. For snacks, *Chemo's Panadería and Pastelería* does a fair empanada. The **Internet café** Cibermaster is at Av Bolognesi 403 and Av Espinar 229.

Quillabamba to Huancacalle

From Quillabamba, it's four to five hours to Huancacalle (s/10), taking the road back down to Chaullay, then up the Vilcabamba valley. At the moment there are three buses daily, at 9am, 11am and 1pm.

Just a few minutes before Huancacalle lies **Pucyura**, one of the older and larger villages in the valley. In years gone by all visitors had to register with the police here and present their passports, though as the threat from the Sendero Luminoso (see p45) has all but vanished this rule has been relaxed. Pucyura was also the location of the first church in the valley, built by Friar Diego Ortiz following the peace treaty between the Spaniards and Titu Cusi in 1568; the modern church you see today stands on the site of the original.

Huancacalle   [see Map 23, p246]

Built in the prettiest part of the Vilcabamba valley, **Huancacalle** is a typical Andean village, the kind of place where the people smile and greet you as you walk past and where the pigs and chickens roam free and the donkeys and dogs are untethered. Huancacalle is also the traditional starting point of the walk to the ruins of Vilcabamba and is fairly used to catering for trekkers. While there are no camping shops or pizza restaurants, this is the place where mules and guides can be hired and last-minute provisions acquired.

There is a hostel in Huancacalle, the *Sixpac Manco Hostal* (☎ 812714) at the very end of the village, sponsored by the author and Vilcabamba expert Vincent Lee (see p32) and run by the Cobos family, the best-known guides in the village. They charge s/10/15 (com/att) and s/3 per meal. As alternatives there are a couple of gloomy **cafés** in town, where s/2 will get you a plate of rubbery meat and potatoes. There's also a place to *camp* next to the unfinished visitors' centre, which seems to have been abandoned and is in an advanced state of disrepair.

HUANCACALLE → UTUTO
[MAP 23, p246; MAP 24, p247; MAP 25, p249]

The trek kicks off with a lengthy but not particularly arduous uphill tramp of about 2½ hours, most of it along a snaking dirt road from the centre of Huancacalle (3181m/10,434ft) to the Abra Ccolpa Casa ('Salty Pass'; 3900m/12,792ft). To follow every twist and turn in the road would be time-consuming but, by taking the short cuts marked on the map you would have a more direct route to the pass.

A short way out of Huancacalle take the right fork in the road and leave it to follow the trail. After a zigzagging bend the path rejoins the road, leaving it just before a bridge near the VIIth Station of the Cross, one of fourteen crucifixes standing at intervals by the roadside. Go over the next bridge, then continue with the Río Vilcabamba on your right. You will pass the VIIIth and IXth Stations of the Cross, rejoining the road once and crossing it twice before joining it again near the XIth Station of the Cross, to pass through the village of San Francisco de la Vitoria de Vilcabamba, often referred to just as Vilcabamba, or as **Vilcabamba La Nueva** to distinguish it from Manco's capital.

This was the first Spanish settlement founded in the Spanish province of Vilcabamba and was its first capital. It was moved in the late 16th century from its original site near Vitcos to its current location near the source of the Río Vilcabamba to service a now-exhausted silver mine that lies nearby. The central feature of Vilcabamba is the large Italian Catholic mission and its adjoining church, a modern construction embellished with a door portraying the life of San Francisco. The church is built on the site of the original 16th-century edifice, whose ancient bell-tower still stands. There is no accommodation in Vilcabamba, though you should have no trouble obtaining permission to camp. There are also two small shops here, the last you'll see for a couple of days.

From Vilcabamba La Nueva the road wends its way northwards and upwards before petering out at **Abra Ccolpa Casa** (the pass). At the pass, the dividing line between the low Andes and the Amazon basin is a little, modern shrine to Santa Rosa de Lima, built at the northern end of a small, flat grassy plateau – the overgrown remains of an Inca plaza. There are even the remains of a little Inca shrine here on the plateau's south-eastern corner, though now it's not much more than a heap of mossy stones.

From Ccolpa Casa the path continues north-west past what was once a school but is now a ruined hut, recognizable by its damaged doors, one green and one red. The path continues past a football pitch and undulates across the puna to **Mollipunku**, an ancient Inca crossroads where paths from both left (to Chalca) and right merge with yours; Inca paving slabs and steps still protect the pathway here. Infrequent blue signs for 'El Camino a Espíritu Pampa' also point the way.

About 25 minutes later you reach and cross the Río Chalca on Puente Antiguo (Mankechaca), where the trail splits. The upper and more obvious path climbs to **Pampaconas** (3340m/10,955ft), a windswept and rather chilly village with a little group of ruins including another Inca platform nearby. Be warned: just before Pampaconas is a deep bog into which some of the Spanish invaders of 1572, Bingham in 1911 and countless others have plunged. (*Continued on p248*)

❏ **Walking times on Maps 23-32 (Vilcabamba Trail)**
Note that on all of the trail maps in this book the times shown alongside each map refer only to time spent actually walking. For the trail times in the Vilcabamba section you may find the pace a little faster than for the Inca Trail timings. When planning your walking for the day you should add about 30-50% to allow for rest stops.

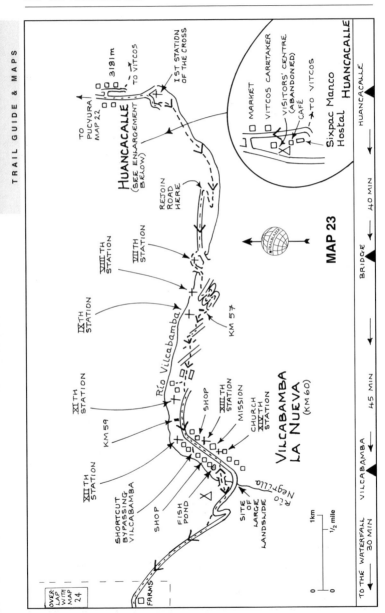

MAP 23

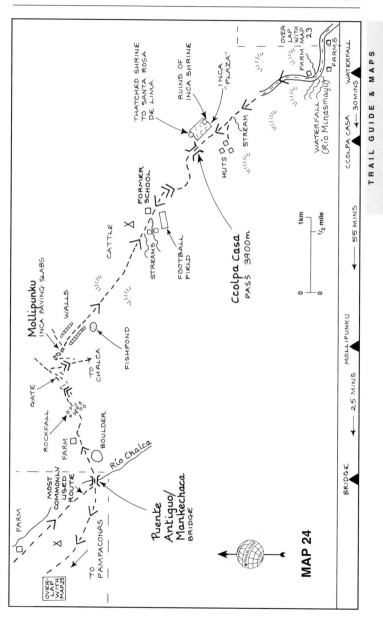

MAP 24

Puente Antiguo/Mankechaca
BRIDGE

Río Chalca

Mollipunku
INCA PAVING SLABS

Ccolpa Casa
PASS 3900m

Thatched shrine to Santa Rosa de Lima

Ruins of Inca shrine

Inca "Plaza"

Huts

Stream

Waterfall (Río Minasmayu)

Over lap with map 23

Farms

Waterfall

Former school

Football field

Streams

Cattle

Walls

To Chalca

Fishpond

Gate

Rockfall

Boulder

Farm

Most commonly used route

To Pampaconas

Farm

Overlap with map 25

0   1km
0   ½ mile

BRIDGE ◄—— 25 MINS ——► MOLLIPUNKU ◄—— 55 MINS ——► CCOLPA CASA ◄—— 30 MINS ——► WATERFALL

Pampaconas

Pampaconas features regularly in 16th-century records. It was to this spot that a wife and sister of Manco, Cura Ocllo, was taken by the Spaniards following their destruction of Vilcabamba in 1539. To prevent the Spaniards raping her, Cura covered herself in excrement and 'filthy matter' so that 'the men who were trying to rape her would be nauseated'. The tactic provided only a temporary reprieve, however, for Cura was killed in anger by the Spaniards shortly afterwards following yet another rejection of a peace treaty by Manco.

Pampaconas was also a centre for worship. Not only did the Incas hold various sun-worshipping ceremonies on the grassy plateau but Titu Cusi also gave permission for the Spanish to erect the first Christian cross in Vilcabamba here, under which missionaries were allowed to preach to the heathen locals. During the invasions in 1539 and 1572, the Spaniards were forced to leave their horses behind here, the path beyond being too forested. Bingham had to do the same in 1911, though today the path ahead is open to horses all the way to Espíritu Pampa.

(Continued from p245) Indeed, the bog is so renowned around here that unusually it even has its own name, **Oncoy Cacha**.

The more commonly used alternative to the Pampaconas route is to walk on the lower and more direct path, the start of which, though not immediately obvious from the Puente Antiguo, lies just two minutes away and is not difficult to find: just walk through the grassy field along the riverbank below the main path and you'll soon see it leading off to the north, along the valley towards **Ututo** where it rejoins the trail from Pampaconas. Take note that there's some extremely boggy ground around Ututo, one of the largest settlements in the Pampaconas valley, though if you can find a dry patch of ground it's an excellent place to *pitch a tent* for the night.

UTUTO → URPIPATA   [MAP 26, p250; MAP 27, p251; MAP 28, p253]

This is perhaps the most pleasant and certainly the easiest stage of the walk, an undemanding and largely downhill march through increasingly dense but always gorgeous cloud forest.

The forest begins as soon as you cross the large concrete bridge (which is a bit worse for wear but generally safe) at Ututo. This first stretch on the Pampaconas' eastern banks is very pretty indeed, a sun-dappled, mossy path adorned with the occasional Inca stairway and punctuated by a few clearings where cows and horses look on and graze.

According to Vincent Lee, the Spaniards were unaware of this particular trail, and instead tried to carve out a path along the cliffs and through the forest on the opposite bank: this explains why they took eight days to reach Vilcabamba from Pampaconas, while walkers today can do it in just over two.

After the Puente de Cedro (Cedrochaca in Quechua), there follows an uphill climb before the path bends to the west towards the tiny clearing of **Tambocarahuina**. Whilst the clearing itself is unremarkable, it does provide an

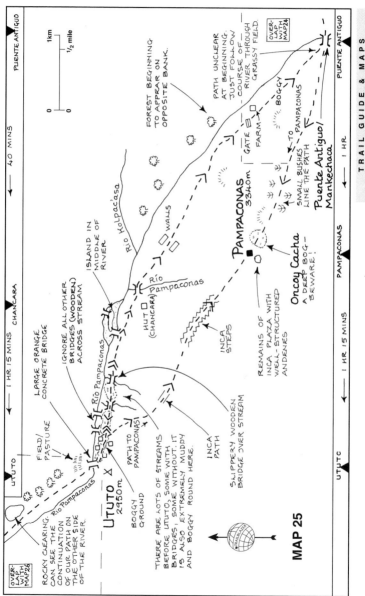

MAP 25

PUENTE ANTIGUO

40 MINS

1 HR 15 MINS CHANCARA

UTUTO

OVER-LAP WITH MAP26

PATH UNCLEAR AT BEGINNING. JUST FOLLOW COURSE OF RIVER THROUGH GRASSY FIELD.

FOREST BEGINNING TO APPEAR ON OPPOSITE BANK.

Río Kolpac'asa

ISLAND IN MIDDLE OF RIVER

LARGE ORANGE CONCRETE BRIDGE

IGNORE ALL OTHER BRIDGES (WOODEN) ACROSS STREAM

Río Pampaconas

Río Pampaconas

HUT (CHANCARA)

WALLS

INCA STEPS

REMAINS OF INCA PLAZA WITH WEAK-STRUCTURED ANDENES

PAMPACONAS 3340m

Oncoy Cacha A DEEP BOG - BEWARE!

GATE FARM

BOGGY

SMALL BUSHES LINE THE PATH

Puente Antiguo/ Mankechaca.

TO PAMPACONAS

FIELD/ PASTURE

UTUTO 2950m

BOGGY GROUND

PATH TO PAMPACONAS

INCA PATH

SLIPPERY WOODEN BRIDGE OVER STREAM

ROCKY CLEARING. CAN SEE THE CONTINUATION OF OUR PATH ON THE OTHER SIDE OF THE RIVER.

Río Pampaconas

THERE ARE LOTS OF STREAMS BEFORE UTUTO, SOME WITH BRIDGES, SOME WITHOUT. IT IS ALSO EXTREMELY MUDDY AND BOGGY ROUND HERE.

OVER-LAP WITH MAP24

PUENTE ANTIGUO

1 HR.

1 HR 15 MINS PAMPACONAS

UTUTO

0 1km
0 ½ mile

TRAIL GUIDE & MAPS

excellent view of the slender ridge above the scattered farms of **Tambo**, a little
way to the north. Lee has identified this ridge as the site of the Inca bastion
known as **Huayna Pucará**, or the new fort (see box p252).

At the end of elongated Tambo, the path descends along a series of switchbacks to the Río Zapatero and the one-hut settlement of the same name, before
continuing to the village of **San Fernando**. Then you come to three rivers – the

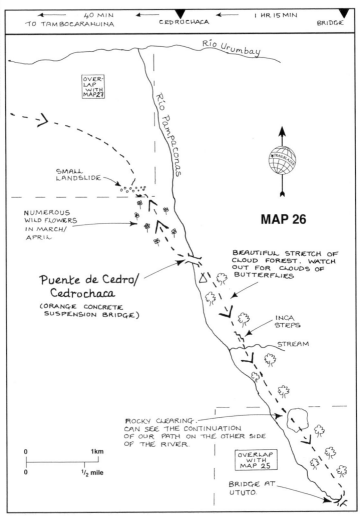

← 40 MIN
TO TAMBOCARAHUINA

▼ ← CEDROCHACA

← 1 HR 15 MIN

▼ BRIDGE

Río Urumbay

OVER-
LAP
WITH
MAP 27

Río Pampaconas

SMALL
LANDSLIDE

NUMEROUS
WILD FLOWERS
IN MARCH/
APRIL

MAP 26

TRAILBLAZER

Puente de Cedro/
Cedrochaca
(ORANGE CONCRETE
SUSPENSION BRIDGE)

BEAUTIFUL STRETCH OF
CLOUD FOREST. WATCH
OUT FOR CLOUDS OF
BUTTERFLIES

INCA
STEPS

STREAM

ROCKY CLEARING.
CAN SEE THE CONTINUATION
OF OUR PATH ON THE OTHER SIDE
OF THE RIVER.

OVERLAP
WITH
MAP 25

BRIDGE AT
UTUTO.

0   1km
0   1/2 mile

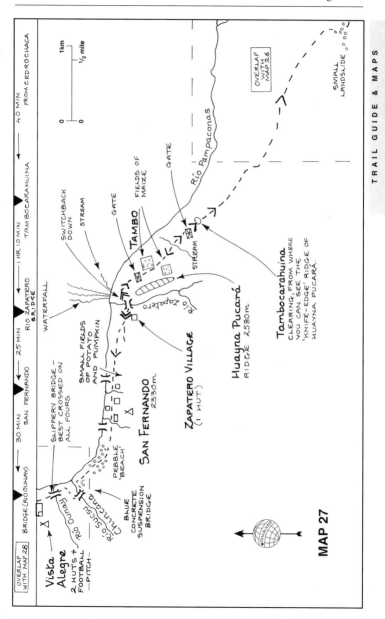

MAP 27

Huayna Pucará

According to accounts of the Spanish invasion of 1572, it was at Huayna Pucará that the Incas planned to launch a major assault on the advancing Spanish army. Boulders were lined up along the crest of the ridge above the path, ready to topple down onto unsuspecting Spanish heads as they passed along the path beneath the fort, while archers were positioned on the other side of the river, ready to kill off any who survived this initial onslaught.

Unfortunately for the Incas, one of their number defected to the Spanish side just before the ambush, and told them of the trap that had been set. Under cover of darkness, troops climbed stealthily up the hillside; now it was the Spaniards who had the element of surprise on their side. As dawn broke, the Incas awoke to find Spanish troops in position above their fort. Realizing they'd been rumbled, they put up a rearguard action before eventually retreating in despair, leaving the huge boulders perched and primed directly above the path – where, if you scramble up the slopes to the top of the ridge above Tambo, you can still find them today. After this defeat, the Inca army put up no further resistance.

Sucsu Chincana, Ounay and Vista Alegre – quite close together. Cross the first on a concrete suspension bridge. The latter two are spanned by very slippery wooden bridges, and some trekkers prefer to wade through the rivers instead; those that decide to tackle the bridges should do so on all-fours. Immediately after the second river is the small but aptly named settlement of **Vista Alegre** ('Happy View'), a few small houses and a football pitch. If it's getting late you may wish to stop here for the night, as the Spanish did in 1572; the next place to camp is at **San Cristóbal**, just over an hour further on.

After negotiating these three rivers you'll again find yourself heading due north on an undulating path following the natural contours of the valley walls. The forest begins to press ever closer on both sides now and if nobody has walked this way for a few weeks you may find you have to resort to the machete in places. The path here is also prone to landslides and you may have to scramble higher to cross debris safely before picking your way back to the main path. But having gradually climbed away from the river after about two hours you'll come upon the settlement of **Urpipata** lying just beneath the crest of the hill – an ideal spot to camp for the night. Lee has identified Urpipata as the site of

Machu Pucará

According to Titu Cusi, the Incas launched their first concerted attack against the advancing Spaniards in 1539 at Machu Pucará, and enjoyed their greatest success here too. From their hideout above the path they ambushed the invading army, dropping boulders onto them from a great height and killing anywhere between 13 Spaniards (according to the Spaniards) and 36 (according to the Incas). Ten days later, however, Pedro Pizarro climbed the hill with 100 soldiers, and forced the Incas into retreat. In the second invasion of 1572, however, the Spaniards encountered no such trouble and found the place abandoned.

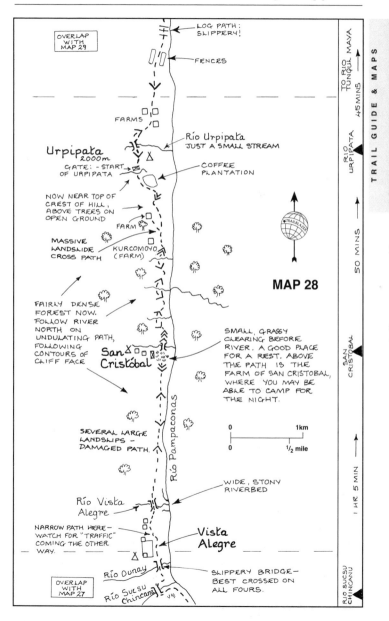

OVERLAP WITH MAP 29

LOG PATH: SLIPPERY!

FENCES

FARMS

Urpipata
2000m

GATE: - START OF URPIPATA

Río Urpipata
JUST A SMALL STREAM

COFFEE PLANTATION

NOW NEAR TOP OF CREST OF HILL, ABOVE TREES ON OPEN GROUND

FARM

MASSIVE LANDSLIDE CROSS PATH

KURCOMOYO (FARM)

MAP 28

FAIRLY DENSE FOREST NOW. FOLLOW RIVER NORTH ON UNDULATING PATH, FOLLOWING CONTOURS OF CLIFF FACE

San Cristóbal

SMALL, GRASSY CLEARING BEFORE RIVER. A GOOD PLACE FOR A REST. ABOVE THE PATH IS THE FARM OF SAN CRISTOBAL, WHERE YOU MAY BE ABLE TO CAMP FOR THE NIGHT.

Río Pampaconas

SEVERAL LARGE LANDSLIPS - DAMAGED PATH.

0   1km
0   ½ mile

WIDE, STONY RIVERBED

Río Vista Alegre

NARROW PATH HERE - WATCH FOR "TRAFFIC" COMING THE OTHER WAY.

Vista Alegre

Río Dunay

OVERLAP WITH MAP 27

Río Sucsu Chincana

SLIPPERY BRIDGE - BEST CROSSED ON ALL FOURS.

TRAILBLAZER

Machu Pucará (the Old Fort). Near to Urpipata, to the right of the trail are a few walls that might have once formed part of the fort's defences, though this is mere conjecture. If you're interested, ask your guide or one of the villagers to show you the site.

URPIPATA → ESPÍRITU PAMPA   [MAP 29, p255; MAP 30, p256]

This stage begins much as the previous one finished, with a walk through thick forest and over rivers as you hug the western banks of the valley. Immediately after the bridge over the first river, the **Tunqul Mayu**, there's a particularly well-camouflaged bog, so use a stick to test the ground ahead of you before taking each step. The bridge over the second river, the Río Luca Mayu, is prone to being washed away; if you see a few logs and branches laid across, you're in luck. A fairly steep climb then ensues up to the 'settlement' of **Cedro Casa**, a small cleared patch of ground in front of a thatch hut. Set back from the path, you may well miss it altogether – look for a bend west in the path by a tree that is obvious (at least in March/April) from its glorious orange blossom.

One hour further on and you should find yourself traversing the giant outcrop known as La Roca, from where you can see the village of **Consevidayoc** (1470m/4822ft) a further hour to the north. The imprint of man's hand is all around this village, from the fields of maize and coffee to the recently denuded hills and as a consequence the occasional landslip. In Vincent Lee's opinion Consevidayoc, a fairly large place by the standards of Vilcabamba with its own football field and school, is built on the site of ancient Marcanay, the last resting place of Friar Diego Ortiz. The Spanish destroyed Marcanay utterly when

The Martyrdom of Friar Diego Ortiz
The Inca Titu Cusi fell ill and his friar, Diego Ortiz, gave him medicine. The Inca then died. The chronicler, Sarmiento de Gamboa takes up the story:
'*When his chiefpeople and captains saw that the Inca Don Felipe Titu Cusi Yupanqui was dead, and that the prayers and sacrifices of the said Father Friar Diego Ortiz were of no avail, an Indian named Quispi, who is still living, came to the said Friar, and asked him why his God had not cured the Inca if he was so powerful? And without giving the father time to answer, the Indian struck him. Our Lord permitted that his hand and his arm up to the shoulder should wither. It is dried up to this day, and the Indian knew his sin. The Friar went down on his knees, and turned the other cheek to the smiter. He received another blow and they tied his hands behind his back and dragged him along. They opened a place under the beard with a kind of knife called a* tumi *and fastened a rope in his mouth by which they dragged him, making him suffer an unheard of martyrdom*'. (*Historia de los Incas*, Pedro Sarmiento de Gamboa, 1572, trans. Sir Clements Markham).
Ortiz was dragged before the new Inca, Tupac Amaru, who refused to see him, and the friar was killed. His body was buried upside down, to prevent divine vengeance.
For many years, it seemed as if the martyrdom of Diego Ortiz would ensure his canonization, but he was not to become a saint. Nevertheless, his bones were hallowed and he was venerated.

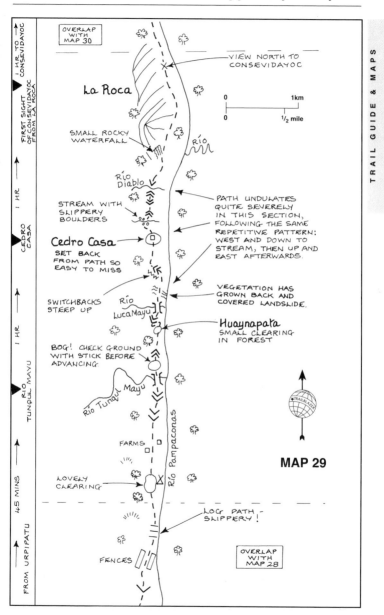

OVERLAP WITH MAP 30

VIEW NORTH TO CONSEVIDAYOC

1 HR. TO CONSEVIDAYOC

FIRST SIGHT OF CONSEVIDAYOC FROM LA ROCA

La Roca

0   1km
0   ½ mile

SMALL ROCKY WATERFALL

RÍO

1 HR.

RÍO Diablo

STREAM WITH SLIPPERY BOULDERS

PATH UNDULATES QUITE SEVERELY IN THIS SECTION, FOLLOWING THE SAME REPETITIVE PATTERN: WEST AND DOWN TO STREAM, THEN UP AND EAST AFTERWARDS.

Cedro Casa

CEDRO CASA

SET BACK FROM PATH SO EASY TO MISS

VEGETATION HAS GROWN BACK AND COVERED LANDSLIDE.

SWITCHBACKS STEEP UP

Río LucaMayu

Huaynapata SMALL CLEARING IN FOREST

1 HR.

BOG! CHECK GROUND WITH STICK BEFORE ADVANCING

RÍO TUNQUL MAYU

Río Tunqul Mayu

Río Pampaconas

FARMS

LOVELY CLEARING

MAP 29

45 MINS

LOG PATH - SLIPPERY!

FROM URPIPATU

FENCES

OVERLAP WITH MAP 28

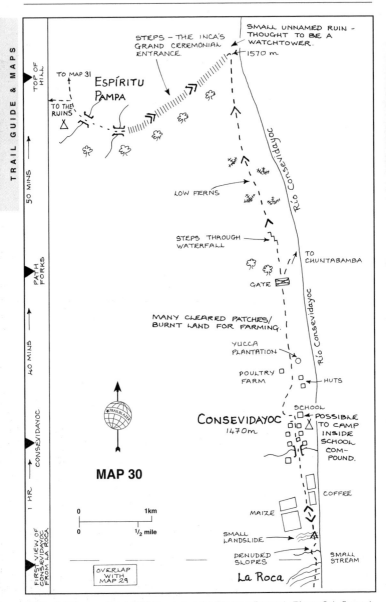

TOP OF HILL

TO MAP 31

TO THE RUINS

ESPÍRITU PAMPA

STEPS – THE INCA'S GRAND CEREMONIAL ENTRANCE.

SMALL UNNAMED RUIN – THOUGHT TO BE A WATCHTOWER.
1570 m

50 MINS

LOW FERNS

Río Consevidayoc

STEPS THROUGH WATERFALL

TO CHUNTABAMBA

PATH FORKS

GATE

MANY CLEARED PATCHES/ BURNT LAND FOR FARMING.

40 MINS

YUCCA PLANTATION

POULTRY FARM

HUTS

Río Consevidayoc

CONSEVIDAYOC
1470m

SCHOOL

POSSIBLE TO CAMP INSIDE SCHOOL COMPOUND.

CONSEVIDAYOC

MAP 30

0   1km
0   1/2 mile

COFFEE

1 HR.

MAIZE

SMALL LANDSLIDE

DENUDED SLOPES

SMALL STREAM

La Roca

FIRST VIEW OF CONSEVIDAYOC FROM LA ROCA

OVERLAP WITH MAP 29

(**Opposite**) Choquequirao (p273): lower plaza (**top**), terraces (**bottom**). (Photos © A. Stewart).

they found out about the horrors inflicted on Ortiz (see box p254), which goes some way to explaining why there are only a few scattered stone ruins here today; they are east of the village by the football field. You can **camp** in the school compound here, if you first get permission from the school director who lives on site. It costs between s/10 and s/15 per group, depending on size and the number of mules in the party.

After Consevidayoc, the path climbs up past a fork in the path: veer left; the right-hand trail leads to Chuntabamba, bypassing Espíritu Pampa altogether.

Slowly the vegetation flanking the path changes from forest to fern; this hill seems to receive little rain in April, the path becomes an arrow-straight line of baked, cracked orange clay. At last the trail turns westwards over the crest of the hill, and one minute later the lush valley of **Espíritu Pampa** moves into view.

The descent to the 'Plain of the Spirits', which is what 'Espíritu Pampa' means, is certainly a dramatic one, down a steep, wide ceremonial stairway. At the bottom, cross two streams and you arrive at a large farm by a small church-cum-school. Below the farm there is an excellent spot for **camping**, the perfect base for exploring the ruins.

The ruins of Espíritu Pampa

The map on p259 depicts the central area of the site only, where the most impressive ruins lie. If you have your own machete it's a lot of fun searching among the undergrowth for some of the other buildings here; there are said to be over 400 ruins. Watch out for snakes. Please, though, be very careful not to disturb any of the stones of the ruins as Vilcabamba has not been fully investigated by archaeologists.

If you'd like a more complete picture of the pampa, check out the maps and drawings by Vincent Lee at the back of his books, *Forgotten Vilcabamba* and *Sixpac Manco*.

Although the ruins are not particularly spectacular, this abandoned city does exude a certain amount of charm, particularly the way the jungle has gradually encroached and reclaimed the area. The building blocks are green with moss, vines and creepers grasp the ruins while trees now grow through them, their roots like flying buttresses emerging from the stones.

However you decide to explore the site, don't miss the following: the carefully carved **baths** and the bridge over the Inca-built **canal** on the way into the city; the football-field-sized **plaza** with the large **Vilca stone** in its north-eastern corner; the intact and rather impressive green mossy wall a couple of minutes to the south of the plaza and, further on, the **Eromboni Pampa**, home of the Palace of Fourteen Ashlars.

With such scant remains, it's quite difficult to imagine what life was like for the inhabitants of Vilcabamba. But it cannot have been easy. Most of the city's

---

(Opposite) Top left: On the trail to Vilcabamba. (Photo © Henry Stedman). **Top right:** Sixteenth century bell-tower at Vilcabamba La Nueva (see p245). (Photo © Alexander Stewart). **Bottom:** Eromboni Pampa at Espíritu Pampa. (Photo © Henry Stedman).

The last Inca capital?

At first sight, the ruins at Vilcabamba seem unimpressive. There's a distinct lack of majesty about the place and the few ruined buildings that survive appear rather mundane and unworthy of a capital city. This lack of grandeur has prevented many scholars down the years – Hiram Bingham included – from believing that this really was the city founded by Manco Inca in the 16th century.

Most visitors to Espíritu Pampa today are similarly underwhelmed. Yet there are enough clues in even these crumbling walls to put up a pretty good case for this being Vilcabamba. For a start, one must remember that the Incas were now living in severely reduced circumstances, their empire lost, their wealth appropriated and, presumably, many of their finest stonemasons and craftsmen gone. This would explain why the ruins cannot compare with those in Cusco or Machu Picchu. Secondly, capital or not, there is little doubt that the masonry on show is Inca in origin. The lintels, the fine ashlars (squared stones used to face walls), the baths and canals all seem distinctly Inca in concept and design. Ironically, perhaps the most persuasive evidence that these are Inca ruins is provided by the one monument that is almost completely free of any Inca embellishments: the Vilca stone in the south-east corner of the plaza is so reminiscent of Ñusta España and the Sacred Rock at Machu Picchu that it seems only logical to assume that the same people were behind the construction of all three sites: Espíritu Pampa, therefore, must be of Inca origin.

But is it Manco's capital? The fact that the ruins are spread over such a wide area and are so numerous suggests that this settlement was certainly large enough to be the capital. Then there is the grand ceremonial stairway that even now, almost 500 years later, never fails to impress visitors. It is a typically majestic piece of Inca work, albeit one tempered by the reality of the Incas' diminished position; though Manco had relinquished most of his empire and had been forced to flee into inhospitable jungle, it seems he couldn't resist making this one defiant gesture. Then there are the terracotta roof tiles, imitations of the Spanish tiles the Incas would have seen in Cusco, discovered by Bingham and others at Espíritu Pampa. This helps to date the town, for if it were a town built before the conquest the builders would not have used tiles, but straw or turf. Gene Savoy argues in his book, *Antisuyu*, that the presence of the tiles suggests that this is an Inca town built after the conquest and that it's Manco's jungle capital, Vilcabamba.

If the ruins at Espíritu Pampa fail to convince, perhaps the walk you have taken to get here will. By comparing contemporary accounts of the Spaniards' march to Vilcabamba with the – admittedly meagre – ruins you find along the path today, it is possible to tally one with the other. Perhaps the most convincing of these ruins en route is Huayna Pucará (see p252), where one finds a number of boulders lined up by the Incas for dropping on the enemy below, as described in contemporary accounts of the battle. Then there is Pampaconas, which not only has ruins of its own but unusually has even retained the same name as that used by Spanish chroniclers.

Of course some doubts do remain: the village of Marcanay, mentioned frequently in contemporary accounts, may or may not have been on the site of modern Consevidayoc – the ruins there are not conclusive – while those of Machu Pucará, or the Old Fort are negligible and maybe not even of Inca origin. Nevertheless, as John Hemming says in the conclusion of *Conquest of the Incas*:

'Unless someone can discover another ruin that so exactly fulfils the geographical and topographical details known about Vilcabamba, and that also contains imitation Spanish roofing tiles, the lost city of Vilcabamba has finally been located at Espíritu Pampa.'

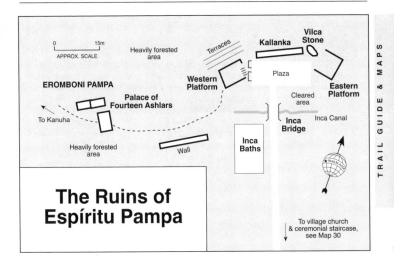

The Ruins of Espíritu Pampa

EROMBONI PAMPA

Palace of Fourteen Ashlars

To Kanuha

Heavily forested area

Wall

Western Platform

Terraces

Kallanka

Vilca Stone

Plaza

Eastern Platform

Cleared area

Inca Bridge

Inca Canal

Inca Baths

Heavily forested area

0   15m
APPROX. SCALE

To village church
& ceremonial staircase,
see Map 30

residents were used to living at altitudes some 2000m higher than Espíritu Pampa, and the low altitude and humid climate must have left many feeling unwell. The diseases, poisonous snakes and spiders of the forest constituted a constant threat, as did the Spanish just a few days' march away. Furthermore, the uneven terrain, though easy to defend, was difficult to farm.

Yet the city must have had its advantages too. According to some reports there was enough pasture for grazing, and the tropical forest provided its own crops, including coca, cotton, sugar, honey, cassava, sweet potatoes and maize, as well as rabbits, turkeys, pheasants and other fowl. Also the city was built to a comfortingly familiar Inca blueprint and in light of their deep mistrust of the Spanish, it's easy to see why so many natives chose to remain at Vilcabamba under Manco and his successors. Indeed, as the Spanish historian Martin de Murúa reports:

'The Incas enjoyed scarcely less of the luxuries, greatness and splendour of Cuzco in that distant land of exile. For the Indians brought with them whatever they could get from outside for their contentment and pleasure. And so for that time they enjoyed the good life there.'

ESPÍRITU PAMPA → CHAUNQUIRI   [MAP 31, p260; MAP 32, p261]

This is the shortest stage, but also one of the more exhausting. Not only are the climbs and descents steeper and more frequent, but the steaming jungle heat quickly saps the strength too.

From in front of the church/school a path leads down to a sturdy suspension bridge over the Río Espíritu Pampa and on to the smaller **Río Chuntabamba** and a junction with the path from Consevidayoc. The first concrete buildings since Vilcabamba La Nueva, a two-storey house and a *posta de salud* (health sta-

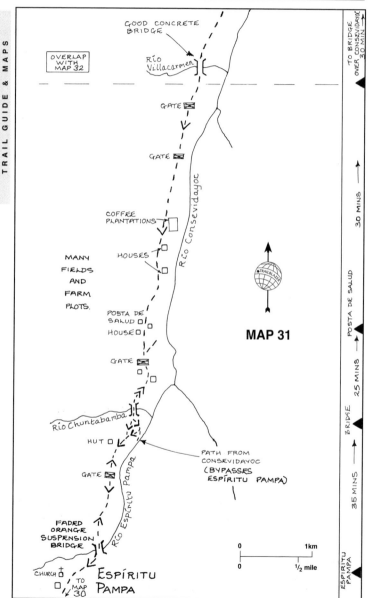

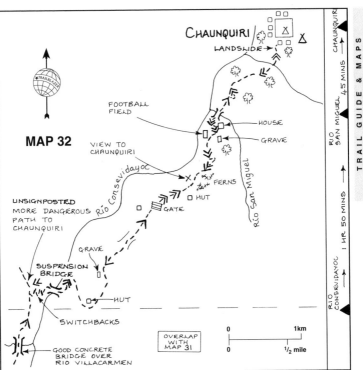

tion), lie an hour outside Espíritu Pampa to the left of the path. About an hour later, having passed through numerous plantations of coffee, oranges and maize, you'll reach an unsigned fork in the trail. Though both paths lead eventually to Chaunquiri, the upper path is much more dangerous and a number of locals have died on that route in the past few years. You should take the lower path down to the Consevidayoc, cross the bridge, and clamber up the other side of the valley.

The path on this side rises and falls with tiresome regularity on its way north; however, by way of encouragement, just 45 minutes after the bridge the tin roofs of Chaunquiri appear glinting in the sunlight ahead. To get there you first have to descend rather rapidly down the southern walls of the **San Miguel valley** to the river of the same name. From there it's a further 45 minutes, much of it uphill, to your final destination.

Chaunquiri

Shabby, a little untidy and centred around a muddy football pitch, ramshackle **Chaunquiri** would rarely, under normal circumstances, appeal to tourists. After

Vilcabamba's giant rats
In the early part of 2000 a remarkable discovery was made in the forests around Vilcabamba by the North American zoologist, Dr Louise Emmons. As she was walking through the undergrowth she scared a tree weasel, which dropped its lunch in her lap. Lunch turned out to be a completely new genus of mammal, never before known to science. It's a rat the size of a cat that lives in trees, and has been called *Cuscomys ashaninka*, after Cusco and the Ashanika, the local people. It's heartening to know that there are still secrets waiting to be discovered in the forests of Peru.

four days of climbing, staggering and wading through jungle, however, to most walkers this place is akin to paradise. There's no accommodation here, though there is running water in the **toilet block** (in the pink building by the secondary school). It's in the south-eastern corner of the square; ask for the key from the teacher). There are two cheap **cafés**, open on market days only. Though there's no accommodation, nor any pizzas or cold beer, the great bonus is that it does have transport to villages and towns where these things exist in abundance.

Leaving Chaunquiri You may be able to hitch a lift to **Kiteni** on one of the delivery trucks that occasionally call into the village, usually on a Friday. These don't turn up every week, however, and your best bet is to wait until Saturday afternoon, when trucks start to leave the market for Kiteni (s/5), a jungle town 34km and two hours away. (Kiteni, incidentally, is where they say Tupac Amaru, see pp106-7, was captured.) From there you can catch a bus or truck to Quillabamba (7-9 hours, s/10). There may even be some direct trucks from Chaunquiri to Quillabamba (s/12, 12 hours), especially on a Sunday.

For those who get stuck in Kiteni there are a couple of basic hostels in the middle and at the southern end of town, including the imaginatively named ***Kiteni Hostal***, where rooms go for just s/10 per night. It is possible to walk to Kiteni from Chaunquiri, of course, though this is a dreary, tiring, full-day's walk along a hot and winding jungle road. Another option is to walk to Yuveni, 9km from Chaunquiri, where your chances of catching a lift are slightly – but only slightly – improved.

The Choquequirao trek

INTRODUCTION

In many ways Choquequirao was the original 'lost city' of the Incas, the first fabled ruins hidden away in remote forested mountains on a dramatic ridge-top to come to light. It had been known about since at least the 18th century, but was only rarely visited despite several 'rediscoveries' over the years (see 'Background' below). To Hiram Bingham, who made his way here in 1909, it was the epiphany that inspired him to seek out the great sites of Machu Picchu and Espíritu Pampa. Indeed, before their discovery, Choquequirao was the only known major ruin in the region.

Located on a ridge at 1750m/5740ft above a deep canyon through which the sacred Apurímac rages, and surrounded by sheer, snow-capped peaks, it's an awe-inspiring place. As awareness about Choquequirao grows, it's becoming an increasingly popular trekking destination, not least because it makes a pretty good substitute for Machu Picchu and is not subject to the nuisance of the Inca Trail trekking regulations. The authorities have also moved to boost the appeal of Choquequirao by simplifying the trek by replacing a treacherous old cable bridge with one of steel and concrete. But the drama of the region's uncompromising wild landscape remains undiminished and many of Bingham's descriptions of the rigours and joys of the approach remain true to this day. A recent donation of €5 million (US$5.7 million) by the French government has also been made to help develop the site, but you'll see nothing like the crowds that throng the Inca Trail. In fact, you're unlikely to encounter many other people at all.

The trek is slightly tougher than the Inca Trail because it comprises a series of very stiff descents and gruelling climbs, and is lower and therefore hotter too. But anyone with a bit of stamina, who's relatively fit, could tackle it. It's best done during the dry season (May to September), but can be done throughout the year. The route is easy to follow and the trek can be undertaken independently although you may want to consider hiring an arriero to help carry the load.

The route can also be incorporated into two longer, more arduous treks: one that continues to Vilcabamba and the other to Machu Picchu via the Yamana and Santa Teresa valleys. For more information, see p276.

BACKGROUND

Little is known about the origin of Choquequirao, but its name translates as 'Cradle of Gold'. Only marginally more is known about the first explorers who uncovered the ruins, in search of the gold of its name, which they believed the Incas had buried there to keep it from the grasping hands of the Spanish conquistadors.

The earliest report of the site is to be found in the writings of the prospector Juan Arias Diaz Topete who recorded the location of an uninhabited town, 'Chuquiquirao', during one of three expeditions to the region in 1710. Over a century later, in 1834, the French explorer and treasure-seeker Eugene, Comte de Sartiges, approached the site. A village headman issued a warning to the Comte: 'Tell the white men that to get where we live, the roads are so bad that they will die on the journey, and that we have no chicken eggs to give them.' Undeterred, the Comte de Sartiges employed a team of porters to hack and burn their way across the mountains from Mollepata via a long and circuitous route. He endured great hardships on the expedition, lost a man and mules over a cliff and resorted to drinking rum all day to stave off the cold. He described the scenery as some of the finest in the Americas, but cursed the path and conditions: 'I do not believe that man could ever live in this valley, however fertile it is, because of the voracious mosquitoes that have taken possession of it. It was impossible to breathe, drink or eat without absorbing large quantities of these insufferable creatures.'

Although he reached Choquequirao, the Comte de Sartiges's expedition produced neither detailed documentation of the site nor any gold. But this did not deter the many treasure-hunters that followed him. None of them found any gold either.

The first known drawings of the site were produced in 1847 by the French Consul in Peru, Léonce Angrand; the originals of these maps languished in the vaults of the Bibliothèque Nationale in Paris until their publication in 1972. For a long time Choquequirao was thought to be the site of Manco Inca's final capital, Vilcabamba, particularly after the Peruvian naturalist and cartographer Antonio Raimondi, lent his prestige and academic weight to the theory. He had spent the late 1860s scouring the upper Vilcabamba valley for the ruins of the capital with no results, leading him to declare that the site had already been found at Choquequirao, the only major Inca ruin known in the area at that time.

Hiram Bingham enjoyed his first taste of a 'lost city' at Choquequirao when he blazed a trail to the site in 1909, an experience that inspired his search for Machu Picchu. Having been persuaded by the prefect of Apurímac to mount an expedition and undertake some serious documentation of the ruins, Bingham

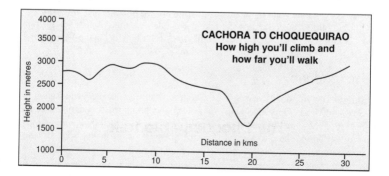

CACHORA TO CHOQUEQUIRAO
How high you'll climb and how far you'll walk

Height in metres

Distance in kms

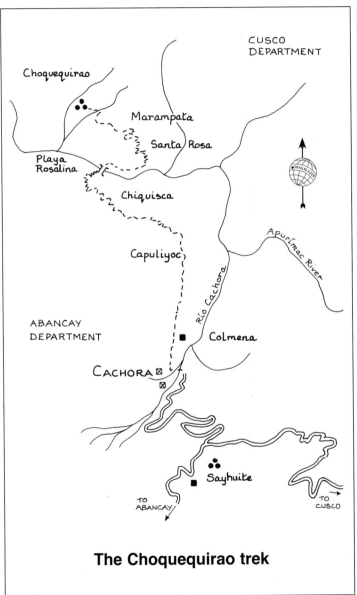

The Choquequirao trek

pioneered a new and much more direct approach to the site from the south, which avoided the mountain ranges but did involve crossing the Apurímac river on a precarious wire bridge: 'The bridge was less than 3ft wide but 273ft long. It swayed in the wind on its six strands of telegraph wire. To cross it seemed like tempting fate. So close to death did the narrow cat-walk of the bridge appear to be, and so high did the rapids throw the icy spray, that our Indian bearers crept across one at a time, on all fours and obviously wishing they had never been ordered by the prefect to carry our luggage… It must have seemed to them the height of folly for any one voluntarily to use this bridge.'

His route reduced to a matter of days what had previously taken weeks to accomplish, and has been used as the way to Choquequirao ever since.

PREPARATIONS

The trek can be undertaken through an agency or done independently. Either way you'll need a tent and adequate food as there are no hotels or stores along the length of the route. Campsites are shown on the maps in this section. If you undertake the trek independently you should consider hiring an **arriero**; climbing the sheer valley sides in the dry heat is tough enough without being laden down with equipment and food. This can be done in Cachora or Colmena (see opposite), or you could try Esteban Huaman, who lives in Yanama (☎ 084 812575) but will meet you in Cachora at the start of your trek. He's genial and reliable, and like most arrieros only speaks Spanish and Quechua.

The trek requires no special **equipment**. You should, however, make sure that you have the capacity to carry several litres of water since the points at which you can refill bottles are far apart and the heat of the Apurímac valley makes you dehydrate very quickly once you begin to exert yourself. You should also carry sufficient insect repellent, since large sections of the track are plagued by sand-flies and mosquitoes.

As a final piece of preparation, read about the ruins in advance to get the most from your visit. Vincent Lee's excellent *Forgotten Vilcabamba* and Hugh Thomson's *The White Rock* are good places to start.

TIMING AND GETTING TO THE TRAILHEAD

The Choquequirao trek takes four days, two to the ruins and two back to the start at Cachora. There is more than enough of interest at Choquequirao to justify spending a day exploring the site, and then you'd also get to see the sun rise and set over the ruins.

To get to Cachora catch an early morning bus from Cusco to Abancay and ask to be dropped off at the Cachora turn-off. Buses leave throughout the early morning until around 7am and the drive takes 3½-4 hours, following the Apurímac river through a spectacular, sheer-sided gorge. Two hours from Cusco the road crosses the Cunyac bridge over the Apurímac, the border between the departments of Cusco and Abancay. The road climbs up and away from the river, passing Sayhuite to arrive at the signposted junction for Cachora. There is

Sayhuite
Some 45km east of Abancay, near the junction for Cachora, you'll see a sign for the archaeological site of Sayhuite pointing in the other direction towards the community of Concachaca, a few hundred metres away. Here stands the enigmatic Sayhuite monolith, an elaborately carved boulder approximately 4m in diameter and over 2m tall. The delicate reliefs represent aspects of Andean culture and appear to show a complex map of some kind; some think it represents the construction plans for Tahuantinsuyo, the Inca Empire. Elaborate buildings, animals and geometrical patterns can be made out amidst the intricate carvings, which have unfortunately been damaged by exposure to the elements and by souvenir hunters and vandals. It costs s/5 to visit the stone.

a large sign for Choquequirao at the junction. Occasionally there are taxis waiting here to ferry people ¹/₂-³/₄ hour along the winding dirt track to Cachora (s/5 fare), 4km away. Alternatively, it's a two-hour walk downhill through eucalyptus groves, or an hour if you cut across the bends in the road.

Cachora [Map 33, p268]
Cachora sits in an idyllic spot cupped on three sides by steep sloping ridges at the head of the Cachora valley. It's a picturesque Andean town, which enjoys fertile soils, a reliable water supply, reasonably good weather and stunning views north of the snow-capped peaks of the Vilcabamba range including the imposing Padrayoc (5482m/17990ft).

On the southern edge of the town plaza is the Comisaria PNP building, where you should probably register if trekking alone or independently (although it's not obligatory to do so). The *Hospedaje Judith Catherine* (☎ 084-320202, beds s/10) is on the main street. You can hire **arrieros** from around the central plaza and buy basic provisions from the handful of hole-in-the-wall shops on the main street.

CACHORA → CAPULIYOC [MAP 33, p268]

In the north-western corner of the plaza a dirt road heads down the valley past the light-blue **health centre building** and winds down to a crossroads. Carry straight on and make the gentle climb up the left-hand side (W) of the valley, crossing a stream as you go. This road is narrow and often muddy, and may be impassable to small minibuses or 4WD vehicles after heavy rain.

Shortly after a **gate**, you'll come to a fork. The lower branch descends for 1km to the farmhouses of **Colmena**, where you can hire arrieros and horses. From Colmena, you can cross the Cachora river and climb up the western side of the valley to rejoin the original road heading north. Eventually it will be extended all the way to Capuliyoc, but at the time of writing it peters out beside the lone hut at Pucaira, 8km from Cachora, beyond the giant boulder marking the start of the Choquequirao National Park.

The stream in a deep U-shaped hollow shortly after Pucaira is the last place to fill **water** bottles until Chiquisca, at least four hours away. *(Continued on p270)*

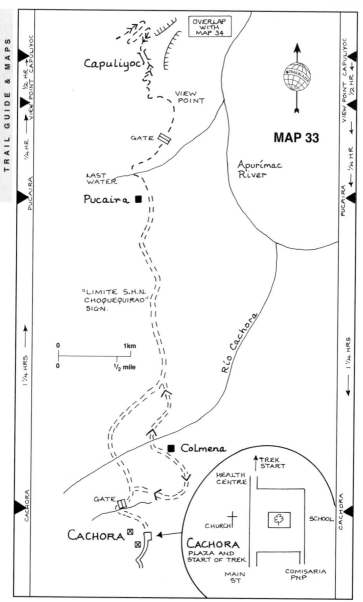

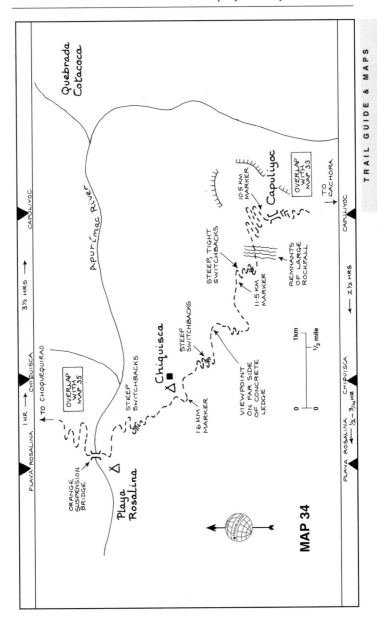

MAP 34

TRAIL GUIDE & MAPS

(Continued from p267) The track then passes through a **gate** and curves around a rocky promontory which gives outstanding views of the surrounding valleys and ridges. A battered sign warns of rock fall here, so take care. You can also make out **Capuliyoc pass** (2800m/9185ft) ahead, around half an hour away at the top of a sharp final 50m push. Sometimes you can buy soft drinks and water at a shack up here. Capuliyoc is a narrow wind-beaten arête, whipped by clouds which frequently shroud the vertiginous cliffs and jagged peaks nearby. On clear days, however, you can just make out with binoculars the hazy outline of Choquequirao, balanced on top of a forested ridge away to the west, but even with the naked eye you can't miss the dramatic canyon-like Apurímac valley, one of the deepest ravines in the Americas.

CAPULIYOC → PLAYA ROSALINA [MAP 34, p269]

From the Capuliyoc pass, the path drops steeply into the Apurímac valley on a series of switchbacks, descending amidst tough grasses and cutting across the remnants of a large rockfall.

About 2km after the pass, the path edges around a rocky prow and across a **concrete ledge** with handrail to a spectacular viewpoint. From here you can make out the campsite at Chiquisca and the suspension bridge that spans the Apurímac river beyond. Rather depressingly, you can also pick out the steep zigzags up the apparently sheer valley opposite – part of the trek.

As the path descends for the next 4km, you'll notice changes in temperature and vegetation as the scrub and cacti make way for trees festooned with bromeliads. Passing the **16km marker**, the path curves right and goes by a thatched shack, where there's space to camp but no water supply. A much better bet is **Chiquisca**, in the wooded area just below, where a local family will let you *camp* beneath cherimoya, lemon and papaya trees by their house for free. There's running water and even a cold shower, and the family sells soft drinks, bottled water and can rustle up a cooked meal for a fee. There is a second, more spacious campsite about 50m further down the track, where the tour groups tend to stay.

Chiquisca to Playa Rosalina

An early start will give you the most of the shade and morning cool; the valley bottom becomes unbearably hot later and the ascent of the far side of the valley can be exhausting in direct sun.

❑ **Apurímac River**
'The sound of the Apurímac rises faintly from the gorge, like a murmur from outer space...
'Apurímac River! Apurímac River!' the Runa children repeat with tenderness and a
touch of fear.' (**José María Arguedas**, *Los Ríos Profundos*)

The Apurímac river rises near Arequipa and eventually flows into the Amazon as a raging torrent 250ft wide and 80ft deep. The rapids and churning water along its length led to the Indians giving it its Quechua name, Apu-rimac, which literally translates as 'The God Who Speaks', or 'Great Speaker'.

Beyond Chiquisca the path descends steeply for half an hour in a series of hairpins for 2km to the riverside and **Playa Rosalina** (45 minutes from Chiquisca), a tumbledown hut amidst boulders and stubby trees. You could camp here but the place is infested with sand-flies. The Apurímac is very strong, but you can get water and wash in the sheltered spots. Nearby a concrete **suspension bridge** spans the river, linking the departments of Abancay to the south and Cusco to the north. This is the lowest point on the trek and you must now begin the long climb to Choquequirao.

PLAYA ROSALINA → CHOQUEQUIRAO   [MAP 35, p272]

On the north side of the Apurímac, you'll soon be labouring up a long sequence of switchbacks, which become shorter and tighter as they weave beneath a cliff and up past slopes scarred by recent rockfall.

About two hours beyond the bridge the path climbs above a crop of bright green sugar cane cultivated for the production of *cañazo*, the lethal spirit beloved by the local people. Above this field is **Santa Rosa**, where you can camp in a cleared area; there's a water source nearby, but the pitch is prone to sand-flies. Push on for 10 minutes beyond the small shrine to a second slightly larger, more pleasant *campsite*, next to a narrow stream and free from sand-flies, which boasts sumptuous views of the valley. At the farm here, you may be able to hire mules if you haven't already done so and could do with a little extra help, but they'll be more expensive than at the trailhead and you'll probably be too exhausted to haggle.

The long, strenuous climb continues past the 23.5km rock, where the track crosses a stream and zigzags up a forested ridge that rises ahead of you. This lengthy ascent can seem endless in the absence of landmarks by which to gauge your progress. After 2-2¹/₂ hours from Santa Rosa the path passes through a rustic gate and rounds a wooded prow to emerge at **Marampata** (2850m/9350ft), a village on a steep hillside that is home to three families. You can *camp* on the terraces by the houses and enjoy the exceptional, panoramic views. By now the valley is too steep to see the Apurímac at its foot. A series of hanging valleys block out each succeeding drop from sight, hiding the true extent of the chasm. You can, however, see the outline of Choquequirao on an adjacent ridge top.

Marampata to Choquequirao

From Marampata the path undulates eastwards for 45 minutes before turning into a subsidiary valley. Here you'll find the **Choquequirao checkpoint**, although it's still 1.5km to the ruins where the warden is likely to be; he'll soon find you to collect the fee when you pitch camp. The ruins themselves are clearly visible from this point across the gorge. The Upper and Lower Plaza straddle a ridge about 500m above a number of recently uncovered terraces that merge into thick forest; they seem to be clinging to a sheer slope that disappears into a bottomless ravine.

Skirt around the side-valley and pick your way on boulders across the Sunchumayo river, which tumbles down in a series of huge shelves. Take care

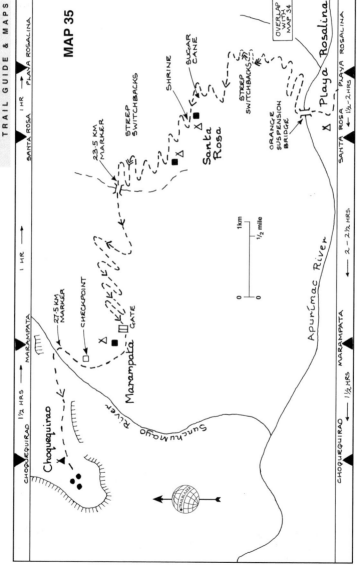

MAP 35

CHOQUEQUIRAO ½ HRS → MARAMPATA → 1 HR → SANTA ROSA → 1 HR → PLAYA ROSALINA

23.5 KM MARKER

STEEP SWITCHBACKS

SHRINE

SUGAR CANE

Santa Rosa

STEEP SWITCHBACKS

ORANGE SUSPENSION BRIDGE

Playa Rosalina

OVERLAP WITH MAP 34

27.5 KM MARKER

CHECKPOINT

Marampata GATE

Choquequirao

Sunchumayo River

Apurímac River

1km
½ mile
0

CHOQUEQUIRAO ← 1½ HRS — MARAMPATA ← 2 – 2½ HRS — SANTA ROSA ← 1½–2 HRS — PLAYA ROSALINA

after heavy rain when the river can rise, making the crossing precarious. A little further on, two large huts for staff and archaeologists mark the entrance to the site, and after 15 minutes, you emerge from the forest at the north-eastern end of the long curved terraces beneath the Lower Plaza. A 2m-wide stone road runs along the base of these terraces to a rough path leading up to the Lower Plaza. Ninety minutes after the initial checkpoint you arrive in the heart of Choquequirao.

You'll probably arrive in the late afternoon so still have time to explore the site as darkness falls. This means that you should catch what is often a spectacular sunset from the midst of the ruins.

At present you're allowed to *camp* on the broad east-facing terraces below the Lower Plaza, an amazing vantage point that not only catches the morning sun, but affords breathtaking views back up the Apurímac valley to the Capuliyoc pass. The fee (collected by the warden) is s/10 per person and s/3 per arriero or porter, but this will inevitably go up as visitor numbers rise – or be discontinued altogether. The authorities are acting quickly to preserve the site in light of a projected increase in tourists, and a new campsite might be in the offing further down the slope; campers might even be restricted to Marampata.

CHOQUEQUIRAO

Although only about a third of Choquequirao has been cleared, there's still plenty to see. The site is potentially larger than Machu Picchu, but has fewer buildings. Despite the degree to which the area is still overgrown, or perhaps even because of it, the site itself is utterly spectacular and reinforces the belief that the Incas chose to build in dramatic locations in part for their aesthetic value.

The **terraces** you could see on the way from Marampata are the lowest feature at the site, lying about 350m below the Ridge Group of ruins, on a steep slope of between 35 and 45 degrees. Recent restoration work has revealed tumbledown walls and a single building standing in the centre of the terraces. It's very basic and has no niches or other features, leading archaeologists to suggest that it was a storage facility. Above the terraces and beyond a stretch of forest are the 350m-long **curved terraces**, where you first entered the site. A similarly curved **stone road**, known as 'The Avenue of the Cedars', runs the length of the terraces.

Four sets of stairs link the terraces, but there's no apparent stairway connecting either the stone road or the terraces to the **Lower Plaza** itself, where the majority of the high-status ceremonial and residential buildings are located. This is also where much of the current restoration is taking place. A great hall looking out over the Apurímac valley, a lesser hall and three double-sided two-storey buildings stand at the northern end of the plaza, and the extensive use of double-jamb doorways on these principal buildings emphasizes their importance. The stonework is not as good as that found at Machu Picchu, something US explorer Gary Ziegler attributes to the fragile metamorphic rock found at Choquequirao, which is an inferior building material to the granite and andesite of Machu Picchu.

An intricate water channel runs from the Lower Plaza along the western edge of the ridge to a 'fountain', probably the site's water supply, on the **Upper Plaza**. Rustic structures at the southern end of the plaza face an array of terraces and niched retaining walls. The rougher stonework and the absence of any double-jamb doorways implies that they are not as significant as those of the Lower Plaza. But the retaining wall on the western edge of the Upper Plaza is impressive for its position above a terrifying cliff-drop plummeting over 1750m/5740ft to the Apurímac river. At the south-western end of the plaza is the **Giant Stairway**, eight small terraces built around a large outcrop and several big boulders. Like many of the features at Choquequirao its purpose remains unknown.

Back at the southern end of the Lower Plaza is a collection of what appear to be small shrines featuring double-jamb niches. Next to these is a sizeable double-jamb doorway through which a path climbs to the top of what Bingham described as the **Truncated Hilltop**. This was a ceremonial square, or *Usno*, and was undoubtedly the focus of the site, as demonstrated by its elaborate entrance and the ring of stones around it. Even the gentle curve of the terraces seems to draw the eye there. Its use is unknown but it may have been a platform for celestial observation or for communication with other sites.

A faint track leads south-west of the Truncated Hilltop along a narrow ridge to the '**Outlier**', two well-crafted oblong buildings stand opposite each other across a small courtyard. The purpose of these buildings is also unknown, although the high quality masonry suggests that they were significant.

Below the Truncated Hilltop, 50-100m to the south-east, is the **Ridge Group**. This large collection of buildings and terraces was only explored and mapped in 1996 by Vincent Lee and still remains uncleared. The slope is heavily forested and the outlines of the dilapidated structures merely hint at what lies beneath.

 So whose was it?

As yet, there's no conclusive archaeological evidence to tell us who built Choquequirao or why. Neither are there any references to the site in the Spanish chronicles. But what we do know is that the site most closely resembles Inca country estates and ceremonial centres such as Pisac and more pertinently, Machu Picchu, with which there are plenty of other comparisons to be made. Vincent Lee points to the ridge-top location and the way that the Apurímac relates to Choquequirao as the Urubamba does to Machu Picchu. He observes that although the setting of Choquequirao, three times as far above the Apurímac as Machu Picchu is above the Urubamaba, is probably more spectacular, the latter remains the finer site by virtue of its superior architecture. Nonetheless, the fancy buildings and double-jamb doorways of the Lower Plaza suggest that Choquequirao was also possibly a royal residence or ceremonial centre. If, as widely thought, Pachacutec built Machu Picchu, it's fair to surmise that Choquequirao was either also built during his reign or by someone powerful who admired his work. In a recent archaeological report, Lee himself favours the latter possibility, suggesting that Topa Inca, Pachacutec's successor, was 'the probable suspect' responsible for the site.

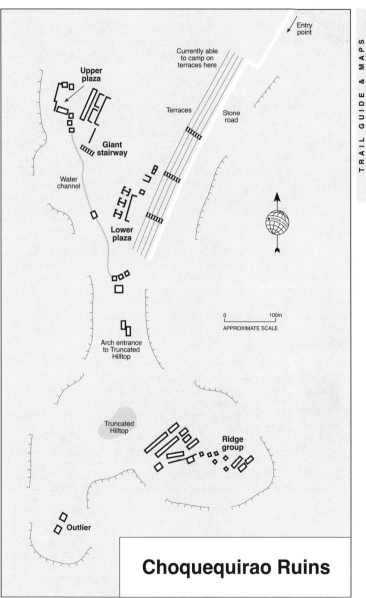

Entry point

Currently able to camp on terraces here

Upper plaza

Terraces

Stone road

Giant stairway

Water channel

Lower plaza

0   100m
APPROXIMATE SCALE

Arch entrance to Truncated Hilltop

Truncated Hilltop

Ridge group

Outlier

Choquequirao Ruins

OPTIONS FROM CHOQUEQUIRAO

From Choquequirao you have three options. The first and most common is to **retrace your steps to Cachora**. Back at the main road, you can catch a bus (departs around 5.30am and 11am), or flag down a colectivo or taxi to Cusco, four hours away.

Alternatively you have a choice of two trek extensions: to Huancacalle and Vilcabamba; or to Machu Picchu via the Yanama and Santa Teresa valleys. The trek from **Cachora to Espíritu Pampa** (Vilcabamba) takes at least two weeks whilst the 100km trek from **Cachora to Machu Picchu** takes at least a week.

Both routes begin with a descent beyond Choquequirao past the unrestored ruins at **Pincha Unuyoc** before heading over to a campsite high on the far side of the valley. The following day the path crosses the San Juan pass and descends to the traditional Andean village of **Yanama**, which has no road or rail connections to the outside world. From here the path to Huancacalle heads west for between seven and nine hours to the 4600m/15,090ft Choquetacarpo pass. From the pass it's a further four to five hours' trek north to Huancacalle. Once at Huancacalle you can begin the trek to Espíritu Pampa (see p244).

The route to Machu Picchu bears east from Yanama along the Río Yanama, before climbing to the Apacheta pass (4800m/15745ft) and then descending into the Santa Teresa valley. From here you pick up the Santa Teresa route to Machu Picchu at Ccolpapampa (see p231).

Both routes are very beautiful, but they're also strenuous and isolated, and should only be undertaken by experienced trekkers after thorough preparation and research. For more detailed information visit the SAE (see box p118) or consult one of the trekking agencies in Cusco (see box pp140-1); details of the maps required can be found on p31.

Pincha Unuyoc
Buried in the jungle on the far side of the ridge behind Choquequirao is a mass of more than 50 terraces, spilling down the forested slopes. The name Pincha Unuyoc means 'Water bursting forth' and is a reference to a natural spring (now a silted-up cave), which once provided the site's water via a canal. In size and scale Pincha Unuyoc resembles Intipata on the Inca Trail. However, its buildings are of a higher quality, leading Vincent Lee to suppose that the site could have been, 'a high-status relaxation spa in the midst of what may have been a vertical garden for exotic or ornamental plants.'

The Lost City?

INTRODUCTION

I felt infinitely small in the centre of that navel of rocks, the navel of a deserted world, proud, towering high, to which I somehow belonged. I felt that my own hands had laboured there at some remote point in time, digging furrows, polishing rocks.

Pablo Neruda, *Memoirs*

For many people, the words Machu Picchu conjure up an image of a lost Inca city, swathed in the green creepers of an encroaching jungle, hidden behind the years, waiting to be discovered by intrepid explorers armed with machetes and attended by armies of porters. It was like this, there's no doubt – all you have to do is look at the photographs of the Hiram Bingham expedition to be reminded of Indiana Jones from the film *Raiders of the Lost Ark* – but today, sadly, some of the mystique has gone. You can now make a day trip to the site by train, and if you want to spend the night near the ruins there is a reasonable hotel close to the old stones.

With the multitudes that flock each day to this 'lost' city, come inevitable problems: overcrowding, erosion, garbage and hotels built like concrete bunkers. In 2003, Unesco even threatened to strip the site of its World Heritage status unless the Peruvian authorities took action. Two years later the government responded with a US$130 million preservation plan and a proposal of a daily limit of 2500 tourists. This represents about the current number of visitors per day, so the measure might not be deemed good enough, but at the time of writing Unesco had yet to deliver its verdict on the scheme.

Even so, Machu Picchu hasn't been ruined yet – it would take the most insensitive of philistines not to be impressed by the sight of the sun rising over the rim of the mountains that enclose this awe-inspiring place. This *is* still a Lost City and still a place of magic especially when you come upon it after three days hiking in the wilderness.

Practicalities

Machu Picchu is 2400m (7800ft) above sea level, and it nestles on a ridge between Machu Picchu mountain and the sugar loaf of Huayna Picchu. When the sun's out it burns, so bring sun-barrier cream and a hat. It can also get cold up here when the sun's not out, and it sometimes rains unpredictably, so bring a jumper and a waterproof. Insect repellent's a good idea too.

ARRIVAL

You've either come off the trail or up from Aguas Calientes by bus or foot (see p168). If you're going back to Cusco in the afternoon check the train timetable as it changes often. They normally have the times at the reception desk in the hotel; see p302 for the timetable at the time of writing. For more information about getting back from Machu Picchu see p293.

ORIENTATION

If you've just come off the Inca Trail, to the right of the path at the top of the ruins is a zigzag path down to the entrance booth. Here you must leave your kit at a left-luggage store (US$0.50) because you won't be allowed in the ruins with it (some people claim this is to stop base jumpers from sneaking their parachutes in and launching themselves off into the valley below). Smaller day packs are still permitted within the site. The large ugly bungalow you can see by the entrance is the restaurant and hotel. If you've come up by bus from Aguas Calientes you'll be dropped off in the car park in front of the hotel. The entrance to the ruins is just up some stairs to the right of a map of Machu Picchu.

Passing through the entrance booth and around a shoulder of rock, you'll walk by a plaque commemorating Hiram Bingham as the 'scientific discoverer' of Machu Picchu. After this you reach an open area. Straight ahead are a couple of thatched cottages between which most visitors enter the site. Before this there is a path uphill, indicated by little white arrows painted on stones. If you follow these (back up the little hill you just climbed down if you've come along the trail) you'll get to a place just below a thatched hut on the top of a promontory. This is the Watchman's hut, the best place to start your tour – see 'A guide to the ruins' (see p283).

OPENING TIMES AND TICKETS

The ruins are open 7am-5.30pm daily. Entrance costs US$20 (US$10 for students). There is no longer a discount for those who are returning for a second day. If you've walked the trail the price of one day's entrance is included in your s/192 (roughly US$60 trail fee, which you should have paid already. The ruins are a lot quieter before 10.30am and after 3.30pm. Saturday and Monday tend to be the busiest days, as tour groups often visit Machu Picchu on the days before or after seeing the Sunday markets at Pisac.

Guides of varying quality are available for hire at the site entrance and cost around US$15 for a 2¹/₂-hour private tour of the ruins.

WHERE TO STAY

You can't camp in the ruins – so don't try. The only *campsite* (US$2 per tent) is at the foot of the hill: cross over the Urubamba via the bridge at Puente Ruinas, and it's to the right (E) in a cleared stretch of pasture alongside the river, which you'll be sharing with sand-flies and glow-worms; a stone blockhouse nearby has cold running water and showers. Don't leave kit unattended at this campsite or you'll lose it.

Machu Picchu Sanctuary Lodge (aka The Tourists' Hotel; Km7, Carretera Hiram Bingham; ☎ 241777/211038, 📠 247111, 🖥 res-mapi@peruorientex press.com.pe, www.monasterio.orient-express.com), is the only hotel right by these legendary ruins. They can, therefore, charge what they like and recently prices have skyrocketed to US$474/567/768 (sgl/dbl/suite). I'm not sure there should be a hotel here at all, but if you haven't got qualms about its being so close to what should be a pristine site, it's an adequate-enough place. You can make bookings for Machu Picchu Sanctuary Lodge at Hotel Monasterio in Cusco (see p148).

There is a much wider selection of places in Aguas Calientes (see p167).

WHERE TO EAT

You can have an excellent buffet breakfast and an overpriced canteen lunch at **Machu Picchu Sanctuary Lodge**. The 'all you can eat' breakfast is expensive but worth it at US$23. Lunch, too, is expensive at US$23 and isn't worth it; pick up an overpriced hot dog or burger instead from the **café** above the lavatories. There's also a cheapish **restaurant** a 10-minute walk down the road in a building on your left. You are not allowed to take food inside the ruins.

History

People have been arguing about what Machu Picchu was and why it was built almost from the moment Hiram Bingham rediscovered it in 1911. It all seems a bit clearer now, since a lot of light was thrown into this dark corner of history by an old copy of a 16th-century document found by the scholars Luis Miguel Glave, María Remy and John Rowe in the library of a Cusco monastery.

MACHU PICCHU REVEALED TO THE WORLD

A young graduate from Yale University named Hiram Bingham had been bewitched by the stories of lost Inca cities ever since visiting a pre-Hispanic ruin called Choquequirau (see p273). (Bingham was originally an expert on Bolívar, not an archaeologist, and he was rather at a loss for what to do when he made it to his first ruin. In the best tradition of the amateur he did his best, helped by a book published by the Royal Geographical Society with the quaint title *Hints to Travellers*.) Bingham raised enough money to lead a seven-man expedition to Peru under the auspices of Yale University and the National Geographic Society. In 1911 he and his team started to explore the uncharted hills around the ancient Inca capital, Cusco.

Uncharted is not the right word: these hills weren't completely unknown territory. The mountain Machu Picchu appears on a map in the 1910 edition of a book on the Incas written by the English historian, Clements Markham, and Bingham himself used a map of the area prepared by Antonio Raimondi. There had even been some reports of ruins around the lower Urubamba. Bingham describes both the failure of a Frenchman, Charles Wiener, to find them in 1875, and what he rather unfairly referred to as the 'treasure hunting' of a Peruvian called Lizárraga.

So in July 1911, Bingham and his team headed out of Cusco down the Urubamba, and almost immediately they discovered a major Inca site which they named Patallacta (it's the site on the corner where the Cusichaca river meets the Urubamba, see p188). After walking a little up the Cusichaca, the team also discovered Huayllabamba and Paucarcancha. Bingham and his companions then travelled on. On July 23, just a week into the expedition, they camped off the trail at Mandorpampa. A local man, one Melchor Artega, was suspicious of these foreigners, and came over to see what was going on. When they explained that they were looking for ruins, Artega told them that there were some fine ones up in the hills above their camp.

The next day it rained. No one else in the expedition wanted to climb up the steep side of the Urubamba canyon, so Bingham went on his own, accompanied by the expedition's guard, Sergeant Carrasco, and Artega. After an unpleasant crossing of the Urubamba on a flimsy log bridge and a perilous climb through snake-infested forest, he reached a grass-covered hut. There he was welcomed by two men, Richarte and Álvarez, who had been living up on the hillside for four years to escape the army and taxes. They gave Bingham water and fed him, and he describes not really wanting to have a look at the ruins because he was tired, the water was cool and the heat of the day was great. But he did have a look. And the rest, as they say, is history.

Keeper of the royal bridge
FELIPE HUAMÁN POMA DE AYALA (c1590)

WHAT BINGHAM FOUND IN THE JUNGLE

Bingham named the ruins Machu Picchu because that was the name of the mountain on which they were found. Machu means old or big, and Picchu is the name of the area. The sugar-loaf mountain that overlooks the ruins is called Huayna Picchu (small Picchu).

Bingham believed that he'd stumbled upon the rebel Incas' stronghold, Vilcabamba (see p258), the site of the last independent Inca state and their place of final refuge in the days when the Spanish were hunting them down. For a number of reasons it's now thought that these ruins aren't Vilcabamba, not least because the routes the Spanish took to get to Vilcabamba don't match the routes you'd need to take to get to

Machu Picchu, and the descriptions of the site of Vilcabamba don't fit with the geography around Machu Picchu. But what Bingham did find is no less impressive: he'd discovered not only a lost city of the Incas but a whole lost province that the Incas had miraculously concealed from the Spanish conquistadors. (No one knows how they managed to pull this off). Within the mountains now enclosed by the Machu Picchu Historical Sanctuary are numerous Inca roads and ruins, towns, cities, forts and outposts – everything from humble mud-and-rock structures to castles of magnificent dressed stone – which have only survived the centuries because no one knew they were there.

It's now thought that Vilcabamba is much further into the jungle at a place known as Espíritu Pampa; a description of the Vilcabamba Trail to Espíritu Pampa begins on p238. Bingham would not really mind if he knew this as he also rediscovered Espíritu Pampa.

MACHU PICCHU AS PACHACUTEC'S ROYAL FRONTIER

According to the old papers found by Rowe and his colleagues, the lower Urubamba valley was conquered by the Inca Pachacutec in his expansionist wars of the 15th century. It's likely, then, that Pachacutec built the hilltop city of Machu Picchu to celebrate his greatness; he decorated the banks of the Urubamba with Ollantaytambo for the same reason. Machu Picchu was the royal estate at the end of the line, also perhaps a religious centre, the capital of a frontier province, and an impregnable watchtower that guarded the route from Antisuyu to the civilized uplands of Cusco.

The Urubamba route to Antisuyu became less important in later years. All traffic for the *cejas de la selva* (the eyebrows of the jungle) headed down the Lucumayo, and Machu Picchu became a backwater rather than a frontier. By the time of the conquest, it's probable that Machu Picchu was already just an abandoned shell, and when the archaeologists arrived there wasn't much they could dig up. It's not clear why the city was quite so thoroughly deserted. Perhaps the water ran out – there were hardly enough springs to provide water for Bingham's expedition, so water must have been very scarce when the city was fully inhabited. Perhaps the Incas evacuated the place to create an uninhabited buffer zone between their rebel capital of Vilcabamba and the Spaniards' base in Cusco.

At any rate, Rowe's document says that by the time of the conquest, part of the area was used for growing coca. It was given to Hernando Pizarro when the Spanish carved up the old empire, and it passed from him to the encomienda of a man called Arias Maldonado.

OTHER THEORIES

Tour guides give explanations as to Machu Picchu's past, varying from the plausible to those which have now been disproved by research, and on to the absurd. But it's not just a case of guides making it up to impress the tourists: not everyone agrees on the interpretation of Rowe's document, and it's likely archaeologists will come up with other tenable theories.

Incorrect

The idea that Machu Picchu was a convent of *acllas* (Inca nuns) was based on evidence that 80% of the bones that Bingham dug up were those of women. This has been disproved by recent re-examination of the bones, which showed that the sexes were equally represented.

Alternatively, you might read that Machu Picchu is laid out to resemble both a condor and a cayman (South American crocodile) and that Huayna Picchu is carved into the shape of a large puma. You can believe that if you want to, but I don't. If the Incas had wanted to make Machu Picchu look like a condor or a puma they'd have done a much better job.

Unlikely

An interesting theory of Bingham's suggests that Machu Picchu was between 800 and 1000 years old by the time of the Spanish invasion.

According to legend, the Incas had their origin in a sacred cave called Tambo-toqo (see p86), and the mythical first Inca, Manco Capac, built a three-windowed temple on this site to celebrate its significance. Bingham suggested – quite sensibly – that the Temple of the Three Windows in Machu Picchu (see p287) commemorated Manco Capac's temple. However, he went on to suggest that the structure in Machu Picchu was, in fact, the actual one built by Manco Capac, and that Machu Picchu is therefore the primeval home of the Incas. There is little evidence to support this theory and much against it: few pre-Inca objects have been found, the style of the Temple of the Three Windows is 15th-century Inca (not 5th century), and anyway Machu Picchu is completely the wrong side of Cusco to be Tambo-toqo.

Plausible

Some say that Machu Picchu was an **agricultural outpost** of the Incas. It was used, they say, to maximize the rare and valuable growing zone between the jungle and the high valleys of Cusco, a suggestion backed by the large tracts of land in the district that have been irrigated and terraced for agriculture. Other people expand on this, suggesting that the area around Machu Picchu was a place where sacred plants were grown by priests.

There are theories that Machu Picchu is a big **observatory**. It's recently been discovered that at dawn on the winter solstice (21 June) the sun shines right through the middle of the window in the Torreón (see p292), casting a shadow. This isn't the only building that was built with an eye on the heavens. The Temple of the Moon, on the far side of the sugar-loaf mountain that dominates Machu Picchu, was built to face the Pleiades (also worshipped by the Incas), and some say the Intihuatana (see p288) is a place where the sun could be ceremonially tied and prevented from falling lower in the sky in winter.

Johan Reinhard, a respected anthropologist, suggests an interesting idea in his short book *The Sacred Centre*. Reinhard thinks Machu Picchu was the focal point of a constellation of sacred geographical features: the city is built on a spur of one of the Inca's most important mountains, Salcantay; it perches above the sacred river Urubamba and it is on a sighting line from other important mountains, Pumasillo and Veronica. Machu Picchu is, like Cusco, the focus of religion. The city should not be looked at as a citadel but as a religious symbol, a sacred centre. This theory links in with what we know about the Inca religion – the sacredness of certain spots (*huacas*) and the sacred lines (*ceques*) which joined them to other spots. It's true, too, that there is a large amount of ornate Inca architecture in these hills. If Reinhard is right, this means that the Inca Trail is more than just a road – it's a sacred route of pilgrimage.

Of course, these theories aren't necessarily contradictory. It's possible that Machu Picchu was a citadel built to the glory of Pachacutec, on a place found to be sacred in Inca religion, designed in a way so that the heavens could be observed, accessible only after a ritual journey.

A guide to the ruins

This was the habitation, this is the site:
here the fat grains of maize grew high
to fall again like red hail.

The fleece of the vicuña was carded here
to clothe men's loves in gold, their tombs and mothers,
the king, the prayers, the warriors.

Up here men's feet found rest at night
near eagles' talons in the high
meat-stuffed eyries.
Pablo Neruda, from *The Heights of Machu Picchu.*

This walking tour covers the main buildings at the site and summarizes what's known about (or guessed about) each one. The rest is up to your imagination. The best place to start is up at the Watchman's hut – for directions from the entrance booth, see 'Orientation' p278.

AROUND THE WATCHMAN'S HUT AND FUNERARY STONE

This lone hut gives such a perfect view over Machu Picchu that it has been called the **Watchman's Hut**. It guards any entrance to the site from the road to Intipunku (p200), the trail up Machu Picchu mountain, or the road to the Inca Bridge (see p286). It's unlikely that this was a hut for a mere gatekeeper as the stonework's too good. The oddly shaped rock nearby is known as the **Funerary Stone**, but it's probably a sacrificial altar. The Incas often sacrificed llamas, and sometimes even humans. In the festival of Inti Raymi (see p62), there's a llama sacrificed (allegedly – it still looked pretty alive to me), and the remains of the occasional human sacrifice have been found in such places as the volcano of El Misti near Arequipa. Note the strange carvings in the stone of a ring and something a bit like a staircase: no one knows what they're for, but there's one of these rings carved in a rock in Vilcabamba (see p257) and the Incas often carved

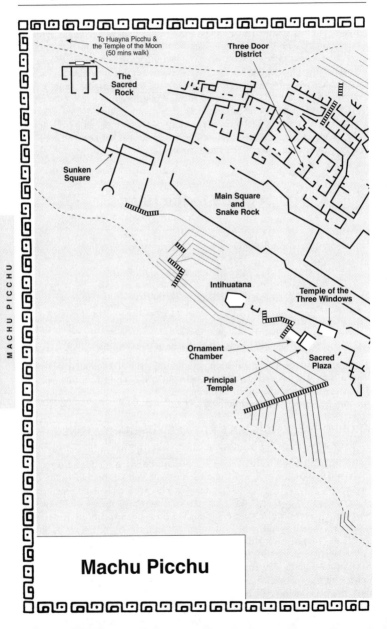

To Huayna Picchu &
the Temple of the Moon
(50 mins walk)

Three Door
District

The
Sacred
Rock

Sunken
Square

Main Square
and
Snake Rock

Intihuatana

Temple of the
Three Windows

Ornament
Chamber

Sacred
Plaza

Principal
Temple

Machu Picchu

MACHU PICCHU

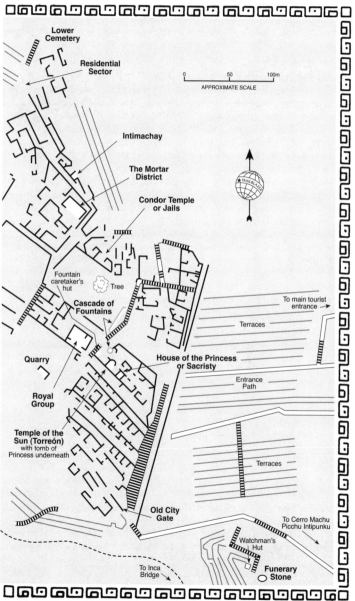

Lower Cemetery

Residential Sector

0   50   100m
APPROXIMATE SCALE

Intimachay

The Mortar District

Condor Temple or Jails

Fountain caretaker's hut

Tree

Cascade of Fountains

To main tourist entrance →

Terraces

Quarry

House of the Princess or Sacristy

Royal Group

Entrance Path

Temple of the Sun (Torreón) with tomb of Princess underneath

Terraces

Old City Gate

To Cerro Machu Picchu Intipunku

Watchman's Hut

To Inca Bridge

Funerary Stone

their huacas with stair-like designs, Qenko (see p158), for example. The rock was named the Funerary Stone because Bingham found and excavated many tombs near here, which leads some to think that this stone was the place where the privileged dead were laid out for embalming – a Funerary Stone. Because of these finds, the area around here is often called the upper cemetery.

Machu Picchu's districts

Looking out over the city you can see the division of the land into terraces (an agricultural zone) and buildings (an urban zone). The terraces in the agricultural area were primarily for growing foodstuffs, and there are many more at nearby Choquesuysuy (p207) and Huinay Huayna (p199). Dr Ann Kendall thinks that there were about 677 hectares (1670 acres) of land under cultivation in the Sanctuary, and that there was a four-fold over-capacity. In other words, the Machu Picchu area was a breadbasket.

There are other suggestions as to what the terracing was for. Some have suggested that they were a defence measure against potential attackers, and others have suggested they were for decoration: the Chronicles say that the terraces at Ollantaytambo were used for growing flowers.

From the terracing you can clearly see another division of the city; the division into Hanan and Hurin districts to the left and right of the main plaza. The Incas often divided their towns into these two sections, which were probably inhabited by different clan groups. There's an interesting theory that every feature in one district (Sun Temple, etc) has a mirror image in the other district.

This is the ideal place from which to take a picture of Machu Picchu.

The Inca Bridge and Machu Picchu mountain

If you're looking down at the town, the path for the **Inca Bridge** goes off from your left, snaking around the top of the amphitheatre of terraces. The 20-minute path leads along a sheer rockface to an abyss. In Inca times, there was a wooden drawbridge across this void that could be drawn up in times of trouble. There's a rudimentary reconstruction in place at the moment, but you can't cross it; a barrier blocks your way some distance before. Nonetheless, you can still see the dramatic continuation of the path carved into the vertical cliff face as well as astonishing views down the Urubamba valley.

The path for **Machu Picchu mountain** (cerro Machu Picchu) is on the right if you head back up towards Intipunku. It takes about an hour to get to the top and it's a tiring climb.

THE MOAT AND GATE

You can see from the Watchman's Hut a moat and long stairway that divides the agricultural terraces from the buildings. Walk along the path in front of the Hut to the top of the **moat**. According to Bingham, there are 150 steps in the main staircase in the moat and about 3000 in the whole city. Because this is the main route by which an army could approach Machu Picchu, many think that the moat was a defence feature. Precipices and rock walls guarded the city's other flanks. However, those who prefer to regard Machu Picchu as a sacred rather than a military city see it as an architectural way of excluding the outside profane world from the inside sacred city.

The **Old City Gate** is at the top of the moat, and is an impressive trapezoidal arch with a vast lintel. When Bingham discovered this doorway it was in the process of collapse, so what you see has been repaired. If you stand in the gateway, there is a large wall to your left that overlooks you, which may be to protect the door from attackers. If you were standing here with a battering ram, there'd be nowhere to hide from any rocks and arrows thrown at you. Go through the door and look up at the big ring above the lintel and at the bars sunk in the doorposts to the left and right. These probably provided a method of securing the door.

Bingham found the remains of 41 containers of liquid refreshment in this place and thought that the chicha sellers of the old city were stationed here, selling drink to tired travellers.

THE QUARRY

Walk on through the gateway and along the street and you'll see in front of you a place where there are large boulders lying around. Go down some steps to get there. Bingham found tombs around here and thought this was a cemetery, but it's now thought that this place was the **quarry** for the stones used to build the city. You can see some rocks that are in the process of being split: tiny stones have been fed into small cracks. These stones kept the cracks open, which were then worked apart until eventually the rock was split. This 'Inca work-in-progress' is eagerly pointed out to tourists by guides, but it was in fact an experiment conducted by a modern researcher, Dr Manuel Chávez Ballón.

THE SACRED PLAZA GROUP

Walk on through the quarry and straight ahead rising above the rest of the city, you'll see a mound on top of which is the Intihuatana. You're about to walk into the Sacred Plaza at its base.

The Sacred Plaza was named by Bingham because Machu Picchu's finest buildings are set around it. On one side the **Principal Temple**, on another the **Temple of the Three Windows**, and looming above it the **Intihuatana** itself.

Bingham's archaeologists dug up the floor of the Sacred Plaza as a good place to look for artefacts but found nothing. They did, however, find an enormous amount of smashed pottery on the ground outside, beneath the Temple of the Three Windows, which leads many to think that pots were ritually broken here and thrown out of the window as part of some ceremony.

The three-windowed temple is a very important place – Bingham used it as the centrepiece in his theory that Machu Picchu was about a thousand years older than anyone else had thought (see p282). The three windows refer to the creation myths of the Incas.

An enormous amount of effort has gone into the building of this place: look downwards out of one of the windows and you'll see that the terrace on which this place was built has been clad in massive, beautifully carved rocks. If you can't quite see from this angle, look back at it when you're walking along the other side of the city.

The principal temple was thus called because it is so impressively built. The ranks of regular bricks have slipped a bit in the years as a result of subsidence. (Some researchers believe there's a serious risk of landslide in the area). In front of them there's a large altar.

Walk to the left of this temple and along a path. You'll see on your right the doorway of the **Ornament Chamber**. Put your head in and have a look at the corners of this room – they're not built from stone blocks but carved from rock – one of these stones has 32 angles in three dimensions. This isn't building, it's sculpture.

THE INTIHUATANA

Continue walking past the ornament chamber and you'll start to climb the stairs up to the **Intihuatana** (see photo opposite). The importance of this place is emphasized by its architecture: you have to climb to reach it, and you can't go straight there, you have to turn corners. You get almost the same sense of awed anticipation as you do climbing to Intipunku to get a first sight of Machu Picchu.

Inti means sun and *hata* means to tie, and 'intihuatana' has been translated as 'hitching post of the sun'. The word doesn't appear in the ancient vocabularies of Quechua; it seems it was first noted by the 19th-century North American traveller, George Squier. Squier came across an Intihuatana in Pisac and thought that it might be a place where the sun was ritually stopped, perhaps when it reached its lowest point in the winter skies, and encouraged to rise higher once more.

Spanish priests, when they came across these sacred rocks of the Incas, used to lop the tops off them or ritually exorcize them, and it's rare for one to survive relatively intact. I say relatively, because in September 2000 the Intihuatana was damaged by a crane. The US publicity firm, J Walter Thompson, was filming an advertisement for Cusqueña beer, when a crane they were using chipped a chunk out of the old stone. There's a rich symbolism in the fact that this ancient monument, which survived the Spanish invasion and centuries lost in the jungle, has now been damaged by the forces of modern capitalism.

Unlike the Torreón (see p292), no one has yet found a precise astrological function for the Intihuatana – the various edges and angles are carved into the mother rock with considerable exactitude but no one knows why. Some archaeologists don't think of it as a ritual hitching post; it's been renamed simply as a *gnomon* (a carved block), although a gnomon is also the name for the arm on a sundial.

(**Opposite**): The Intihuatana, before being damaged by a film company. (Photo © Bryn Thomas). (**Overleaf**): Machu Picchu revealed, with Huayna Picchu rising in the background. (Photo © Alexander Stewart).

AROUND THE SACRED ROCK

Pass through the space around the Intihuatana, and go down the other side. As you're walking, look down at the minute terraces on your left, apparently too small to be purely for agriculture, yet on such a steep slope that it's doubtful whether they were either necessary or effective for defence purposes.

In front of you to the left is the **Sunken Square**. This area has been carefully terraced to make a little enclosed square apart from the main plaza, and in one corner there are the remains of what looks like a tomb under a large rock. It's often overgrown, and by looking at it you can get an idea of what Machu Picchu must have looked like when Bingham first stumbled up here – that is, unless they've cut the plants back again.

The **Sacred Rock** is to your right, tucked away under the shadow of Huayna Picchu, across the main square. There's a path that leads to it. This rock's called 'sacred' because it has been exposed in such a way that its shape is emphasized, fronted by a plaza and enclosed on two sides with well-built Inca houses. Why it's been exposed like this isn't clear, and you'll hear some bizarre theories: that the rock is a statue of Pachamama, the earth goddess, that it's a puma or that it's a guinea pig. The most likely theory is that the shape of this rock mimics the mountains around it. The plaza makes you want to look at the rock from one side, and you'll notice that it's a good representation of the mountain Putucusi that looms behind. Some, however, have pointed out that the rock's an even better copy of Pumasillo (Puma's Claw), a mountain many miles away on the opposite horizon behind you.

HUAYNA PICCHU

The path for Huayna Picchu leaves from the caretaker's little hut to the left of the Sacred Rock. It's a tough 45-minute climb to the top, and in places the path takes you up near-vertical faces with ropes and steps driven into the rock. Tiny terraces cover the top of Huayna Picchu. There's a small viewing platform and above that a narrow tunnel leading up to the very top. The view of the sunrise from the summit is even better than that from Intipunku.

A side path on Huayna Picchu branches left around the western side of the mountain to the **Temple of the Moon**, about 50 minutes' detour down a very steep path (with the occasional ladder). The Temple of the Moon has very high-quality Inca stonework and was orientated to face the Pleiades, which were worshipped by the Incas. Bingham missed the site and it didn't come to light until 1936. Fire damaged the whole mountain in 1997, and it was out of bounds until late 1998.

MACHU PICCHU

(Opposite) Top left: The Torreón and below it the sculpted chamber known as the Tomb of the Princess. **Top right**: View across the main square to the Machu Picchu residential sector from the Temple of the Three Windows. (Photos © Alexander Stewart).
Bottom: The Torreón, photographed on the June solstice. (Photo © Richard Danbury).

> ❏ *From the narrow saddleback on which the ruined city stands, the precipices plunge headlong into the raging brown river, fifteen hundred feet below. Looking up makes you even giddier than looking down, for all around the valley are black snow-streaked mountains, looming over you through the driving clouds, and right ahead, at the end of the ridge, towers an appalling berg of rock, like the fragment of a fallen moon. This is called Huayna Picchu. The Incas, who must have been able to climb like flies, built a watchtower on top of it, to guard the approach to the citadel.*
> **Christopher Isherwood**
> *The Condor and the Cows*, 1949.

The trail opens early, at 7am, and closes at 1pm. Everybody must be off the mountain by 3pm, and it's best to get up here before the crowds arrive at around 10am.

You must register at the small caretaker's hut at the bottom of the climb on both the way in and the way out, otherwise the authorities will start searching for you, beginning at the bottom of the cliffs. Do take care in the wet, as the path becomes very slippery.

THE THREE DOOR DISTRICT AND LOWER CEMETERY

Turn right from the Sacred Rock and walk behind a large boulder. You'll come to a flat rock that hangs a little over the precipice leading down to the Urubamba below. There's an unforgettable view from the edge of it.

Continue walking and follow some little white arrows painted on rocks, and the path will take you to the **Three Door District** (so named because it's got three main doors). This is a clan group area of Machu Picchu, and the houses are arranged in a small labyrinth. Note the pillars sticking out of the building's gables, and also the little carved projecting holes that run along the edge. To these the Incas tied the thatch that made up their roofs – you can see reconstructions of this in the Watchman's Hut, the huts around the sacred rock and the storehouses on the way out.

Looking downhill you can see a terraced area connected to the three-door district by tiny paths and stairways. This is the **lower cemetery**, another area where Bingham found many tombs, but it's very steep – you should only visit it if you have a head for heights and are sure-footed.

THE MORTAR DISTRICT

Back up in the main housing district, the next clan group to the south (straight on) is the **Mortar District**. It got its name because Bingham found some interesting solid stone circles carved into rocks set into the floor of one of these houses, which he thought were mortars used for crushing maize in the house of an important chief. They don't bear much relation to the mortars commonly used by local people today so this theory isn't believed any more, but what they are actually for, no one knows. This district's sometimes called the Industrial Sector.

THE CONDOR TEMPLE OR JAILS

Leave the Mortar District, and go down a flight of stairs bordering the main plaza. Look back across at the marvellous stonework of the Temple of the Three Windows, if you haven't already. At the bottom of the stairs, turn left, and then right. This is the district that Bingham thought contained the **jails** of the city. He noticed the small alcoves with tying places bored into the niche frames at about the height for manacling a prisoner to the rock. People no longer think these were jails; it seems that death was a punishment for many crimes against Inca laws, and there would be no need of jails. It's thought by some that these niches used to contain something sacred and holy: mummies, perhaps, guarded by a taboo stick tied onto the rings.

On the floor further around the corner is a rock that looks a little like a condor with a white ruff, which gives this area its other name: **the Condor Temple**. The flaring boulders above the rock are supposed to be the condor's wings. There's also an altar in a natural fissure in the rock here, a bit like the one in Qenko (see p158). The condor was a sacred bird, sometimes a messenger or an embodiment of the huacas, especially of the *apus* (mountain spirits). Different birds could represent different things, the smallest bird representing a small mountain and the largest – condors – the sacred mountains of Salcantay, Veronica and Pumasillo. However, not every bird was a messenger – some were just birds, and it took an expert to be able to tell the difference.

THE FOUNTAINS AND THE ROYAL GROUP

Come out of the Condor Temple group and make your way up the large flight of stairs to a **cascade of fountains**. These little square structures with water flowing through them are probably something to do with the ritual worship of water: there are similar structures in Phuyu Pata Marca, Sayac Marca and Tambo Machay. Bingham again thought them something different, believing that they were the main water supply for the city. The spring that used to feed these now feeds the hotel, and rather prosaically they can be switched on and off like a tap.

At the head of the cascade is the most carefully worked fountain. Uphill from this is the **Fountain Caretaker's Hut**, which, like the Watchman's Hut, is too ornate to be that of a mere caretaker. It is likely to be a place associated with water worship like the fountains it oversees. There are niches and stone pegs inside for hanging things, and there's a theory that it's where a priest supervised the rituals of water worship. It's good to sit in the place and absorb the atmosphere.

On the right (looking from below) of the caretaker's hut is **The Royal Group**. This is an area of particularly fine buildings, which Bingham took to be the place where the most important person lived. The stone is nicely carved, but what draws most attention is the massive lintel over the main door. It weighs about three tons and was probably placed where it is by being dragged up an earth mound, which was then swept away. There's also an enclosed area in this group, possibly a garden, which the historian, Garcilaso de la Vega, describes as being common in the dwellings of people of high status, and often filled with golden statues (see p135).

THE TORREÓN OR SUN TEMPLE GROUP

The circular tower to the left of the Fountain Caretaker's Hut (if you're looking uphill) is the **Torreón**.

The Torreón was probably a Sun Temple but it does not have the six chambers you normally find in a sun temple. Reminding you of the Serpent Window in the Coricancha in Cusco is a window with holes drilled in the frame. These holes were probably for fixing shadow-casters or aids to astronomy, but some have suggested they concealed snakes – hence the name. It's recently been noted that at dawn on the winter solstice (21 June) the sun shines through the window in the circular wall highlighting the rock in the middle of the temple (see photo opposite p289). You can't enter the temple as it's been roped off.

Beneath the Torreón is a wonderful place, where the rocks have been carved in three-dimensional asymmetry so that they look as if they're made of putty. This is called the **Tomb of the Princess**, or the Royal Tomb, but that's misleading because no bodies were found here. All the same it's likely that this was an important place for the Incas, judging from the work involved in enlarging and shaping this fissure. Just around the corner from the Tomb there is a flight of eight stairs carved from the living rock, leading to a beautiful double-framed door. There are two of these doors in Ollantaytambo, and they are very impressive, indicating an important dwelling. Note the bars recessed deeply into both door frames, similar to the ones in the Old City Gate.

To the right of the stairs is an entrance into a particularly fine walled building called **The Sacristy** or **House of the Princess**. The walls of Inca buildings are especially remarkable and here both the internal and external walls are amazing pieces of workmanship, especially when you consider that the Incas didn't have iron, only small brass crowbars. Bingham described it as 'the most beautiful wall in all America'.

THE WAY OUT

If you stand at the top of the cascade of fountains facing out into the void, you can see two or three thatched huts away to your right, at the same level as you are. A path leads there. This is the way out to Machu Picchu Sanctuary Lodge (The Tourists' Hotel, see p279), the car park and the buses back to the valley floor.

Moving on

Transport for Cusco leaves from Aguas Calientes in the valley below Machu Picchu.

MACHU PICCHU TO AGUAS CALIENTES (see p167)

The **walk** down from Machu Picchu to Aguas Calientes takes around an hour (follow the *Camino Peatonal* signpost on the edge of the car park), or you can take the **bus**. The bus ticket office is next to the bus stop, near the left-luggage office, and the fare is US$4.50. Buses leave approximately every 15 minutes, though there's no service down between 9am and 12 noon, and the last bus departs at 5.30pm.

AGUAS CALIENTES TO CUSCO

From Aguas Calientes the only way back to Cusco is by **train**. The timetable depends on the class of train and upon the vagaries of the Peruvian railway system. See pp301-2 for details of times and prices at the time of writing. To save time, get off the train in Poroy just before the switchbacks down to Cusco and catch a bus (s/5) from the station forecourt; the train takes an hour from here and the bus 10-15 minutes. Or to save money, catch the train only as far as Ollantaytambo, which is half the Cusco fare, and take a local bus from there.

APPENDIX A: QUECHA AND SPANISH

QUECHUA

There are very few readily available Quechua–English dictionaries or phrasebooks except for Ronald Wright's *Quechua Phrasebook* (Lonely Planet Publications). If you've access to a large library, however, have a look at the *Tri-lingual Dictionary: Quechua of Cusco/English/Spanish* by Esteban S Hornberger and Nancy H Hornberger (three volumes, Quechua Community Ministry, 1977). This is a good book, but it sometimes goes over the top with religious vocabulary and doesn't translate words such as 'chicha'!

There are many different ways of spelling Quechua. In most of this book I've followed Dr Ann Kendall and used the Hispanic spelling because many maps use it, but in this section I've tried to use the version which is easiest for English speakers to pronounce (which also happens to be the accepted standard alphabet). Pronunciation of Quechua words is difficult, as the language includes glottal stops, aspirations and plosives not found in most European languages. Stress, as in Spanish, almost always falls on the second last syllable. Letters to watch out for are Q, Q', Qu, Qh, K, K' (glottalizations).

SPANISH

Peruvian Spanish differs from Castilian (Spanish Spanish) in pronunciation and vocabulary but is basically the same language.

The letters for an English speaker to watch out for are the LL (pronounced as an English Y), C (pronounced as an S when followed by E and I, otherwise K), H (silent), HU (pronounced a bit like W), Ñ (the ~ puts an I noise after the N), Q (pronounced K). Unlike Castilian, the S is pronounced as an S not a TH, and the V is usually a V not a B. The rule of thumb about stress is that it goes on the penultimate syllable, unless there's an accent, in which case it goes where the accent indicates.

ENGLISH	QUECHUA	SPANISH
Hello and goodbye		
Greeting!	*Napaykullayki!*	*¡Buenos días!*
How are you?	*Allillanchu?*	*¿Cómo está usted?*
See you later	*Ratukama*	*Hasta luego*
Goodbye (final)	*Kacharpari*	*Adiós*
sir	*tayta*	*señor*
madam	*mama*	*señora*
Excuse me (polite)	*Munayniykimanta*	*Con permiso*
oi!	*yaw!*	*¡oiga!*
Politeness		
Please	*Ama hiinachu kay, allichu*	*Por favor*
Thanks	*Añáy*	*Gracias*
Can I stay here? (spend the night)	*Puñupayukuykimanchu*	*¿Puedo pasar la noche aquí?*
Yes and no		
yes	*arí, riki* (certainly!)	*sí*
no	*mana, ama* (don't!)	*no*
impossible	*mana atina*	*imposible*
that's good	*allinmi*	*está bien*
that's bad	*manan allinchu*	*no está bien*

ENGLISH	QUECHUA	SPANISH
Directions		
Where is...?	*maypin ...?*	*¿dónde está...?*
...the river	*...mayu*	*...el río*
...the village	*..llaqta, marka*	*...el pueblo*
...the path	*...ñan*	*...el camino, el sendero*
...the pass	*...q'asa*	*...la abra*
...the bus/truck	*...omnibus /karro*	*...el bus/el camión*
...the railway	*...ferrocarril*	*...el ferrocarril*
...the toilet	*...bañu*	*...los baños*
...the hotel	*...qorpa huasi*	*...el hotel*
...the house	*...huasi*	*...la casa*
...water	*...unu*	*...agua*
...food	*...mikuna*	*...la comida*
here	*kaypi*	*aquí*
there	*chaypi*	*allí, allá*
over there	*haqay*	*por ahí*
up	*huichay*	*arriba*
down	*uray*	*abajo*
left	*lloq'e*	*izquierda*
right	*paña*	*derecho*
near	*sispa*	*cerca*
far (far off)	*karu*	*lejos*
straight ahead	*dirichu*	*derecho*
everywhere, nowhere, anywhere	*maypipas*	*en todos partes, en ninguna parte, dondequiera*
When?		
When?	*hayk'aq?*	*¿cuándo?*
now (soon)	*kunan*	*pronto*
right now	*kunallan, kunanpacha!*	*ahora mismo*
later	*qhepata*	*más tarde*
never	*manan hayk'aqpas*	*nunca*
Weather		
heat of the sun	*ruphay*	*calor del sol*
rain	*para*	*lluvia*
wind	*wayra*	*viento*
freezing wind	*qasa*	*viento helado*
snow	*rit'i*	*nieve*
How much?		
How much is...?	*hayk'atan kubrawanki...?*	*¿cuánto cuesta...?*
that one	*...haqay, chay*	*...eso/a*
...it to hire a guide	*...pusawasqaykimanta*	*...arrendar un guía?*
...it to hire a horse	*...caballoykikunamanta*	*...arrendar un caballo?*
...it to hire a llama	*...llamaykikunamanta*	*...arrendar una llama?*
...it for a week	*...sapa semanan*	*...por semana*
...it for a day	*...sapa p'unchay*	*...por día*
Will you sell me...?	*icha ... ta bendiwankiman?*	*¿me vende ...?*
...money	*...qolqe*	*...dinero*

ENGLISH	QUECHUA	SPANISH

Food and drink (see pp58-60)

meat (dried meat)	*aycha, (ch'arki)*	*carne (charqui)*
fish	*challwa*	*pescado*
chicken	*huallpa*	*pollo*
egg	*runtu*	*huevo*
bread	*t'anta*	*pan*
soup	*chupi*	*sopa*
maize (corn)	*choqllo, sara*	*maíz, choclo*
potato	*papa*	*papa*
fruit	*ruru, añawi*	*fruta*
roast	*kanka*	*asado*
boil	*t'impuy*	*hervir*
fry	*theqtichiy*	*freír*
raw	*hanku*	*crudo*
cooked	*chayasqa*	*cocido*
coca	*kuka*	*coca*
beer	*sirwisa*	*cerveza*
fizzy drink		*bebida gaseosa*
hot (temperature)	*q'oñi*	*caliente*
spicy	*haya*	*picante*
cold	*chiri, khutu*	*frío*
cold food	*kharmu*	*comida fría*

Quantity

more	*aswan*	*más*
less	*aswan pisi*	*menos*
a little	*chika, pisi*	*un poco, poquito*
big, large	*hatun*	*grande*
small, little	*huch'uy*	*pequeño/a*
normal sized	*tinku*	*tamaño normal*

Numerals

1	*huk*	*uno*
2	*iskay*	*dos*
3	*kinsa*	*tres*
4	*tawa*	*cuartro*
5	*pisqa*	*cinco*
6	*soqta*	*seis*
7	*qanchis*	*siete*
8	*pusaq*	*ocho*
9	*isqon*	*nueve*
10	*chunka*	*diez*
20	*iskay chunka*	*viente*
30	*kinsa chunka*	*trienta*
100	*pachak*	*ciento*
200	*iskay pachak*	*dos cientos*
1000	*waranqa*	*mil*
2000	*iskay waranqa*	*dos mil*

ENGLISH	QUECHUA	SPANISH
Help!		
Help me!	*yanapaway!*	*¡socorro!*
Take me to a hospital	*uspitalman pusaway*	*lévame al hospital*
Ouch!	*achakáw!*	*¡ay!*
It hurts	*nanan*	*me duele*
I'm cold	*chiriwashan*	*tengo frío*
I'm hungry	*yarqawashan*	*tengo hambre*
I'm thirsty	*ch'akiwashan*	*tengo sed*
I'm tired	*sayk'usqa kan*	*estoy cansado*
Tie up your dog	*atahay alqoykita*	*ate su perro*

APPENDIX B: GLOSSARY

AMS	acute mountain sickness
abra	mountain pass
aclla	Inca nun
acllahuasi	convent
alpaca	type of llama bred for its wool
altiplano	high plateau
amauta	keeper of Inca oral history
andene	terrace
anticucho	heart (beef) kebabs
Antis	Inca word for the tribes of the rainforest
Antisuyu	the forested eastern district of the Inca Empire
apachita	cairn; pile of stones
apu	mountain spirit
arriero	muleteer, donkey man
audiencia	a seat of government of Spanish South America
awaska	everyday cloth worn by the majority of people
ayllu	Inca kinship group
cabildos	town councils
cacique	Spanish word for a local leader in the time of the Incas
calle	street
cambista	money-changer
cambio	bureau de change, exchange bureau
campesino	Peruvian peasant
cancha	block of houses in an Inca town
caudillos	the military leaders at the time of Peruvian independence
cejas de la Selva	'eyebrows of the jungle' (the eastern slopes of the Andes, covered by the edge of the rainforest
ceques	sacred lines radiating from the centre of the Sun Temple
cerro	mountain
ceviche	traditional Peruvian dish of marinated raw fish
cevicherías	seafood restaurants selling ceviche
chacos	Royal Hunts
chasqui	relay-running message carrier

chicha	drink of fermented maize
Chinchaysuyu	the northern quarter of the Inca Empire
chullo	locally knitted hat
chuño	type of traditional freeze-dried potato
ciudadela	Enclosure surrounded by a large wall, inside which there are labyrinths of storage rooms, a large platform (which doubles as a burial place) and audience rooms called *audiencias*
colectivo	South American form of transport, half-taxi, half-bus
Collasuyu	the far southern quarter of the Inca Empire
Convención (La)	the district further into the jungle beyond Machu Picchu
conquistadors	the Spanish conquerors of Peru
Coricancha	Inca Sun Temple
Corregidores	Crown agents
correo	post office
Coya	the Inca's sister and his official wife
Cuntisuyu	the south-western quarter of the Inca Empire
Curaca	Inca name for local noble
cuy	guinea pig
Encomendero	man who owns an encomienda
encomienda	plot of land governed by a Spaniard
guanaco	type of wild llama
HACO/HAPO	very serious forms of mountain sickness
Hanan	Inca clan division, also a part of an Inca town, the opposite of Hurin
huaca	sacred spot
huayna	small or young
Hurin	an Inca clan division, also a part of an Inca town, the opposite of Hanan
Inca	(see Sapa Inca)
Inti	the sun, the Sun God
Intihuatana	the 'hitching post of the sun', an Inca ceremonial stone
Inti Raymi	a re-creation of the Inca festival of the winter solstice
jirón	street
llama	a South American relative of the camel
llipta	A mixture of lime or quinoa and potash chewed with a quid of coca leaves
machay	cave
machu	old, big
mamacona	mother superior in an Inca convent
mercado	a purpose-built indoor market
mestizo	mixed blood
mit'a	Inca tax, often paid in labour
mitimaes	Inca settlers
nevado	snow-capped peak
orejones	'big-ears', the Spanish name for Inca nobles
Pachamama	an earth goddess
pampa	plain
panaca	the tradition of preserving the estate of a dead person
parillada	plate of grilled meat
pirka	basic method of Inca construction
posta de salud	health station
pucará	Inca fort
pueblos jóvenes	shanty towns
puna	high grassland

Punchao	a sacred idol of the sun from Cusco's Sun Temple, now lost
Qenko	sacred spot near Cusco
qollqa	Inca storehouse
qompi	fine fabric woven for the Inca
quebrada	river gorge
Quechua	a name for the Inca language; the Incas' descendants currently living in Peru
quinoa	an Andean grain
quipus	strings and knots used by the Incas for record-keeping
raccay	ruins
Runasimi	the Quechua word for their language
Sapa Inca	the ruler of the Incas (also just 'Inca')
suyu	a division of the Inca Empire
Tahuantinsuyu	Inca name for the Inca Empire
tambo	an inn, way-station or rest-house
tarjeta telefónica	telephone card
taxista	taxi driver
Tiahuanaco	a pre-Inca Peruvian culture
tumi	an Andean knife
urpu	the characteristic pot form ie a fat belly, a curved base and long spout
usno	raised ceremonial square in Inca city
vicuña	rare wild relative of the llama with beautiful wool
Villac Umu	chief of the caste of priests in the Inca state religion
Viracocha	the creator of the Incas, also the name of one of the early Incas

APPENDIX C: PERUVIAN EMBASSIES

Argentina
Av Del Libertador No 1720
1425 Capital Federal, Buenos Aires
(☎ 011-4802 2000, 🖷 011-4802 5887)

Australia
40 Brisbane Ave, Suite 8
Ground Floor Barton Act 2600
Canberra (PO Box 106 Red Hill)
(☎ 02-6273 8752, 🖷 02-6273 8754,
🖳 embassy@embaperu.org.au)

Australia (Sydney consulate)
Level 3, 30 Clarence St
New South Wales 2000
(☎ 02-9262 6464, 🖷 02-9290 2939)

Austria
Gottfried-Keller-Gasse 2/8-35
1030 Vienna
(☎ 01-713 4377, 🖷 01-712 7704)

Belgium
Avenue de Tervuren 179
1150 Bruxelles
(☎ 02-733 3185, 🖷 02-733 4819)

Bolivia
Calle Fernando Guachalla Cdra.3
Sopocachi, La Paz
(☎ 02-353550, 🖷 02-367640)

Brazil
SES Av das Nacoes, Lote 43
70428-900, Brasilia DF
(☎ 061-242 9933, 🖷 061-244 9344,
🖳 www.embperu.org.br)

Canada
130 Albert St, Suite 1901
Ottawa, Ontario, K1P 5GA
(☎ 613-238-1777, 🖷 613-232-3062,
🖳 emperuca@bellnet.ca)

Chile
Av Andres Bello 1751
Providencia, Santiago
(☎ 02-235 6451, ▤ 02-235 8139,
▢ embstgo@entelchile.net)

China
Sanlitun, Bangong Lou 1-91,
Diplomatic Building, 100600, Beijing
(☎ 010-6532-3477, ▤ 010-6532-2178,
▢ www.embperu.cn.net)

Colombia
Carrera 10 No 93-48, Bogotá
(☎ 01-218 9212, ▤ 01-623 5102)

Denmark
Rosenvaengets Alle 20, 2nd TV
2100 Copenhagen
(☎ 035-265848, ▤ 035-268406)

Ecuador
Av República de El Salvador 495 e Irlanda
Quito
(☎ 02-468410, ▤ 02-252560)

Finland
Annankatu 31, 33C 44 00100 Helsinki
(☎ 09-693-3681)

France
50, Avenue Kleber, 75116 Paris
(☎ 01-53 70 42 00, ▤ 01-47 04 32 55,
▢ amb.perou@noos.fr)

Germany
Godesberger Allee 125, 53175 Bonn
(☎ 0228-373045, ▤ 0228-379475)

Israel
37 Rehov Ha-Marganit
Shinkun Vatikim, 52584 Ramat Gan
(☎ 03-613 5591, ▤ 03-751 2286)

Japan
4-4-27 Higashi, Shibuya-ku
Tokyo 150-0011
(☎ 03-3406 4243, ▤ 03-3409 7589)

Netherlands
Nassauplein 4, 2585 EA, La Hague
(☎ 070-365 3500, ▤ 070-365 1929)

New Zealand
Level 8 Cigna House, 40 Mercer St
Wellington, PO 2566
(☎ 04-499 8087, ▤ 04-499 8057,
▢ embassy.peru@xtra.co.nz)

Russia
Smolensky Boulevard 22/14.KV
15 Moscow
(☎ 0095-248-7738)

South Africa
Infotech Building Suite 202
1090 Arcadia St, 0083 Hatfield, Pretoria
(☎ 012-342 2390, ▤ 012-342 4944)

Spain
C/Príncipe de Vergara No 36
5 to Derecha, 28001 Madrid
(☎ 091-431 4242, ▤ 091-431 2493)

Switzerland
Thunstrasse 36, 3005 Berma
(☎ 031-351 8555, ▤ 031-351 8570)

Thailand
Glas Haus Bldg, 16th Floor
No 1 Sukhumvit 25 Rd, Bangkok 10110
(☎ 02-260-6243, ▢ www.peruthai.th.com)

UK
52 Sloane St, London SW1X 9SP
(☎ 020-7235 1917, ▤ 020-7235 4463,
▢ www.peruembassy-uk.com)

USA (Washington consulate)
1700 Massachusetts Ave NW
Washington DC 20036
(☎ 202-833-9860, ▤ 202-659-8124,
▢ www.peruemb.org)

USA (Miami consulate)
444 Brickell Ave
Suite M-135
Miami, Florida 33131
(☎ 305-374-1305, ▤ 305-381-6027,
▢ www.consulado-peru.com)

USA (New York consulate)
215 Lexington Ave 21st Floor
New York, NY 10016
(☎ 212-481-7410, ▤ 212-481-8606)

APPENDIX D: TRAIN INFORMATION & TIMETABLES

Until recently, trains were the cheapest form of transport between the major destinations in Peru. All that changed, however, with the privatization of the rail network in 1999, for while the trains remain the most pleasant and safest form of transport, they are certainly no longer the cheapest. Though some dirt-cheap 'local' trains still ply the main routes, the owners of the rail network, Peru Rail, now forbid non-locals from taking them. It is not just foreigners who are no longer permitted to take these cheaper trains: even Peruvians from outside the local area are barred.

Fortunately, buses provide a cheap alternative to the trains on almost every major route. Unfortunately, the one place where the buses cannot go, and where you are left with virtually no other option but to take the train is, of course, to Aguas Calientes, the village below Machu Picchu.

There are currently three standards of **tourist train** servicing the line to Aguas Calientes. The relatively no-frills **Backpacker** is the cheapest at US$41.65 one way or US$65.45 round trip. One step up for its complimentary snacks and drinks is the **Vistadome** (US$59.50 one way/US$101.15 round trip), so called for its panoramic windows. The most luxurious, though, is the **Hiram Bingham** (US$476 round trip/one way not available), which departs daily except Sundays from the village of Poroy, at the top of the switchbacks. The ticket includes onboard meals in the plush dining cars, cocktails and drinks, live entertainment, guides, all bus transfers (between Cusco and Poroy, and Aguas Calientes and Machu Picchu), entrance to Machu Picchu and afternoon tea in the Machu Picchu Sanctuary Lodge.

There are two ways to cut costs. First, rather than travelling all the way between Aguas Calientes and Cusco by train, stop off in Ollantaytambo instead, and complete the rest of your journey by bus (train fares for a journey beginning or ending in Ollantaytambo tend to be half that for the full trip between Cusco and Aguas Calientes). Buses to and from Cusco pull in and leave from the train station at Ollantaytambo. Secondly, a local train (US$12) with two coaches tacked on for tourists leaves Aguas Calientes at 5.45am from the 'local' train station (see p168) and terminates at Ollantaytambo, from where you can catch the bus.

Fail to get a ticket for this service, and the only alternative is to sit back in the comfy seats of one of the more luxurious trains, enjoy the free soft drink they provide, gaze at the gorgeous scenery and remember that, whilst extortionate by Peruvian standards, these fares are no more than you'd expect to pay in Europe and America for a similar journey.

Please note that timetables and services are subject to change at very short notice and should be used as an approximate guide at best. For a more up-to-date schedule, call in at the train stations or visit Peru Rail's **website** (⌨ www.perurail.com); you can make bookings by email on it. You could also check with the SAE (see box p118) for the latest information.

Cusco to Machu Picchu

Services are daily, except for the Hiram Bingham which does not run on Sundays.

	Cusco	Poroy		Ollantaytambo		Puente Ruinas	Aguas Calientes
	Dep	Arr	Dep	Arr	Dep	Arr	Arr
Hiram Bingham	n/a	n/a	09.00	10.47	10.52	12.39	n/a
Vistadome	06.00	06.40	06.45	08.05	08.15	n/a	09.38
Backpacker	06.15	07.05	07.10	08.35	08.40	n/a	10.12

Machu Picchu to Cusco

Services are daily except for the Hiram Bingham, which does not run on Sundays.

	Aguas Calientes		Ollantaytambo		Poroy	Cusco
	Dep	Arr	Dep	Arr	Dep	Arr
Hiram Bingham*	18.15	20.03	20.08	22.03	n/a	n/a
Vistadome	15.05	16.34	16.39	18.02	18.12	19.05
Backpacker	15.30	17.13	17.16	18.52	19.02	19.58

* Note that only on the journey up from Cusco does the Hiram Bingham stop at Puente Ruinas, the station below Machu Picchu. On the return journey it starts at Aguas Calientes.

Sacred Valley to Machu Picchu

Those based in the Sacred Valley might be interested in the option of taking the shorter, yet similarly spectacular journey from Urubamba to Aguas Calientes. The daily Vistadome service costs US$41.65/69.02 (one way/round trip). During the high season (April to October), there is also a daily Backpacker service, which runs from Ollantaytambo to Machu Picchu and back for US$51.17 (round trip only).

	Urubamba	Ollantaytambo	Aguas Calientes			Ollantaytambo	Urubamba
	Dep	Arr	Dep	Arr	Dep	Arr	Dep	Arr
Vistadome	06.10	07.00	07.05	08.19	08.35	10.01		
Vistadome			10.40	11.56	13.20	14.37		
Vistadome			14.55	16.16	17.00	18.21	18.28	19.25
Backpacker			10.03	11.31	17.25	19.05		

Between Cusco and Puno

Trains leave Cusco for Puno from Huanchac Station on Mondays, Wednesdays and Saturdays at 08.00, arriving Juliaca at 16.35, departing 16.50, and get to Puno at 18.00.

Trains leave Puno on Mondays, Wednesdays and Saturdays at 08.00, arriving Juliaca at 09.10, departing 09.25, and get to Cusco at 18.00.

There are two classes: First Class costs US$89.25 (this includes a three-course lunch) one-way, and Tourist Class (Turismo), which costs US$14.28 one-way.

Between Puno and Arequipa

Currently the train only runs if 40 passengers or more have made reservations, which effectively means it tends to be out of action unless there's been a group booking or a private charter. Check 🖥 www.perurail.com for details.

APPENDIX E: BIBLIOGRAPHY

Some contemporary sources

Comentarios reales que tratan del origen de los Incas, Garcilaso de la Vega 1609
  trans Livermore, Texas 1966, trans CR Markham 1869

The Discovery and Conquest of Peru, Pedro De Cieza de León, Duke University Press,
  1998, trans Alexandra & Noble Cook

History of the Incas, Pedro Sarmiento de Gamboa, Dover/Constable and Co, London 1999
  (reprint of 1907 Hakluyt Markham translation)

Historia del descumbriento y conquista del Perú, Agustín de Zarate, 1555, trans
  JM Cohen, Harmonsworth, 1968

Historia del Nuevo Mundo, Bernabé Cobo, 1653, trans Ronald Hamilton, *History
  of the Inca Empire* and *Inca Religion and Customs,* Univ of Texas, Austin 1979 and 1990

Instrucción del Inga Don Diego de Castro Tito Cussi Yupangui, Titu Cusi 1570,
  in *En el encuentro de dos mundos: los Incas de Vilcabamba,* María del Carmen, Martín
  Rubio, ed, Madrid 1988

Letter to a King (El Primera Coronice y Buen Gobierno), Felipe Huamán Poma de Ayala
  1613, facsimile edition, *Travaux et mémoires de l'institut de' ethnologie,* Paris 1936, vol 23

Relación del descumbriento y conquista de los reinos del Perú, Pedro Pizarro, 1571, trans
  PA Means, *Relation of the Discovery and Conquest of the Kingdom of Peru,* Cortes
  Society, New York, 1921

Verdadera relación de la conquista del Perú, Francisco de Xerex (Pizarro's scribe), July
  1534, trans CR Markham, *Reports on the Discovery of Peru,* Hakluyt Society, first series
  47, 1872

Modern historians of the Incas

Conquest of Peru, William Prescott, New York, 1847
Conquest of the Incas, John Hemming, Macmillan 1970, Penguin 1983, Papermac 1993
Everyday life of the Incas, Ann Kendall, BT Batsford, 1973
The Incas of Peru, Clements Markham, Smith Elder & Co, 1910
Realm of the Incas, Max Milligan, Idlewild, 2003

Inca studies

Inca Architecture and Construction at Ollantaytambo, Jean-Pierre Protzen, OUP, 1993
Inca Road Systems, John Hyslop, Academic Press New York, 1984
Inca Architecture, Louise Margolies & Graziano Gasparini, Univ of Indiana, Bloomington,
  1984
Inca Settlement Planning, John Hyslop, University of Texas Press Austin, 1990
Monuments of the Incas Edward Ranney and John Hemming, New York Graphic Society,
  New York, 1982
Discovering the Inca Ice Maiden, Johan Reinhard, National Geographic, Washington 1998
The Social Life of Numbers, Gary Urton, University of Texas, Austin 1997
Rain of the Moon: Silver in Ancient Peru, Heidi King, Metropolitan Museum of Art, New
  York 2000
Mathematics of the Incas, Code of the Quipu, Marcia and Robert Ascher, Dover
  Publications, New York 1981
The Incas, Terence D'Altroy, Blackwell, Oxford 2002
Ritual Sacrifice in Ancient Peru, Ed Benson & Cook, University of Texas Press, Austin, 2001

Machu Picchu and the Inca sites around it

An introduction to the Archaeology of Cusco, John H Rowe, Papers of the Peabody
  Museum of American Archaeology, Harvard University vol 22, No 2, 1944
Ancient Cuzco, Heartland of the Inca, University of Texas Press, Austin, 2004

Archaeological Explorations in the Cordillera Vilcabamba, Paul Fejos, Publications in Anthropology No 3, The Werner Gren Foundation, 1944

Archaeological Investigations of Late Intermediate Period and Late Horizon Period at Cusichaca, Peru, Ann Kendall, in *Current Archaeological Projects in the Central Andes*, edited by Ann Kendall, BAR Int Series 210, 1984

Exploring Cusco, Peter Frost, Nuevas Imágenes, 2000

Inca Planning North of Cuzco between Anta and Machu Picchu and along the Urubamba Valley, Dr Ann Kendall, BAR Int Series, 421, Oxford, 1988

Lost City of the Incas, Hiram Bingham, Duell, Sloan and Pearce, 1948

Lost City of the Incas, Hiram Bingham, Weidenfeld & Nicholson, 2002, a reprint with photos

Machu Picchu, John Hemming. Readers' Digest, 1981

Machupicchu, Devenir Histórico y Cultural, Efraín Chevarría Huarcaya, UNSAAC, 1992

Machu Picchu Historical Sanctuary, Jim Bartle and Peter Frost, Nuevas Imágenes, 1995

The Sacred Centre Johan Reinhard, Nuevas Imágenes, 1995

Machu Picchu – A Civil Engineering Marvel, Kenneth R Wright and Alfredo Valencia Zegarra, American Society of Civil Engineers, 2000

The Machu Picchu Guidebook, Ruth Wright and Alfredo Zegarra, Johnson Books, Boulder, 2004

The Ancient Incas, Chronicles from National Geographic, Arthur Schlesinger, Chelsea House, Philadelphia, 1999

Inca Architecture and Construction at Ollantaytambo, Jean-Pierre Proetzen, OUP, 1993

Vilcabamba

Forgotten Vilcabamba – Final Stronghold of the Incas, Vincent R Lee, Sixpac Manco Publications, 2000

Sixpac Manco: travels among the Incas, Vincent R Lee, Sixpac Manco publications, 1985

Antisuyu, Gene Savoy, Simon and Schuster, 1970

Books on ancient Peru

Art of the Andes, Rebecca Stone-Miller, Thames and Hudson, 1995

Chavín and the Origins of Andean Civilisation, Richard Burger, Thames and Hudson, 1992

Peruvian Prehistory, Keatinge (ed), CUP, 1988

The Ancient Civilisations of Peru, J Alden Mason, Penguin, 1957

The Ancient Kingdoms of Peru, Nigel Davies, Penguin, 1997

The Cities of the Ancient Andes, Adriana von Hagen and Craig Morris, Thames and Hudson, 1998

The Incas and their Ancestors, Michael Moseley, Thames and Hudson, 1992

The Pre-Hispanic Cultures of Peru, Justo Caceres Macedo, Lima, 1998

Modern Peru

A Fish in the Water, Mario Vargas Llosa, Faber and Faber, 1994

Fujimori's Peru, John Crabtree and Jim Thomas (ed), Institute of Latin American Studies, 1998

Shining Path, Simon Strong, Harper Collins, 1992

The Peru Reader, Latin America Bureau, 2003

The Mystery of Capital, Hernando de Soto, Bantam, London, 2000

Latin America

A History of Latin America, George Pendle, Penguin, 1963

Ancient South America, Karen Bruhns, CUP, 1994

The Penguin History of Latin America, Edwin Williamson, Penguin, 1992

Quechua
Quechua Phrasebook, Lonely Planet Publications, 2002
Tri-Lingual Dictionary: Quechua/English/Spanish, Esteban S Hornberger, Nancy H
  Hornberger, Quechua Community Ministry, 1977

Travel narratives
Cut Stones and Crossroads, Ronald Wright, Penguin, 1984
Cuzco: A Journey to the Ancient Capital of Peru, Clements Markham, 1856
Inca Kola, Matthew Parris, George Weidenfeld & Nicholson, 1990
Inca Land, Hirham Bingham, London Constable & Co, 1922, and National Geographic,
  2003
Memoirs, General William Miller, London, 1828
Peregrinations of a Pariah Flora Tristan, Folio, 1986 (trans)
Peru. Travel and Exploration in the Land of the Incas, E George Squier, New York, 1877
The Condor and the Cows, Christopher Isherwood, Random House, 1948
The White Rock: an Exploration of the Inca Heartland, Hugh Thomson, Phoenix, 2002
Three Letters From the Andes, Patrick Leigh Fermor, John Murray, 2005
Voyage a Travers L'Amerique du Sud, Paul Marcoy (Laurent Sant-Criq), Paris, 1869

Other books
Death in the Andes, Mario Vargas Llosa, trans Faber and Faber, 1996
Royal Hunt of the Sun, Peter Shaffer, Longman, 1991
The Bridge of San Luis Rey, Thornton Wilder, Penguin, 1969
Canto General, Pablo Neruda (trans Jack Schmitt), Univ of California Press, Berkley, 1991
The Dancer Upstairs, Nicholas Shakespeare, Harvill 1995, Picador, 1997
To the Last City, Colin Thubron, Chatto & Windus, 2002

Health and medicine
Altitude Illness: Prevention & Treatment by Stephen Bezruchka MD, Cordee, 1994
Bugs, Bites and Bowels Dr Jane Wilson Howarth, Cadogan, 2002
Medical Handbook for Mountaineers Peter Steele, Constable, 1993
Medicine for Mountaineering Ed James Wilkerson MD, The Mountaineers, 1985

Flora and fauna
Annotated Checklist of Peruvian Birds, Theodore Parker III and others, Buteo Books, 1982
Birds of the High Andes by Jon Fjeldsa and Niels Krabbe, Apollo Books, 1990
A Field Guide to the Birds of Peru, James F Clements, Ibis Publishing, 2001
Peru Travellers' Wildlife Guide, David Pearson and Les Beletsky, Arris Books, 2005
Orquídeas del Perú, Moisés Cavero and others, Centro de Datos para la Conservación del
  Perú, Lima 1991

APPENDIX F: LICENSED TOUR OPERATORS (CUSCO)

Below is a comprehensive list of the tour operators that had official licences at the time of writing. Note that inclusion is no guarantee of quality but it does mean that the operator has achieved a basic level of service and satisfied a number of official requirements. These licences are renewed every year at the end of February. Be aware that licences are only issued to Peruvian trekking companies – never to overseas or foreign tour operators. For up-to-date contact listings and web addresses, it's worth looking at the Andean Travel website (🖳 www.andeantravelweb.com), which contains a full list of licensed operators and is updated regularly.

A Cross Adventure Av Tupac Amaru, ☎ 241674, 🖳 duliacusco@yahoo.es
Adventure Paradises Calle Procuradores 44, Office 02, ☎ 241507,
   🖳 advparadises@hotmail.com
Adventure's Paradise Expeditions Calle Saphi 578-A, ☎ 253097,
   🖳 cinthyab_82@hotmail.com
Alfa Tours Av El Sol 346, Office 104, ☎ 221722
Amazin Adventures Av Collasuyo 517, Urb Miravalle, ☎ 237733
Amazonas Explorer Av Collasuyo 910, Urb Miravalle, ☎ 252846,
   🖳 www.amazonasexplorer.com
American Inka's Territory Urb José Carlos Mariategui D-38 2do p.- Wanchaq, ☎ 229456,
   🖳 m_malaga_nadal@hotmail.com
American Travel Express Calle Procuradores 351,Office 115, ☎ 249372, 🖳 at@peru.com
Andean Adventures Urb Lucrepata E-13, ☎ 263498, 🖳 www.andeanadventuresperu.com
Andean Discoveries Tour Operator Urb Lucrepata D-4, ☎ 239572,
   🖳 www.andeandiscoveries.com
Andean Explorer's Cusco Calle Triunfo 338, Second Floor, ☎ 242975,
   🖳 andean_explorers@hotmail.com
Andean Express Calle Simón Bolívar I-8, Bancopata- Santiago, No phone listed
Andean Land Adventures Urb Ttio Z-21, ☎ 228997, 🖳 andeanla@terra.com.pe
Andean Life Calle Plateros 372, ☎ 221491,🖳 www.andeanlife.com
Andes Journey's Portal de Panes 123, Office 106, ☎ 235940, 🖳 andes_journeys@hotmail.com
Andes Nature Tours Calle San Andres 270, Office 4-A, ☎ 242522, 🖳 ant@terra.com.pe
Andina Travel Treks & Eco Adventure Plazoleta Santa Catalina 219, ☎ 251892,
   🖳 andinatravel@terra.com.pe, www.andinatravel.com
Apumayo Expediciones Calle Garcilaso 265, Office 3, ☎ 246018, 🖳 www.apumayo.com
Arroyo Viajes Y Turismo Calle Francisco Bolognesi V-16, Zarzuela, ☎ 224362,
   🖳 arroyo@hotmail.com
Auqui Mountain Spirit José Gabriel Cosio 307, Urb Magisterial, ☎ 251278,
   🖳 vroger@qenqo.rcp.net.pe
Base Camp Calle Herrajes 148, ☎ 231104, 🖳 basecamp@terra.com.pe
Big Foot Tours Calle Triunfo 392, Office 213, 2nd Fl, ☎ 238568, 🖳 www.bigfootcusco.com
BM Calle Plateros 394, ☎ 432454, 🖳 bmtours_1@hotmail.com
Brama Tours Calle Atocsaycuchi 647, ☎ 228090, 🖳 bramatours@speedy.com.pe
C & C Peru Travel Calle del Medio 131, ☎ 246254
Camping Tours Calle Triunfo 392, Office 209, ☎ 241869, 🖳 campingtours@hotmail.com
Cocatambo Inversiones Av Tomas Turu Tupac 119, ☎ 433306,
Colibri Travel Calle Triunfo 392, Office 209, ☎ 247849, 🖳 www.colibritour.com
Columbia Travel Av El Sol 816, Office 217, ☎ 248755, 🖳 columb_travel@hotmail.com
Condor Travel Calle Saphi 848, A, ☎ 225961, 🖳 www.condortravel.com.pe
Continental Tours Calle Plateros 329, ☎ 236919, 🖳 contitur@terra.com.pe

Culturas Peru Viajes y Servicos Calle Triunfo 393, Interior 202, ☎ 243629,
   🖳 www.culturasperu.com
Cusco Explorer's Calle San Jorge Ochao 241, Second Floor, ☎ 245443/9683577,
   🖳 cuscoexplorer@yahoo.com
Destinos Turisticos Portal de Panes 123, Office 101, ☎ 260099, 🖳 destinos@terra.com.pe
Di-Mare Tours Agencia de Viajes Avenida Pardo 545, Interior 'E', ☎ 231714,
   🖳 machaska@hotmail.com
Dos Manos Calle Suecia 368, ☎ 235620, 🖳 www.dosmanosperu.com
Eco Andes Adventures Corner Tandapata and Atocsaycuchi 667, ☎ 241598,
   🖳 www.ecoandesadventures.com
Ecotime Peru Urb Santa Teresa chico D-19, ☎ 244823, 🖳 ecotimeperu@hotmail.com
Eco Adventures Cusco Calle Siete Cuartones 231, ☎ 244823,
   🖳 info@ecoaventures@terra.com
Eco Service Tours Calle Garcilaso 210, Office 111, ☎ 231288, 🖳 ecoaventures@terra.com
Eco Tourism Ch'aska Calle Plateros 325, Second Floor, Office 'A', ☎ 240424,
   🖳 www.chaskatours.com
EcoInka Av Pardo 545 –Office 01, ☎ 224050, 🖳 www.ecoinka.com
El Dorado Expeditions Portal Comercio 141, Office 3, Second Floor, ☎ 255305,
   🖳 dorado_expeditions@hotmail.com
Emperadores Tours Calle Procuradores 190, ☎ 231183, 🖳 empetcusco@hotmail.com
Enigma Adventure Calle Garcilaso 210, Office 103, ☎ 222153, 🖳 www.enigmaperu.com
Epitours Adventure Procuradores 351, ☎ 805332, 🖳 epitours_adventure@hotmail.com
Eric Adventures Calle Plateros 324, ☎ 228475, 🖳 www.ericadventures.com
Exotic Adventures in Peru Calle Plateros 325, Second Floor, ☎ 243826,
   🖳 www.exotic-adventures.com
Expeandes Pasaje Ciro Alegria H-15 Santa Monica, ☎ 247152, 🖳 expeandes_ag@terra.com
Expediciones Tambo Calle Tullumayo 245, ☎ 241950, 🖳 pablo@tamboperu.com
Expediciones Vilca Calle Plateros 363, ☎ 244751, 🖳 manuvilca@terra.com.pe
Explorandes Av Garcilaso 316-A, ☎ 238380/245700, 🖳 www.explorandes.com
Export Tour Av Pardo 721, ☎ 221641, 🖳 www.exporttour.com
Fiesta Tours International Calle Santa Catalina 366, ☎ 228177, 🖳 www.fiestatoursperu.com
Forever Young Av Santa Rosa, ☎ 271085, 🖳 foreveryoung5@yahoo.com
Frontier Expeditions Calle Plateros 364, ☎ 243432, 🖳 frontier@planet.com.pe
GAP Adventures Portal Comercio 177, Office 13, ☎ 228716, 🖳 www.gap.ca
Gregory's Tours Portal Comercio 177, ☎ 807142, 🖳 gregorystours@terramail.com.pe
Highway Expeditions Calle Almagro 407, 🖳 highwaycusco@hotmail.com
Highlander's Expedition Av Pardo 915, (no phone listed)
Hiking Peru Portal de Panes 123, ☎ 247942, 🖳 info@hikingperu.com
Hugo Paullo Alfaro Portal de Panes 123, Office 301, ☎ 237649,
   🖳 southerncrosspaullo@terra.com.pe
Illapa Culturas Andinas Inversiones Calle Turquezas E-11, ☎ 251084,
   🖳 www.illapa.com
Inca Explorers Calle Ruinas 427, ☎ 241070, 🖳 www.incaexplorers.com
Inka Sunrise Travel Agency Calle Huayruropata 1206, ☎ 263267
Inka Natura Travel Calle Recardo Palma J-1, Urb Santa Monica, ☎ 243408,
   🖳 www.inkanatura.com
Inka's Golden Travel Adventure Calle Plataros 334, ☎ 248284,
   🖳 inkas_golden@hotmail.com
Inka's Mysteries Travel Service Calle Triunfo 392 Office 217-A, ☎ 261296,
   🖳 www.inkasmysteries.com
Inka's Peru Tours Jr Cajamarca N-2, San Borja, ☎ 238532

Inka's Peru Trek Calle Triunfo 392, Office 215, ☎ 260747, 🖳 inka@peru.com
Inka's Travel Services Urb Los Nogales N-14, San Sebastian, ☎ 242428, 🖳 www.inkastravelservices.com
Inka Wasi Travel Service Calle Triunfo 392, ☎ 260781, 🖳 www.inkawasitravel.com
Inkaways Urb Santa Ursula C-19, ☎ 223865, 🖳 www.inkaways.com
Instinct Calle Procuradores 50, ☎ 233451, 🖳 www.instinct-travel.com
Inti Kuntur Calle Triunfo 393, Office 204, ☎ 246235, 🖳 intikuntur@hotmail.com
Inversiones Turisticas Flamenco Portal Confituria 265, Office 2, ☎ 224176
Inversiones X-treme Turbulencia Expeditions Calle Plateros 358, No phone listed
Jenly Adventures Calle del Medio 127, ☎ 380577, 🖳 jenlyadventures2002@yahoo.es
K'intu Expeditions Portal de Panes 123, 2nd Floor, ☎ 240746, 🖳 kintuexp@hotmail.com
Let's Travel Peru Calle Simón Bolívar F-22 Bancopata, ☎ 246116, 🖳 letstravelperu@yahoo.com
Llama Path Calle San Juan de Dios 250, No phone listed
Liz's Explorer Calle del Medio 114–B, ☎ 246619, 🖳 www.lizexplorer.com
Loreto Tours Calle del Medio 111, ☎ 228264, 🖳 loretotours@planet.com.pe
Lucero's Tour Urb Campina Alta C-6 San Sebastian, ☎ 270060, 🖳 lucerostour@hotmail.com
M.A. Travel Agency Portal del Panes 109, Second Floor, ☎ 245550, 🖳 matravelagency@yahoo.com
Machete Tours Calle Tecsecocha 161, ☎ 224829, 🖳 www.machetetours.com
Machu Picchu Union World Calle San Bernardo 122, No phone listed
Marcelo's Travel Adventure Portal Comercio 145, No phone listed
Manu Expeditions Urb Magesterio G-5, 2nd Floor, ☎ 226671, 🖳 www.manuexpeditions.com
Marle's Travel Adventure Calle Nuevea Alta 850-F, 2nd Floor, ☎ 242972, 🖳 marlestravel@hotmail.com
Maura Travel Av Simón Bolívar E-3, (no phone listed)
Mayuc Cusco Portal Confituria 211, ☎ 232666, 🖳 www.mayuc.com
Mely Tours Urb Santa Beatriz G-1, ☎ 806001, 🖳 melytours@hotmail.com
Moroni Tours Prolongacíon Jerusalen F-10, ☎ 222616
Nao Tour Av Luis Uzátegui 925, ☎ 243066, 🖳 naoka@terra.com
Naty's Travel Agency Calle Panpa de la Alianza 149, 2nd Floor, ☎ 261811, 🖳 www.natystravel.com
Nice Tour Peru Calle Meloc 487, ☎ 9621146, 🖳 nicetourperu@hotmail.com
Pachamama Tour Expeditions Urb El Ovalo Lote C-22, ☎ 805924, 🖳 chachanite@yahoo.com
Panorama Cusco Travel Portal de Panes 123, ☎ 243221
Personal Travel Service Portal de Panes 123, Office 109, ☎ 244036, 🖳 ititoss@terra.com.pe
Peru Alive Tour Operators Av La Convención 210, ☎ 232970, 🖳 perualive@terra.com
Peru Ancash Travel Portal de Panes 123, Office 205, ☎ 228860, 🖳 www.peruatravel.com
Peru Travel Expeditions Tambo de Montero 117, ☎ 260146
Peru Travel and Services Calle del Medio 123, No phone listed
Peru Treks and Adventure Calle Garcilaso 265, Office 11, Second Floor, ☎ 805863, 🖳 www.perutreks.com
Peruvian Andean Treks Av Pardo 705, ☎ 225701, 🖳 www.andeantreks.com
Peruvian Cross Av Industrial O-1, ☎ 244110, 🖳 peruviancross@hotmail.com
Peruvian Highland Travel Calle Plateros 347, ☎ 234908, 🖳 peruvianhighland@terra.com.pe
Peruvian Highland Trek Calle del Medio 139, ☎ 242480, 🖳 peruvianhighlandtreks@hot mail.com
Peruvian Odyssey Pasaje Pumachupan 831, ☎ 222105

Peruvian Sacred Adventures Hilario Mendivil G-303, ☎ 251920
Peruvian Trek Santa Catalina Angosta 127, ☎ 255483
Peruvian Tucan Trek Calle Inca 492, ☎ 242525, 🖳 tucanperu@terramail.com.pe
Puma's Adventure Calle Triunfo 392, Office 207, ☎ 247293,
    🖳 pumas_adventure@yahoo.us
Puma's Trek Peru Portal Comercio 141, Office 4, ☎ 256044,
    🖳 pumastrekperu@hotmail.com
Q'ente Calle Garcilaso 210, ☎ 238245, 🖳 www.qente.com
Qori Travel Service Calle Heladeros 157, ☎ 242578, 🖳 qoriqio@terra.com.pe
Qosqo Mistico Viajes y Servicios Calle Procuradores 48, ☎ 243388,
    🖳 www.qosqomistico.com
Quechua Tours Av Collasuyo 2818, ☎ 234643
R R General Tours Calle Romeritos 204, No phone listed
Reserva Ecologica Yanayaco Lodge Calle Tecsecocha 424, ☎ 248122
Royal Crown Adventures Calle Garcilaso 265, Office 8, ☎ 248858
Saca Expeditions Calle Triunfo 392, Office 218, ☎ 246041, 🖳 info@sacaexpeditions.com
Sacred Valley Adventures Jr Grau 706, ☎ 201212
SAS Travel Adventure (South American Sites) Portal de Panes 167, ☎ 255205,
    🖳 www.sastravelperu.com
Servicios Turísticos Cusco Tours Cuesta del Almirante 232, ☎ 247412,
    🖳 cuscotour@hotmail.com
Siwar Tours Portal de Carnes 260, Office 203, ☎ 252724, 🖳 siwartour@hotmail.com
Sky Viajes y Turismo Calle Santa Catalina Ancha 366-3C, ☎ 261818, 🖳 www.skyperu.com
Spectacle Bear Exploring Tours Calle Garcilaso 210, Office 109, ☎ 239696
Sunrise Expeditions Calle Suecia 300-C, ☎ 272436
Suri Travel Calle Espaderos 105-A, ☎ 222000, 🖳 suritravelcuso@yahoo.es
T y G Travel Calle Plateros 365, ☎ 241969
Tambo Trek Calle Tullumayo 245, Second Floor, ☎ 237718, 🖳 www.tamboperu.com
Tari Tours Conj Hab Fovipal Dpto 314, ☎ 239132, 🖳 taritourscusco@hotmail.com
Teqsi Travel Services Av Luis Uzátegui J-15, ☎ 227194
Tesoros Del Perú Calle Maruri 228, Office 404, ☎ 252230, 🖳 inters@viabcp.com
The Great Andean Pathways Tour Operator Calle Peru W-18, ☎ 439499
Thin Air Outfitters Av Santa Ana Lote 17, ☎ 233677
Tierra De Los Andes Calle Turquezas E-11-Urb Kennedy A, ☎ 247277,
    🖳 terandes@terra.com.pe
Tour Operator Wayki Trek Expedition Av Paz Soldan Q-30, ☎ 9684409
Tranastawa Urb Villa Union D-2-Huancaro, ☎ 262291
Trek Peru Jr Ricardo Palma N-9, ☎ 252899 / 261501, 🖳 www.trekperu.com
Tropical American Adventure Calle Chihuampapa 591-A, ☎ 233505,
    🖳 etorre@terra.com.pe
Tourismo Kasiri Calle Garcilaso 210, Office 210, ☎ 239681, 🖳 info@kipachiperu.com
Turpuno Av El Sol 327B, ☎ 228431, 🖳 www.turpuno.com
United Mice Calle Plateros 351, ☎ 221139, 🖳 www.unitedmice.com
Viajes Colón Urb Vallecito-Huancaro A-1-4, ☎ 261759
Vida Andina Adventure Tour Jr Luis Uzátegui Arce 751, ☎ 233004,
    🖳 vidaandina@terra.com.pe
Vida Tours Calle Ladrillos 425 (inside Hotel Arqueologo), ☎ 227750, 🖳 www.vidatours.com
Wayki Trek Calle Procuradores 351, ☎ 224092, 🖳 www.waykitrek.net
Welcome South America Travel Urb La Colina B-18, ☎ 222231, 🖳 welsat@terra.com.pe
Willka Mayu Peru Tours Av El Sol 679, ☎ 253666
World Wide Travel Calle Procuradores 366, ☎ 246603, 🖳 www.worldwideperu.com

INDEX

Town plan key

		(*i*)	Tourist Information	△	Camping Site
⌂	Where to stay	$	Bank	●	Other
○	Where to eat / drink	🏛	Museum	✍	Internet
✉	Post Office	✝	Church / Cathedral	☻	Bus Station

UPDATE – AUGUST 2006

This update is arranged to mirror the main parts of the book and you can make best use of it by using both page numbers and headings. In its preparation I was helped enormously by Joseph, Benedict, Eleanor, Alex Stewart (again!), Joy Durighello, Shawn McLaughlin and Rob Fenichel, Andean Trails (🖥 www.andeantrails.co.uk), the South American Explorers' Club (🖥 www.saexplorers.org) and Lew Brown. And Bryn. And Melissa.

To contact me with further updates, recommendations or comments write c/o Trailblazer (address on p2) or email me at richard.danbury@trailblazer-guides.com. A free copy of the next edition or imprint will be sent for the most useful letters.

Page 11 – Possible new trail charges
I'm getting reports that the Peruvian authorities are planning to charge people to walk to Vilcabamba, Choquequirao and Santa Teresa. It'd be sensible to check the current regime before you leave. The South American Explorers' Club (🖥 www.saexplorers.org) is a good source of information. (One would hope such charges benefit the local community).

Page 49 – García's second term
Toledo is no longer president. In a hard-fought election in 2006, Alan García beat Ollanta Humala. García was of course notorious for having damaged the country's economy when he was president for the first time in the late 1980s, so people are holding their breath a little to see what happens this time round. He and his administration say they've learnt the lessons of defaulting on their international debt, and he inherits an economy in a better shape than the one he left. García's a populist, and one of his first actions on taking office has been to try and change the constitution to bring back the death penalty – albeit for murders of children, but a move that leaves some disturbed as it'll apparently entail withdrawing from the Inter American court of Human Rights. The most significant current issue in Peruvian politics is a free trade agreement which Toledo signed with the Americans. The campesinos hate it, and have gone on strike in protest (recently disrupting the train service to Machu Picchu).

Fujimori ended up in Chile, and the Peruvians are seeking his extradition. The case is mired in the Chilean courts. The aftershocks of the Fujimori era are still being felt, and as recently as August 2006 a former America television broadcaster was found guilty of taking money from Fujimori's henchman, Montesinos.

Page 52 – The environment
The Camisea pipeline was built. It was heralded as a responsible piece of economic development, showing due regard to local populations and the fragile ecosystems through which it's built. However, in March 2006 a bit of it ruptured, and some NGOs remain suspicious about whether it poses a serious threat to indigenous communities.

Peruvian glaciers continue to melt. In the last 30 years, the country's lost 25% of its glaciers. Latest predictions suggest that all the glaciers will be gone by 2015. This depressing state of affairs is probably down to climate change.

Page 92 – Inca roads
More than one numerate reader has pointed out a mistake on page 92. I wrote that the Inca road network, 33,000km in length, was enough to circle the earth two and a half times. Actually, they'd only go round about two thirds of the earth. Mea culpa!

Page 97 – The Incas and Easter Island
A reader has pointed out to me (see the review for this book on Amazon.com) that my box on Easter Island and Thor Heyerdahl is inaccurate. Heyerdahl didn't prove that you could float from the Peruvian coast to Easter Island – he avoided the most difficult bit by being towed

out to sea past the Humboldt Current. And I'm asked to stress that Heyerdahl's theories aren't held to be credible. Nevertheless, I think it's all intriguing stuff.

Page 119 – Lima accommodation

Casa Andina (🖳 www.casa-andina.com) have opened hotels in Lima and Cusco. They sound good, and I'd very much like to hear what people think of them.

Page 124 – Miraflores (mid range)

Paul Saroli, manager of *Hotel San Antonio Abad*, has been praised for his trip-planning abilities.

❑ Rates of exchange – p56	
	Peru Nuevo Sol
Aus$1	s/2.49
Can$1	s/2.88
Euro€1	s/4.11
NZ$1	s/2.05
UK£1	s/6.11
US$1	s/3.24

🖳 www.oanda.com/convert/
classic or www.xe.com/ucc

Page 131-2 – Cusco: history

Cusco remains a focus for occasional local discontent. In 2006 there was a brief siege at the Coricancha, where disgruntled coca farmers held tourists hostage. They were protesting against Government policies to eradicate coca-growing. No one was hurt.

Page 139 – Cusco: banks and cambios

Bank Weise charge 3.5% commission, so they're no longer a great deal. Interbank on Avenida El Sol charges no commission for USD cheques changed into Soles.

Page 140 – Cusco: tour agencies

A reader writes in to warn that some tour companies have been less than straightforward. If you ask them for a porter to carry your main pack, they can charge you around US$60. Then when you turn up on the trail, there's no porter for you. There's a suspicion that the extra money is pocketed by the tour company but it could just be old fashioned inefficiency. A reader writes in to warn that if you want a porter to carry your kit, ask for the tour company to arrange it but say that you'll pay the porter directly yourself.

On a happier note, I've had a recommendation for a company that's particularly knowledgeable about Choquequirao. **Aracari Travel Consulting** (☎ 511 242 6673, 🖳 www.aracari.com) is in Lima at Avenida Pardo 610 of 802, Miraflores.

Page 144 – Cusco: equipment rental Soqllaq'asa, Calle Plateros 365 has shut.

Page 144 – Cusco: hiking provisions The supermarket at Plateros 346 has closed.

Page 145 – Cusco accommodation *Casa Andina* has opened. See Lima, above.

Page 277 – Machu Picchu

The area around Machu Picchu is beset by mud slides and fires both of which disrupt the train service to the ruins. There were slides in April 2004 and October 2005, and a fire in August 2006. They may be caused by climate change, but more likely it's something that has been happening in this area for ages. It's not helped by the number of tourists wandering around these hills. UNESCO were so disturbed by the way the Sanctuary was being managed that they threatened to put Machu Picchu on the list of endangered World Heritage Sites; they relented (July 2006) after the Peruvian authorities drew up a plan to protect it. Some NGOs find the plan suspect, partly because the cap on visitor numbers per day remains high: 2500 people a day will still be let into the park.

There's a growing movement in Peru to ask Yale to return the artefacts found at Machu Picchu by Hiram Bingham. One report suggests that the Peruvians are going to sue the university. It's likely to become a cause célèbre, rather like the campaign to return the Elgin Marbles, currently held in the British Museum, to Greece.

Page 304 – Bibliography

Cochineal Red, Hugh Thomas, Weidenfeld & Nicolson, London 2006. Fascinating description of Llactapata, recently re-discovered ruins on the next hill down from Machu Picchu.

TRAILBLAZER'S BRITISH WALKING GUIDE SERIES

We've applied to destinations which are closer to home Trailblazer's proven formula for publishing definitive route guides for adventurous travellers. Britain's network of long-distance trails enables the walker to explore some of the finest landscapes in the country's best walking areas and they are an obvious starting point for this series. These are guides that are user-friendly, practical, informative and environmentally sensitive.

● **Unique mapping features** In many walking guidebooks the reader has to read a route description then try to relate it to the map. Our guides are much easier to use because walking directions, tricky junctions, places to stay and eat, points of interest and walking times are all written onto the maps themselves in the places to which they apply. With their uncluttered clarity, these are not general-purpose maps but fully-edited maps **drawn by walkers for walkers**.

● **Largest-scale walking maps** At a scale of just under 1:20,000 (8cm or 3¹/₈ inches to one mile) the maps in these guides are bigger than even the most detailed British walking maps currently available in the shops.

● **Not just a trail guide – includes where to stay, where to eat and public transport** Our guidebooks are a complete guide, not just a trail guide. They include: what to see, where to stay, where to eat: pubs, hotels, B&B, camping, bunkhouses, hostels. There is detailed public transport information for all access points to each trail so there are itineraries for all walkers, both for hiking the route in its entirety and for day walks.

West Highland Way *Charlie Loram*   2nd edn out now
ISBN 1 873756 90 9, 192pp, 53 maps, 16pp colour, £9.99, $17.95

Hadrian's Wall Path *Henry Stedman*   2nd edn out now
ISBN 1 873756 85 2, 192pp, 60 maps, 16pp colour, £9.99, $17.95

Pennine Way *Ed de la Billière & Keith Carter*   1st edn out now
ISBN 1 873756 57 7, 256pp, 140 maps, 16pp colour, £9.99, $16.95

Coast to Coast *Henry Stedman*   2nd edn out now
ISBN 1 873756 92 5, 224pp, 110 maps, 16pp colour, £9.99, $17.95

Pembrokeshire Coast Path *Jim Manthorpe*   1st edn out now
ISBN 1 873756 56 9, 208pp, 96 maps, 16pp colour, £9.99, $16.95

Offa's Dyke Path *Keith Carter*   1st edn out now
ISBN 1 873756 59 3, 208pp, 53 maps, 16pp colour, £9.99, $16.95

Cornwall Coast Path *Edith Schofield*   2nd edn out now
ISBN 1 873756 93 3, 224pp, 100 maps, 16pp colour, £9.99, $17.95

The Ridgeway *Nick Hill*   1st edn Nov 2006
ISBN 1 873756 88 7, 176pp, 60 maps, 16pp colour, £9.99, $17.95

North Downs Way *John Curtin*   1st edn Oct 2006
ISBN 1 873756 96 8, 192pp, 53 maps, 16pp colour, £9.99, $17.95

South Downs Way *Jim Manthorpe*   2nd edn Jan 2007
ISBN 1 873756 95 X, 192pp, 60 maps, 16pp colour, £9.99, $17.95

'*The same attention to detail that distinguishes its other guides has been brought to bear here*'. **The Sunday Times**

TRAILBLAZER GUIDES – TITLE LIST

For more information about Trailblazer, for where to find your nearest stockist, for guidebook updates or for credit card mail order sales visit:

www.trailblazer-guides.com

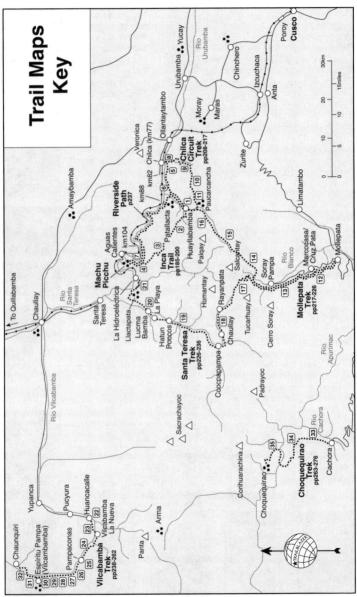

Peru

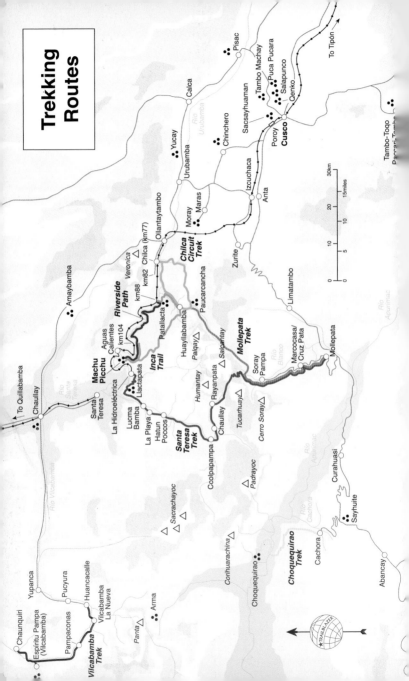